Blockchain Applications

A Hands-On Approach

Arshdeep Bahga • Vijay Madisetti

Blockchain Applications: A Hands-On Approach

Published by Arshdeep Bahga & Vijay Madisetti

ISBN: 978-0-9960255-6-0

Book Website: www.blockchain-book.com

Contents

Preface

About the Book

In the US, the services sector provides employment to about 100 million, while the manufacturing sector provides employment to about 20 million. In the services sector, retail (15 million employees), professional and business services (16 million employees), health care (14 million), hospitality (12 million), federal and local governments (20 million), educational services (2 million), and financial services (8 million) form the main business sectors. All these sectors are highly automated, and driven by sophisticated business processes forming an integral part of the digital economy. While the applications themselves may be distributed over the Internet in time and space, the core business, regulatory, and financial aspects of the digital economy are still centralized, with the need for centralized agencies (such as banks, customs authorities, and tax agencies) to authenticate and settle payments and transactions. These centralized services often are manual, difficult to automate, and represent a bottleneck to facilitating a frictionless digital economy. The next revolutionary step in the services and manufacturing economy of the future is the development of automated distributed applications that do not depend on these traditional centralized agencies for controlling, facilitating and settling multi-party transactions that may themselves be subject to complex contractual constraints. The blockchain technology is an integral part of these next steps that promises a smart new world of automation of complex services and manufacturing processes.

Blockchain is a distributed and public ledger which maintains records of all the transactions on a blockchain network comprising suppliers of products and services and consumers. A blockchain network is a peer-to-peer network and does not require a central authority or trusted intermediaries to authenticate or to settle the transactions or control the underlying infrastructure. Bitcoin was an early generation blockchain network that was introduced in 2008 where the primary application of the blockchain network was the use of electronic cash or cryptocurrency called Bitcoin. A second generation blockchain network called Ethereum was introduced in 2013. Ethereum allows a single programmable blockchain network to be used for developing different types of applications where each application takes the form of a smart contract which is implemented in a high-level language and deployed on the blockchain network.

With the blockchain's ability to establish trust in a peer-to-peer network through a distributed consensus mechanism rather than relying on a powerful centralized authority, the technology is being seen by the industry experts as one of the greatest innovations since the invention of the Internet. The blockchain technology has the potential to disrupt FinTech, manufacturing, supply chain, logistics, and healthcare industries by making transactions faster, cheaper, more secure and transparent without the need for a central authority or a trusted intermediary. Recognizing the potential of the blockchain, several financial and technology firms have invested billions of dollars to bring blockchain technology to capital markets. Industry surveys predict that blockchain technologies could reduce the infrastructural costs for financial institutions by $15-20 billion a year by 2022.

There are very few books that can serve as a foundational textbook for colleges looking to create new educational programs in these areas of blockchain, smart contracts, and decentralized applications. Existing books are primarily focused on the business side of blockchain, or describing vendor-specific offerings for blockchain platforms. Recent studies from PwC and CapGemini have determined that only ten percent of the financial industry is comfortable with the technical aspects of blockchain, and FinTech and RegTech industries are struggling to identify its impact on their business and how they should react to it.

We have written this textbook, as part of our expanding "A Hands-On Approach"[TM] series, to meet this need at colleges and universities. This book is also written for use within industries in the FinTech and RegTech space that may be interested in rolling out products and services that utilize this new area of technology. The book can serve as a textbook for senior-level and graduate-level courses on financial and regulation technologies, business analytics, Internet of Things, and cryptocurrency, offered in Computer Science, Mathematics and Business Schools.

The typical reader is expected to have completed a couple of courses in programming using traditional high-level languages at the college-level, and is either a senior or a beginning graduate student in one of the science, technology, engineering or mathematics (STEM) fields. The reader is provided the necessary guidance and knowledge to develop working code for real-world blockchain applications. Concurrent development of practical applications that accompanies traditional instructional material within the book further enhances the learning process, in our opinion. Furthermore, an accompanying website for this book contains additional support for instruction and learning (www.blockchain-book.com).

The book is organized into three main parts, comprising a total of ten chapters. Part I provides an introduction to blockchain, applications of blockchain, design patterns, and architectures for blockchain applications. A blockchain stack comprising a decentralized computation platform, a decentralized messaging platform, and a decentralized storage platform is described. While in this book we describe a specific realization of the blockchain stack based on the Ethereum blockchain platform, the same blockchain concepts can be applied to other blockchain platforms as well, such as Eris and Multichain. We describe a blockchain application design methodology that includes analysis, design and implementation stages. Templates for blockchain applications are provided. The blockchain stack and application design methodology form the pedagogical foundation of this book.

Part II introduces the readers to various tools and platforms for blockchain, and the architectural and programming aspects of these platforms. We chose the Ethereum blockchain platform for this book. For smart contract implementations, we chose the Solidity programming language. Other blockchain platforms and programming languages, may also be easily used within the blockchain stack described in this book. The reader is introduced to Ethereum tools such as Geth, PyEthApp, TestRPC, Mist Ethereum Wallet, MetaMask, Web3 JavaScript API, and the Truffle Dapp framework. The types of Ethereum accounts are described along with examples of setting up and working with the accounts. In the smart contracts chapter, we describe the structure of smart contracts and how to implement, compile, deploy and interact with smart contracts. Implementation examples of various smart contracts and the commonly used patterns are provided. In the chapter on decentralized applications (Dapps), we describe with the help of examples and case studies the steps involved in implementing Dapps using the Truffle Dapp framework. The chapter on mining provides an in-depth study of the consensus mechanism in a blockchain network, the steps involved in mining, the structure of a block, mining proof of work algorithm, mining rewards and state storage in Ethereum. The chapter on Whisper decentralized messaging platform introduces the reader to the structure of whisper envelope and message, whisper communication patterns, whisper wire protocol and routing approaches. The chapter on Swarm decentralized storage platform introduces the reader to the swarm architecture and concepts and the incentive mechanisms in swarm.

Part III focuses on advanced topics such as the security and scalability related challenges for the blockchain platforms.

Through generous use of hundreds of figures and tested code samples, we have attempted to provide a rigorous "no hype" guide to blockchain. It is expected that diligent readers of this book can use the canonical realizations of blockchain application templates and patterns described in this book to develop their own blockchain applications. We adopted an informal approach to describing well-known concepts primarily because these topics are covered well in existing textbooks, and our focus instead is on getting the reader firmly on track to developing robust blockchain applications as opposed to more theory.

While we frequently refer to offerings from commercial vendors, this book is not an endorsement of their products or services, nor is any portion of our work supported financially (or otherwise) by these vendors. All trademarks and products belong to their respective owners and the underlying principles and approaches, we believe, are applicable to other vendors as well. The opinions in this book are those of the authors alone.

Please also refer to our books "Big Data Science & Analytics: A Hands-On Approach[TM]", "Internet of Things: A Hands-On Approach[TM]" and "Cloud Computing: A Hands-On Approach[TM]" that provide additional and complementary information on these topics. We are grateful to the Association of Computing Surveys (ACM) for recognizing our book on cloud computing as a "Notable Book of 2014" as part of their annual literature survey. We are also grateful to the universities worldwide that have adopted these textbooks as part of their program offerings for providing us feedback that has helped us in improving our offerings.

Book Website

For more information on the book, copyrighted source code of all examples in the book, lab exercises, and instructor material visit the book website: www.blockchain-book.com

Acknowledgments

From Arshdeep Bahga
I would like to thank my father, Sarbjit Bahga, for inspiring me to write books and sharing his valuable insights and experiences on authoring books. This book could not have been completed without the support of my mother Gurdeep Kaur, wife Navsangeet Kaur, son Navroz Bahga and brother Supreet Bahga, who have always motivated me and encouraged me to explore my interests.

From Vijay Madisetti
I thank my family, especially Anitha and Jerry (Raj), and my parents (Prof. M. A. Ramlu and Mrs. Madhavi Saroja Ramlu) for their support.

From the Authors
We would like to acknowledge the instructors who have adopted our earlier books in the "A Hands-On Approach"[TM] series, for their constructive feedback.

About the Authors

Arshdeep Bahga
Arshdeep Bahga is a researcher in cloud computing, IoT and big data analytics. Arshdeep completed Masters degree in Electrical & Computer Engineering from Georgia Institute of Technology in 2010. He worked as Research Scientist with Georgia Tech from 2010-2016. Arshdeep has authored several scientific publications in peer-reviewed journals. Arshdeep received the 2014 Roger P. Webb - Research Spotlight Award from the School of Electrical and Computer Engineering, Georgia Tech.

Vijay Madisetti
Vijay Madisetti is a Professor of Electrical and Computer Engineering at Georgia Institute of Technology. Vijay is a Fellow of the IEEE, and received the 2006 Terman Medal from the American Society of Engineering Education and HP Corporation.

Companion Books from the Authors

Cloud Computing: A Hands-On Approach

Recent industry surveys expect the cloud computing services
market to be in excess of $20 billion and cloud computing jobs to
be in excess of 10 million worldwide in 2014 alone. In addition,
since a majority of existing information technology (IT) jobs is
focused on maintaining legacy in-house systems, the demand for
these kinds of jobs is likely to drop rapidly if cloud computing
continues to take hold of the industry. However, there are very
few educational options available in the area of cloud computing
beyond vendor-specific training by cloud providers themselves.
Cloud computing courses have not found their way (yet) into
mainstream college curricula. This book is written as a textbook
on cloud computing for educational programs at colleges. It can
also be used by cloud service providers who may be interested in
offering a broader perspective of cloud computing to accompany
their customer and employee training programs.

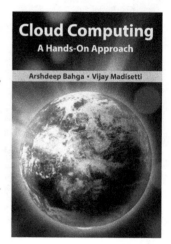

Additional support is available at the book's website:
www.cloudcomputingbook.info

Internet of Things: A Hands-On Approach

Internet of Things (IoT) refers to physical and virtual objects
that have unique identities and are connected to the Internet
to facilitate intelligent applications that make energy, logistics,
industrial control, retail, agriculture and many other domains
"smarter". Internet of Things is a new revolution of the Internet
that is rapidly gathering momentum driven by the advancements
in sensor networks, mobile devices, wireless communications,
networking, and cloud technologies. Experts forecast that by
the year 2020 there will be a total of 50 billion devices/things
connected to the Internet. This book is written as a textbook
on Internet of Things for educational programs at colleges and
universities, and also for IoT vendors and service providers who
may be interested in offering a broader perspective of Internet
of Things to accompany their customer and developer training
programs.

Additional support is available at the book's website:
www.internet-of-things-book.com

Big Data Science & Analytics: A Hands-On Approach

Big data is defined as collections of datasets whose volume, velocity or variety is so large that it is difficult to store, manage, process and analyze the data using traditional databases and data processing tools. Big data science and analytics deals with collection, storage, processing and analysis of massive-scale data. Industry surveys predict that there will be over 2 million job openings for engineers and scientists trained in the area of data science and analytics alone, and that the job market is in this area is growing at a 150 percent year-over-year growth rate. We have written this textbook to meet this need at colleges and universities, and also for big data service providers who may be interested in offering a broader perspective of this emerging field to accompany their customer and developer training programs.

The book is organized into three main parts, comprising a total of twelve chapters. Part I provides an introduction to big data, applications of big data, and big data science and analytics patterns and architectures. Part II introduces the reader to various tools and frameworks for big data analytics, and the architectural and programming aspects of these frameworks, with examples in Python. Part III introduces the reader to various machine learning algorithms with examples using the Spark MLlib and H2O frameworks, and visualizations using frameworks such as Lightning, Pygal and Seaborn.

Additional support is available at the book's website: www.big-data-analytics-book.com

Part I

BLOCKCHAIN TECHNOLOGY

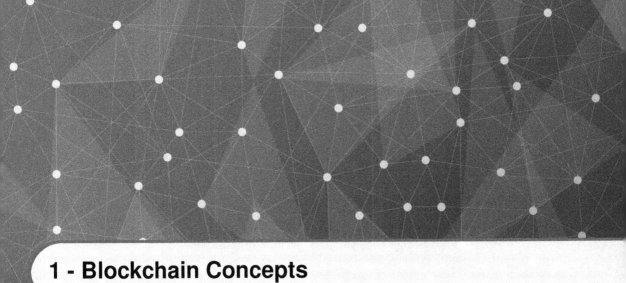

1 - Blockchain Concepts

This chapter covers

- Blockchain Introduction
- Blockchain Evolution
- Blockchain Structure
- Blockchain Characteristics
- Blockchain Stack
    - Decentralized Computation Platform - Ethereum
    - Decentralized Storage Platform - Swarm
    - Decentralized Messaging Platform - Whisper
    - Smart Contracts
    - Decentralized Applications (Dapps)
    - Tools & Interfaces
- From Web 2.0 to the Next Generation Decentralized Web
- Domain Specific Blockchain Applications
- Blockchain Benefits & Challenges

1.1 Blockchain

In the US, the services sector provides employment to about 100 million, while the manufacturing sector provides employment to about 20 million. In the services sector, retail (15 million employees), professional and business services (16 million employees), health care (14 million), hospitality (12 million), federal and local governments (20 million), educational services (2 million), and financial services (8 million) form the main business sectors. All these sectors are highly automated, and driven by sophisticated business processes forming an integral part of the digital economy. While the applications themselves may be distributed over the Internet in time and space, the core business, regulatory, and financial aspects of the digital economy are still centralized, with the need for centralized agencies (such as banks, customs authorities, and tax agencies) to authenticate and settle payments and transactions. These centralized services often are manual, difficult to automate, and represent a bottleneck to facilitating a frictionless digital economy. The next revolutionary step in the services and manufacturing economy of the future is the development of automated distributed applications that do not depend on these traditional centralized agencies for facilitating and settling complex multi-party transactions that may themselves be subject to complex contractual constraints. The blockchain technology is an integral part of these next steps that promises a smart new world of automation of complex services and manufacturing processes.

Blockchain is a distributed and public ledger which maintains records of all the transactions. A blockchain network is a truly peer-to-peer network and it does not require a trusted central authority or intermediaries to authenticate or to settle the transactions or to control the network infrastructure. With the blockchain's ability to establish trust in a peer-to-peer network through a distributed consensus mechanism rather than relying on a powerful central authority, the technology is being seen by the industry experts as one of the greatest innovations since the invention of the Internet. Blockchain has the potential to disrupt not just the financial technology (FinTech) industry but also other industries such as manufacturing, supply chain, logistics, and healthcare.

The current blockchain technology was introduced by Satoshi Nakamoto in the paper titled, "Bitcoin: A Peer-to-Peer Electronic Cash System" [1], less than a decade ago. In this paper, Nakamoto proposed a peer-to-peer version of an electronic cash system which allowed online payments to be sent from one party to another, without the need for a trusted third party or a financial institution. Due to the absence of a trusted third party, some mechanism is required to prevent "double-spending". Double-spending can occur when a party manages to successfully spend the same money more than once. In a financial system with a central authority that maintains a ledger of all transactions, any attempts to do double spending can be identified and prevented, however, in a peer-to-peer and trustless network, it becomes a challenging task.

To prevent double-spending without a trusted central authority, Nakamoto identified two key requirements: (1) publicly announcing all transactions, (2) having a system for the participants to agree on the transactions and their sequence. These requirements led to the development of the blockchain, which is a distributed data structure comprising a chain of blocks. Blockchain acts as a distributed database or a public ledger which maintains records of all transactions on a peer-to-peer network. A blockchain is maintained by a network of nodes and every node executes and records the same transactions. The blockchain structure is replicated among the nodes in the network. Any node in the network can read the transactions. The transactions are time-stamped and bundled into blocks where each block is identified by its cryptographic hash. The blocks form a linear sequence where each block references the hash of the previous block, forming a chain of blocks called the blockchain.

New blocks are created and added to the blockchain in a process called mining. The nodes in the blockchain network that perform the mining operations are called miners. New transactions are broadcast to all the nodes on the network. Each miner node creates its own block by collecting the new transactions and then finds a proof-of-work (by performing complex mathematical computations) for its block. The miners validate the transactions and reach a consensus on the block that should be added next to the blockchain. The newly mined block (called the winning block) is then broadcast to the entire network. The winning block is the one that contains a proof-of-work (PoW) of a given difficulty.

Since the miner nodes dedicate their computational resources for maintaining the blockchain network and mining new blocks, they are given incentives in the form of some units of a cryptocurrency. The miners on a blockchain network compete to do a complex mathematical computation and the miner that wins each round is the one whose block is added next to the chain. A mining reward is given to the miner whose block is added to the chain. The mining rewards serve two purposes: (1) they provide incentives to the nodes for supporting the network, (2) they provide a way to generate and distribute new cryptocurrency into circulation as there is no central authority in the network to issue new cryptocurrency.

1.1.1 Blockchain Evolution

As mentioned earlier, Bitcoin was the first generation blockchain network which was introduced by Satoshi Nakamoto in 2008. The primary application of this first generation blockchain network was the electronic cash or cryptocurrency using Bitcoin. The Bitcoin network made use of the blockchain technology to record transactions which transfer Bitcoin cryptocurrency. The blockchain facilitated transactions on a trustless peer-to-peer network. As the popularity of Bitcoin grew, the developer community proposed several enhancements to the Bitcoin protocol and came up with alternative types of coins (alt-coins) where each type of coin had its own blockchain network. Vitalik Buterin, in 2013, proposed the second generation blockchain network called Ethereum [2]. In the Ethereum Whitepaper, Buterin proposed that instead of separate blockchain networks for different types of cryptocurrencies, a single programmable blockchain network can be used to develop different types of applications. Each application on this second generation blockchain network takes the form of a "smart contract". The smart contract, implemented in a high-level language, would be deployed on the network. In 2014, Ethereum Foundation was setup and the development of the Ethereum blockchain network was initially funded by an online public crowd sale. Late in 2014, Gavin Wood published the Ethereum Yellow paper which provided the formal specification of a blockchain protocol [3]. Gavin Wood also implemented the first functional implementation of Ethereum and proposed the Solidity language that may be used to write smart contracts.

1.1.2 Blockchain Structure

Figure 1.1 shows the structure of a blockchain comprising a sequence of blocks where each block is identified by its cryptographic hash (the *nonce* field) and references the hash of its parent block. The cryptographic hash of a block is used to verify that a sufficient amount of computation has been carried out on this block and the block contains a valid proof-of-work (PoW). Each block maintains records of all the transactions on the network received since the creation of its previous block. Instead of storing the information on all the transactions within the block itself, a special data structure called a Merkle tree is used to store the transactions and only the hash of the root of the Merkle tree is stored in the block. In Chapter-7, we provide the details on all the fields in a block and the Merkle tree structure.

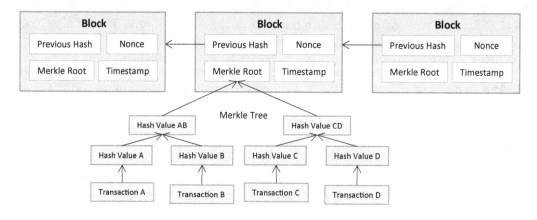

Figure 1.1: Blockchain structure

1.1.3 Blockchain Characteristics

- **Immutability**: Blockchain is an immutable and durable data structure which maintains a record of the transactions on a trustless peer-to-peer network. The transactions are bundled into blocks and the blocks are added to the blockchain through a consensus among the peers. Once a transaction is recorded in a block, it cannot be altered or deleted as long as a majority of the computational power of the network is not controlled by peers who collude to alter the blockchain.
- **No Central Authority**: A blockchain network is a truly peer-to-peer network with no central authority to process and settle the transactions. The absence of a central authority can result in lower transaction charges and faster settlement times.
- **Secure and Transparent**: Blockchain provides greater transparency than centralized financial systems. The transactions in a blockchain network are made public and can be viewed by any node in the network. Each node keeps a copy of all the transactions which are bundled into blocks. While each miner on the network can create its own block, only the block which has a proof-of-work of a given difficulty is accepted to be added to the blockchain. The consensus mechanism ensures that all the nodes agree on the same block to contain the canonical transactions. Blockchain offers enhanced security as compared to centralized systems as every transaction is verified by multiple miners. The integrity of the transaction data recorded in the blocks is

protected through strong cryptography. In addition to the transaction data, each block contains a cryptographic hash of itself and the hash of the previous block. Any attempts to modify a transaction would result in a change in the hash and would require all the subsequent blocks to be recomputed. This would be extremely difficult to achieve as long as the majority of miners do not cooperate to attack the network.

- **Privacy**: While the transactions on a blockchain network are publicly announced to all the nodes, the privacy of the transacting parties is maintained by keeping their public keys anonymous. Each party has a public-private keypair associated with it. The account address is derived from the public key. The private key is encrypted with the password which is provided while creating the account. For sending transactions to other accounts, the private key and the account password are required. While the public can see the public keys of the transacting parties, the real identities of the parties are not revealed.

- **Scalable and Available**: A blockchain network is maintained by peers located around the world. While the peers can join and leave the network, the network remains available. The blockchain structure itself is replicated across the peers. The computational power of the network can scale-up as more and more peers join the network.

1.2 Blockchain Application Example: Escrow

Before we go into the specifics of blockchain and the related tools and platforms, let us look at a simple example of how a blockchain platform can be used to create a complex financial contract between two parties. The example is an Escrow, which is a contractual agreement between two parties, where a third party holds and regulates the payment of the funds from one party to another. An Escrow can be used by a buyer and seller to make the transaction more secure. The payment is held in a secure escrow account and released only when all of the terms of the agreement are met.

Figure 1.2 shows an example of an escrow contract between a buyer and a seller. The buyer and the seller have their own accounts on a blockchain platform. The buyer sets up an Escrow smart contract and makes a deposit. While initializing the contract, the buyer provides the address of the seller, an expiry time of the contract and a value (in the form of a cryptocurrency). The escrow contract is deployed on a blockchain network and the deposit is held in the contract account. The seller then ships the item to the buyer. Buyer checks the delivered item and releases the escrow. When the escrow is released, the deposit held in the escrow contract is sent to the buyer.

Box 1.1 shows an implementation of the Escrow contract in the Solidity programming language. At this stage, we will not go into all the implementation details of the smart contract and the Solidity language, but describe the structure of the contract and how to interact with the contract. A tutorial on the basics of Solidity language is provided in Appendix-1. Smart contracts are covered in detail in Chapter-5.

A smart contract includes state variables and a set of executable functions. The functions are executed when transactions are made to these functions. The transactions include input parameters which are required by the functions in the contract. Upon the execution of a function, the state variables in the contract change depending on the logic implemented in

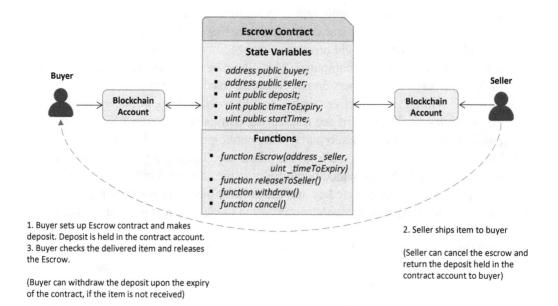

Figure 1.2: Escrow contract structure and transactions

the function. A special function, called the constructor, with the same name as the contract name, is used to initialize the contract.

In the Escrow contract shown in Box 1.1, we have state variables *buyer* and *seller* which store the addresses of the buyer and seller. The state variable *deposit* stores the amount of deposit sent by the buyer, the state variables *timeToExpiry* stores the time duration after which the contract will expire and the variable *startTime* stores the timestamp when the contract is initialized. The buyer sets up the escrow contract and pays the deposit by sending a transaction to the contract constructor (*Escrow* function). The deposit is held in the contract account. When the buyer receives the item from the seller, the buyer releases the deposit by sending a transaction to the *releaseToSeller* function. If the buyer doesn't receive the item, the buyer can withdraw the deposit when the escrow contract expires by sending a transaction to the *withdraw* function. If the seller doesn't have the item in stock or wants to cancel the escrow contract, the seller can do so by sending a transaction to the *cancel* function. The *isExpired* is a utility function to check if the contract has expired or not.

■ **Box 1.1: Escrow contract implemented in Solidity**

```
contract Escrow {
  address public buyer;
  address public seller;
  uint public deposit;
  uint public timeToExpiry;
  uint public startTime;



  //Buyer sets up the escrow contract and pays the deposit
```

```
function Escrow(address _seller, uint _timeToExpiry) {
  buyer = msg.sender;
  seller = _seller;
  deposit = msg.value;
  timeToExpiry = _timeToExpiry;
  startTime = now;
}


//Buyer releases deposit to seller
function releaseToSeller() {
  if (msg.sender == buyer){
    suicide(seller); //Finish the contract and send all funds to seller
  }
  else{
    throw;
  }
}


//Buyer can withdraw deposit if escrow is expired
function withdraw() {
  if (!isExpired()) {
    throw;
  }

  if (msg.sender == buyer){
    suicide(buyer); // Finish the contract and send all funds to buyer
  }
  else{
    throw;
  }
}


// Seller can cancel escrow and return all funds to buyer
function cancel() {
  if (msg.sender == seller){
    suicide(buyer);
  }
  else{
    throw;
  }
}

function isExpired() constant returns (bool) {
  if (now > startTime + timeToExpiry){
    return true;
  }
  else{
    return false;
  }
}
}
```

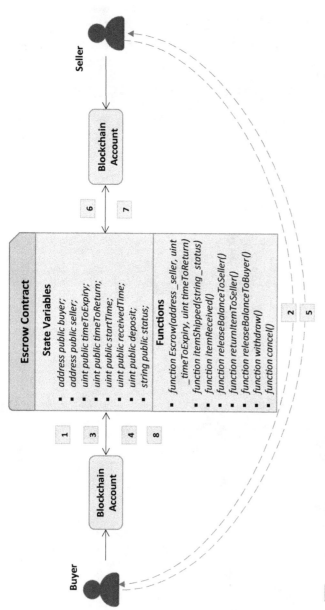

Escrow Contract

State Variables
- *address public buyer;*
- *address public seller;*
- *uint public timeToExpiry;*
- *uint public timeToReturn;*
- *uint public startTime;*
- *uint public receivedTime;*
- *uint public deposit;*
- *string public status;*

Functions
- *function Escrow(address _seller, uint _timeToExpiry, uint timeToReturn)*
- *function itemShipped(string _status)*
- *function itemReceived()*
- *function releaseBalanceToSeller()*
- *function returnItemToSeller()*
- *function releaseBalanceToBuyer()*
- *function withdraw()*
- *function cancel()*

1   Buyer sets up Escrow contract and makes deposit. Deposit is held in the contract account.

2   Seller ships item to buyer and updates item shipment information.

3   Buyer checks the delivered item and releases 20% of the Escrow deposit.

4   If the buyer is satisfied with the item, the buyer releases the balance deposit to the seller.

5   If the buyer is not satisfied with the item, the buyer can return the item.

6   Seller releases the balance deposit to buyer upon receiving the item returned by the buyer. Seller keep 20% as restocking fees.

7   Seller can cancel the escrow and return the deposit held in the contract account to buyer.

8   Buyer can withdraw the deposit upon the expiry of the contract, if the item is not received.

Figure 1.3: Advanced Escrow contract structure and transactions

To demonstrate the power and flexibility of the blockchain platform, let us now extend the basic Escrow smart contract and add some additional conditions. Let us provide the buyer the option of returning the item within a certain time period after the item is received, if the buyer is not satisfied with the item. When the buyer receives the item, the buyer releases 20% of the amount to the seller. The buyer gets a certain number of days to use and evaluate the item. If the buyer is satisfied with the item, the buyer releases the balance (i.e. 80% of the escrow deposit) to the seller. However, if the buyer is not satisfied with the item, the buyer can return the item. When the seller receives the item returned by the buyer, the seller can then release the balance amount (i.e. 80% of the escrow deposit) to the buyer. The remaining amount already paid to the seller (i.e. 20% of the escrow deposit) remains with the seller as the restocking penalty paid by the buyer.

Figure 1.3 shows the structure of the advanced escrow contract and the interactions between the buyer and seller. Box 1.2 shows the advanced version of the Escrow contract with these additional conditions. The buyer sets up the Escrow contract and pays a deposit equal to the value of the item. The seller ships the item to the buyer and updates the shipment information by sending a transaction to the *itemShipped* function. The buyer confirms receipt of the item by sending a transaction to the *itemReceived* function. In this function, 20% of the deposit is released to the seller. The buyer can use and evaluate the item for a certain time period (defined by the *timeToReturn* state variable).

If the buyer is satisfied with the item, the buyer releases the balance deposit to the seller by sending a transaction to the *releaseBalanceToSeller* function. However, if the buyer is not satisfied, the buyer returns the item and updates the contract by sending a transaction to the *returnItemToSeller* function. Upon receiving the item, the seller refunds the balance deposit to the buyer by sending a transaction to the *refundBalanceToBuyer* function.

■ **Box 1.2: Advanced escrow contract implemented in Solidity**

```
contract Escrow {
  address public buyer;
  address public seller;
  uint public timeToExpiry;
  uint public timeToReturn;
  uint public startTime;
  uint public receivedTime;
  uint public deposit;
  string public status;


  //Buyer sets up the escrow contract and pays the deposit
  function Escrow(address _seller, uint _timeToExpiry,
               uint _timeToReturn) {
    buyer = msg.sender;
    seller = _seller;
    deposit = msg.value;
    timeToExpiry = _timeToExpiry;
    timeToReturn = _timeToReturn;
    startTime = now;
    status = "Escrow Setup";
```

```
}

//Seller updates item shipment information
function itemShipped(string _status) {
  if (msg.sender == seller){
    status = _status;
  }
  else{
    throw;
  }
}


//Buyer releases partial deposit to seller
function itemReceived(string _status) {
  if (msg.sender == buyer){
    status = _status;
    receivedTime = now;

    //Pay 20% to seller
    if (!seller.send(deposit/5)){
        throw;
      }
  }
  else{
    throw;
  }
}


//Buyer releases balance deposit to seller
function releaseBalanceToSeller() {
  if (msg.sender == buyer){

    //Finish the contract and send all funds to seller
    suicide(seller);
  }
  else{
    throw;
  }
}


//Buyer returns the item
function returnItemToSeller(string _status) {
  if (msg.sender != buyer){
    throw;
  }

  if (now > receivedTime + timeToReturn){
    throw;
  }
```

```
    status = _status;
  }


  //Seller releases balance to buyer
  function releaseBalanceToBuyer() {
    if (msg.sender != seller){
      throw;
    }

    // Finish the contract and send remaining funds to buyer
    //20% restocking penalty previously paid to seller
    suicide(buyer);
  }


  //Buyer can withdraw deposit if escrow is expired
  function withdraw() {
    if (!isExpired()) {
      throw;
    }

    if (msg.sender == buyer){
      suicide(buyer); // Finish the contract and send all funds to buyer
    }
    else{
      throw;
    }
  }


  // Seller can cancel escrow and return all funds to buyer
  function cancel() {
    if (msg.sender == seller){
      suicide(buyer);
    }
    else{
      throw;
    }
  }


  function isExpired() constant returns (bool) {
    if (now > startTime + timeToExpiry){
      return true;
    }
    else{
      return false;
    }
  }
}
```

Till now we looked at the implementation of the Escrow smart contract and how the seller and buyer can interact with the contract by sending transactions to the contract. For compiling and deploying the contract on the Ethereum blockchain platform, we can use different Ethereum clients such as Go-Ethereum client (*geth*), Python Ethereum Client (*pyethapp*) or the Ethereum Mist Wallet application. These clients are described in detail in Chatper-3.

While one can interact with the contracts using the Ethereum clients, having a web-based user interface (UI) for a contract makes it convenient for the end-users. Decentralized applications (Dapps) provide this functionality. A Dapp is backed by one or more smart contracts and provides a web-based user interface for the contracts. A Dapp can be accessed in an Internet browser using the URL or the address of the server from which it is served. Blockchain users can connect their blockchain accounts to the Dapp (either through a wallet application or a browser extension) and send transactions to the underlying smart contracts.

Let us look at an example of a Dapp for the Escrow example. Figures 1.4 - Figures 1.12 show the screenshots of the web interface of the Escrow Dapp. For each step as shown in Figure 1.3, we have a separate tab in the Dapp's web interface. For example, Figure 1.4 shows the first step in which the buyer initializes the Escrow contract and pays the deposit.

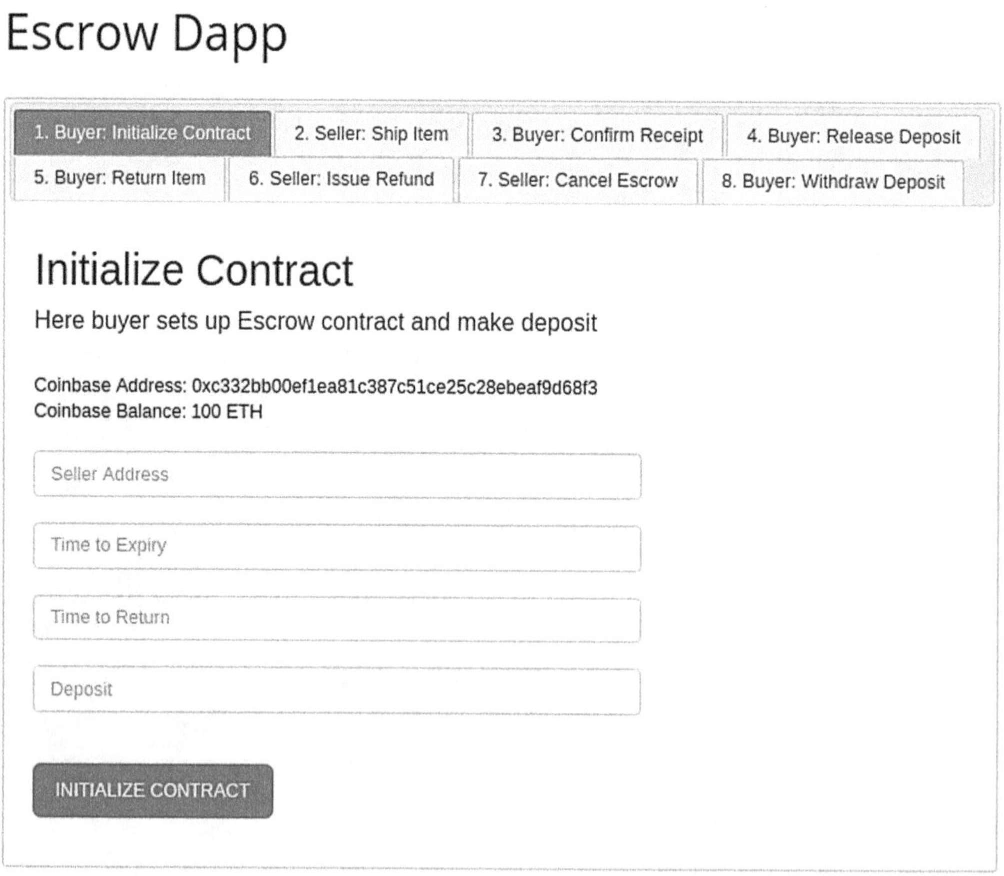

Escrow Dapp

| 1. Buyer: Initialize Contract | 2. Seller: Ship Item | 3. Buyer: Confirm Receipt | 4. Buyer: Release Deposit |
| 5. Buyer: Return Item | 6. Seller: Issue Refund | 7. Seller: Cancel Escrow | 8. Buyer: Withdraw Deposit |

Initialize Contract

Here buyer sets up Escrow contract and make deposit

Coinbase Address: 0xc332bb00ef1ea81c387c51ce25c28ebeaf9d68f3
Coinbase Balance: 100 ETH

Seller Address

Time to Expiry

Time to Return

Deposit

INITIALIZE CONTRACT

Figure 1.4: Escrow Dapp: Buyer initializes contract

Figure 1.5 shows the Escrow contract's state information as viewed in the Dapp.

Escrow Contract

Contract Address	0xbf6d7681429f3056150b55d8d8f2b46b6819517a
Buyer Address	0xc332bb00ef1ea81c387c51ce25c28ebeaf9d68f3
Seller Address	0xc3c2afb5ffe96ebdb2d2d8e4987d409d0d2baa50
Time To Expiry	2000
Time To Return	1000
Start Time	1477565094
Received Time	-
Deposit	2.0 ETH
Status	Contract initialized

Figure 1.5: Escrow Dapp: Viewing contract's state information

Figure 1.6 shows the Dapp interface where the seller can update the item shipment information.

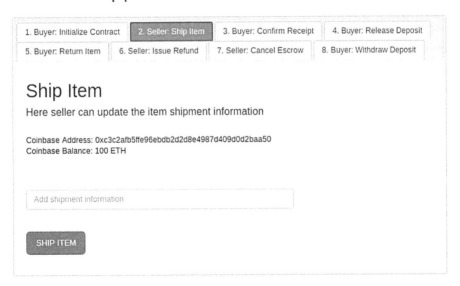

Figure 1.6: Escrow Dapp: Seller updates shipment information

Figure 1.7 shows the Dapp interface where the buyer can confirm receipt of the item and release 20% of the Escrow deposit.

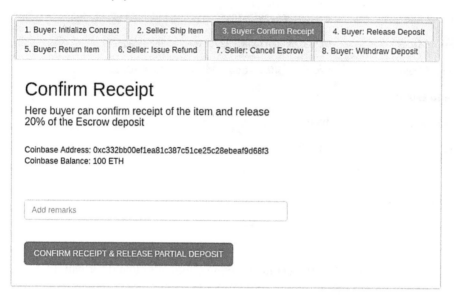

Figure 1.7: Escrow Dapp: Buyer confirms receipt and releases partial deposit

Figure 1.8 shows the Dapp interface where the buyer can release the balance deposit to the seller, if satisfied with the item,

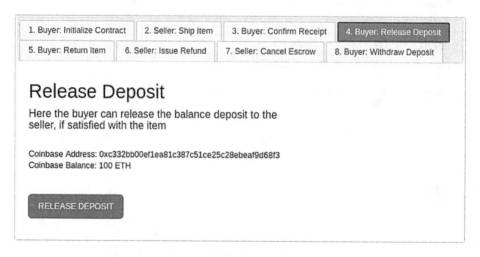

Figure 1.8: Escrow Dapp: Buyer releases balance deposit

Figure 1.9 shows the Dapp interface where the buyer can update the item return information, if not satisfied with the item.

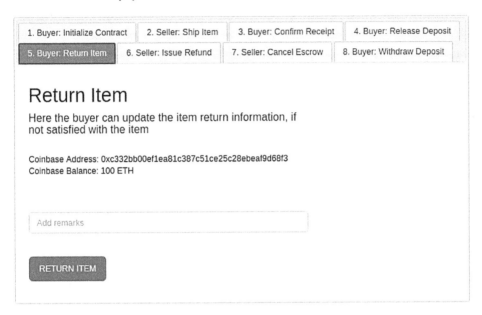

Figure 1.9: Escrow Dapp: Buyer updates item return information

Figure 1.10 shows the Dapp interface where the seller can release the balance deposit to the buyer upon receiving the item returned by the buyer.

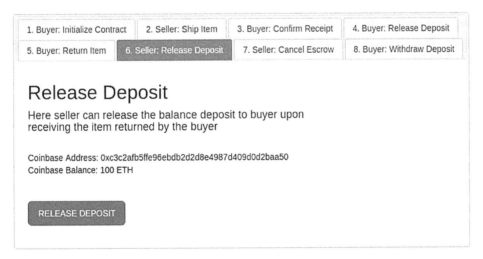

Figure 1.10: Escrow Dapp: Seller release balance deposit to buyer

Figure 1.11 shows the Dapp interface where the seller can cancel the escrow and return the deposit held in the contract account to the buyer.

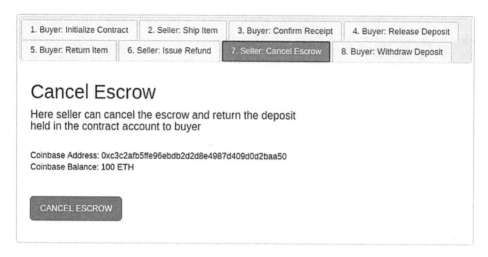

Figure 1.11: Escrow Dapp: Seller can cancel contract

Figure 1.12 shows the Dapp interface where the buyer can withdraw the deposit upon the expiry of the contract if the item is not received.

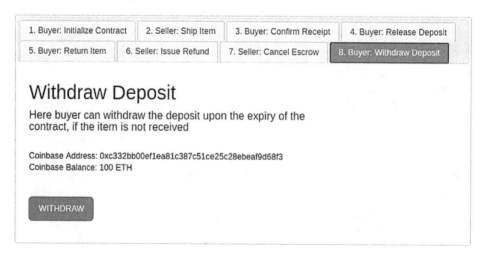

Figure 1.12: Escrow Dapp: Buyer can withdraw deposit

Key concepts to learn from the Escrow example:

1. We have two types of accounts on a blockchain platform - user accounts and contract accounts. Both types of accounts are identified by an address and have a balance (in a cryptocurrency). We will describe these Ethereum accounts in detail in Chapter-4.
2. Smart contracts are used for programming the blockchain and developing different blockchain applications. Smart contracts are implemented in a high-level language and deployed on a blockchain network. We describe smart contracts in detail in Chapter-5.
3. Users interact with the smart contracts by sending transactions to the contracts. A transaction includes the input parameters for the contract function to which the transaction is being sent. A value (in a cryptocurrency) can optionally be sent with the transaction. We describe various ways of interacting with smart contracts in detail in Chapter-5.
4. Access to the functions in a contract can be restricted to specific users. This can be done by checking addresses of the users who sent the transactions and throwing exceptions for unauthorized users. We describe smart contract patterns (for instance, access restriction, withdrawal and automatic expiration) in detail in Chapter-5.
5. User-friendly interfaces can be developed and made accessible to users as decentralized applications (Dapps). We describe Dapps in detail in Chapter-6.
6. The transactions sent to a contract are validated by the miners on the blockchain network. The miners bundle the transaction into blocks and in each mining round, one of the blocks gets selected to be added next to the blockchain. We describe the mining process in detail in Chapter-7.

1.3 Blockchain Stack

Blockchain technology has been designed to solve the double spending problem to establish consensus in a decentralized and trustless peer-to-peer network. The blockchain structure is well-suited for maintaining a record of all the transactions on the network. However, blockchain is not designed for storing large volumes of data or messaging between the peers. For developing decentralized applications that work on a blockchain network, other specialized solutions are required for storage and messaging. In this section, we describe a blockchain stack that forms the foundation of this book. Figure 1.13 shows the blockchain stack with the chapter numbers highlighted for the various blocks in the stack. The successive chapters in the book describe these blocks in detail along with hands-on examples and case studies. The key blocks in the stack include (1) a decentralized computation platform, (2) a decentralized messaging platform and (3) a decentralized storage platform. While in this book we describe a specific realization of the blockchain stack based on the Ethereum blockchain platform [9] the same blockchain concepts can be applied to other blockchain platforms as well, such as Eris [11] and Multichain [10].

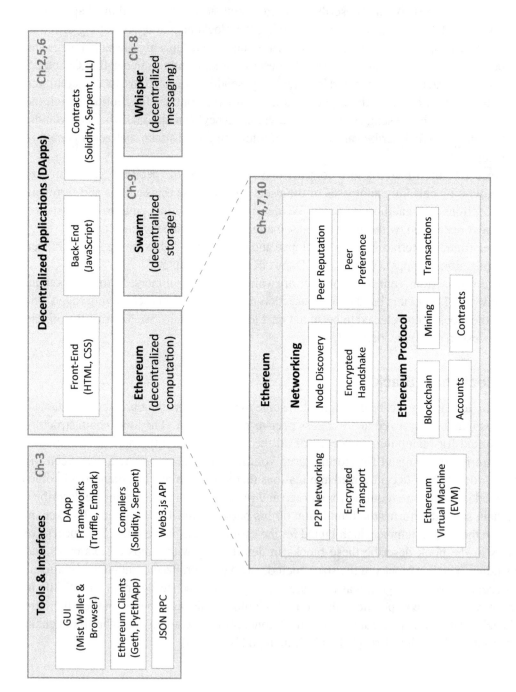

Figure 1.13: Blockchain stack

Let us look at each block in the blockchain stack one-by-one:

1.3.1   Decentralized Computation Platform - Ethereum

Ethereum is an open and programmable blockchain platform. Ethereum allows development of decentralized blockchain applications through the use of smart contracts that perform arbitrarily complex computations. Anyone can signup for the platform and create an Ethereum account. Users can create and deploy smart contracts to the Ethereum platform and build decentralized applications. The platform is not owned or controlled by any entity and is powered by the peers who run the Ethereum nodes. The key components of Ethereum include a runtime environment for smart contracts and a peer-to-peer network protocol. Let us look at the key concepts related to the Ethereum platform in more detail:

Ethereum Virtual Machine

Ethereum Virtual Machine (EVM) is the runtime environment for smart contracts in Ethereum. The nodes in the Ethereum network run the EVM. The EVM runs as a sandbox and provides an isolated execution environment. All the nodes in the blockchain network perform the same computations, thus providing redundancy in the execution of smart contracts. While this massive amount of redundancy is not an efficient approach for execution, but this is required to maintain consensus in the network where there is no centralized authority or a trusted third-party.

Figure 1.14: Ethereum account types

Accounts

Ethereum has two types of accounts - Externally Owned Accounts (EOAs) and Contract Accounts. EOAs are the accounts which are owned and controlled by the users. Each EOA has an Ether balance associated with it. These accounts can send transactions to other EOAs or contract accounts. Each Externally Owned Account (EOA) has a public-private keypair associated with it. The account address is derived from the public key. When a new EOA is created, a JSON keyfile is created which has the public and private keys associated with the account. The private key is encrypted with the password which is provided while creating the account. For sending transactions to other accounts, the private key and the account password are required. The contract accounts are controlled by the associated contract code which is stored with the account. The contract code execution is triggered by transactions sent by EOAs or messages sent by other contracts. Figure 1.14 shows the elements of the two types of Ethereum accounts. In Chapter-4, we describe the Ethereum accounts in detail.

Blocks

The transactions in a blockchain network are bundled into blocks and executed on all the participating nodes. A block contains a transaction list, the most recent state, a block number, and a difficulty value. If there are conflicting transactions on the network (for example, transactions that do double spending), only one of them is selected to become a part of the block. The blocks are added to the blockchain at regular intervals. In Chapter-7, we describe in detail the structure of a block and the process of creation of new blocks.

Transactions & Messages

Transactions are the messages which are sent by Externally Owned Accounts (EOAs) to other EOAs or contract accounts. Each transaction includes the address of the recipient, transaction data payload, and a transaction value. When a transaction is sent to an EOA, the transaction value is transferred to the recipient. When a transaction is sent to a contract account, the transaction data payload is used to provide input to the contract function to be executed. Transactions are signed by the sender's private key. Transactions are selected and included in the blocks in the mining process. The state of the network is changed only by the transactions which are selected for inclusion in the blocks. The transactions on a blockchain network can be read by all the participating nodes in the network. Contracts deployed on a blockchain network can send messages to other contracts. The difference between a transaction and a message is that a message is produced by a contract while a transaction is produced by an EOA.

Mining

The transactions on a blockchain network are verified in a process called mining. The participating nodes in the network are given incentives in the form of Ethers for performing the mining operations. Miners compete to do complex mathematical computations and the node that wins (i.e., whose block is selected to be added next to the chain) earns a reward in Ethers. Miners produce blocks which are verified by other miners for validity. A valid block is one which contains proof-of-work (PoW) of a given difficulty. In Ethereum, a proof-of-work algorithm called Ethash is used. The PoW algorithm finds *nonce* input to the algorithm so that the result is below a certain difficulty threshold. The time for finding a new block can be controlled by manipulating the difficulty. A successful PoW miner is the one whose block is selected to be next on the blockchain. Once a winning block is selected, all other nodes update to that new block. In Chapter-7, we describe the mining process in detail.

Ether

Ether is the currency which is used in the Ethereum blockchain network. The miners in the Ethereum network receive mining rewards in the form of Ethers. The base unit of Ether is called Wei (where 1 Ether = 10^{18} Wei).

Gas

Gas is the name of the crypto-fuel which is consumed for performing the operations on a blockchain network. All the transactions on the network are charged a certain amount of gas.

While sending a transaction, the sender sets a gas price which represents the fee the sender is willing to pay for gas. The senders of the transactions are charged a gas fee, which is paid to the miners and the balance is refunded to the sender. The gas fee paid is proportional to the amount of work that is needed to execute the transaction, in terms of the number of atomic instructions.

1.3.2 Decentralized Storage Platform - Swarm

Swarm is a decentralized storage platform and content distribution service for Ethereum. Swarm has been designed to serve as a decentralized and redundant store of Ethereum's public record, and also to store and distribute Dapp code. Swarm is a peer-to-peer storage platform which is maintained by the peers who contribute their storage and bandwidth resources. Being a peer-to-peer system, Swarm has no single point of failure and is resistant to faults and distributed denial of service (DDoS) attacks. Swarm is also censorship-resistant as it is not controlled by any central authority. Swarm has a built-in incentive system for peers who pool in their storage and bandwidth resources. Swarm has been designed to dynamically scale up to serve popular content and has a mechanism to ensure the availability of the content which is not popular or frequently requested. In Chapter-9, we will describe the Swarm storage platform in detail.

1.3.3 Decentralized Messaging Platform - Whisper

Whisper is a communication protocol that allows decentralized applications (Dapps) to communicate with each other. With Whisper, Dapps can publish messages to each other. Whisper messages are transient in nature and have a time-to-live (TTL) set. Each message has one or more topics associated with it. The Dapps running on a node inform the node about the topics to which they want to subscribe. Whisper uses topic-based routing where the nodes advertise their topics of interest to their peers. Topics are used for filtering the messages which are delivered to a node which are then distributed to the Dapps running on the node. In Chapter-8, we will describe the Whisper communication protocol in detail.

1.3.4 Smart Contracts

A smart contract is a piece of code that resides on a blockchain and is identified by a unique address. A smart contract includes a set of executable functions and state variables. The function code is executed when transactions are sent to the function. The transactions include input parameters which are required by the functions in the contract. Upon the execution of a function, the state variables in the contract change depending on the logic implemented in the function. Figure 1.15 shows the structure of a smart contract.

Smart contracts can be written in various high-level languages (such as Solidity or Python). Language-specific compilers for smart contracts (such as Solidity or Serpent compilers) are used to compile the contracts into bytecode. Once compiled, the contracts are uploaded to the blockchain network which assigns a unique address to each contract. Any user on the blockchain network can trigger the functions in the contract by sending transactions to the contract. The contract code is executed on each node participating in the network as part of their verification of new blocks. Contracts deployed on a blockchain network can send messages to other contracts. A message contains the address of the sender,

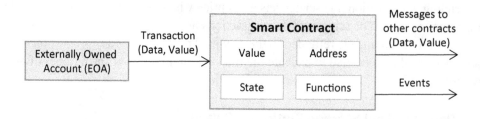

Figure 1.15: Smart Contract structure

address of the recipient, value to transfer, and a data field which contains the input data to the recipient contract. The difference between a transaction and a message is that a message is produced by a contract while a transaction is produced by an EOA. In Chapter-5, we describe the steps involved in implementing smart contracts along with examples and case studies.

1.3.5 Decentralized Applications (Dapps)

A Decentralized Application (or Dapp) is an application that uses smart contracts. Dapps provide a user-friendly interface to smart contracts. A cryptocurrency application is an example of a Dapp that runs on a blockchain network. A decentralized application (Dapp) comprises smart contracts and files for web user interface front-end (HTML, JavaScript, stylesheets and images). Building a Dapp involves the following steps:

1. Implement smart contracts in a high-level language.
2. Compile the contracts with language-specific compilers to generate the contract binary.
3. Deploy the contracts on Ethereum Blockchain network using Ethereum clients.
4. Build web applications that interact with the smart contracts.

Figure 1.16 shows the structure of a Dapp and Figure 1.17 shows the Dapp creation workflow. In Chapter-6, we describe the steps involved in implementing Dapps along with examples and case studies.

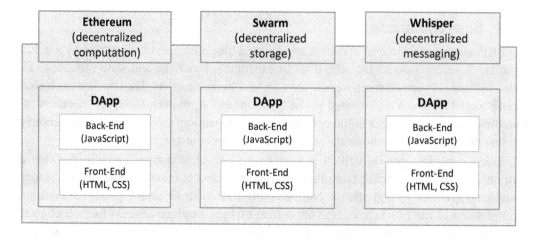

Figure 1.16: Dapp structure

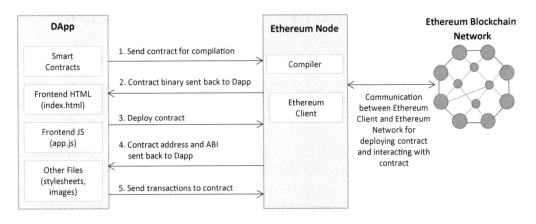

Figure 1.17: Dapp creation workflow

1.3.6   Tools & Interfaces

The tools and interfaces required for developing applications on the Ethereum blockchain platform are described in detail in Chapter-3. For now, let us briefly look at the types of tools and interfaces for development of blockchain applications:

Ethereum Clients

Ethereum clients allow us to setup an Ethereum node on our computer. An Ethereum client is like a Java Virtual Machine (JVM) and allows us to run Ethereum programs. With an Ethereum client, we can participate in the Ethereum network and perform tasks such as creating accounts and contracts, sending Ether to other accounts, sending transactions to contracts, mining on Ethereum network and other tasks related to the Ethereum Blockchain network. Ethereum provides clients in various launguages including the Go (*go-ethereum*), C++ (*cpp-ethereum*), Python (*pyethapp*), JavaScript (*ethereumjs-lib*), Ruby (*ruby-ethereum*), Java (*Ethereum(J)*), Haskell (*ethereumH*) and Rust (*Parity*). For the examples in this book, we have used the Go (*geth*) and Python (*pyethapp*) clients.

Graphical User Interfaces

The Mist Ethereum Wallet application provides a graphical user interface for performing tasks such as managing Ethereum accounts, sending Ether to other accounts, deploying contracts, sending transactions to contracts and viewing account transactions. The standard way of accessing and interacting with Dapps deployed on the Ethereum platform is through the Mist Browser. However, for users who do not want to install the Mist Browser and download the entire Blockchain, the MetaMask Chrome extension provides a user-friendly option to interact with the Dapps from Chrome browser. MetaMask allows you to run Ethereum Dapps in your browser without running a full Ethereum node [31].

Compilers

Ethereum provides various high-level languages for implementing contracts, including Solidity which is similar to JavaScript, Serpent which is similar to Python and Lisp Like Language (LLL) which is similar to Assembly. For the examples in this book, we use Solidity which is the most popular language for Ethereum and has more community support available as compared to Serpent and LLL.

Dapp Frameworks

Dapp frameworks such as Truffle [33] or Embark [34] simplify the steps involved in the creation of Dapps as shown in Figure 1.17. For the Dapp examples in this book, we have used the Truffle framework.

Web3 JavaScript API

Web3 is a JavaScript API created by the Ethereum Foundation which provides methods for interacting with the Ethereum network [32]. Web3 allows Dapps to work with the Ethereum network. Web3 provides a JavaScript object *web3* which includes various sub-objects such as *eth* (which contains the Ethereum Blockchain related methods), *shh* (which contains Whisper protocol related methods that allow DApps to communicate each other), *admin* (which contains various admin related methods), *net* (which contains methods related to the peer-to-peer network), *currentProvider* (which contains methods related to the current provider), *miner* (which contains methods related to mining), *version* (which provides version information for the node) and other sub-objects including *db, debug, personal, providers* and *txpool*.

JSON RPC

The Ethereum JSON-RPC is a stateless and lightweight remote procedure call (RPC) protocol that is used by Ethereum clients implemented in different programming languages to interact with an Ethereum node [13]. The Ethereum JSON-RPC defines Ethereum blockchain related methods, Whisper protocol related methods and other methods related to the peer-to-peer network.

1.4 From Web 2.0 to the Next Generation Decentralized Web

The blockchain technology stack described in the previous section enables a transition from Web 2.0 to the next generation decentralized web. In the context of Ethereum, the term Web 3.0 is often used to refer to this next generation decentralized web [14], however, we would use the term NextWeb in this book instead of Web 3.0, as the term Web 3.0 has also been used in the context of Internet of Things. Figure 1.18 shows the difference between a Web 2.0 application and a Dapp. Most Web 2.0 applications are centralized in nature and are deployed on one or more server instances under the control of a single organization or a cloud platform. For example, e-Commerce, Business-to-Business, Banking and Financial web applications can have a multi-tier deployment architectures with presentation, logic and storage tiers. The presentation tier includes the web interfaces for the applications which are implemented in languages such as HTML, CSS and JavaScript. The logic tier (or application tier) includes implementation of the application logic in the form of patterns such as Model-View-Controller (MVC). For the logic tier, specialized web frameworks such as Django, NodeJS or Ruby-on-Rails are used. This tier includes one or more application servers which work under a load balancer. The storage tier includes databases (relational or non-relational) and static storage. The databases can either be deployed on one or more servers or managed by a cloud service provider. Similarly, for static storage, a cloud storage platform can be used. While web applications can be distributed in nature with different services within the application running on separate server instances within one or more data centers, the computing and storage infrastructure used by these applications is usually under the control of one organization. Web applications use the HTTP or HTTPS protocol for interaction between the user and the application and also for communication between different components of the applications.

Dapps, in contrast to web applications, are decentralized in nature with no single entity or organization controlling the infrastructure on which the applications are deployed. In the context of Ethereum, Dapps are backed by smart contracts which are deployed on the Ethereum blockchain platform that is maintained by the Ethereum nodes or peers worldwide. A Dapp itself is deployed on a central server which is either a full Ethereum node or can communicate with an Ethereum node. However, the server only serves the Dapp's web interface. The Dapp logic is controlled by the associated smart contracts which are deployed on the blockchain platform. Dapps provide friendly interfaces to smart contracts where the users can submit transactions to the contracts from a web interface. A Dapp's web interface forwards the transactions to the blockchain platform and displays the transaction receipts or state information in the smart contracts in the web interface. Dapps use a decentralized messaging protocol such as Whisper for communication and decentralized storage platforms such as Swarm for static storage.

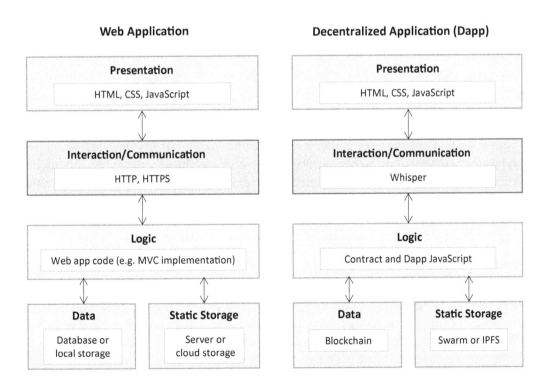

Figure 1.18: Web App vs DApp

1.5 Domain Specific Blockchain Applications

The applications of blockchain span a wide range of domains including (but not limited to) FinTech, Internet of Things, industrial & manufacturing, energy, supply chain & logistics, and healthcare. In this section, we provide an overview of various applications of blockchain for each of these domains. In the later chapters, the reader is guided through reference implementations and examples that will help the readers in developing these applications.

1.5.1 FinTech

Financial Technology, in short FinTech, is a term used for companies that use new technologies to make financial services more efficient. By making use of modern software and web technologies, FinTech companies aim to disrupt the traditional applications, processes, business models and products in the financial services industry. Blockchain is being seen as a key enabling technology for FinTech. Blockchain being a distributed and global ledger which is not under the control of a single organization, is useful in many ways for FinTech applications. Let us look at some FinTech sectors and specific applications in these sectors that can benefit from blockchain.

Banking

Blockchain can solve multiple challenges for the banking industry by providing faster, cheaper, more secure and transparent transactions. Blockchain is a distributed and shared ledger which maintains records of all transactions. The transactions are verified by the miners on a blockchain network, combined into blocks and added to the blockchain. Blockchain can provide a verifiable record of every transaction done on the network without the need for a centralized authority. While traditional transaction processing methods require third parties or trusted intermediaries to process and validate the transactions, blockchain platforms are maintained by a network of peers distributed across the globe. By eliminating the need for intermediaries and decentralizing trust, blockchain reduces settlement times and transaction processing fees. Banks can make use of blockchain technology for various services such as currency remittances, cross-border payments, and trading. R3, a financial innovation firm has formed a consortium of over 50 of the world's leading financial institutions. R3 has created a distributed ledger platform called Corda to record, manage and synchronize financial agreements between regulated financial institutions [17]. Hyperledger is another such effort [18] which aims to advance cross-industry blockchain technologies through a collaboration of leading players in financial, banking and other sectors.

Insurance

Blockchain has the potential to disrupt the insurance industry by streamlining the claims process, simplifying the payment of premiums, and reducing claim frauds. Insurance agreements between the insurance companies and customers can be recorded on the blockchain in the form of smart contracts. Customers can pay insurance premiums and submit claims by sending transactions to the insurance smart contracts. Smart contracts can automatically verify the identities of the customers, validate insurance claims and settle the claims. Blockchain can also enable innovative insurance solutions such as parametric insurance and peer-to-peer insurance. Parametric insurance solutions leverage IoT and blockchain technologies, to automate the release of payments when certain conditions are met (such as a fire incident in a house). Peer-to-peer insurance platforms can be developed using the blockchain technology. In this model of insurance, the policyholders form small groups and a part of their insurance premium is paid into a cashback pool and the other part to an insurance company. If no claim is made, the group members get a cashback at the end of the year. Minor claims are paid from the group fund while major claims are paid by the insurance company. The peer-to-peer model of insurance can make insurance easier and cheaper for customers.

Payments and Transactions

Blockchain platforms can be used for developing applications for mobile payments, peer-to-peer money transfer, user-to-device and device-to-device transactions. Payments and transactions can be done on a blockchain platform in the form of a cryptocurrency. For example, the Ethereum blockchain platform supports the Ether cryptocurrency. Users registered on the blockchain platforms can use mobile applications for blockchain wallets to make payments to other users or devices (such as Internet of Things devices). Such applications can help us in moving towards cashless economies where all transactions are done online without the need for physical cash. Financial transactions done through blockchain platforms are secure as each transaction is verified by the miners who mine the blocks. Blockchain provides a decentralized and public record of transactions which once confirmed and added to the blockchain cannot be tampered with. In Chapter-6, we provide implementation case studies of user-to-device and device-to-device transactions through decentralized applications deployed on the blockchain.

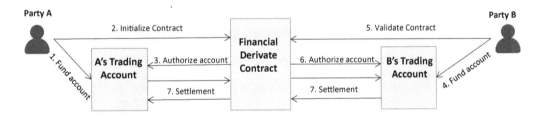

Figure 1.19: Using blockchain and smart contracts for financial derivatives

Trading and Investments

Blockchain can be used for developing trading and investment platforms which can automate financial services through the use of smart contracts, replacing traditional investment brokers and advisors. The potential benefits of blockchain for trading and investments include faster settlement times, greater transparency and lower collateral requirements. In Chapter-6, we provide implementation case studies of Dapps for financial derivative instruments such as Call Option and Interest Rate Swap. For these Dapps, either the concerned parties (e.g. buyer and seller) can transact directly using their blockchain account or setup separate trading accounts managed by smart contracts as shown in Figure 1.19. In the latter approach, each party maintains sufficient balance in their trading account to facilitate the payments. Separate smart contracts are used for financial derivative instruments. The derivative contracts can be initialized by either party and then verified by the other party. Each party authorizes the derivative contract to deposit/withdraw money to/from their trading account. Thus, when the derivative contract is exercised, the contract itself can automatically deposit or withdraw money to/from trading accounts without additional permissions from the two parties.

Peer-to-peer Lending & Crowdfunding

Blockchain can be used for developing peer-to-peer (P2P) lending platforms. P2P lending platforms help in connecting borrowers and investors around the world. For the borrowers, such platforms make credit more affordable and for the investors, they make investing more rewarding. A simple peer-to-peer lending solution can be implemented using a smart contract deployed on a blockchain platform. The smart contract acts as an agreement between a borrower and an investor and captures the lending terms such as the credit, annual percentage rate (APR), term, equated monthly installment (EMI) through the state variables in the contract.

Crowdfunding platforms can also be developed using the blockchain technology. Such platforms allow individuals and businesses to create funding campaigns and raise funds from individuals who collectively contribute to the campaigns. This model of fundraising provides alternative sources of investments for projects and business which are less likely to get funded by traditional methods like banks or venture capitalists. In Chapter-6, we provide an implementation case study of a decentralized application (Dapp) for crowdfunding. With such a Dapp, users can create their own crowdfunding campaigns. A smart contract is used to maintain the campaign information and accept funds from the backers of the campaign. Users registered on the blockchain platform can connect their wallets to the Dapp and fund a campaign by sending a transaction to the campaign smart contract through the Dapp's web interface. At the end of the campaign, the contract checks if the funding goal is met and the campaign is successful. If successful, the funds are transferred from the contract account to the beneficiary account. If a campaign fails, the funds raised are refunded.

1.5.2   Internet of Things

Internet of Things (IoT) refers to things that have unique identities and are connected to the Internet. The "Things" in IoT are the devices which can perform remote sensing, actuating and monitoring. IoT devices can exchange data with other connected devices and applications (directly or indirectly), or collect data from other devices and process the data either locally or send the data to centralized servers or cloud-based application back-ends for processing the data, or perform some tasks locally and other tasks within the IoT infrastructure, based on temporal and space constraints (i.e., memory, processing capabilities, communication latencies and speeds, and deadlines).

IoT systems can leverage blockchain platforms to enable device-to-device and consumer-to-device transactions. Blockchain can also be used for device tracking and coordination. With blockchain, various types of decentralized applications (Dapps) for IoT can be built to allow the consumers to transact with the devices directly without the need for a trusted intermediary. IoT devices can have smart contracts associated with them which are deployed on the blockchain. These contracts can store information on the device identities and usage patterns. Users who wish to avail the services of the IoT devices can transact with the smart contracts associated with the devices. Blockchain can be used to monetize the data collected or generated by the IoT devices. The IoT device owners can sell the data to interested parties by accepting micropayments to the device smart contracts.

Let us now look at some IoT applications that can benefit from blockchain:

Smart Locks

IoT and blockchain technologies can be used to develop smart locks. Smart locks can be used to rent real-world physical objects (such as houses, cars or bikes). Slock.it has developed a smart lock technology called Slocks which enables real-world physical objects to be controlled by the blockchain [20]. The owners of a Slock who want to rent their real-world physical objects set a deposit amount and a price for using the objects. Users can find the Slocks using the mobile app and then make a payment in Ethers to rent the objects. After the transactions are validated on the Ethereum blockchain network, the users get permission to open or close the Slocks with their smartphone. A smart contract is automatically enforced between the owner and the user. After the object is returned, the deposit minus the cost of the rental is returned to the user.

Smart Parking

IoT and blockchain technologies can be used for smart parking systems to enable direct consumer-to-parking-meter or vehicle-to-parking-meter transactions. For example, a smart parking meter can have its own blockchain account and an associated smart contract to manage the transactions sent to the meter. A smart contract for a parking meter can manage information related to the meter such as the meter ID, location, and per-minute rate. Users can pay directly to a contract account associated with a parking meter from their blockchain wallet applications. Parking meters equipped with sensors can detect when a car is parked in a parking lot and when it is moved out. Thus, users can be charged only for the duration of use of the parking slot. Such parking meters can be much cheaper to maintain as compared to meters which process electronic (credit card or debit card) payments since there is no centralized authority or an intermediary involved. Changing the rate for a meter is as simple as sending a transaction to the smart contract associated with the meter with the new rate. The parking meter smart contract can also store information related to the usage of the meter. Planners and decision makers can analyze such information to provide insights into the usage patterns and can make informed decisions on future parking infrastructure.

Smart Appliances

Modern homes have a number of appliances such as TVs, refrigerators, music systems, washers, etc. Managing, controlling and maintaining these appliances can be cumbersome. Blockchain and IoT technologies can be used to make the home appliances smarter and more responsive to their operating conditions. For example, a blockchain-enabled smart washer can detect when it is running low on detergent and place an order for detergent by sending a transaction to a smart contract associated with a detergent supplier. The detergent supplier can communicate the delivery details to the washer when the order is shipped. Similarly, a smart refrigerator can keep track of the items stored (using RFI or NFC tags) and place an item replenishment order when an item is low on stock. Blockchain-enabled smart appliances can monitor their operating state, diagnose problems and automatically place service requests or part replacement orders by sending transactions to the smart contracts associated with the service vendors. The service vendors can check if an appliance is in warranty and process the service requests.

Connected Vehicles

IoT and blockchain technologies can be used to enable smart applications for connected vehicles. For example, identification information of the vehicles, warranty, insurance, vehicle maintenance history and owners' information can be stored on the blockchain. Connected vehicles can monitor their state, diagnose problems and automatically place service requests by sending transactions to the smart contracts associated with the automobile companies or service dealers. Insurance claims' processing can be automated using the blockchain, thus reducing settlement times and claim frauds. Self-driven cars of the future can leverage blockchain for user-to-vehicle micropayments. Users can rent cars by paying to the smart contracts associated with the cars without the need for subscribing to the car-rental service providers. Blockchain-enabled self-driven cars would be able to avail a variety of services by making vehicle-to-infrastructure transactions such as smart parking systems, smart tolls and car charging stations.

1.5.3   Industrial & Manufacturing

Blockchain platforms for industrial and manufacturing systems can be used for developing smart manufacturing and diagnostics applications. We proposed a Blockchain platform for Industrial Internet of Things (BPIIoT) [22]. With the use of blockchain technology, the BPIIoT platform enables peers in a decentralized, trustless, peer-to-peer network to interact with each other without the need for a trusted intermediary.

IoT technologies are promising for industrial and manufacturing systems and the experts have forecast a trillion dollar impact on these sectors by IoT. IoT technologies are being adopted for manufacturing automation, remote machine diagnostics, prognostic health management of industrial machines and supply chain management. A recent on-demand model of manufacturing that is leveraging IoT technologies is called Cloud-Based Manufacturing (CBM) [23]. CBM enables ubiquitous, convenient, on-demand network access to a shared pool of configurable manufacturing resources that can be rapidly provisioned and released with minimal management effort or service provider interaction [24, 25]. The BPIIoT platform acts as a key enabler for cloud-based manufacturing, enhancing the functionality of existing CBM platforms, especially towards integrating legacy shop floor equipment into the cloud environment.

Figures 1.20 shows how BPIIoT platform can enhance the functionality of Cloud-based Manufacturing (CBM) platforms, by providing a decentralized, trustless, peer-to-peer network for manufacturing applications. CBM is a service-oriented manufacturing model in which service consumers are able to configure, select, and utilize configurable manufacturing resources. CBM leverages the four key cloud computing service models: Infrastructure-as-a-Service (IaaS), Platform-as-a-Service (PaaS), Hardware-as-a-Service (HaaS), and Software-as-a-Service (SaaS) [26]. BPIIoT is based on a blockchain network on which smart contracts are deployed. The smart contracts act as agreements between the service consumers and the manufacturing resources to provide on-demand manufacturing services. BPIIoT enables integrating legacy shop floor equipment into the cloud environment and allows developing decentralized and peer-to-peer manufacturing applications.

The key enabler component for the industrial machines in the proposed BPIIoT platform is the IoT device. Figure 1.21 shows the architecture of the IoT device. The IoT device enables existing machines to communicate with the cloud as well as the blockchain network.

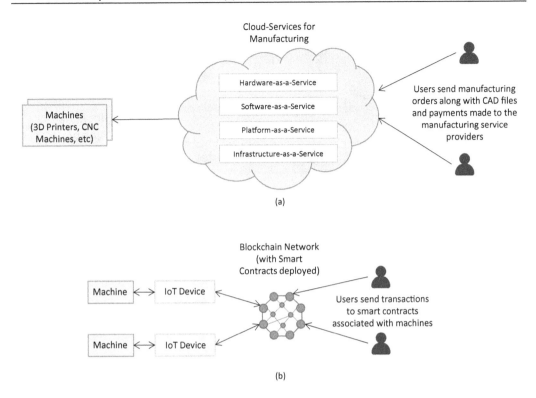

Figure 1.20: (a) Cloud-based manufacturing (CBM) model (b) Blockchain for Industrial Internet of Things

The IoT device is a 'plug and play' solution that allows machines to exchange data on their operations to the cloud, send transactions to the associated smart contracts and receive transactions from the peers on the blockchain network. The IoT device includes an interface board (based on Arduino) and a single-board computer (based on Beaglebone Black or Raspberry Pi). The interface board has digital input/output and analog input capability. Sensors and actuators interface with the digital or analog pins on the interface board. The interface board has a serial interface to the single-board computer (SBC). The sensor bridge between the interface board and the SBC enables the SBC to capture sensor data from the interface board and also send control signals to the actuators. The sensor and actuator connectivity drivers are installed on the SBC. The device manager on the SBC allows the users to configure the SBC using a web interface and also view the device status and statistics. The I/O block on the SBC enables connectivity to external systems over digital, analog, serial and USB connections. The blockchain service on the SBC communicates with the blockchain network and sends/receives transactions to/from the network. Each IoT device has its own account on the blockchain network and maintains a blockchain wallet on the SBC. The controller service performs various actions which can be configured through the device management interface. For example, an action can be to capture data from the sensor bridge and publish it to the cloud through the cloud bridge. Another action can be to monitor the machine status and operating environment and send transactions to the associated smart contracts on the blockchain network (such as a transaction to order replacement of a part).

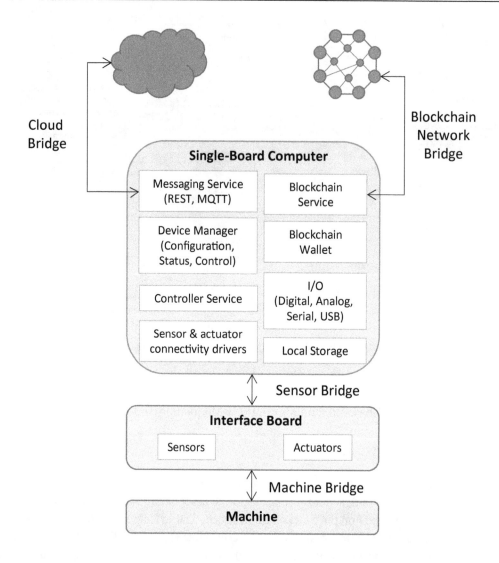

Figure 1.21: Blockchain platform for Industrial Internet of Things (BPIIoT)

Let us now look at some industrial and manufacturing applications that can benefit from blockchain:

On-Demand Manufacturing

Blockchain platforms for industrial and manufacturing systems, such as the BPIIoT platform, can enable a marketplace of manufacturing services where the machines will have their own blockchain accounts and the users will be able to provision and transact with the machines directly to avail manufacturing services in a CBM-like on-demand model. Such platforms can enable peer-to-peer networked manufacturing applications where the peers will be able to avail manufacturing services (such as CNC machining or 3D printing) by sending transactions to the machines.

Smart Diagnostics & Machine Maintenance

Blockchain platforms can be used for developing smart diagnostics and self-service applications for machines where the machines will be able to monitor their state, diagnose problems, and autonomously place service, consumables replenishment, or part replacement requests to the machine maintenance vendors. Smart contracts between manufacturers and vendors for procurement of supplies and service of machines can help in automating the machine maintenance tasks.

Traceability

Blockchain platforms can be used for developing traceability applications for manufactured products. Smart contracts between the consumers and manufacturers can keep production records, for example, which factory and which machines within the factory were used for manufacturing a particular product. In the case of product recalls (either due to manufacturing defects or faulty parts) after the products are delivered, traceability applications can help in identifying the affected products.

Supply Chain Tracking

Blockchain platforms can be used for developing supply chain tracking applications. The Blockchain and smart contracts can keep a formal registry of products and track their possession through different points in a supply chain. Such applications can also enable automated financial settlements on delivery confirmations.

Product Certification

Blockchain platforms can be used for developing product certification applications. The manufacturing information for a product (such as the manufacturing facility details, machine details, manufacturing date and parts information) can be recorded on the blockchain. This information can help in proving the authenticity of the products, thus eliminating the need for physical certificates which can be prone to tampering and forging.

Consumer-to-Machine & Machine-to-Machine Transactions

Blockchain platforms can enable machine-to-machine transactions for manufacturing services. For example, a consumer can send a request for manufacturing a product by sending a transaction to a manufacturer's smart contract along with the payment made in a cryptocurrency (such as Ethers). The manufacturer's smart contract can then send transactions to smart contracts associated with individual machines (consumer-to-machine transactions). If services of different machines are required for manufacturing a product, the machines can send microtransactions to other machines (machine-to-machine transactions).

Tracking Supplier Identity & Reputation

Blockchain platforms can be used for developing supplier identity and reputation management applications which track various performance parameters (such as delivery times, customer reviews and seller ratings) for sellers. Such applications can be used by consumers to find the sellers that can meet their manufacturing requirements and by manufacturers for finding suppliers for consumables. Smart contracts can also help in automatically negotiating best prices for consumables and supplies in real-time based on the seller reputations.

1.5.4   Registry of Assets & Inventory

Blockchain platforms can be used for developing applications for maintaining records of manufacturing assets and inventory. These applications can keep records of the asset identification information and the transfer of assets through the supply chain, eliminating the need for manual paper records.

1.5.5   Energy

Let us now look at some applications of blockchain for energy systems:

Solar Charging Stations

Solar charging stations for electric vehicles can use blockchain platforms to enable the user to station micropayments without the need for an intermediary or a payment gateway. Such a system will have a smart contract for solar charging stations to manage the transactions sent to the stations. The smart contract can manage information related to the station such as the station ID, location, and per-minute rate. Users can pay directly to a contract account from their blockchain wallet applications.

MicroGrids

A microgrid is a localized grouping of electricity generation sources and loads. With microgrids, local electricity generation sources such as renewable energy sources (solar or wind) can be connected to energy consumers in a locality. By using blockchain platforms with microgrids, users can buy and sell renewable energy to their neighbors. TransActiveGrid has developed a combination of software and hardware technologies that enable users to buy and sell solar energy from each other securely and automatically, using smart contracts and the blockchain [21]. Smart contracts can be used by energy producers and consumers for buying and selling energy. The energy producers can set the rates at which they are willing to sell energy. Similarly, consumers can set their preferences for buying energy. Consumers can buy energy by sending transactions to the smart contracts associated with the producers. Once a transaction is confirmed, the associated hardware in the system can actually release the energy from the producer to the consumer. Blockchain-enabled smart meters can be used for real-time metering of local energy generation and usage. Such microgrids can also serve as fallback options in case the centralized grid fails due to natural disasters.

1.5.6   Supply Chain & Logistics

Let us now look at some applications of blockchain for supply chain and logistics:

Supply Chain Tracking

Blockchain and IoT technologies can be used for supply chain tracking. For example, food items can be tracked from their point of origin to the consumer. Smart contracts can be used to maintain the tracking information of the food items. Tracking can be automated with the use of IoT systems equipped with RFID, NFC or BLE tags. Thus, as the food items move from the farms to the shelves in the grocery stores, their time-stamped locations can be recorded within the smart contracts deployed on a blockchain platform. Tracking the food items in this manner makes it easier to trace the origin and the path taken by the items as they move through the supply chain. In the case of recalls, the food items can be easily identified and removed.

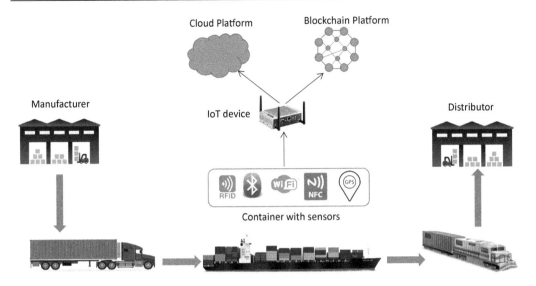

Figure 1.22: Shipment tracking with blockchain and IoT

Shipment Tracking

Blockchain and IoT technologies can be used for tracking shipments as shown in Figure 1.22. Let us take the example of a container that is shipped by a manufacturer in one country to a distributor in another country. The container is first shipped via a truck from the manufacturer's facility to the nearest port. From there it gets transported to the destination port. At the destination port, the container is picked up and transported via rail to the distributor's city and finally transported via truck from the railway station to the distributor's facility. In this case, there are multiple modes of transportation and multiple stakeholders involved. By using IoT technologies and RFID, NFC or BLE tags, we can identify the location of the container as it moves from the source to destination. The time-stamped location information can be recorded within a smart contract and the access to this information can be provided to all the stakeholders. The benefit of this approach is that the shipment tracking can be automated and cryptographically verifiable receipts of the shipment can be issued as the container is transferred from one party to another. In such a system, time-stamped transactions sent to the smart contract can serve as proof-of-shipment and proof-of-delivery. Smart contracts can provide an auditable trail of information and also streamline the processing of shipments at the customs as they move from one country to another. Smart contracts can be used to maintain and furnish necessary information about the container, the consignee, and consignor to speed up the customs clearances.

1.5.7 Records & Identities

Blockchain technology can be used to maintain records for a wide range of applications. Blockchain acts as a distributed database or a global ledger which maintains records of all transactions on a blockchain network. The state information in a blockchain platform is maintained using smart contracts. Proof-of-existence decentralized applications (Dapps) can be developed to verify the existence of the records at particular times. Records stored on the blockchain cannot be tampered by any means. The proof of existence is irrefutable and public for everyone to see.

Blockchain can also be used for identity applications that require the identity of a user to be verified. Blockchain platform users are identified by public-private key-pairs. The transactions sent to the blockchain platform are cryptographically signed by the private keys of the users. Thus a user's identity can be verified by checking if a transaction is signed by the correct private key.

Let us look at some records and identity applications that can benefit from blockchain:

Document Verification

Document verification applications can be developed using blockchain and smart contracts. A document verification application can be used to store a cryptographic hash of any document on the blockchain. Users can verify the existence and validity of a document whose hash is stored on the blockchain. Such an application doesn't store the documents anywhere. While adding a new document, its cryptographic hash is computed on the client side. The document hash along with a timestamp is then submitted to the smart contract associated with the application. Once these details for a document are added to the contract, any user can later verify if the document existed at that time. The cryptographic hash of a document depends on the document's content. Any changes in the document will change its hash. Thus users can securely verify the existence of a document and be assured that the same document existed at a particular moment in time.

Marriage Certificates

Marriage records and certificates can be stored on the blockchain. These records are time-stamped and immutable. A smart contract can be created to maintain records of marriage such as partner information, marriage date and proof of marriage. Marriage records can be securely verified by sending transactions to the smart contracts that maintain the records.

Birth Certificates

Just like marriage records, birth information and birth certificates can be stored on the blockchain. Smart contracts can be created to store birth information such as baby name, date and time of birth, birth location and parent names. The birth records can be verified by anyone by sending a transaction to the smart contracts that maintain the birth records.

Automobile Records

Automobile records can be stored on the blockchain. Smart contracts can be created to store identification information of the automobiles. Furthermore, the warranty, insurance, vehicle maintenance history and owners' information can be stored on the blockchain.

Land Registry

Decentralized applications backed by smart contracts can be used for land registries. Such Dapps can store land records and ownership information on the blockchain. This can ensure greater transparency and reduce manual errors in maintaining land records. The proof of ownership of a piece of land at a particular moment in time can be verified by sending a transaction to the land registry Dapps. Land ownership transfers can be simplified as there is no need for a third party, such as expensive legal counsel. Ownership transfer can be as simple as a transaction sent to the land registry Dapp cryptographically signed by the landowner. Since the blockchain is a decentralized and public ledger, maintaining land registries on the blockchain can reduce costs and increase efficiency.

Copyright Protection

Decentralized applications backed by smart contracts can be created for protecting the copyrights of the content owner. The owner of a content (such as a photo, music, video or a document) can store the ownership information of the content along with the content hash to the copyright protection Dapps. Content owners can use copyright protection Dapps to issue time-stamped copyright certificates to their clients. In the case of copyright infringement, the content owners can prove the ownership of the content with the content copyright information stored on the blockchain.

1.5.8   Healthcare

The healthcare ecosystem consists of numerous entities including healthcare providers (primary care physicians, specialists, hospitals, for instance), payers (government, private health insurance companies, employers), pharmaceutical, device and medical service companies, IT solutions and services firms, and patients. The process of provisioning healthcare involves healthcare data that exists in different forms (structured or unstructured), is stored in disparate data sources (such as relational databases, file servers, for instance) and in many different formats. To promote more coordination of care across the multiple providers involved with patients, their clinical information is increasingly aggregated from diverse sources into Electronic Health Record (EHR) systems. Physicians diagnose patients based on information from many sources such as laboratory tests and medical devices (such as CT and MRI scanners). In the diagnosis process, physicians retrieve and analyze the health information from the EHR. Chronic disease patients are typically seen by multiple physicians at different sites. Care is so distributed that the provider network around the average primary care physician includes some 200 other physicians. Information sharing among them is critical to high-quality care. Physicians often seek expert advice from consulting specialists and this process depends on accurate and timely information sharing.

Due to lack of common software architectures and data storage formats, interoperability problems exist between health-IT systems. Lack of interoperability in health-IT systems poses challenges to the flow of information between the healthcare stakeholders. Blockchain being a decentralized and shared system can be used to store healthcare information. Smart contracts can be created to store different types of healthcare information, such as the patient demographic information, medical history, admission and discharge information, vital signs and services rendered. Access to the Protected Health Information (PHI) or Personally Identifiable Information (PII) stored on the blockchain can be restricted to only the concerned healthcare stakeholders.

Blockchain can be used to store healthcare data in two ways: (1) state information within smart contracts, (2) decentralized storage platform that forms a part of the blockchain stack. Smart contracts store the data within their state variables. For example, state variables in a smart contract for maintaining patient records can store information such as patient ID, name, gender, date of birth and address. Since blockchain and smart contracts are not designed to store large amounts of data and big files, such information can be stored on a decentralized storage platform (such as Swarm). In this approach, while the data is stored off the blockchain

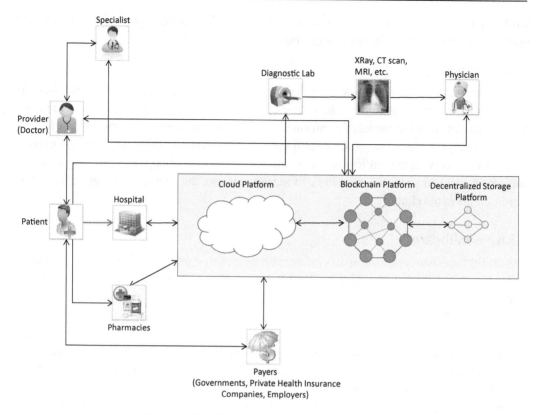

Figure 1.23: Using blockchain for healthcare

within a storage platform, the hash of the data (which is used to uniquely identify the data) is stored on the blockchain as state variables within a smart contract. For example, an X-Ray image file can be stored on a storage platform such as swarm and the swarm-hash of the file can be stored within a smart contract. The benefit of this approach is that while standardized data fields can be stored as state variables in a smart contract, the abstract data types and large files can be stored off the blockchain and pointers to the data (content-hash) stored with the smart contracts.

Let us now look at some healthcare applications that can benefit from blockchain:

Master Patient Index

Master Patient Index (MPI) is a database that stores demographic and essential medical information about patients in a healthcare organization. MPI serves as a consistent data store that stores essential information on patients who are seen in differents departments of an organization. The benefit of MPI is that the patient information is stored only once and is easier to maintain rather than each department storing the same information in their own systems. A smart contract deployed on the blockchain can be used as an MPI. Access to the information within the smart contract can be restricted. Patients can have their own accounts on the blockchain and can keep their information in the MPI up to date.

Electronic Health Records

Electronic Health Record (EHR) systems capture and store information on patient health and provider actions including individual-level laboratory results, diagnostic, treatment, and demographic data. EHRs also maintain information such as patient visits, allergies, immunizations, lab reports, prescribed medicines, vital signs, for instance. EHRs can use blockchain, smart contracts and decentralized storage platforms for storing various types of healthcare information. For example, information on patient-provider interactions can be captured through transactions sent to a smart contract. The smart contract can verify the identities of the concerned stakeholders and validate the information submitted for storage.

Provider Directory

Blockchain and smart contracts can be used for creating a provider directory which includes information on the participating providers registered with a payer. The provider directory can include names, addresses, and affiliations of the providers. Blockchain can enable interoperability between different provider directories.

Medical Insurance Claims

Smart contracts between providers and payers can speed up processing of medical insurance claims and minimize claim frauds. Healthcare providers can create a claim by sending transactions to the smart contracts between the providers and payers. The payers can verify the claims, patient and provider identities and the patient-provider interactions and then approve or deny payments. Claims processing can even be automated by using smart contracts. For example, a smart contract can be used to record the services rendered by a provider to a patient and initiate payment to the provider as soon as the information on a patient-provider interaction is submitted to the contract.

1.6 Blockchain Benefits & Challenges

In this section, we discuss the key benefits and challenges of the blockchain technology. The benefits of blockchain are as follows:

- **Decentralized & Trustless**: Blockchain is a public ledger of all transactions on the network which is maintained by different decentralized nodes. Blockchain technology enables a decentralized and trustless peer-to-peer network where the peers do not need a trusted intermediary for interacting with each other. Since a blockchain network is not controlled by a central authority and all the transactions are verified and validated by a consensus among the peers, the peers do not need to trust each other.
- **Resilient**: Blockchain network is resilient to failures, as it is a decentralized peer-to-peer network with no single point of failure. The blockchain itself is an immutable and durable ledger and the transactions once recorded on the blockchain after a consensus among the peers cannot be altered or deleted.
- **Scalable**: Blockchain network is highly scalable in nature as it is maintained by a network of peers. The computing capability of the network scales up as more and more peers (or miners) join the network.
- **Secure & Auditable**: All the transactions in a blockchain network are secured by strong cryptography. Furthermore, the transparent nature of the public ledger

maintained by a blockchain network makes it secure and auditable as everyone on the network knows about all the transactions and the transactions cannot be disputed.

- **Autonomous**: Blockchain can enable different entities (e.g. IoT devices) to communicate with each other and do transactions autonomously. For example, an IoT device can have its own account on a blockchain network and transact with other devices autonomously without a trusted third-party.

While the blockchain technology looks promising for different industries and domains, there are various challenges that need to be addressed to ensure its widespread adoption. The key challenges are as follows:

- **CAP & Blockchain**: For distributed data systems, a trade-off exists between consistency and availability. These trade-offs are explained with the CAP Theorem, which states that under partitioning, a distributed data system can either be consistent or available but not both at the same time. Blockchain gives up on consistency to be available and partition tolerant. Blockchain is a distributed ledger which is eventually consistent, i.e. all nodes eventually see the same ledger. In Ethereum, the block-time (time after which a new block is mined) is roughly 17 seconds, which is much faster than Bitcoin which has a block time of 10 minutes. A consequence of fast block-time is reduced security, therefore many blockchain applications require multiple confirmations for newly mined blocks to secure the transactions from double-spending. Faster block-time also leads to a high number of stale blocks to be produced. Stale blocks are competing blocks produced by miners which do not contribute to the main chain. High stale rate reduces security of the main chain [2]. To counter this problem the "Greedy Heaviest Observed Subtree" (GHOST) protocol has been proposed [6]. The GHOST protocol is described in detail in Chapter-10.

- **Smart Contract Vulnerabilities**: Smart contracts can have software vulnerabilities which can be exploited by hackers. In June 2016, an attacker managed to drain more than 3.6 million Ether from the Slock.it backed Decentralized Autonomous Organization (DAO) into a "child DAO". The attacker managed this by exploiting a "recursive call bug" vulnerability in the DAO smart contract. Since smart contracts are meant to be agreements between transacting parties on a blockchain and not legally enforceable outside the network, such attacks can put the organizations, miners and even the blockchain network at risk [5].

- **Awareness**: Blockchain is a nascent technology and is mostly adopted in the financial sector (Bitcoin being the most popular application). Lack of awareness about the blockchain technology in other sectors is affecting its widespread adoption.

- **Regulation**: Since blockchain does away with the need for a centralized authority or a trusted intermediary for validating the transactions, there remain regulatory hurdles in the widespread adoption of the technology. New government and industry regulations are required for decentralized systems such as blockchain. Furthermore, there is a need to ensure legal enforceability of smart contracts to avoid disputes among the transacting parties.

- **Privacy**: Since blockchain is a public ledger and anyone can view all the transactions on a blockchain network, there remain privacy concerns for the transacting parties.

- **Efficiency**: Since all the nodes in a blockchain network perform the same computations in an attempt to mine the next block for the blockchain, this is not an efficient approach.

Due to this redundancy in execution, the contribution of an individual node to the overall network is very small even though the node may be performing very hard computations. The proof-of-work algorithms used by blockchain networks have been criticized for consuming large amounts of electricity as the miners have to expend significant computational resources and energy to perform complex mathematical computations for computing the PoW *nonce*.

Summary

In this chapter we introduced the reader to the concept of a smart new world based on a frictionless digital economy. We described some basic blockchain concepts and the evolution of blockchain platforms in the past decade. Blockchain is a distributed and public ledger which maintains records of all the transactions with no centralized agency controlling the infrastructure. The current blockchain technology was introduced by Satoshi Nakamoto, the creator of Bitcoin. To prevent double-spending without a trusted central authority, Nakamoto identified two key requirements: (1) publicly announcing all transactions, (2) having a system for the participants to agree on the transactions and their sequence. These requirements led to the development of the blockchain, which is a distributed data structure comprising a chain of blocks. Bitcoin is a first generation blockchain network in which the primary application is the electronic cash or cryptocurrency called Bitcoin. Vitalik Buterin proposed a second generation of the blockchain network in 2013, called Ethereum, which has been designed as a programmable blockchain network that can be used to develop different types of applications. The blockchain structure includes a sequence of blocks where each block is identified by its cryptographic hash and references the hash of its parent block. Next, we described a blockchain stack that includes (1) a decentralized computation platform, (2) a decentralized messaging platform and (3) a decentralized storage platform. A specific realization of the blockchain stack based on the Ethereum blockchain platform was described. Next, we described domain specific blockchain applications for FinTech, Internet of Things, industrial and manufacturing, energy, supply chain and logistics, and healthcare domains. Finally, we described the benefits and challenges in the development and deployment of blockchain platforms.

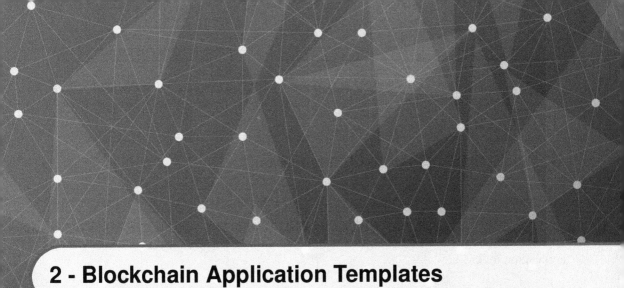

2 - Blockchain Application Templates

This chapter covers

- Blockchain Application Components
- Design Methodology for Blockchain Applications
- Blockchain Application Templates
  - Many-to-one
  - Many-to-one for IoT applications
  - Many-to-many or peer-to-peer
  - One-to-one for financial applications

In this chapter, we propose a novel design methodology for blockchain applications using smart contracts and decentralized applications that utilizes four different types of design templates.

2.1   Blockchain Application Components

In Chapter-1, we described the typical blockchain stack as including a decentralized computation platform (Ethereum), a decentralized messaging platform (Whisper) and a decentralized storage platform (Swarm). We also briefly described smart contracts and decentralized applications (Dapps). Let us now look at how these all fit together and how a blockchain application looks like.

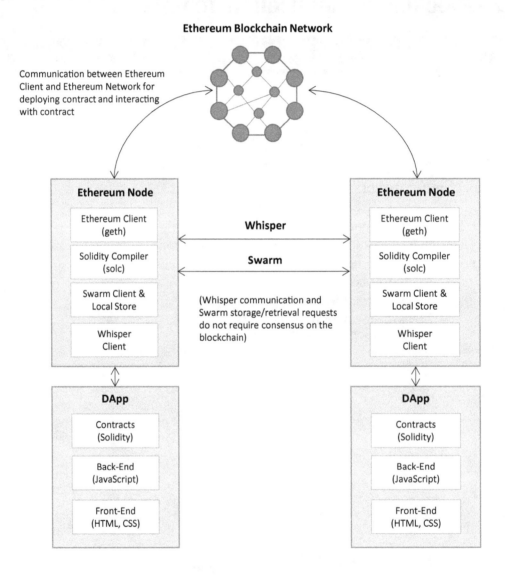

Figure 2.1: Blockchain components

Figure 2.1 shows the various components of the Ethereum blockchain platform. Blockchain applications are either in the form of smart contracts or Dapps. A smart contract is a piece of code which is deployed on the blockchain and is uniquely identified by an address. A smart contract implementation includes state variables, functions, modifiers, and events. Smart contracts are implemented in a high-level language such as Solidity. In Appendix-A, we cover the basics of the Solidity language. In Chapter-5 we describe the steps involved in implementing and deploying smart contracts. While smart contracts can directly be used by end users who can send transactions or calls to the smart contracts through Ethereum clients, however, to provide a more user-friendly interface to smart contracts, Dapps can be developed and applied over these smart contracts. A Dapp includes a front-end user interface which is implemented in HTML and CSS and a back-end which is typically implemented in JavaScript. Users can submit transactions to the smart contract associated with a Dapp from the Dapp's web interface itself. The Dapp's web interface forwards the transactions to the blockchain platform and displays the transaction receipts or state information in the smart contracts in the web interface. In Chapter-6, we will describe the steps involved in implementing Dapps along with examples and case studies.

A Dapp is deployed on an Ethereum node which serves the Dapp's web-based user interface. The Dapp logic is controlled by the associated smart contracts which are deployed on the blockchain platform. Dapps which have special storage requirements can make use of decentralized storage platforms such as Swarm. Similarly, Dapps which have special messaging requirements can leverage a decentralized messaging platform such as Whisper. While the smart contracts are deployed on the Ethereum blockchain, Swarm storage and Whisper messaging work off the chain as they do not require a consensus on the blockchain. In chapters 8 and 9, we will introduce Whisper and Swarm platforms and how Dapps can leverage these platforms. An Ethereum node comprises an Ethereum client (such as Geth), compilers for smart contract programming languages (such as *solc* compiler for Solidity), and clients for Swarm and Whisper platforms. In Chapter-3, we will describe the steps involved in setting up an Ethereum node.

2.2 Design Methodology for Blockchain Applications

Figure 2.2 shows the stages involved in designing and implementing industrial-strength blockchain applications. In the analysis stage, we analyze the requirements of the blockchain application to be developed and identify the entities involved, their roles and relationships. The entities can either be physical (such as users or objects) or virtual (such as concepts). In the design stage, we model the entity attributes as state variables and interactions between them as functions. At this stage, we also capture the dependencies and constraints. In the implementation stage, we implement the smart contract for the blockchain application (including state variables, functions, modifiers, and events) in a high-level language such as Solidity. If a user-friendly interface to the application is required, we implement the Dapp which is backed by the smart contract. For the Dapp, we implement the front-end (in HTML and CSS) and backend (in JavaScript).

Let us now apply this design methodology towards the development and deployment of a crowdfunding application. Using such an application, a crowdfunding campaign can be setup. Backers interested in supporting the funding campaign can send transactions to the contract along with the value (in Ether) to contribute to the campaign.

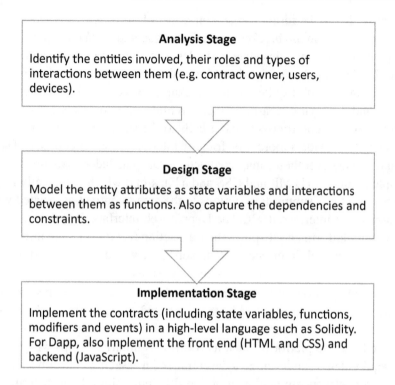

Analysis Stage

Identify the entities involved, their roles and types of interactions between them (e.g. contract owner, users, devices).

Design Stage

Model the entity attributes as state variables and interactions between them as functions. Also capture the dependencies and constraints.

Implementation Stage

Implement the contracts (including state variables, functions, modifiers and events) in a high-level language such as Solidity. For Dapp, also implement the front end (HTML and CSS) and backend (JavaScript).

Figure 2.2: Steps involved in designing and implementing blockchain applications

Figure 2.3 shows the analysis stage for this application. The entities involved include a campaign owner, the campaign itself and the campaign backers. The funding campaign owner creates a campaign and the campaign backers contribute to the campaign. Next, we identify the types of interactions between the entities involved. The campaign backers fund the campaign created by a campaign owner. Upon completion of the campaign, the campaign owner checks if the campaign goal has been reached. If the campaign succeeds, the funds collected are transferred to the campaign owner. However, if the campaign fails, the funds collected are returned to the backers.

Figure 2.4 shows the design stage for this application. We model the entity attributes as state variables and interactions between them as functions. For a crowdfunding campaign, the attributes include the campaign goal, campaign duration, amount raised, campaign status and number of backers. Similarly, for a campaign backer, the attributes include the address of the backer and the amount contributed. The interaction between a campaign backer and the campaign is modeled as the *fund* function. A campaign backer can contribute to the campaign by sending a transaction to the *fund* function along with the value to contribute (in Ether). The interaction between the campaign owner and the campaign is modeled as the *checkGoalReached* function. Upon the completion of the campaign, the campaign owner can send a transaction to the *checkGoalReached* function to check if the campaign succeeded or failed, and withdraw the funds (if succeeded) or issue refunds (if failed).

Analysis Stage

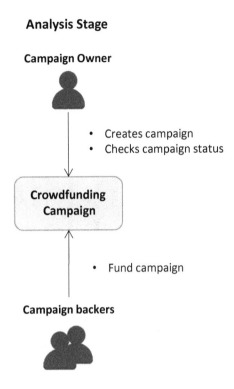

Figure 2.3: Analysis stage for crowdfunding application

Design Stage

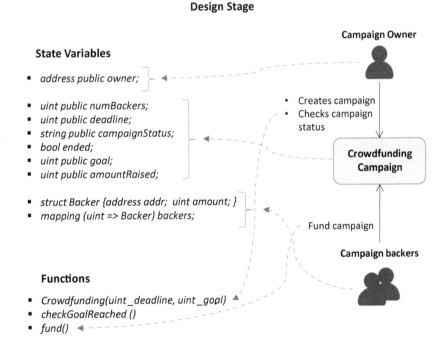

Figure 2.4: Design stage for crowdfunding application

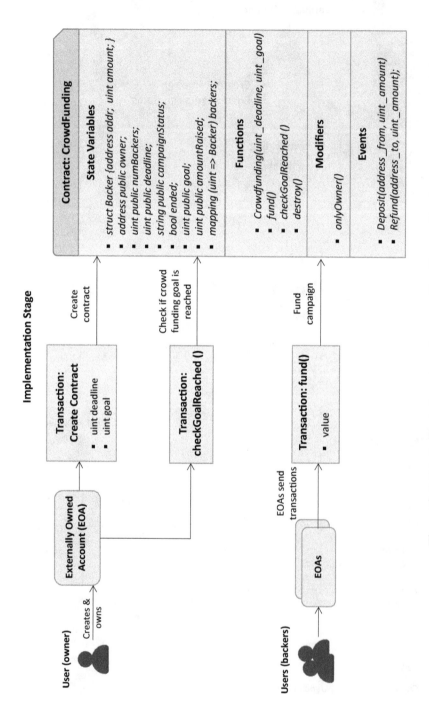

Figure 2.5: Implementation stage for crowdfunding application

Figure 2.5 shows the implementation stage for this application. In this stage, we implement the crowdfunding smart contract based on the state variables and functions identified in the design stage. A function modifier *onlyOwner* is implemented and applied to the *checkGoalReached* function, to restrict access to this function. We also implement two events to log the deposits and refunds. In Chapter-5, we provide the complete implementation of the smart contract for the crowdfunding application. In Chapter-6, we provide an implementation of a Dapp for crowdfunding.

2.3   Blockchain Application Templates

In this section, we propose key blockchain application templates based on an analysis of the examples covered in this book. For each template, we have also listed the related applications for which we have provided complete implementations in this book. The readers may choose one or more of these templates to assist their development and deployment activities.

2.3.1   Many-to-One

This template can be used for applications in which a user (who is the owner of a contract) sets up the contract for a specific purpose. For example, the purpose can be to raise funds from the public, sell tickets for an event, conduct voting, etc. All other users who interact with the contract have the same role, for example, backers of a crowdfunding campaign, buyers of event tickets, voters, etc. Figure 2.6 shows the structure of the template and the entities involved. We have used this template for Crowdfunding, Event Registration, Voting, and Name Registration applications which are described in Chapters 5 and 6.

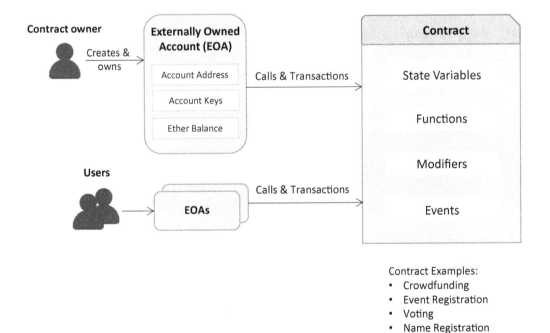

Figure 2.6: Template-1: Many-to-one

2.3.2   Many-to-One for IoT Applications

This template can be used for applications in which the contract owner sets up a contract that allows users to control an IoT device. The IoT device can be used for several purposes such as to open or close a lock, to turn a switch on or off, etc. Figure 2.7 shows the structure of the template and the entities involved. We have used this template for Solar Charging Stations and Smart Switch applications which are described in Chapters 5 and 6.

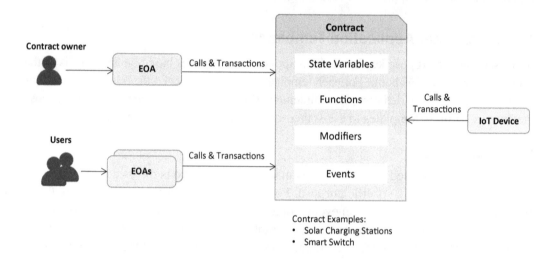

Figure 2.7: Template-2: Many-to-one for IoT applications

2.3.3   Many-to-Many or Peer-to-Peer

This template can be used for applications in which the contract owner sets up a contract that allows two types of users to conduct business through the contract. For example, the users may have the roles of buyer/seller, producer/consumer or creator/verifier. Figure 2.8 shows the structure of the template and the entities involved. We have used this template for Product Sales, Stock Photos and Document Verification applications which are described in Chapters 6 and 9.

2.3.4   One-to-One for Financial Applications

This template can be used for applications which involve financial contracts between two parties such as financial derivative applications. One of the parties sets up a contract and the other party verifies and accepts the contract. Once the contract is verified and activated, either party can execute the contract. Separate trading accounts are created for each party which are backed by a smart contract. Each party maintains a sufficient balance in their trading account to facilitate the payments. Separate smart contracts are used for different financial applications (such as financial derivative instruments). The contracts can be initialized by either party and then verified by the other party. Each party authorizes the financial contract to deposit/withdraw money to/from their trading account. Thus, when the contract is exercised, the contract itself can automatically deposit or withdraw money to/from the trading accounts without additional permissions from the two parties. Figure 2.9 shows the structure of the template and the entities involved. We have used this template for Call Option and Interest Rate Swap applications which are described in Chapters 6.

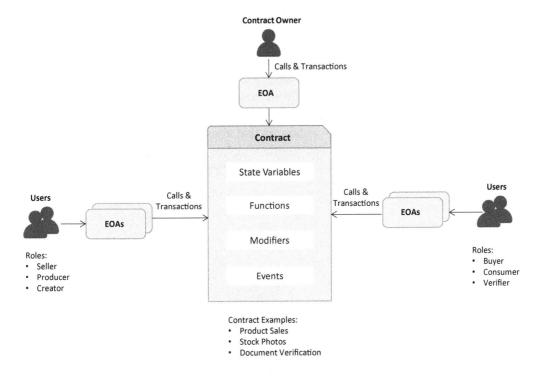

Figure 2.8: Template-3: Many-to-many or peer-to-peer

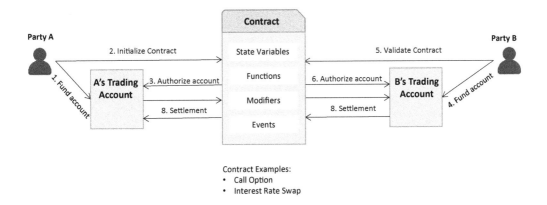

Figure 2.9: Template-4: One-to-one for financial applications

Summary

In this chapter, we described a powerful (yet simple!) design methodology for blockchain applications that includes analysis, design and implementation stages. In the analysis stage, we analyze the requirements of the blockchain application to be developed and identify the entities involved, their roles and relationships. In the design stage, we model the entity attributes as state variables and the interactions between them as functions. In the implementation stage, we implement the smart contract for the blockchain application (including state variables, functions, modifiers, and events) in a high-level language such as Solidity. Next, we proposed a few useful blockchain application templates. The many-to-one template can be used for applications in which a user (who is the owner of a contract) sets up the contract for a specific purpose. The many-to-one template for IoT applications can be used for applications in which the contract owner sets up a contract that allows users to control an IoT device. The many-to-many or peer-to-peer template can be used for applications in which the contract owner sets up a contract that allows two types of users to conduct business through the contract. The one-to-one template for financial applications can be used for applications which involve financial contracts between two parties such as financial derivative applications.

Part II

BLOCKCHAIN COMPONENTS & APPLICATIONS

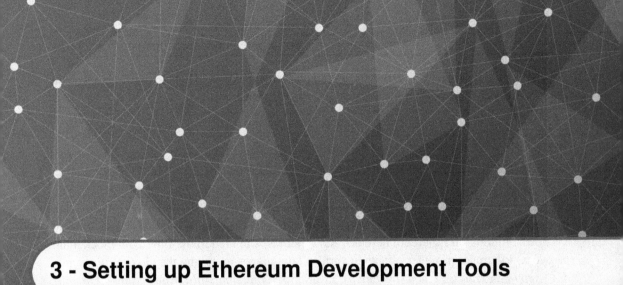

3 - Setting up Ethereum Development Tools

This chapter covers

- Ethereum Clients
  - Go-Ethereum Client (geth)
  - Python Ethereum Client (pyethapp)
- Solidity Ethereum Language
- TestRPC
- Mist Ethereum Wallet
- MetaMask
- Web3 JavaScript API
- Truffle

In this chapter we describe the Ethereum development tools and how to setup a blockchain development environment to run the examples in this book.

3.1   Ethereum Clients

Ethereum clients allow you to setup an Ethereum node on your computer. An Ethereum client is like a Java Virtual Machine (JVM) and allows you to run Ethereum programs. With an Ethereum client, you can participate in the Ethereum network and perform tasks such as creating accounts and contracts, sending Ether to other accounts, sending transactions to contracts, mining on Ethereum network and other tasks related to the Ethereum blockchain network. Ethereum provides clients in various launguages including the Go (*go-ethereum*), C++ (*cpp-ethereum*), Python (*pyethapp*), JavaScript (*ethereumjs-lib*), Ruby (*ruby-ethereum*), Java (*Ethereum(J)*), Haskell (*ethereumH*), and Rust (*Parity*). For the examples in this book, we have used the Go (*geth*) and Python (*pyethapp*) clients.

3.1.1   Go-Ethereum Client (geth)

The Go-Ethereum client, commonly called *geth*, is the Ethereum's official client [28]. The box below shows the commands for setting up an Ethereum node and the *geth* client:

```
■ Setting up Ethereum node and Geth client
sudo apt-get install software-properties-common
sudo add-apt-repository -y ppa:ethereum/ethereum
sudo add-apt-repository -y ppa:ethereum/ethereum-dev
sudo apt-get update
sudo apt-get install ethereum
```

Box 3.1 shows the *geth* client commands and Box 3.2 shows the *geth* client options. For interacting with the Ethereum network, the *geth* client provides an interactive JavaScript console and also JSON-RPC based APIs which are exposed by HTTP, WebSocket and IPC.

```
■ Box 3.1: Geth commands
import    import a blockchain file
export    export blockchain into file
upgradedb      upgrade chainblock database
removedb Remove blockchain and state databases
dump      dump a specific block from storage
monitor   Geth Monitor: node metrics monitoring and visualization
account   manage accounts
wallet    ethereum presale wallet
makedag   generate ethash dag (for testing)
gpuinfo   gpuinfo
gpubench  benchmark GPU
version   print ethereum version numbers
init      bootstraps and initialises a new genesis block (JSON)
console   Geth Console: interactive JavaScript environment
attach    Geth Console: interactive JS environment (connect to node)
js        executes the given JavaScript files in the Geth JavaScript VM
```

■ Box 3.2: Geth options

```
ETHEREUM OPTIONS:
  --datadir "/home/ubuntu/.ethereum"  Data directory for the
            databases and keystore
  --keystore: Directory for the keystore
            (default = inside the datadir)
  --networkid "1": Network identifier
            (integer, 0=Olympic, 1=Frontier, 2=Morden)
  --olympic:   Olympic network: pre-configured pre-release test network
  --testnet:   Morden network: pre-configured test network with
            modified starting nonces (replay protection)
  --dev:  Developer mode: pre-configured private network
            with several debugging flags
  --genesis:  Insert/overwrite the genesis block (JSON format)
  --identity: Custom node name
  --fast: Enable fast syncing through state downloads
  --lightkdf: Reduce key-derivation RAM & CPU usage at some
            expense of KDF strength
  --cache "128":   Megabytes of memory allocated to internal
            caching (min 16MB / database forced)
  --blockchainversion "3": Blockchain version (integer)

ACCOUNT OPTIONS:
  --unlock  Comma separated list of accounts to unlock
  --password: Password file to use for non-inteactive password input

API AND CONSOLE OPTIONS:
  --rpc: Enable the HTTP-RPC server
  --rpcaddr "localhost": HTTP-RPC server listening interface
  --rpcport "8545":   HTTP-RPC server listening port
  --rpcapi "eth,net,web3":: API's offered over the HTTP-RPC interface
  --ws:  Enable the WS-RPC server
  --wsaddr "localhost":  WS-RPC server listening interface
  --wsport "8546":   WS-RPC server listening port
  --wsapi "eth,net,web3"::  API's offered over the WS-RPC interface
  --wsorigins:: Origins from which to accept websockets requests
  --ipcdisable::   Disable the IPC-RPC server
  --ipcapi "admin,eth,debug,miner,net,shh,txpool,personal,web3"
            API's offered over the IPC-RPC interface
  --ipcpath "geth.ipc":  Filename for IPC socket/pipe within the
            datadir (explicit paths escape it)
  --rpccorsdomain:   Comma separated list of domains from which to
            accept cross origin requests (browser enforced)
  --jspath "."::   JavaScript root path for `loadScript` and
            document root for `admin.httpGet`
  --exec::  Execute JavaScript statement (only in combination
            with console/attach)
  --preload: Comma separated list of JavaScript files to preload
            into the console

NETWORKING OPTIONS:
  --bootnodes: Comma separated enode URLs for P2P discovery bootstrap
  --port "30303": Network listening port
```

```
--maxpeers "25": Maximum number of network peers
                (network disabled if set to 0)
--maxpendpeers "0": Maximum number of pending connection
                attempts (defaults used if set to 0)
--nat "any": NAT port mapping mechanism (any|none|upnp|pmp|extip:<IP>)
--nodiscover: Disables the peer discovery mechanism
                (manual peer addition)
--nodekey:   P2P node key file
--nodekeyhex:   P2P node key as hex (for testing)

MINER OPTIONS:
--mine:  Enable mining
--minerthreads "4":  Number of CPU threads to use for mining
--minergpus: List of GPUs to use for mining (e.g. '0,1'
                will use the first two GPUs found)
--autodag:   Enable automatic DAG pregeneration
--etherbase "0": Public address for block mining rewards
(default = first account created)
--targetgaslimit "4712388": Target gas limit sets the
        artificial target gas floor for the blocks to mine
--gasprice "20000000000":  Minimal gas price to accept
                for mining a transactions
--extradata: Block extra data set by the miner
                (default = client version)

GAS PRICE ORACLE OPTIONS:
--gpomin "20000000000": Minimum suggested gas price
--gpomax "500000000000"   Maximum suggested gas price
--gpofull "80":  Full block threshold for gas price calculation (%)
--gpobasedown "10":  Suggested gas price base step down ratio (1/1000)
--gpobaseup "100":  Suggested gas price base step up ratio (1/1000)
--gpobasecf "110":  Suggested gas price base correction factor (%)

VIRTUAL MACHINE OPTIONS:
--jitvm: Enable the JIT VM
--forcejit:  Force the JIT VM to take precedence
--jitcache "64":  Amount of cached JIT VM programs

LOGGING AND DEBUGGING OPTIONS:
--metrics:   Enable metrics collection and reporting
--fakepow:   Disables proof-of-work verification
--verbosity: Logging verbosity
--vmodule:   Per-module verbosity
```

To setup a full Ethereum node, you can run the *geth* client as follows:

■ **Running Ethereum node and Geth client**
```
geth -fast console
```

The fast option enables fast syncing of the Ethereum blockchain through state downloads, without having to process all the history of the Ethereum network. The console command opens an interactive JavaScript console where you can run JavaScript commands and the management API provided by *geth* to interact with the Ethereum network. Within the *geth*

JavaScript console, you can create new accounts, check account balances, send Ether to other accounts, create and deploy contracts, send transactions to contracts and perform other operations to interact with the Ethereum network. To work on the Ethereum test network (testnet) instead of the main network, you can add the *–testnet* option to the above command.

For the examples in this book, we use an Ethereum private blockchain network. A private blockchain is useful for testing smart contracts and Dapps, without having to use real Ether on the main Ethereum blockchain. Before creating the private blockchain, we create a new directory to hold the blockchain files and then create two Ethereum accounts as follows:

```
■ Create Ethereum accounts
mkdir /home/ubuntu/ethchain
geth -datadir "/home/ubuntu/ethchain" -dev account new
```

After creating the Ethereum accounts, you can list the accounts as follows.

```
■ List Ethereum accounts
geth -datadir "/home/ubuntu/ethchain" -dev account list
```

Note the account addresses and create a genesis block JSON file as shown in Box 3.3. The genesis block JSON file contains information on the first block of the blockchain. Ethereum provides the flexibility to specify your own genesis block file to create a new blockchain. The fields in the genesis JSON file include:

- **nonce**: The nonce field is a 64-bit hash, which along with mixhash field is used to verify that a sufficient amount of computation has been carried out on this block and the block contains a valid proof-of-work (PoW).
- **mixhash**: The mixhash field is a 256-bit hash, which along with nonce field is used to verify that the block contains a valid proof-of-work.
- **difficulty**: This field specifies a difficulty value for mining. A block is only valid if it contains a valid proof-of-work (PoW) of a given difficulty. If the difficulty value is high, the miners have to perform more calculations to mine a block, hence the block generation time increases as the difficulty increases. For the private blockchain, we keep this value low so that the blocks can be mined faster (and also the transactions are processed faster).
- **alloc**: The alloc field allows pre-allocating Ether to Ethereum accounts created previously. Note that the Ether allocated and also mined by the miners on a private blockchain are not real Ether and do not work on any other blockchain.
- **coinbase**: The coinbase field specifies the address of the account to which all the rewards for mining of the block and the execution of contracts are transferred. This value can be anything in the genesis file as it is set by the miner who mines the block.
- **timestamp**: This is the UNIX timestamp value at the creation of the block. If the time interval between the last two blocks is large, the difficulty value decreases, so that the next block is mined faster. For the genesis block, we set this value to zero.
- **parentHash**: Each block in a blockchain is linked to its parent through the parentHash, which is the hash of the parent block header. In the case of genesis block (first block on the blockchain), the parentHash is zero.
- **extraData**: Optional 32-byte extra data can be provided in the genesis block.

- **gasLimit**: The gas limit value is the limit of Gas expenditure per block.

■ **Box 3.3: Genesis File**

```
{
  "nonce": "0x0000000000000042",
  "difficulty": "0x4000",
  "alloc": {
    "684363c3b24ea557ef0276597e8abe5bb21fda7a": {
      "balance": "1000000000000000000000000"
    },
    "be26b442b05af34b8e91b2cedf2d7ef5a6630409": {
      "balance": "1000000000000000000000000"
    }
  },
  "mixhash":
  "0x0000000000000000000000000000000000000000000000000000000000000000",
  "coinbase": "0x0000000000000000000000000000000000000000",
  "timestamp": "0x00",
  "parentHash":
  "0x0000000000000000000000000000000000000000000000000000000000000000",
  "extraData": "0x",
  "gasLimit": "0xffffffff"
}
```

With the genesis file created, now let us use the genesis block JSON to seed a private blockchain, as shown in the box below:

■ **Create Private Blockchain**

```
geth -datadir "/home/ubuntu/ethchain" -dev -unlock 0,1 -mine
-minerthreads 2 -rpc -rpcaddr 0.0.0.0 -rpccorsdomain "*"
-rpcport 8101 init "/home/ubuntu/genesis.json"
```

Once the private blockchain is created, you can run the following command to run a *geth* instance and start mining on the private blockchain. Note that we unlock accounts with indexes 0 and 1 and use two mining threads. We also specify the HTTP-RPC server settings.

■ **Run Miners**

```
geth -datadir "/home/ubuntu/ethchain" -dev -unlock 0,1 -mine
-minerthreads 2 -rpc -rpcaddr 0.0.0.0
-rpccorsdomain "*" -rpcport 8101
```

Next, you can attach a *geth* console to the *geth* instance connected to the private blockchain as follows:

■ **Run Geth console**

```
geth -datadir "/home/ubuntu/ethchain"
-dev attach ipc:/home/ubuntu/ethchain/geth.ipc
```

Within the *geth* JavaScript console, you can check if the accounts created previously have been pre-allocated Ether as specified in the genesis block JSON file.

■ **Check account balance**
```
> web3.fromWei(eth.getBalance(eth.accounts[0]), "ether");
10000
> web3.fromWei(eth.getBalance(eth.accounts[1]), "ether");
10000
```

3.1.2 Python Ethereum Client (pyethapp)

The Python Ethereum client called *pyethapp* includes two components [29]:

* *pyethereum*: This is the Python core library of the Ethereum project that implements the blockchain, the Ethereum virtual machine, and mining.
* *pydevp2p*: This is the peer-to-peer (p2p) networking library for the Ethereum project. This library implements the RLPx network layer and provides features such as node discovery, network formation, peer preference strategies, peer reputation, encrypted handshake and encrypted transport.

The box below shows the commands for setting up the *pyethapp* client:

■ **Setting up pyethapp client**
```
sudo apt-get install build-essential automake
sudo apt-get install pkg-config libtool libffi-dev libgmp-dev
sudo pip install pyethapp
```

Box 3.4 shows the *pyethapp* client commands and Box 3.5 shows the *pyethapp* client options.

■ **Box 3.4: pyethapp commands**

```
account: Manage accounts.
blocktest  Start after importing blocks from a file.
config:  Show the config
export:  Export the blockchain to FILE.
import:  Import blocks from FILE.
run: : Start the client ( --dev to stop on error)
```

■ **Box 3.5: pyethapp options**

```
--profile [livenet|testnet]: Configuration profile.  [default: livenet]
-C, --Config TEXT:         Alternative config file
-c TEXT:                   Single configuration parameters
-d, --data-dir TEXT        Data directory
-l, --log_config TEXT      log_config string
--log-json / --log-no-json:  Log as structured json output
--log-file PATH:           Log to file instead of stderr.
-b, --bootstrap_node TEXT: Single bootstrap_node
-m, --mining_pct INTEGER:  pct cpu used for mining
--unlock TEXT:             Unlock an account (prompts for password)
--password FILENAME:       Path to a password file
```

To setup a full Ethereum node, you can run the *pyethapp* client as follows:

■ **Running Ethereum node and pyethapp client**
```
pyethapp run --console
```

Like the *geth* client, the *pyethapp* client also provides various account management commands. You can create a new Ethereum account with *pyethapp* as follows:

■ **Creating an Ethereum account with pyethapp**
```
$ pyethapp -d "/home/ubuntu/ethchain" account new
INFO:config setup default config path=/home/ubuntu/ethchain
INFO:config writing config path=/home/ubuntu/ethchain/config.yaml
INFO:app    using data in path=/home/ubuntu/ethchain
INFO:config loading config path=/home/ubuntu/ethchain
INFO:app    registering service service=accounts
Password to encrypt private key:
Repeat for confirmation:
INFO:accounts    adding account
Account creation successful
   Address: 943ac3596b1fd225976a461d8ce931f295519b6f
      Id: None
```

To list the accounts you can use the following command:

■ **Listing Ethereum accounts with pyethapp**
```
$ pyethapp -d "/home/ubuntu/ethchain" account list
    Address (if known)                   Id (if any)   Locked
  #1 106082fe9ffddb0bb07be253e58e34bad764be35            yes
  #2 943ac3596b1fd225976a461d8ce931f295519b6f            yes
```

To setup a private blockchain, a custom genesis block JSON file can be created as described in the previous section. To seed a private blockchain using a genesis file, the following command can be used:

■ **Creating a private blockchain with pyethapp client**
```
pyethapp -d "/home/ubuntu/ethchain" -c
  eth.genesis=/home/ubuntu/genesis.json run --console
```

For interacting with the Ethereum network, the *pyethapp* client provides an interactive IPython console and also JSON-RPC based APIs. Within the *pyethapp* interactive console you can check if the accounts created previously have been pre-allocated Ether as specified in the genesis block JSON file as follows:

■ **Checking account balance within pyethapp console**
```
In [1]:  eth.latest.get_balance(eth.services.accounts[0].address)
Out[1]:  1000000000000000000000000000L
In [2]:  eth.latest.get_balance(eth.services.accounts[1].address)
Out[2]:  1000000000000000000000000000L
```

3.2 Ethereum Languages

Ethereum provides various high-level languages for implementing contracts, including Solidity which is similar to JavaScript, Serpent which is similar to Python, and Lisp Like Language (LLL) which is similar to Assembly. For the examples in this book, we use Solidity for the most part, as it is the most popular language for Ethereum and has more community support available as compared to Serpent and LLL.

3.2.1 Solidity

Solidity is a JavaScript like high level language for implementing smart contracts [12]. Solidity can be installed as follows:

■ **Installing Solidity**
```
sudo add-apt-repository ppa:ethereum/ethereum
sudo apt-get update
sudo apt-get install solc
```

Box 3.6 lists the command line options for the Solidity compiler (*solc*).

■ **Box 3.6: Solc options**
```
--version:  Show version and exit.
--optimize: Enable bytecode optimizer.
--optimize-runs n (=200): Estimated number of contract runs
                     for optimizer tuning.
--add-std: Add standard contracts.
--libraries libs:   Direct string or file containing library addresses.
-o [ --output-dir ] path: If given, creates one file per component and
 contract/file at the specified directory.
--combined-json abi,asm,ast,bin,bin-runtime,clone-bin,devdoc,
     interface,opcodes,userdoc: Output a single json document
     containing the specified information.
--gas:   Print an estimate of the maximal gas usage for each function.
--assemble: Switch to assembly mode, ignoring all options and
          assumes input is assembly.
--link:  Switch to linker mode, ignoring all options apart from
       --libraries and modify binaries in place.
--ast:  AST of all source files.
--ast-json:  AST of all source files in JSON format.
--asm:  EVM assembly of the contracts.
--asm-json:  EVM assembly of the contracts in JSON format.
--opcodes:  Opcodes of the contracts.
--bin:  Binary of the contracts in hex.
--bin-runtime:   Binary of the runtime part of the contracts in hex.
--clone-bin: Binary of the clone contracts in hex.
--abi:  ABI specification of the contracts.
--interface: Solidity interface of the contracts.
--hashes:   Function signature hashes of the contracts.
--userdoc:   Natspec user documentation of all contracts.
--devdoc:   Natspec developer documentation of all contracts.
--formal:   Translated source suitable for formal analysis.
```

Contracts implemented in Solidity can either be compiled using the *solc* compiler via command line or using the *web3.eth.compile.solidity()* function provided in the interactive JavaScript console of the Ethereum clients such as *geth*. Appendix-A provides an introduction to the Solidity language. Examples of smart contracts implemented in Solidity are described in detail in Chapter-5.

3.3 TestRPC

While Ethereum clients such as *geth* and *pyethapp* are good options for working with the main Ethereum blockchain, TestNet or a private blockchain, however, for development and testing of contracts and Dapps, we recommend using TestRPC which is a Node.js based Ethereum client. TestRPC simulates Ethereum client behavior and creates an in-memory blockchain [27]. With TestRPC, the transactions are processed instantly unlike other clients, making it very useful for development and testing as you do not need to wait for the next block to be mined for the transactions to be processed. TestRPC can be installed as follows:

■ **Installing TestRPC**
```
npm install -g ethereumjs-testrpc
```

Box 3.7 lists the TestRPC options.

■ **Box 3.7: TestRPC options**
```
--accounts: Specify the number of accounts to generate at startup.
--blocktime: Specify blocktime in seconds for automatic mining.
            Default is 0 and no auto-mining.
--deterministic: Generate deterministic addresses based on a
            pre-defined mnemonic.
--mnemonic: Use a specific HD wallet mnemonic to generate
            initial addresses.
--port: Port number to listen on. Defaults to 8545.
--hostname: Hostname to listen on. Defaults to Node's
            server.listen() default.
--seed: Use arbitrary data to generate the HD wallet
        mnemonic to be used.
--gasPrice: Use a custom Gas Price (defaults to 1)
--gasLimit: Use a custom Gas Limit (defaults to 0x47E7C4)
--fork: Fork from another currently running Ethereum
        client at a given block.
--debug: Output VM opcodes for debugging
```

Box 3.8 shows how to run TestRPC.

■ **Box 3.8: Running TestRPC**
```
~$ testrpc -h 0.0.0.0
EthereumJS TestRPC v2.2.4

Available Accounts
==================
```

```
(0)  0x98b884a883e5f71d58d702154fe9aa9917057a93
(1)  0xb30cc4f0800578a37c5dfae2aa1e6fcce67a2e5f
(2)  0x8fe80b08ebc497cd4fe381282bb9f190fcaa73a4
(3)  0x34c7409b2b4a76717bc3d3d7bfe0f315d7385d01
(4)  0xb90e3dded19d24be5ff73ec005d9010bfbbe52f4
(5)  0x9bf6e5804a1fbcbfc66e3d3dc4fa38078ac1ef7c
(6)  0xae12dfd1dcd9e5c3e753630139b1b32843644f07
(7)  0x666e54b7cea94927108eff8e2926132abc7d3d12
(8)  0xe5eb80ba7c7e8d144c6b55c3b3e7efcc946dc066
(9)  0x21cd66edd7c7bd9ea85a9cb4d429575d41f298a7


Private Keys
====================
(0)  86ad2cb071c28a5f03a3934491707370511722ca4156e2e705cdc729dcf2d815
(1)  8b0fa9616cb8429672c448cb162a16d9d15031a29d2dd4257577c3f4e3a3b476
(2)  b70165f21f7c0d842336795b15cc64313a40adc9973f35eb06a339796f9bf229
(3)  69d4e9526f6d717dd1cc54cbbd50b4d6f2c62674bf6b4445716640148db8b3de
(4)  477d62e4de8f7688d3980f8171c0c7db339249eb4480ecb4b376d8a203252640
(5)  c7b24354489ec4652042c3ec42c05b3f2d4d3230c0302c17ea2442faf14eb313
(6)  207cc4b698903243ebb6acdf5411835f57a5e395149deda8fcd477d04bc3c0ce
(7)  a57e74409a5aa96c19620b7424db36bcd1be1e9d7d4403a1f3c25e2d13a769e2
(8)  8214dbe6711978cb7fd8a76b64c92fe76a2f46dad4133d9717021180453e1316
(9)  51dd6c7b5b7a3d08d713e30270b2ceeab568897a0747cd156959cc642ebaec0d


HD Wallet
====================
Mnemonic:       right blame topic indicate dial
                negative service velvet sister negative business absurd
Base HD Path:   m/44'/60'/0'/0/{account_index}

Listening on 0.0.0.0:8545
```

When you run TestRPC, it creates 10 Ethereum accounts and pre-allocates 100 Ether to each account. The account addresses, account private keys, the HD wallet mnemonic to generate initial addresses, RPC hostname and port are emitted in the output.

3.4   Mist Ethereum Wallet

The Mist Ethereum Wallet application allows you to perform tasks such as managing Ethereum accounts, sending Ether to other accounts, deploying contracts, sending transactions to contracts and viewing account transactions. The Mist Ethereum Wallet application can be downloaded from [30].

When you download and run the wallet application binary, it will connect to the Ethereum main network by default. You can switch to the test network (Testnet) from the (Develop->Network) menu option in the wallet application.

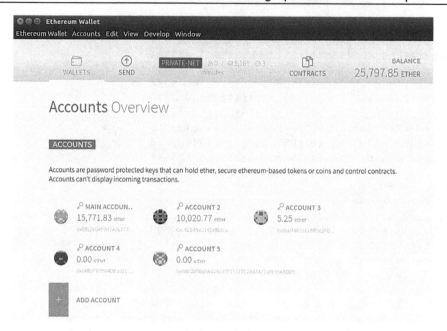

Figure 3.1: Mist Ethereum wallet application showing Ethereum accounts

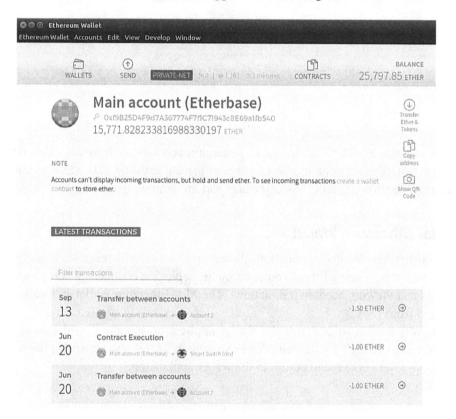

Figure 3.2: Viewing account details using Mist Ethereum wallet application

To connect the wallet application to a private blockchain, first run an Ethereum client as follows:

■ **Running geth client to work with Mist wallet**
```
geth -datadir "/home/ubuntu/ethchain" -dev -unlock 0,1
  -mine -minerthreads 2 -rpc -rpcaddr 0.0.0.0
  -rpccorsdomain "*" -rpcport 8101
  -ipcpath "/home/ubuntu/.ethereum/geth.ipc"
```

Note that the IPC path used in the above command is the one that the Mist Ethereum wallet uses. After running the Ethereum client, run the wallet application. Figure 3.1 shows a screenshot of the Mist Ethereum wallet application connected to a private blockchain network (Private-Net). You can view information related to the sync status of the node, the number of peers connected and account balances. Figure 3.2 shows the details of an Ethereum account as viewed in the Mist Ethereum wallet application. Chapter-4 has more details on using Mist Ethereum wallet application for creating accounts, deploying contracts and sending transactions.

3.5 MetaMask

While Dapp frameworks (such as Truffle, described later in this chapter) allow you to create and deploy Dapps, the users need a way to connect their Ethereum wallets to the Dapps so that they can interact and transact with the Dapps. The standard way of accessing and interacting with a Dapp is through the Mist Browser. However, for users who do not want to install the Mist Browser and download the entire blockchain, the MetaMask Chrome extension provides a user-friendly option to interact with the Dapps from the Chrome browser. MetaMask allows you to run Ethereum Dapps in your browser without running a full Ethereum node [31]. MetaMask includes a secure identity vault for managing your account identities. With MetaMask, you can either create a new wallet (or vault) or restore an existing wallet as shown in Figure 3.3. To restore an existing wallet, the HD mnemonic that was used seed the initial addresses is required. For example, if you are working with TestRPC, an HD mnemonic is emitted when you run TestRPC as shown in Box 3.8. After creating or restoring a wallet you can view the account details as shown in Figure 3.4(a) and the list of accounts as shown in Figure 3.4(b). Figure 3.5(a) shows how to send a transaction using MetaMask and Figure 3.5(b) shows the transaction confirmation page. The RPC hostname and port for the blockchain network can be configured in the MetaMask settings as shown in Figure 3.6(a). When using TestRPC, the default RPC hostname is "localhost" and port is 8545. You can switch to the Ethereum main network or test network from MetaMask as shown in Figure 3.6(b).

In Chapter-6, we will describe examples of using MetaMask for interacting with Dapps built with the Truffle framework. When you access a Dapp from the Chrome browser and enable the MetaMask extension, it injects the Web3 JavaScript API directly into the Dapp context and allows you to transact with the Dapp using your wallet account.

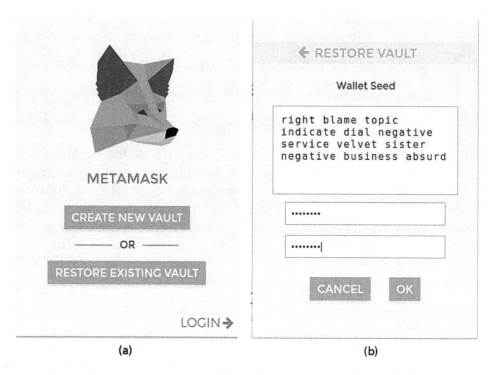

Figure 3.3: (a) Setting up a vault with MetaMask (b) Restoring an existing vault

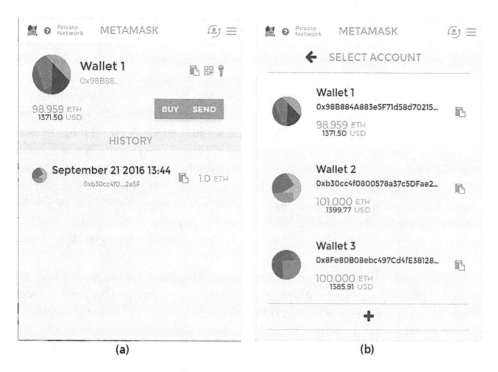

Figure 3.4: (a) Viewing account details using MetaMask (b) Selecting an account

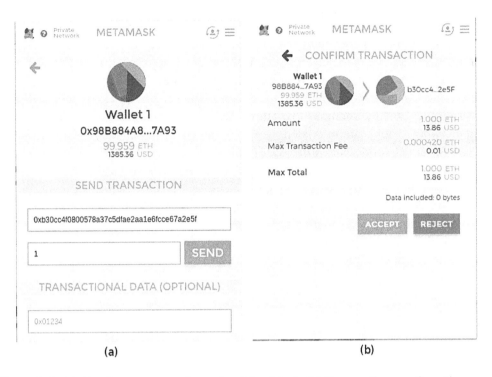

Figure 3.5: (a) Sending a transaction using MetaMask (b) Transaction confirmation page

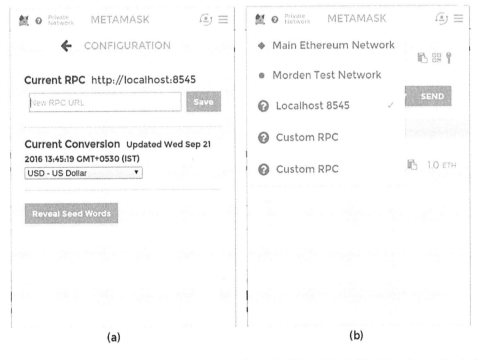

Figure 3.6: (a) Configuring RPC hostname and port in MetaMask (b) Selecting a blockchain network in MetaMask

3.6   Web3 JavaScript API

Web3 is a JavaScript API created by the Ethereum Foundation which provides methods for interacting with the Ethereum network [32]. Web3 allows Dapps to work with the Ethereum network. Web3 provides a JavaScript object *web3* which includes various sub-objects such as *eth* (which contains the Ethereum blockchain related methods), *shh* (which contains Whisper protocol related methods that allow Dapps to communicate each other), *admin* (which contains various admin related methods), *net* (which contains methods related to the peer-to-peer network), *currentProvider* (which contains methods related to the current provider), *miner* (which contains methods related to mining), *version* (which provides version information for the node) and other sub-objects including *db, debug, personal, providers* and *txpool*. Web3 also provides various utility functions (such as *web3.fromWei()* for converting Wei to Ether) which we will describe as we use them in the examples in the book. Box 3.9 shows the *web3* object as viewed from the *geth* JavaScript console.

▪ Box 3.9: Web3 object

```
> web3
{
  admin: {
    datadir: "/home/arshdeep/ethdata",
    nodeInfo: {

      enode: "enode://74e9655a22ac60e3bb542f2a2ecaa5b208a89eb
          d1f2b5c61cfeaa233d53e79e070653bf74a42388b4229c5
          60fbf1c9936af68361770afc7f91eb93a6eca26d18@192.168.1.1:54686",

      id: "74e9655a22ac60e3bb542f2a2ecaa5b208a89ebd1f2b5c61c
          feaa233d53e79e070653bf74a42388b4229c560fbf1c9936af
          68361770afc7f91eb93a6eca26d18",

      ip: "192.168.1.1",
      listenAddr: "[::]:57046",
      name: "Geth/v1.4.5-stable/linux/go1.5.1",
      ports: {
        discovery: 54686,
        listener: 54686
      },
      protocols: {
        eth: {...},
        shh: "unknown"
      }
    },
    peers: [],
    addPeer: function(),
    exportChain: function(),
    getContractInfo: function(),
    getDatadir: function(callback),
    getNodeInfo: function(callback),
    getPeers: function(callback),
    httpGet: function(),
    importChain: function(),
```

```
      register: function(),
      registerUrl: function(),
      saveInfo: function(),
      setGlobalRegistrar: function(),
      setHashReg: function(),
      setSolc: function(),
      setUrlHint: function(),
      sleep: function(),
      sleepBlocks: function(),
      startNatSpec: function(),
      startRPC: function(),
      startWS: function(),
      stopNatSpec: function(),
      stopRPC: function(),
      stopWS: function()
   },
   currentProvider: {
      newAccount: function(),
      send: function(),
      sendAsync: function(),
      unlockAccount: function()
   },
   db: {
      getHex: function(),
      getString: function(),
      putHex: function(),
      putString: function()
   },
   debug: {
      backtraceAt: function(),
      blockProfile: function(),
      chaindbProperty: function(),
      cpuProfile: function(),
      dumpBlock: function(),
      gcStats: function(),
      getBlockRlp: function(),
      goTrace: function(),
      memStats: function(),
      metrics: function(),
      printBlock: function(),
      seedHash: function(),
      setBlockProfileRate: function(),
      setHead: function(),
      stacks: function(),
      startCPUProfile: function(),
      startGoTrace: function(),
      stopCPUProfile: function(),
      stopGoTrace: function(),
      traceBlock: function(),
      traceBlockByFile: function(),
      traceBlockByHash: function(),
      traceBlockByNumber: function(),
      traceTransaction: function(),
      verbosity: function(),
```

```
    vmodule: function(),
    writeBlockProfile: function(),
    writeMemProfile: function()
},
eth: {
    accounts: ["0xf9b25d4f9d7a367774f7f1c71943c8e69a1fb540",
    "0xc421d5e214ddb07a41d28cf89ee37495aa5edba7"],
    blockNumber: 1199,
    coinbase: "0xf9b25d4f9d7a367774f7f1c71943c8e69a1fb540",
    compile: {
      lll: function(),
      serpent: function(),
      solidity: function()
    },
    defaultAccount: undefined,
    defaultBlock: "latest",
    gasPrice: 20000000000,
    hashrate: 60870,
    mining: true,
    pendingTransactions: [],
    syncing: false,
    call: function(),
    contract: function(abi),
    estimateGas: function(),
    filter: function(fil, callback),
    getAccounts: function(callback),
    getBalance: function(),
    getBlock: function(),
    getBlockNumber: function(callback),
    getBlockTransactionCount: function(),
    getBlockUncleCount: function(),
    getCode: function(),
    getCoinbase: function(callback),
    getCompilers: function(),
    getGasPrice: function(callback),
    getHashrate: function(callback),
    getMining: function(callback),
    getNatSpec: function(),
    getPendingTransactions: function(callback),
    getStorageAt: function(),
    getSyncing: function(callback),
    getTransaction: function(),
    getTransactionCount: function(),
    getTransactionFromBlock: function(),
    getTransactionReceipt: function(),
    getUncle: function(),
    getWork: function(),
    iban: function(iban),
    icapNamereg: function(),
    isSyncing: function(callback),
    namereg: function(),
    resend: function(),
    sendIBANTransaction: function(),
    sendRawTransaction: function(),
```

```
      sendTransaction: function(),
      sign: function(),
      signTransaction: function(),
      submitTransaction: function(),
      submitWork: function()
    },
    isIBAN: undefined,
    miner: {
      makeDAG: function(),
      setEtherbase: function(),
      setExtra: function(),
      setGasPrice: function(),
      start: function(),
      startAutoDAG: function(),
      stop: function(),
      stopAutoDAG: function()
    },
    net: {
      listening: true,
      peerCount: 0,
      version: "1",
      getListening: function(callback),
      getPeerCount: function(callback),
      getVersion: function(callback)
    },
    personal: {
      listAccounts: ["0xf9b25d4f9d7a367774f7f1c71943c8e69a1fb540",
        "0xc421d5e214ddb07a41d28cf89ee37495aa5edba7"],
      getListAccounts: function(callback),
      importRawKey: function(),
      lockAccount: function(),
      newAccount: function(),
      signAndSendTransaction: function(),
      unlockAccount: function()
    },
    providers: {
      HttpProvider: function(host),
      IpcProvider: function(path, net)
    },
    settings: {
      defaultAccount: undefined,
      defaultBlock: "latest"
    },
    shh: {
      addToGroup: function(),
      filter: function(fil, callback),
      hasIdentity: function(),
      newGroup: function(),
      newIdentity: function(),
      post: function()
    },
    txpool: {
      content: {
        pending: {},
```

```
      queued: {}
    },
    inspect: {
      pending: {},
      queued: {}
    },
    status: {
      pending: 0,
      queued: 0
    },
    getContent: function(callback),
    getInspect: function(callback),
    getStatus: function(callback)
  },
  version: {
    api: "0.15.3",
    ethereum: "0x3f",
    network: "1",
    node: "Geth/v1.4.5-stable/linux/go1.5.1",
    whisper: "0x2",
    getEthereum: function(callback),
    getNetwork: function(callback),
    getNode: function(callback),
    getWhisper: function(callback)
  },
  createBatch: function(),
  fromAscii: function(str),
  fromDecimal: function(value),
  fromICAP: function(icap),
  fromUtf8: function(str),
  fromWei: function(number, unit),
  isAddress: function(address),
  isChecksumAddress: function(address),
  isConnected: function(),
  reset: function(keepIsSyncing),
  setProvider: function(provider),
  sha3: function(string, options),
  toAscii: function(hex),
  toBigNumber: function(number),
  toChecksumAddress: function(address),
  toDecimal: function(value),
  toHex: function(val),
  toUtf8: function(hex),
  toWei: function(number, unit)
}
```

3.7 Truffle

A decentralized application (Dapp) comprises smart contracts and files for the web front-end
(HTML, JavaScript, stylesheets and images). Building a Dapp involves the following steps:

1. Implement smart contracts in a high-level language such as Solidity.
2. Compile the contracts with language-specific compilers (such as *solc*) to get the
   contract binary.

3. Deploy the contracts on Ethereum blockchain network using Ethereum clients such as *geth* to get the contract address and ABI.
4. Build web applications that interact with smart contracts using the Web3 JavaScript API.

While it is possible to use the tools and APIs described earlier in this chapter to build Dapps, we recommend using Dapp frameworks such as Truffle [33] or Embark [34] which simplify the above steps. For the Dapp examples in this book, we have used the Truffle framework.

Truffle has built-in capability for smart contract compilation, linking, deployment and binary management. With Truffle, you can automate the testing of contracts. Truffle uses the Mocha testing framework for automated testing and Chai library for assertions. Truffle has inbuilt network management capability to deploy contracts to public or private blockchain networks. An interactive console is provided for directly interacting with contracts. For interacting with the contracts and the Ethereum network, Truffle makes use of the Ether Pudding library [35] which is built on top of Web3. Truffle can be installed as follows:

■ **Installing Truffle**
```
npm install -g truffle
```

Box 3.10 lists the Truffle commands.

■ **Box 3.10: Truffle commands**
```
build             : Build development version of app
compile           : Compile contracts
console           : Run a console with deployed contracts
                    instantiated and available (REPL)
create:contract   : Create a basic contract
create:migration  : Create a new migration marked with the
                    current timestamp
create:test       : Create a basic test
exec              : Execute a JS file within truffle environment
init              : Initialize new Ethereum project,
                    including example contracts and tests
list              : List all available tasks
migrate           : Run migrations
networks          : Show addresses for deployed contracts on each network
serve             : Serve app on localhost and rebuild changes as needed
test              : Run tests
version           : Show version number and exit
watch             : Watch filesystem for changes and rebuild
                    the project automatically
```

To initialize a new Dapp project, run *truffle init* command from within a new directory. This will create the Dapp directory structure including example contracts and tests as shown in Box 3.11.

■ **Box 3.11: Directory structure for a Dapp created with Truffle**

```
.
|-- app
|   |-- images
|   |-- index.html
|   |-- javascripts
|   |   `-- app.js
|   `-- stylesheets
|       `-- app.css
|-- contracts
|   |-- ConvertLib.sol
|   |-- MetaCoin.sol
|   `-- Migrations.sol
|-- migrations
|   |-- 1_initial_migration.js
|   `-- 2_deploy_contracts.js
|-- test
|   `-- metacoin.js
`-- truffle.js
```

Dapps built with Truffle can be deployed to public or private blockchain networks. While developing Dapps with Truffle we recommend using the TestRPC Ethereum client described earlier in this chapter. TestRPC creates an in-memory blockchain and processes the transactions instantly. Once you are confident that your contracts and Dapps work as expected, you can connect your Truffle Dapp to the Ethereum main network or test network using a full Ethereum client such as *geth*.

Box 3.12 shows an example of a Truffle project configuration file. The *build* option in the configuration file contains the build configuration of the Dapp front-end. The *network* option contains settings for various blockchain networks to which the Truffle Dapp can be deployed. For example, in the development stage, you can use the "development" network as shown in the sample configuration with network_id as "default", which uses the RPC settings defined in the *rpc* option. For testing, you can use the Ethereum Modern test network (network_id: 2) and for production, you can use the Ethereum main network (network_id: 1). The *rpc* option contains settings for connecting the Dapp to an Ethereum client. When using TestRPC with Truffle the default value for host is "localhost" and port is 8545.

■ **Box 3.12: Truffle project configuration file**

```
build: {
  "index.html": "index.html",
  "app.js": [
    "javascripts/app.js"
  ],
  "app.css": [
    "stylesheets/app.css"
  ],
  "images/": "images/"
},
networks: {
```

```
  "live": {
    network_id: 1 // Ethereum public network
  },
  "morden": {
    network_id: 2 //Ethereum official test network
  },
  "staging": {
    network_id: 1234, // custom private network
    host: 192.168.1.20,
    port: 8101
  },
  "development": {
    network_id: "default" // use default rpc settings
  }
}
rpc: {
  host: "localhost",
  port: 8545
  // optional config values
  // gas: Gas limit used for deploys. Default is 4712388
  // gasPrice: Gas price used for deploys. Default is 100000000000
  // from: From address used during migrations.
  //       If not specified, defaults to the first available account
  //       provided by your Ethereum client.
}
};
```

After initializing a new Dapp project and editing the Truffle project configuration file, the next step is to implement the smart contracts within the "contracts" directory. Next add the contracts to the "2_deploy_contracts.js" migration file within the "migrations" directory as shown in Box 3.13. The migration file in this example first deploys the "ConvertLib" library and then calls the *autolink()* function to link all libraries available to the contracts that depend on them. Finally, the contract within the Dapp project ("MetaCoin") is deployed.

■ **Box 3.13: Truffle migration file**

```
module.exports = function(deployer) {
  deployer.deploy(ConvertLib);
  deployer.autolink();
  deployer.deploy(MetaCoin);
};
```

Next, we build the Truffle project, run the migrations to deploy the contracts on the blockchain network and serve the Dapp on "localhost" as shown in Box 3.14. In Chapter-6, additional examples of building various Dapps with Truffle are described in detail.

■ **Box 3.14: Building, deploying and serving Truffle Dapp**

```
$ truffle build
Compiling ConvertLib.sol...
Compiling MetaCoin.sol...
```

```
Compiling Migrations.sol...
Writing artifacts to ./build/contracts

$ truffle migrate
Running migration: 1_initial_migration.js
  Deploying Migrations...
  Migrations: 0x3905b9f1f86ffa60d16761f1885d3c17f394f818
Saving successful migration to network...
Saving artifacts...
Running migration: 2_deploy_contracts.js
  Deploying ConvertLib...
  ConvertLib: 0xcd3e71ec4a4ba740fb53ae82d4a32b9bfbd1e984
  Linking ConvertLib to MetaCoin
  Deploying MetaCoin...
  MetaCoin: 0x0d95700432c911356e3597ed41f5bbf51337b26f
Saving successful migration to network...
Saving artifacts...

$ truffle serve
Serving app on port 8080...
Rebuilding...
Completed without errors on Thu Sep 22 2016 15:42:29 GMT+0530 (IST)
```

Summary

In this chapter, we described how to setup an Ethereum node and use the Ethereum development tools. The Ethereum clients allow you to setup an Ethereum node on your computer. Ethereum provides clients in various languages including Go, C++, Python, JavaScript, Ruby, Java, Haskell and Rust. The Go-Ethereum client, commonly called *geth*, is the Ethereum's official client. We described the commands and options for the *geth* client. Next, we described how to setup and list accounts, create a private blockchain, run miners on an Ethereum node, and use the *geth* console. Next, we described the Python Ethereum Client called *pyethapp*. Smart contracts for the Ethereum platform are developed in high-level languages. We described how to setup and use the Solidity compiler for compiling smart contracts. Next, we described TestRPC, which is a Node.js based Ethereum client that simulates Ethereum client behavior and creates an in-memory blockchain. The benefit of using TestRPC is that the transactions are processed instantly unlike than other clients which make it very useful for development and testing. Next, we described how to setup and use the Mist Ethereum Wallet application which allows you to perform tasks such as managing Ethereum accounts, sending Ether to other accounts, deploying contracts, sending transactions to contracts and viewing account transactions. While the standard way of accessing and interacting with a Dapp is through the Mist Browser, however, for users who do not want to install the Mist Browser and download the entire blockchain, the MetaMask Chrome extension provides a user-friendly option to interact with the Dapps from the Chrome browser. Next, we described the Web3 JavaScript API which provides methods for interacting with the Ethereum network. Finally, we described the Truffle framework for Dapp development which has a built-in capability for smart contract compilation, linking, deployment, and binary management.

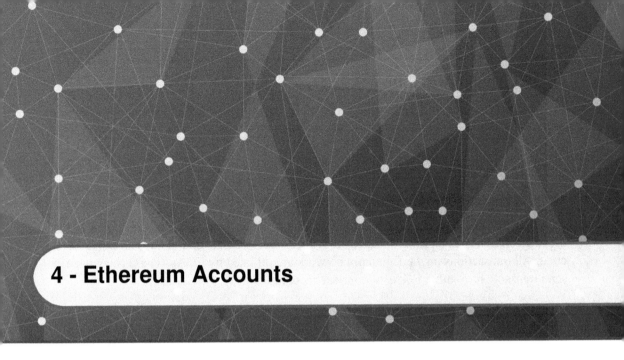

4 - Ethereum Accounts

This chapter covers

- Ethereum account types
- Externally owned accounts
- Contract accounts

4.1 Ethereum Accounts

In this chapter, we will describe the types of Ethereum accounts and their use. We also provide examples of setting up and working with Ethereum accounts. Ethereum has two types of accounts - Externally Owned Accounts (EOAs) and Contract Accounts as shown in Figure 4.1.

4.1.1 Externally Owned Account (EOAs)

Externally Owned Account (EOAs) are the accounts which are owned and controlled by the users. Each EOA has an Ether balance associated with it. EOAs do not have any associated code. All transactions on the Ethereum network are initiated by EOAs. These accounts can send transactions to other EOAs or contract accounts.

4.1.2 Contract Account

Contract Accounts are controlled by the associated contract code which is stored with the account. Each Contract Account has an Ether balance associated with it. The contract code execution is triggered by transactions sent by EOAs or messages sent by other contracts as shown in Figure 4.2. The contract code is executed on all the nodes on the Ethereum network as part of the block verification process. Contract code execution can result in a change of state of the contract (contract storage).

4.2 Keypairs

Each Externally Owned Account (EOA) has a public-private keypair associated with it. The account address is derived from the public key. When a new EOA is created, a JSON keyfile is created which has the public and private keys associated with the account. The private key is encrypted with the password which is provided while creating the account. For sending transactions to other accounts, the private key and the account password are required.

Boxes 4.1 and 4.2 show examples of keyfiles. These keyfiles are stored in the *keystore* directory. To encode the private key, first a key derivation function (KDF) is used to generate a derived key. The supported KDFs include PBKDF2 and Scrypt (mentioned as *kdf* in the JSON file). The *kdfparams* field in the JSON file lists the KDF-dependent static and dynamic parameters. The account password (*pw*) is passed to the KDF along with the *kdfparams* (derivedkey = kdfeval(pw, kdfparams)). The crypto algorithm used for these keyfiles is AES-128-CTR (mentioned as *cipher* in JSON file). The cipher parameters (*cipherparams*) include a 128-bit initialization vector (*iv*) for the cipher. The key for the cipher (enckey) is the leftmost 16 bytes of the derived key (enckey = derivedkey[:16]). The *ciphertext* is computed by passing the private key (*priv*), encryption key (*enckey*) and *cipherparams* to the encryption function of the cipher (c = aes_ctr_encrypt(priv, enckey, cipherparams)). The *mac* field is computed by taking the SHA3 hash of the second-leftmost 16 bytes of the derived key concatinated with the *ciphertext* (mac = sha3(derivedkey[16:32] + c)).

To decode the private key from the JSON file the above steps are reversed. The *derivedkey* is computed by passing the password and the *kdfparams* parsed from the JSON file to the KDF evaluation function. The encryption key (*enckey*) is the leftmost 16 bytes of the derived key. The cipher text parsed from the JSON file is decoded by passing the *ciphertext*, *enckey*

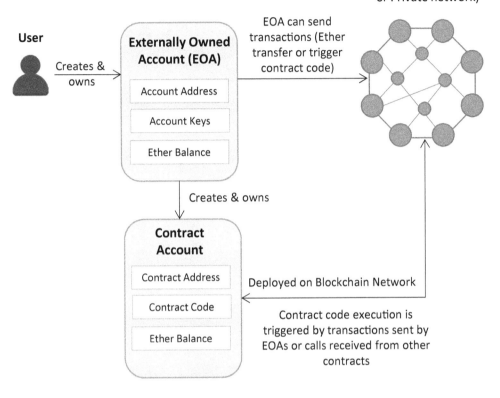

Figure 4.1: Ethereum Accounts

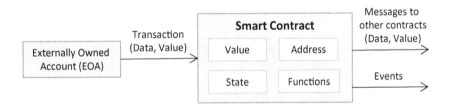

Figure 4.2: Smart Contract execution

and *cipherparams* to the cipher decryption function (o = aes_ctr_decrypt(ctext, enckey, cipherparams)). Next the *mac* provided in the JSON file is compared with a locally computed *mac*. If these MAC values do not match, the user is requested for an alternative password.

■ **Box 4.1: Keystore file using PBKDF2 key derivation function**

```
{
 "address":  "84ff9f7db64dba926718a22cedee4df23093c0d8",
 "crypto":  {
  "cipher":  "aes-128-ctr",
  "ciphertext": "f1b7f9f635828819e99d0f1badec821fbaf25e42b91dbb445bc6b51661404dda",
  "cipherparams":  {
   "iv":  "c96a76a9f702504299f7f83c90a3e284"
  },
  "kdf":  "scrypt",
  "kdfparams":  {
   "dklen":  32,
   "n":  262144,
   "p":  1,
   "r":  8,
   "salt":  "29204bc10fba1e5dd4e4529035ba131ccb12a62d81b344dfa5f0280e9b46dc22"
  },
  "mac":  "728ce567dfa8aa767847cc1e6907a4dbb0182e4c7250030f3fb33b8595b3b14f"
 },
 "id":  "b20814d3-8d4b-41fa-9859-a73494bc7302",
 "version":  3
}
```

■ **Box 4.2: Keystore file using Scrypt key derivation function**

```
{
 "address":  "0xf9b25d4f9d7a367774f7f1c71943c8e69a1fb540",
 "crypto":  {
  "ciphertext": "fc86806be53937328c3993305c87706f8c524533ee17f9ae851995e24bc9b263",
  "cipherparams":  {
   "iv":  "bd9dcb1c70a70d09cf601852eb940bed"
  },
  "kdf":  "pbkdf2",
  "kdfparams":  {
   "dklen":  32,
   "c":  262144,
   "prf":  "hmac-sha256",
   "salt":  "012ae7040fbea8ab164ea66854e4bb8a"
  },
  "mac":  "89fce87d8c357ccc6328671bb2c56b2520b9f2277606dc922325298fe4f9fac9",
  "cipher":  "aes-128-ctr",
  "version":  1
 },
 "id":  "f67c2279-b792-4ac1-c048-008633f5dd6d",
 "version":  3
}
```

4.3 Working with EOA Accounts

In Chapter-3, we described how to setup *geth* client and Mist Ethereum wallet application. In this section, we will describe how to setup and work with Ethereum externally owned accounts (EOAs) using *geth* and Mist Ethereum wallet.

4.3.1 Creating Account

The *geth* client provides the *account* command with various sub-commands for account management including: *new*, *list*, *update* and *import*. To create an account, the *new* command is used as follows:

```
■ Creating an account
$ geth -datadir "/home/ubuntu/ethdata" account new
Your new account is locked with a password.  Please give a password.  Do
not forget this password.
Passphrase:
Repeat passphrase:
Address:   {8b07a633516b5c2fb66c00488a7f62810ccafac7}
```

With the *geth* client, you can provide an optional data directory (–datadir option) to use a non-default path. When an account is created, you will be asked for a password. This password is used to encrypt the private key which is saved in the *keyfile* in the *keystore* directory, in the data directory specified. This password is required to unlock the account while sending transactions from the account. The password must be securely backed up as there is no way to retrieve the password later on, in case you forget the password.

Accounts can also be created from the Mist Ethereum wallet application as shown in Figure 4.3. When you click on the 'Add Account' button, you will be asked for an account password for the new account.

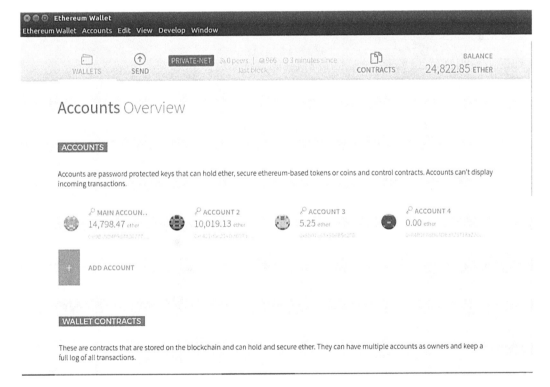

Figure 4.3: Creating an account from Mist Ethereum wallet application

4.3.2   Listing Accounts

To list all the accounts, you can use the *list* command provided by the *geth* client as shown in the box below:

```
■ Listing accounts
$ geth -datadir "/home/ubuntu/ethdata" account list
Account #0:  {f9b25d4f9d7a367774f7f1c71943c8e69a1fb540}
/home/ubuntu/ethdata/keystore/UTC-2016-06-15T08-42-57.750378653Z-
f9b25d4f9d7a367774f7f1c71943c8e69a1fb540

Account #1:  {c421d5e214ddb07a41d28cf89ee37495aa5edba7}
/home/ubuntu/ethdata/keystore/UTC-2016-06-15T09-30-28.486403440Z-
c421d5e214ddb07a41d28cf89ee37495aa5edba7

Account #2:  {8b07a633516b5c2fb66c00488a7f62810ccafac7}
/home/ubuntu/ethdata/keystore/UTC-2016-08-31T05-30-42.333196852Z-
8b07a633516b5c2fb66c00488a7f62810ccafac7
```

The *list* command shows the account indexes, addresses and *keyfile* paths.

To list the accounts within the *geth* interactive console, you can use the *eth.accounts* command as shown in the box below:

```
■ Listing accounts in geth console
> eth.accounts
["0xf9b25d4f9d7a367774f7f1c71943c8e69a1fb540",
 "0xc421d5e214ddb07a41d28cf89ee37495aa5edba7",
 "0x8b07a633516b5c2fb66c00488a7f62810ccafac7"]

> eth.accounts[0]
"0xf9b25d4f9d7a367774f7f1c71943c8e69a1fb540"
```

4.3.3 Updating Accounts

To update an existing account the *update* command can be used as shown in the box below:

```
■ Updating an account
$ geth -datadir "/home/ubuntu/ethdata" account update
8b07a633516b5c2fb66c00488a7f62810ccafac7
Unlocking account 8b07a633516b5c2fb66c00488a7f62810ccafac7 | Attempt 1/3
Passphrase:
I0913 15:34:19.822906 cmd/geth/accountcmd.go:187]
Unlocked account 8b07a633516b5c2fb66c00488a7f62810ccafac7
Please give a new password.  Do not forget this password.
Passphrase:
Repeat passphrase:
```

An account address is provided with the update command. You will be prompted for the account password to unlock the account. Once the account is unlocked, you can provide a new password for the account. The update command also updates the account keyfile to the latest encryption format.

4.3.4 Checking Balance

To check the balance of an account within the *geth* console, use the *eth.getBalance()* function. This function returns the account balance in Wei (where 1 Ether = 10^{18} Wei). You can use the *web3.fromWei()* function to convert the balance in Ether as shown in the box below:

```
■ Checking balance of an account in geth console
> web3.fromWei(eth.getBalance(eth.accounts[0]), "ether")
14708.472816436988330297
```

To check the balances of all the accounts, you can use a JavaScript function as shown in the box below:

```
■ Checking balance of all accounts in geth console
> function checkAllBalances() {
web3.eth.getAccounts(function(err, accounts) {
accounts.forEach(function(id) {
web3.eth.getBalance(id, function(err, balance) {
  console.log("" + id + ":\t balance:   " +
web3.fromWei(balance, "ether") + " ether");
});
});
});
};

> checkAllBalances();
0xf9b25d4f9d7a367774f7f1c71943c8e69a1fb540:
balance:  14708.472816436988330297 ether

0xc421d5e214ddb07a41d28cf89ee37495aa5edba7:
balance:  10019.127183563011669703 ether

0x8b07a633516b5c2fb66c00488a7f62810ccafac7:
balance:  5.25 ether
```

4.3.5 Account Transactions

Till now we looked at how to setup and view accounts. Let us now look at how to send transactions from accounts. The box below shows an example of sending Ether from the coinbase account (*eth.coinbase* or *eth.accounts[0]*) to another account within the *geth* console.

```
■ Sending Ether from one account to another
> eth.sendTransaction({from:eth.coinbase,
  to:eth.accounts[1], value:  web3.toWei(0.05, "ether")})

"0x237018952939e5963f17e74606a9feda6e540a941fbb1543f4b478c97c73b440"
```

To send a transaction with Ether, the *eth.sendTransaction()* function is used, with input parameters including the *from* and *to* account addresses and the *value* in Wei to send. Note that we use the *web3.toWei()* function to convert Ether to Wei. When the transaction is submitted a transaction hash is returned. The amount is transferred from the sender to the receiver account when the transaction is mined.

Figure 4.4 shows how to send Ether using the Mist Ethereum wallet application. When you send the transaction, you will be prompted for the account password as shown in Figure 4.5. You can view the status of the transaction (transaction hash, fee paid, gas used and gas price) from the account details page in the Ethereum wallet as shown in Figure 4.6.

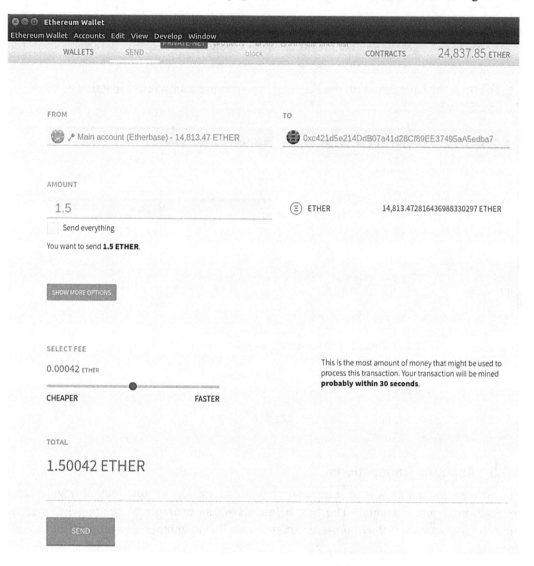

Figure 4.4: Sending Ether using Mist Ethereum wallet

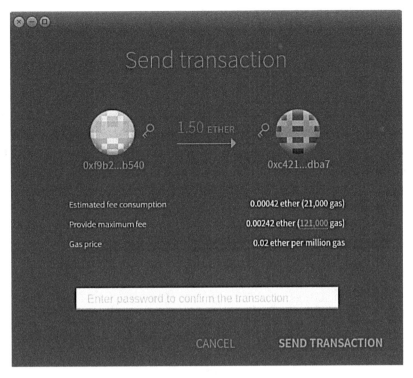

Figure 4.5: Password prompt after initiating a transaction

Transaction

0xd9e2d3f21963eb3f612eef92658c4345ef0b13f46fae194272e4c3d43f810b78

Tuesday, September 13, 2016 4:29 PM
(4 minutes ago, **0** Confirmations)

Amount	1.50 ETHER
From	Main account (Etherbase)
To	Account 2
Fee paid	0.00242 ETHER
Gas used	121,000
Gas price	0.02 ETHER PER MILLION GAS

Figure 4.6: Viewing the status of a transaction

4.4 Working with Contract Accounts

In this section, we will describe how to compile contracts, deploy contracts (create Contract Accounts), and interact with Contract Accounts. Details on contract implementation and contract patterns are described in Chapter-5. For this chapter, let us assume we already have a contract implemented.

To describe the steps involved in compiling and deploying contracts, we will take the example of a smart contract for sharing revenue among the shareholders of a company. Assuming the shareholders of a company already have their accounts on the Ethereum network, the company can use the revenue sharing contract to disburse the revenue equally among the shareholders. Box 4.3 shows the Solidity implementation of the revenue sharing contract (*RevenueShare*).

■ **Box 4.3: RevenueShare contract implemented in Solidity**

```
contract RevenueShare {
  address public creator;
  mapping(uint => address) public shareholders;
  uint public numShareholders;

  event Disburse(uint _amount, uint _numShareholders);

  function RevenueShare(address[] addresses) {
    creator = msg.sender;
    numShareholders = addresses.length;

    for (uint i = 0; i < addresses.length; i++) {
          shareholders[i] = addresses[i];
      }
  }

  function shareRevenue() returns (bool success) {
    uint amount = msg.value / numShareholders;

    for (uint i = 0; i < numShareholders; i++) {
      if (!shareholders[i].send(amount)) throw;
    }

    Disburse(msg.value, numShareholders);

    return true;
  }

  function kill() {
    if (msg.sender == creator) suicide(creator);
  }
}
```

4.4.1 Compiling & Deploying Contract

For deploying the contract we will use the Ethereum *geth* client. Box 4.4 shows the commands for deploying the contract from the *geth* console. To compile the contract from the *geth* console, the *web3.eth.compile.solidity()* function is used. To create a contract we require the contract's compiled code and the Application Binary Interface (ABI). The contract ABI contains definitions of the contract's interfaces. Box 4.5 shows the ABI for the RevenueShare contract. After compiling the contract, we instantiate a JavaScript object which can be used to call the contract, by passing the ABI definition to the *web3.eth.contract()* function. Finally, we create and deploy the contract by calling the *new* method of the contract object created in the previous step and passing as input parameters, an EOA account address (who will be the owner of the contract), the contract's compiled code and a gas limit. When a new contract is deployed, a gas fee is charged from the contract owner's account. When the transaction for deploying a contract is mined on the Ethereum Blockchain network, the contract is assigned an address which is used for sending transactions to the contract account. Box 4.6 shows the contract object after the contract is deployed. The contract object includes the ABI, address, transaction hash and contract interfaces.

■ **Box 4.4: Compiling & deploying the RevenueShare contract**

```
//Contract source converted to a string
var contractSource = "contract RevenueShare { ... } ";

//Compile contract
var contractCompiled = eth.compile.solidity(contractSource);

//List of addresses of shareholders for initializing contract
var addresses = ["0xa5D73d67D7a79Be62e2c77DD877B536775C446DD",
             "0xDa7d00412Ae0FD1A590AdC3718B007872D40F090",
             "0x3a15b505277b2F869ffcB1E9d1E76bD180189E0D"];

//Create contract
var myContract =
  web3.eth.contract(contractCompiled.RevenueShare.info.abiDefinition);

//Deploy contract
var myContractInstance = myContract.new(
    addresses,
    {
        from:web3.eth.accounts[0],
        data:contractCompiled.RevenueShare.code,
        gas: 1000000
    }, function(e, contract){
    if(!e) {
      if(!contract.address) {
        console.log("Contract transaction send:
          TransactionHash: " + contract.transactionHash +
                      " waiting to be mined...");
      } else {
        console.log("Contract mined! Address: " + contract.address);
      }
    }
});

//Contract transaction send: TransactionHash:
```

```
//0xbdc9d77e7350ac7aa13f2fc834c07f92ea247126d
14b6881988b699a3a4e19e0 waiting to be mined...
//Contract mined! Address: 0x15e476ada310dff63fc2c332e051c08a20d157aa
```

■ **Box 4.5: ABI definition of the RevenueShare contract**

```
[{
    constant: true,
    inputs: [],
    name: "creator",
    outputs: [{
        name: "",
        type: "address"
    }],
    type: "function"
}, {
    constant: false,
    inputs: [],
    name: "kill",
    outputs: [],
    type: "function"
}, {
    constant: true,
    inputs: [],
    name: "numShareholders",
    outputs: [{
        name: "",
        type: "uint256"
    }],
    type: "function"
}, {
    constant: true,
    inputs: [{
        name: "",
        type: "uint256"
    }],
    name: "shareholders",
    outputs: [{
        name: "",
        type: "address"
    }],
    type: "function"
}, {
    constant: false,
    inputs: [],
    name: "shareRevenue",
    outputs: [{
        name: "success",
        type: "bool"
    }],
    type: "function"
}, {
```

```
    inputs: [{
        name: "addresses",
        type: "address[]"
    }],
    type: "constructor"
}, {
    anonymous: false,
    inputs: [{
        indexed: false,
        name: "_amount",
        type: "uint256"
    }, {
        indexed: false,
        name: "_numShareholders",
        type: "uint256"
    }],
    name: "Disburse",
    type: "event"
}]
```

■ **Box 4.6: Contract object after the contract is deployed**

```
{
  abi: [{
        constant: true,
        inputs: [],
        name: "creator",
        outputs: [{...}],
        type: "function"
    }, {
        constant: false,
        inputs: [],
        name: "kill",
        outputs: [],
        type: "function"
    }, {
        constant: true,
        inputs: [],
        name: "numShareholders",
        outputs: [{...}],
        type: "function"
    }, {
        constant: true,
        inputs: [{...}],
        name: "shareholders",
        outputs: [{...}],
        type: "function"
    }, {
        constant: false,
        inputs: [],
        name: "shareRevenue",
        outputs: [{...}],
```

```
      type: "function"
}, {
      inputs: [{...}],
      type: "constructor"
}, {
      anonymous: false,
      inputs: [{...}, {...}],
      name: "Disburse",
      type: "event"
}],
address: "0x419f876663b3ebc7643c37dba10b7a62084f072b",
transactionHash: "0xeb98119d6b3c263c6cdb3362dcaca04e5
                  55a68b40a6c70d51446a50a658a19ac",
Disburse: function(),
allEvents: function(),
creator: function(),
kill: function(),
numShareholders: function(),
shareRevenue: function(),
shareholders: function()
}
```

Contracts can also be created and deployed using the Mist Ethereum wallet application. Figure 4.7 shows the Contracts tab in the wallet application with the list of deployed contracts and options to deploy a new contract or watch an existing contract.

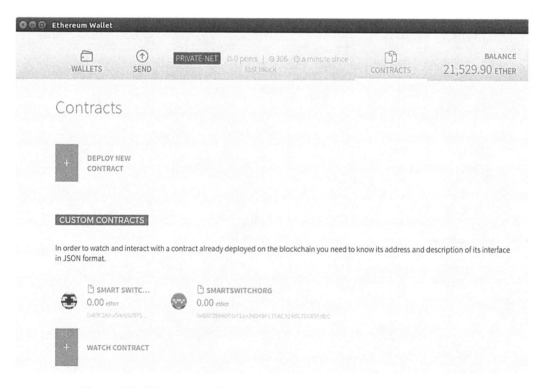

Figure 4.7: Viewing the deployed contracts in Mist Ethereum wallet

Figure 4.8 shows how to deploy a new contract from the Ethereum wallet application. Choose an EOA from which you want to deploy the contract. Next, paste the contract source code, select a gas fee you are willing to pay (the higher the fee you pay, the faster the transaction will be processed) and deploy the contract. Once deployed, you can browse to contract's page as shown in Figure 4.9.

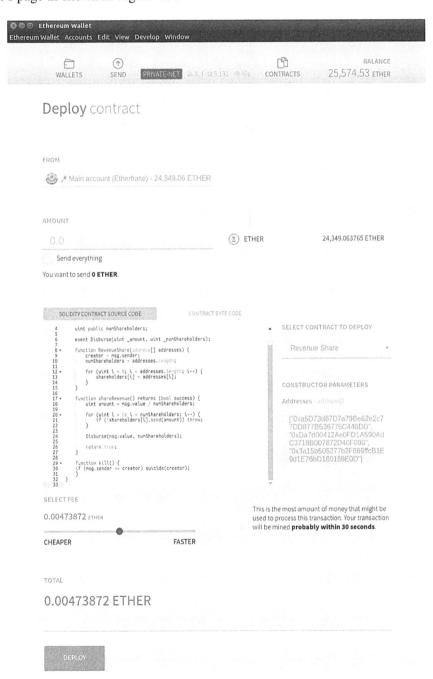

Figure 4.8: Deploying a contract from Mist Ethereum wallet

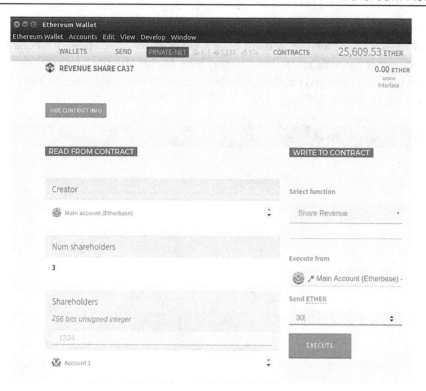

Figure 4.9: Contract's page in Ethereum wallet application

Figure 4.10: Executing a contract

4.4.2 Interacting with Contracts

To interact with the contract within the *geth* console, we will use the JavaScript object (*myContractInstance*) created previously using the *eth.contract()* function. Box 4.7 shows an example of sending a transaction to the *shareRevenue* function of the RevenueShare contract, using the *sendTransaction* function. The account address of the sender and a value (in Wei) is specified for this transaction. When the transaction is submitted, a transaction hash is returned. The transaction changes the state of the contract when it is mined. In the transaction example shown below, when the transaction is mined and the value sent by the sender of the transaction is equally disbursed to the shareholders in the contract. Since the transactions change the state, a gas fee is charged for sending transactions to contract accounts. Another way of interacting with the contracts is using calls, which return the contract's state and do not change the state. For example, to retrieve the number of shareholders in the RevenueShare contract, a call to the *numShareholders* state variable in the contract can be made as shown in the Box 4.7.

> ■ **Box 4.7: Interacting with the RevenueShare contract**
>
> ```
> // Send transaction to contract
> > myContractInstance.shareRevenue.sendTransaction({from: eth.accounts[0],
>                       to: myContractInstance.address,
>                       value: web3.toWei(30, "ether"), gas: 2000000})
>
> // Check shareholder balances
> > web3.fromWei(eth.getBalance(addresses[0]), "ether")
> 10
> > web3.fromWei(eth.getBalance(addresses[1]), "ether")
> 10
> > web3.fromWei(eth.getBalance(addresses[2]), "ether")
> 10
>
> // Send a call to check contract's state variable
> > myContractInstance.numShareholders.call();
> 3
> ```

The Mist Ethereum wallet application can also be used to send transactions to contracts. Figure 4.9 shows how to send a transaction to the *shareRevenue* function of the RevenueShare contract along with a value to be sent to the contract account. When the transaction is sent, the user is prompted for the EOA account password (from which the transaction is sent), as shown in Figure 4.10. The status of the transaction can be tracked from the wallet application as shown in Figure 4.11.

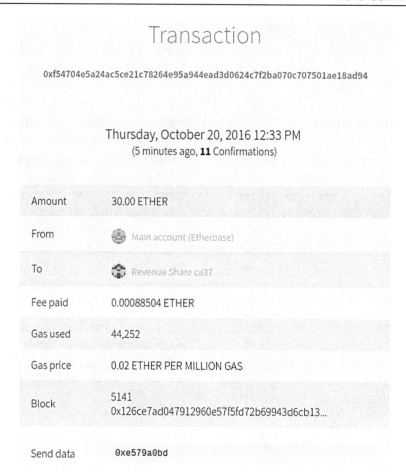

Figure 4.11: Viewing the status of a transaction sent to a contract

4.4.3 Instantiating or Watching a Contract

The JavaScript commands used for interacting with the contract within the *geth* console in
the previous section used the JavaScript contract object (*myContractInstance*). When you
close the *geth* console you will lose the JavaScript object. You can retrieve the contract object
for any contract already deployed on the blockchain network using the contract ABI and the
contract address as shown in Box 4.8.

■ **Box 4.8: Instantiating a deployed contract**

```
var abi = [{ constant: true,inputs: [], name: "creator",
    outputs: [{ name: "", type: "address" }],
    type: "function" }, {constant: false, inputs: [],
    name: "kill", outputs: [], type: "function"}, {
    constant: true, inputs: [], name: "numShareholders",
    outputs: [{ name: "", type: "uint256"}],
    type: "function"}, { constant: true,inputs: [{
        name: "", type: "uint256"}],
```

```
    name: "shareholders", outputs: [{name: "",
        type: "address" }],type: "function"}, {
    constant: false,inputs: [],name: "shareRevenue",
    outputs: [{name: "success",type: "bool"
    }],type: "function"}, {inputs: [{
        name: "addresses",type: "address[]"}],
    type: "constructor"}, {anonymous: false,
    inputs: [{indexed: false,name: "_amount",
        type: "uint256"}, {indexed: false,
        name: "_numShareholders",type: "uint256"
    }], name: "Disburse", type: "event"}];

var MyContract = web3.eth.contract(abi);

var myContractInstance = MyContract.at(
                '0x15e476ada310dff63fc2c332e051c08a20d157aa');
```

Figure 4.12 shows how to watch an already deployed contract from the Mist Ethereum wallet application using the contract ABI and address.

Figure 4.12: Watching an already deployed contract

Summary

In this chapter, we described the two types of Ethereum accounts: Externally Owned Accounts (EOAs) and Contract Accounts. EOAs are the accounts which are owned and controlled by the users. Contract Accounts are controlled by the associated contract code which is stored with the account. Both types of accounts are uniquely identified by an address and have an Ether balance associated with them. Each EOA has a public-private keypair associated with it. For sending transactions to other accounts, the private key and the account password are required. Next, we described how to setup and work with the EOA and Contract Accounts using the *geth* client and the Mist Ethereum wallet application.

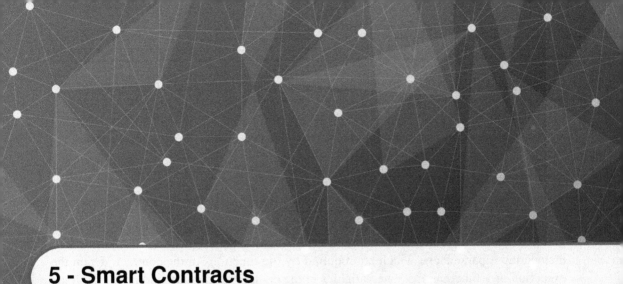

5 - Smart Contracts

This chapter covers

- Smart Contracts
- Structure of a Contract
- Setting up and Interacting with a Contract using Geth Client
    - Compiling & Deploying a Contract
    - Transactions and Calls
    - Interacting with a Contract
    - Gas
    - Logs
    - Events
- Setting up and Interacting with a Contract using Mist Wallet
- Smart Contract Examples
- Smart Contract Patterns
    - Conditions-Effects-Interaction
    - Withdrawal
    - Access Restriction
    - Mortal
    - Automatic Expiration
    - Rejector
    - Circuit Breaker
    - Allow Once per Account

In Chapter-4, we described contract accounts and how to compile, deploy and interact with smart contracts. In this chapter, we will look at developing and deploying smart contracts in more depth. Examples of smart contracts implemented in Solidity are provided. Finally, we describe the smart contract development best practices and commonly used patterns.

5.1   Smart Contract

A smart contract is a piece of code that resides on a blockchain network, and is identified by a unique address. A smart contract includes a set of executable functions and state variables. The functions are executed when transactions are made to these functions. The transactions include input parameters, which are required by the functions in the contract. Upon the execution of a function, the state variables in the contract change depending on the logic implemented in the function.

Contracts can be written in various high-level languages (such as Solidity or Serpent). Language-specific compilers for smart contracts are used to compile the contracts into Ethereum-specific binary format (Ethereum Virtual Machine (EVM) bytecode). Once compiled, the contracts are uploaded to the blockchain network, which assigns a unique address to the contract. Any user on the blockchain network can trigger the functions in the contract by sending transactions to the contract.

The contract code is executed on each node participating in the network as part of the definition of the state transition function, which is a part of the block validation algorithm. Transactions sent to contracts are included in the blocks during the mining process and the contract code spawned by the transactions is executed by all nodes in the network which download and validate the block. The state transition function and the block validation algorithm are described in detail in Chapter-7.

5.2   Structure of a Contract

A contract includes the following:
- **State Variables**: State variables are stored in the contract's storage and are used to maintain the contract's state.
- **Functions**: Functions in a contract include the code which is executed when transactions are sent to the contract. A contract has a special function called a constructor, which is executed only once when the contract is deployed.
- **Modifiers**: Modifiers can be used within a contract to change the behavior of the functions. For example, a modifier can be used to check for a condition before executing a function.
- **Events**: Events are used to track the execution of the transactions sent to the contract.

5.3   Setting up and Interacting with a Contract using Geth Client

In Chapter-4, we described how to compile contracts, deploy contracts (create contract accounts), and interact with contract accounts. Let us look at these steps in more detail with the help of an example of a smart contract to setup a crowdfunding campaign. Box 5.1 shows the Solidity implementation of the CrowdFunding contract. With this contract, a crowdfunding campaign can be setup by specifying a campaign goal and deadline. Backers interested in supporting the funding campaign can send transactions to the contract along with the value (in Ether) to contribute to the campaign. The funds raised are held in the contract account. When the campaign ends, the owner of the campaign can check if the campaign goal has been reached. If the campaign succeeds, the funds are released to the campaign beneficiary (or the owner of the contract). However, if the campaign fails, the backers are issued refunds.

■ **Box 5.1: CrowdFunding contract implemented in Solidity**

```solidity
contract CrowdFunding {
    struct Backer {
        address addr;
        uint amount;
    }

    address public owner;
    uint public numBackers;
    uint public deadline;
    string public campaignStatus;
    bool ended;
    uint public goal;
    uint public amountRaised;
    mapping (uint => Backer) backers;

    event Deposit(address _from, uint _amount);
    event Refund(address _to, uint _amount);

    modifier onlyOwner()
    {
        if (msg.sender != owner) throw;
        _
    }

    function CrowdFunding(uint _deadline, uint _goal) {
        owner = msg.sender;
        deadline = _deadline;
        goal = _goal;
        campaignStatus = "Funding";
        numBackers = 0;
        amountRaised = 0;
        ended = false;
    }

    function fund() {
        Backer b = backers[numBackers++];
        b.addr = msg.sender;
        b.amount = msg.value;
        amountRaised += b.amount;
        Deposit(msg.sender, msg.value);
    }

    function checkGoalReached () onlyOwner returns (bool ended){
        if (ended)
```

```
        throw; // this function has already been called

    if(block.timestamp<deadline)
        throw;

    if (amountRaised >= goal) {
        campaignStatus = "Campaign Succeeded";
        ended = true;
        if (!owner.send(this.balance))
            throw; // If anything fails,
                   // this will revert the changes above
    }else{
        uint i = 0;
        campaignStatus = "Campaign Failed";
        ended = true;
        while (i <= numBackers){
            backers[i].amount = 0;
            if (!backers[i].addr.send(backers[i].amount))
                throw; // If anything fails,
                       // this will revert the changes above
            Refund(backers[i].addr, backers[i].amount);
            i++;
        }
    }
}

function destroy() {
    if (msg.sender == owner) {
        suicide(owner);
    }
}

function () {
    // This function gets executed if a
    // transaction with invalid data is sent to
    // the contract or just ether without data.
    // We revert the send so that no-one
    // accidentally loses money when using the
    // contract.
    throw;
}
}
```

5.3.1   Compiling & Deploying a Contract

To create and deploy a contract on the blockchain, a transaction is sent with an empty address and with the EVM bytecode of the contract as the data field in the transaction. Box 5.2 shows the Python function for creating a contract (excerpt taken from the pyethereum source).

■ Box 5.2: Creating a contract
(code excerpt from pyethereum file - processblock.py)

```python
def create_contract(ext, msg):
  log_msg.debug('CONTRACT CREATION')
  sender = decode_hex(msg.sender) if len(msg.sender) == 40
                                   else msg.sender
  code = msg.data.extract_all()
  if ext._block.number >= ext._block.config['METROPOLIS_FORK_BLKNUM']:
    msg.to = mk_metropolis_contract_address(msg.sender, code)
    if ext.get_code(msg.to):
      if ext.get_nonce(msg.to) >= 2 ** 40:
        ext.set_nonce(msg.to,
                      (ext.get_nonce(msg.to) + 1) % 2 ** 160)
        msg.to = normalize_address(
                 (ext.get_nonce(msg.to) - 1) % 2 ** 160)
      else:
        ext.set_nonce(msg.to,
                      (big_endian_to_int(msg.to) + 2) % 2 ** 160)
        msg.to = normalize_address(
                 (ext.get_nonce(msg.to) - 1) % 2 ** 160)
  else:
    if ext.tx_origin != msg.sender:
      ext._block.increment_nonce(msg.sender)
    nonce = utils.encode_int(ext._block.get_nonce(msg.sender) - 1)
    msg.to = mk_contract_address(sender, nonce)
  b = ext.get_balance(msg.to)
  if b > 0:
    ext.set_balance(msg.to, b)
    ext._block.set_nonce(msg.to, 0)
    ext._block.set_code(msg.to, b'')
    ext._block.reset_storage(msg.to)
  msg.is_create = True
  msg.data = vm.CallData([], 0, 0)
  snapshot = ext._block.snapshot()
  res, gas, dat = _apply_msg(ext, msg, code)
  assert utils.is_numeric(gas)

  if res:
    if not len(dat):
      return 1, gas, msg.to
    gcost = len(dat) * opcodes.GCONTRACTBYTE
    if gas >= gcost:
      gas -= gcost
    else:
      dat = []
      log_msg.debug('CONTRACT CREATION OOG', have=gas,
            want=gcost, block_number=ext._block.number)
      if ext._block.number >= ext._block.config['HOMESTEAD_FORK_BLKNUM']:
        ext._block.revert(snapshot)
        return 0, 0, b''
    ext._block.set_code(msg.to, b''.join(map(ascii_chr, dat)))
    return 1, gas, msg.to
  else:
```

```
return 0, gas, b''
```

In the contract creation function, the sender account's *nonce* field is incremented by one, and then an address is assigned to the contract. The address is defined as the rightmost 160 bits of the Keccak hash of RLP encoding of a list containing the *sender* and the *nonce*. Box 5.3 shows the Python function for generating a contract address (excerpt taken from the pyethereum source).

■ Box 5.3: Generating a contract address (code excerpt from pyethereum file - utils.py)

```
def mk_contract_address(sender, nonce):
    return sha3(rlp.encode([normalize_address(sender), nonce]))[12:]
```

For deploying the CrowdFunding contract, we use the Ethereum *geth* client. Box 5.4 shows the commands for deploying the contract from the *geth* console. To compile the contract from the *geth* console, the *web3.eth.compile.solidity()* function is used. To create a contract, we require the contract's compiled code and the Application Binary Interface (ABI). The contract ABI contains definitions of the contract's interfaces. Box 5.5 shows the ABI for the CrowdFunding contract. After compiling the contract, we instantiate a JavaScript object which can be used to call the contract, by passing the ABI definition to the *web3.eth.contract()* function. Finally we create and deploy the contract by calling the *new* method of the contract object created in the previous step, and pass as input parameters, an EOA account address (who will be the owner of the contract), the contract's compiled code, a gas limit, and the input parameters to the contract's constructor (deadline and goal). When a new contract is deployed, a gas fee is charged from the contract owner's account. When the transaction for deploying a contract is mined on the Ethereum blockchain network, the contract is assigned an address which is used for sending transactions to the contract account. Box 5.6 shows the contract object after the contract is deployed. The contract object includes the ABI, contract address, transaction hash and contract interfaces.

■ Box 5.4: Compiling & deploying the CrowdFunding contract

```
//Copy entire contract source here
> var contractSource = "contract Crowdfunding { ... }";

//Compile the contract
> var contractCompiled = eth.compile.solidity(contractSource);

> var deadline = 1485856567; //timestamp
> var goal = 5000000000000000000; //in Wei

//Create the contract object
> var myContract =
  web3.eth.contract(contractCompiled.Crowdfunding.info.abiDefinition);

//Deploy the contract
> var myContractInstance = myContract.new(
```

```
        deadline,
        goal,
        {
            from:web3.eth.accounts[1],
            data:contractCompiled.Crowdfunding.code,
            gas: 1000000
        }, function(e, contract){
        if(!e) {
          if(!contract.address) {
            console.log("Contract transaction send: TransactionHash: " +
                    contract.transactionHash + " waiting to be mined...");
          } else {
            console.log("Contract mined! Address: " + contract.address);
          }
        }
});

//Contract transaction send: TransactionHash:
//0x69a69e3681e95e677843ad1bc6844a891c771cafb007f86bce6f8ab7417bccb4
//waiting to be mined...

//Contract mined! Address: 0xc79d0f151f6c7f51772a4d9f488c90f5177fee4e

//View receipt of the transaction to deploy the contract
> eth.getTransactionReceipt('0x69a69e3681e95e677843ad1bc6844a
                    891c771cafb007f86bce6f8ab7417bccb4')
{
  blockHash: "0x017ad52708f72616fe32243ebfa6196
            1559d993988abe380601a04fae4c763ee",
  blockNumber: 1975,
  contractAddress: "0xc79d0f151f6c7f51772a4d9f488c90f5177fee4e",
  cumulativeGasUsed: 467112,
  from: "0xa5d73d67d7a79be62e2c77dd877b536775c446dd",
  gasUsed: 467112,
  logs: [],
  root: "3f843a0d94b3e14153412a39b87eaf80efb9
        68dac22b4efd5b1e51d5f91ed0f1",
  to: null,
  transactionHash: "0x69a69e3681e95e677843ad1bc6844
                a891c771cafb007f86bce6f8ab7417bccb4",
  transactionIndex: 0
}
```

■ Box 5.5: ABI definition of the CrowdFunding contract

```
> contractCompiled.Crowdfunding.info.abiDefinition
[{
    constant: false,
    inputs: [],
    name: "checkGoalReached",
    outputs: [{
        name: "ended",
```

```
            type: "bool"
        }],
        type: "function"
}, {
        constant: true,
        inputs: [],
        name: "deadline",
        outputs: [{
            name: "",
            type: "uint256"
        }],
        type: "function"
}, {
        constant: true,
        inputs: [],
        name: "numBackers",
        outputs: [{
            name: "",
            type: "uint256"
        }],
        type: "function"
}, {
        constant: true,
        inputs: [],
        name: "goal",
        outputs: [{
            name: "",
            type: "uint256"
        }],
        type: "function"
}, {
        constant: true,
        inputs: [],
        name: "amountRaised",
        outputs: [{
            name: "",
            type: "uint256"
        }],
        type: "function"
}, {
        constant: false,
        inputs: [],
        name: "destroy",
        outputs: [],
        type: "function"
}, {
        constant: true,
        inputs: [],
        name: "owner",
        outputs: [{
            name: "",
            type: "address"
        }],
        type: "function"
```

```
}, {
    constant: false,
    inputs: [],
    name: "fund",
    outputs: [],
    type: "function"
}, {
    constant: true,
    inputs: [],
    name: "campaignStatus",
    outputs: [{
        name: "",
        type: "string"
    }],
    type: "function"
}, {
    inputs: [{
        name: "_deadline",
        type: "uint256"
    }, {
        name: "_goal",
        type: "uint256"
    }],
    type: "constructor"
}, {
    anonymous: false,
    inputs: [{
        indexed: false,
        name: "_from",
        type: "address"
    }, {
        indexed: false,
        name: "_amount",
        type: "uint256"
    }],
    name: "Deposit",
    type: "event"
}, {
    anonymous: false,
    inputs: [{
        indexed: false,
        name: "_to",
        type: "address"
    }, {
        indexed: false,
        name: "_amount",
        type: "uint256"
    }],
    name: "Refund",
    type: "event"
}]
```

■ Box 5.6: Contract object after the contract is deployed

```
> myContractInstance
{
  abi: [{
      constant: false,
      inputs: [],
      name: "checkGoalReached",
      outputs: [{...}],
      type: "function"
  }, {
      constant: true,
      inputs: [],
      name: "deadline",
      outputs: [{...}],
      type: "function"
  }, {
      constant: true,
      inputs: [],
      name: "numBackers",
      outputs: [{...}],
      type: "function"
  }, {
      constant: true,
      inputs: [],
      name: "goal",
      outputs: [{...}],
      type: "function"
  }, {
      constant: true,
      inputs: [],
      name: "amountRaised",
      outputs: [{...}],
      type: "function"
  }, {
      constant: false,
      inputs: [],
      name: "destroy",
      outputs: [],
      type: "function"
  }, {
      constant: true,
      inputs: [],
      name: "owner",
      outputs: [{...}],
      type: "function"
  }, {
      constant: false,
      inputs: [],
      name: "fund",
      outputs: [],
      type: "function"
  }, {
      constant: true,
```

```
      inputs: [],
      name: "campaignStatus",
      outputs: [{...}],
      type: "function"
}, {
      inputs: [{...}, {...}],
      type: "constructor"
}, {
      anonymous: false,
      inputs: [{...}, {...}],
      name: "Deposit",
      type: "event"
}, {
      anonymous: false,
      inputs: [{...}, {...}],
      name: "Refund",
      type: "event"
}],
address: "0xc79d0f151f6c7f51772a4d9f488c90f5177fee4e",
transactionHash: "0x69a69e3681e95e677843ad1bc6844a
                   891c771cafb007f86bce6f8ab7417bccb4",
Deposit: function(),
Refund: function(),
allEvents: function(),
amountRaised: function(),
campaignStatus: function(),
checkGoalReached: function(),
deadline: function(),
destroy: function(),
fund: function(),
goal: function(),
numBackers: function(),
owner: function()
}
```

5.3.2 Transactions and Calls

Transactions are the messages which are sent by Externally Owned Accounts (EOAs) to other EOAs or contract accounts. Each transaction includes the following fields:

- **nonce**: A scalar value equal to the number of transactions already sent by the sender of the transaction.
- **gasprice**: The price per unit of gas (in Wei) which will be paid for all computations involved in the execution of this transaction.
- **gasLimit or startgas**: A scalar value equal to the maximum amount of gas that can be used in executing the transaction.
- **to**: The 20-byte address of the recipient of the transaction. If the transaction is to create a new contract, this field is empty.
- **value**: A scalar value equal to the number of Wei to be transferred with this transaction. If the transaction is to create a new contract, the value acts as an endowment for the newly created contract account.
- **data**: A byte array containing the input data that is part of the transaction. When the

transaction is sent to a contract, the data field is used to provide the input data to the contract.

- **(v,r,s)**: The (v,r,s) values correspond to the signature of the transaction and are used to determine the sender of the transaction. In Ethereum, the method of signing transactions is similar to the 'Electrum style signatures' [38]. The (v,r,s) tuple is the raw Electrum-style signature of the transaction without the signature made with the private key corresponding to the sending account. From an Electrum-style signature, it is possible to extract the public key, and thereby the address of the sender of the transaction.

When a transaction is sent to an EOA, the transaction value is transferred to the recipient. When a transaction is sent to a contract account, the transaction data payload is used to provide an input to the contract function to be executed. Transactions are signed by the sender's private key. Transactions are selected and included in the blocks in the mining process. The state of the network is changed only by the transactions which are selected for inclusion in the blocks. The transactions on a blockchain network can be read by all the participant nodes in the network. Details on the mining process, transaction validation, and state transition function are described in Chapter-7. Box 5.7 shows an excerpt from the Python implementation of the transaction class (excerpt from the pyethereum source).

▪ Box 5.7: Transaction implementation (code excerpt from pyethereum file - transactions.py)

```python
class Transaction(rlp.Serializable):
    fields = [
        ('nonce', big_endian_int),
        ('gasprice', big_endian_int),
        ('startgas', big_endian_int),
        ('to', utils.address),
        ('value', big_endian_int),
        ('data', binary),
        ('v', big_endian_int),
        ('r', big_endian_int),
        ('s', big_endian_int),
    ]

    _sender = None

    def __init__(self, nonce, gasprice, startgas,
                 to, value, data, v=0, r=0, s=0):
        self.data = None

        to = utils.normalize_address(to, allow_blank=True)
        assert len(to) == 20 or len(to) == 0
        super(Transaction, self).__init__(nonce, gasprice,
                 startgas, to, value, data, v, r, s)
        self.logs = []

        if self.gasprice >= TT256 or self.startgas >= TT256 or \
                self.value >= TT256 or self.nonce >= TT256:
            raise InvalidTransaction("Values way too high!")
```

```
    if self.startgas < self.intrinsic_gas_used:
        raise InvalidTransaction("Startgas too low")

    log.debug('deserialized tx', tx=encode_hex(self.hash)[:8])
```

While transactions change the state of the network, you can use calls to get the state of a contract. The difference between a transaction and a call is that, while a transaction is submitted to the network for inclusion in the blockchain, whereas, a call runs locally. In other words, a call is used when you are interested only in the return value, whereas, a transaction is used when you wish to modify the state of the contract.

5.3.3 Interacting with a Contract

To interact with the contract within the *geth* console, we will use the JavaScript object (*myContractInstance*) created previously. Box 5.8 shows an example of sending a transaction to the *fund* function of the CrowdFunding contract, using the *sendTransaction* function. The account address of the sender and a value (in Wei) is specified for this transaction. When the transaction is submitted, a transaction hash is returned. The transaction changes the state of the contract when it is mined. In the transaction example shown below, when the transaction is mined and the *fund* function executes, the value is sent to the contract account and the sender's address and amount sent is recorded in the contract. Since the transactions change the state, a gas fee is charged for sending transactions to contract accounts. Another way of interacting with the contracts is using calls, which return the contract's state and do not change the state. For example, to retrieve the number of backers of the crowdfunding campaign, a call to the *numBackers* state variable in the contract can be made as shown in Box 5.8.

■ **Box 5.8: Sending transactions and calls to a contract**

```
//Send a transaction to the contract
> myContractInstance.fund.sendTransaction({from: eth.accounts[1],
        value: web3.toWei(1, "ether"), gas: 2000000})
"0x4fbd082414d2c11deaea9a9f9bac1281d521e666c3011b13b22b44f74409b7b6"

//View transaction details
> eth.getTransaction('0x4fbd082414d2c11deaea9a9f9bac1281d5
                    21e666c3011b13b22b44f74409b7b6')
{
  blockHash: "0x25cfe80d2f7f75fbf41760cc6ed8f4c477
            42cc4c55d4a35587f7b1671d650716",
  blockNumber: 2005,
  from: "0xa5d73d67d7a79be62e2c77dd877b536775c446dd",
  gas: 2000000,
  gasPrice: 20000000000,
  hash: "0x4fbd082414d2c11deaea9a9f9bac1281d521e666c
        3011b13b22b44f74409b7b6",
  input: "0xb60d4288",
  nonce: 31,
  to: "0xc79d0f151f6c7f51772a4d9f488c90f5177fee4e",
  transactionIndex: 0,
```

```
    value: 1000000000000000000
}

//Send a call to the contract to get the value of a state variable
> myContractInstance.numBackers.call();
1

> myContractInstance.amountRaised.call();
1000000000000000000
```

5.3.4   Gas

Gas is the name of the crypto-fuel in Ethereum which is consumed for performing the operations on a blockchain network. All the transactions on the network are charged a certain amount of gas. While sending a transaction, the sender sets a gas price which represents the fee, the sender is willing to pay per unit of gas. The gas fee paid is proportional to the amount of work that is needed to execute the transaction, in terms of the number of atomic instructions. If a transaction succeeds, the cost of the gas used (*gasprice * gas_used*) is sent to the block's coinbase account (i.e. to the miner). The cost of the remaining gas (*gasprice * gas_remained*) is refunded to the sender. However, if the transaction fails (or runs out of gas), the cost of the gas used (*gasprice * gas_used*) is sent to the block's coinbase account.

Before a transaction is added to a block, several checks are performed for the transaction, such as checking if the gas limit for the transaction is greater than the intrinsic gas used by the transaction. The intrinsic gas is the amount of gas, the transaction requires to be paid prior to its execution. Intrinsic gas is the sum of: (1) the gas cost paid for every transaction ($G_{transaction}$), (2) gas cost paid for every zero bytes of data or code for a transaction ($G_{txdatazero}$), (3) gas cost paid for every non-zero byte of data or code for a transaction ($G_{txdatanonzero}$), (4) gas cost paid by all contract-creating transactions ($G_{txcreate}$). Box 5.9 shows the Python function for computing intrinsic gas (excerpt taken from the pyethereum source).

■ **Box 5.9: Computing intrinsic gas**
(code excerpt from pyethereum file - transactions.py)

```
class Transaction(rlp.Serializable):

    @property
    def intrinsic_gas_used(self):
        num_zero_bytes = str_to_bytes(self.data).count(ascii_chr(0))
        num_non_zero_bytes = len(self.data) - num_zero_bytes
        return (opcodes.GTXCOST
                + opcodes.GTXDATAZERO * num_zero_bytes
                + opcodes.GTXDATANONZERO * num_non_zero_bytes)
```

Now returning to the CrowdFunding contract, let us look at the gas used for a transaction sent to the contract. Box 5.10 shows the receipt of the transaction sent to the CrowdFunding contract, which contains information related to the transaction execution such as the cumulative gas used in the block immediately after the transaction has been executed and the logs have been created from the execution of the transaction.

■ **Box 5.10: Viewing a transaction receipt and gas used**

```
//View transaction receipt
> eth.getTransactionReceipt('0x4fbd082414d2c11deaea9a9f9bac
                    1281d521e666c3011b13b22b44f74409b7b6')
{
  blockHash: "0x25cfe80d2f7f75fbf41760cc6ed8f4c47742cc4c5
            5d4a35587f7b1671d650716",
  blockNumber: 2005,
  contractAddress: null,
  cumulativeGasUsed: 103252,
  from: "0xa5d73d67d7a79be62e2c77dd877b536775c446dd",
  gasUsed: 103252,
  logs: [{
      address: "0xc79d0f151f6c7f51772a4d9f488c90f5177fee4e",
      blockHash: "0x25cfe80d2f7f75fbf41760cc6ed8f4c47
                742cc4c55d4a35587f7b1671d650716",
      blockNumber: 2005,
      data: "0x00000000000000000000000000a5d73d67d7a79be62e2c77d
            d877b536775c446dd000000000000000000000000000000000000
            0000000000000de0b6b3a7640000",
      logIndex: 0,
      topics: ["0xe1fffcc4923d04b559f4d29a8bfc6cda04eb5b0d3c
            460751c2402c5c5cc9109c"],
      transactionHash: "0x4fbd082414d2c11deaea9a9f9bac1281d5
            21e666c3011b13b22b44f74409b7b6",
      transactionIndex: 0
  }],
  root: "9c53db502649055d31ad10eaa9969f821a60
        afecd10aa8d84aa2613c5bbc9119",
  to: "0xc79d0f151f6c7f51772a4d9f488c90f5177fee4e",
  transactionHash: "0x4fbd082414d2c11deaea9a9f9bac1
        281d521e666c3011b13b22b44f74409b7b6",
  transactionIndex: 0
}
```

5.3.5 Logs

When a transaction sent to a contract is executed, a series of log entries are generated and incorporated into the block. A log entry is a tuple comprising the logger's address (e.g. a contract address), and a series of 32-byte log topics and some number of bytes of data. To retrieve logs from the *geth* client, we can use the *web3.eth.filter()* function as shown in Box 5.11. The filter function takes as input, either a filter string, which can have values 'latest' or 'pending', to watch for changes in the latest block or currently mining block, or filter options. The filter options include:

- **fromBlock**: Number of the earliest block for fetching the logs or use 'latest' or 'pending'.
- **toBlock**: Number of the latest block for fetching the logs or use 'latest' or 'pending'.
- **address**: An address or a list of addresses to only get logs from a particular account(s).
- **topics**: List of log topics.

■ **Box 5.11: Getting logs in geth console**

```
var filterString = 'pending';
var filter = web3.eth.filter(filterString);
// //Watch for state changes
filter.watch(function(error, result){
  if (!error)
    console.log(result);
});

//Output - transaction hash
0x1369363a13994cd77fe31f1b75514f4ae7015fa0b5a6753eeeba3c6063c12bae

var options = {'fromBlock': 'pending',
         'address': '0xc79d0f151f6c7f51772a4d9f488c90f5177fee4e'};

//Watch for state changes and get logs
web3.eth.filter(options, function(error, result){
  if (!error)
    console.log(JSON.stringify(result));
});

//Output
{
"address":"0xc79d0f151f6c7f51772a4d9f488c90f5177fee4e",
"blockHash":"0xd134ca3a65ab817404fea672afbbbc42c6d200
          fe06e9e02d54864b166349535f",
"blockNumber":2386,
"data":"0x0000000000000000000000000a5d73d67d7a79be62e2c77dd877b536775c
      446dd00000000000000000000000000000000000000
      00000000000000de0b6b3a7640000",
"logIndex":0,
"topics":["0xe1fffcc4923d04b559f4d29a8bfc6cda04eb5b0d
          3c460751c2402c5c5cc9109c"],
"transactionHash":"0x131f9863f996b6bfda9811f1e36f47a24
      9f8d6e20f50a0e3bae7867c09d659ad",
"transactionIndex":0
}
```

When the filter string is set to 'latest', it returns the block hash of the last incoming block. When the filter string is set to 'pending', it returns a transaction hash of the most recent pending transaction. When log options are provided, it returns a log object with the following fields (as shown in Box 5.11):

- **logIndex**: Log index position in the block
- **transactionIndex**: Transactions index position this log was created from.
- **transactionHash**: Hash of the transactions this log was created from.
- **blockHash**: Hash of the block where this log was in.
- **blockNumber**: Block number where this log was in.
- **address**: Address from which this log originated.
- **data**: Includes non-indexed arguments of the log.
- **topics**: Includes indexed log arguments.

5.3.6 Events

Events can be added in contracts to track the execution of the transactions sent to the contract. Whenever an event is called in a contract, the arguments to the event are stored in the transaction log. Clients can create watchers (JavaScript callbacks) for the events. A watcher for an event is triggered when the event is called. Box 5.12 shows an example of a watcher for the *Deposit* event of the CrowdFunding contract. When a transaction sent to the *fund* function of the CrowdFunding contract is executed, the Deposit event is called from the *fund* function. The watcher for this event is then triggered. The output of the watcher callback function is also shown.

■ Box 5.12: Watching the Deposit event of the CrowdFunding contract

```
// Watch for a specific event
var event = myContractInstance.Deposit({}, '', function(error, result){
    if (!error){
        console.log(JSON.stringify(result));
    }
});

// Event watcher output
{
"address":"0xee8322d4b92cc4240ea0a994cc0e620eaffb9e8d",
"args": {
        "_amount":"1000000000000000000",
        "_from":"0xa5d73d67d7a79be62e2c77dd877b536775c446dd"
        },
"blockHash":"0x0adc09abb4322a350f375270a7dbbbeed8733e
            616a2967b72985abf60a752f86",
"blockNumber":2199,
"event":"Deposit",
"logIndex":0,
"transactionHash":"0xd1dfac0f572cb7c960042ba57909e4c38dde55
                b002b82f8eb3c0e438877acde2",
"transactionIndex":0}

// Watch for all events
var events = myContractInstance.allEvents('', function(error, result){
  if (!error){
        console.log(JSON.stringify(result));
    }
});
```

The event arguments can be indexed by adding the *indexed* attribute before the argument name while declaring an event in the contract. The arguments which are indexed can be searched from the clients, where the watchers can filter the results based on specific values of the indexed arguments.

Figure 5.1 shows the structure of the CrowdFunding contract and the transactions sent to the contract.

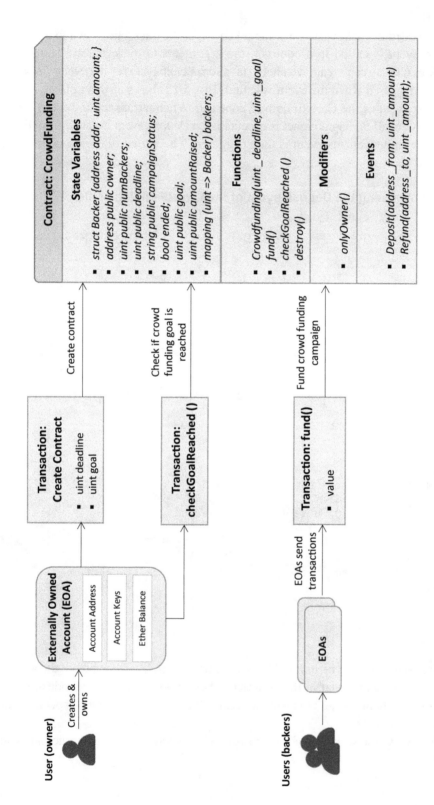

Figure 5.1: CrowdFunding contract structure and transactions

5.4 Setting up and Interacting with a Contract using Mist Wallet

In this section, we will describe the steps involved in setting up and interacting with a contract using Mist Ethereum wallet application. We will take the example of a smart contract for product sales as shown in Box 5.13. With the *ProductSales* contract, the owner of the contract can sell products to buyers. The owner can add a product for sale by sending a transaction with the product ID, product name, inventory, and price. Buyers who already have their Ethereum accounts created, can register with the *ProductSales* contract by sending a transaction to the contract with their name, email and mailing address. A registered buyer can then place an order for a product by sending a transaction to the contract with the product ID, quantity and a value equal to (or greater than) the order amount. If the buyer pays more than the order amount, the balance is refunded when the transaction for a new order is processed.

■ **Box 5.13: ProductSales contract implemented in Solidity**

```solidity
contract ProductSales {

  struct Product {
    uint ID;
    string name;
    uint inventory;
    uint price;
  }

  struct Buyer {
    string name;
    string email;
    string mailingAddress;
    uint totalOrders;
    bool isActive;
  }

  struct Order {
    uint orderID;
    uint productID;
    uint quantity;
    address buyer;
  }

  address public owner;
  mapping (address => Buyer) public buyers;
  mapping (uint => Product) public products;
  mapping (uint => Order) public orders;

  uint public numProducts;
  uint public numBuyers;
  uint public numOrders;

  event NewProduct(uint _ID, string _name, uint _inventory, uint _price);
  event NewBuyer(string _name, string _email, string _mailingAddress);
  event NewOrder(uint _OrderID, uint _ID, uint _quantity, address _from);
```

```
modifier onlyOwner(){
  if (msg.sender != owner) throw;
  _
}

function ProductSales() {
  owner = msg.sender;
  numBuyers = 0;
  numProducts = 0;
}

function addProduct(uint _ID, string _name, uint _inventory,
           uint _price) onlyOwner{
  Product p = products[_ID];
  p.ID = _ID;
  p.name = _name;
  p.inventory = _inventory;
  p.price = _price;
  numProducts++;
  NewProduct(_ID, _name, _inventory, _price);
}

function updateProduct(uint _ID, string _name, uint _inventory,
            uint _price) onlyOwner{
  products[_ID].name = _name;
  products[_ID].inventory = _inventory;
  products[_ID].price = _price;
}

function registerBuyer(string _name, string _email,
            string _mailingAddress) {
  Buyer b = buyers[msg.sender];
  b.name = _name;
  b.email = _email;
  b.mailingAddress = _mailingAddress;
  b.totalOrders = 0;
  b.isActive = true;
  numBuyers++;
  NewBuyer(_name, _email, _mailingAddress);
}

function buyProduct(uint _ID, uint _quantity)
          returns(uint newOrderID){
  // Check if there is sufficient inventory of the product
  if(products[_ID].inventory < _quantity){
    throw;
  }

  // Check if amount paid is not less than the order amount
  uint orderAmount = products[_ID].price*_quantity;
  if(msg.value<orderAmount){
    throw;
  }
```

```
// Check if buyer is registered
if(buyers[msg.sender].isActive != true){
  throw;
}

// Update total orders of the buyer
buyers[msg.sender].totalOrders += 1;

// Generate new order ID
newOrderID = uint(msg.sender) + block.timestamp;

// Create a new order
Order o = orders[newOrderID];
o.orderID = newOrderID;
o.productID = _ID;
o.quantity = _quantity;
o.buyer = msg.sender;

//Update total number of orders
numOrders++;

// Update product inventory
products[_ID].inventory = products[_ID].inventory - 1;

// Refund balance remaining to buyer
if(msg.value>orderAmount){
  uint refundAmount = msg.value - orderAmount;
  if (!msg.sender.send(refundAmount))
    throw;
}

NewOrder(newOrderID, _ID, _quantity, msg.sender);
}

function withdrawFunds() onlyOwner{
  if (!owner.send(this.balance))
    throw;
}

function kill() onlyOwner{
    suicide(owner);
}
}
```

5.4.1 Compiling & Deploying a Contract

Figure 5.2 shows how to deploy a new contract from the Ethereum wallet application. Choose an EOA from which you want to deploy the contract. Next, paste the contract source code, select a gas fee you are willing to pay (the higher the fee you pay, the faster the transaction will be processed) and deploy the contract. Once deployed, you can browse to contract's page to interact with the contract.

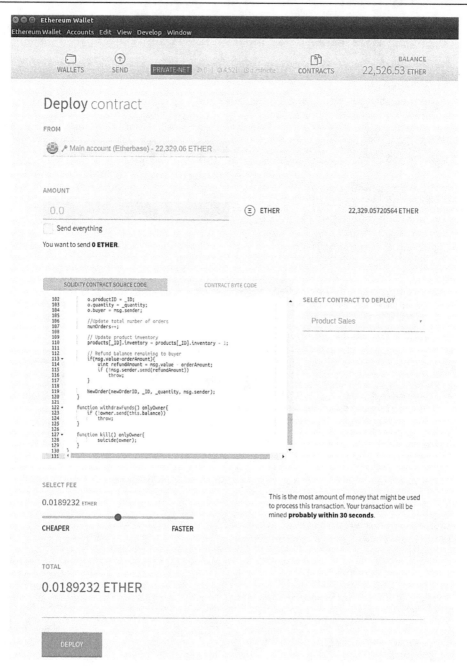

Figure 5.2: Deploying ProductSales contract from Mist Ethereum wallet application

5.4.2   Interacting with a Contract

Figure 5.3(a) shows how to send a transaction to the *addProduct* function of the ProductSales contract along with the input parameters. When the transaction is sent, the user is prompted for the EOA account password (from which the transaction is sent) as shown in Figure 5.3(b). Figure 5.4 shows how to send transactions to the *registerBuyer* and *buyProduct* functions of the contract.

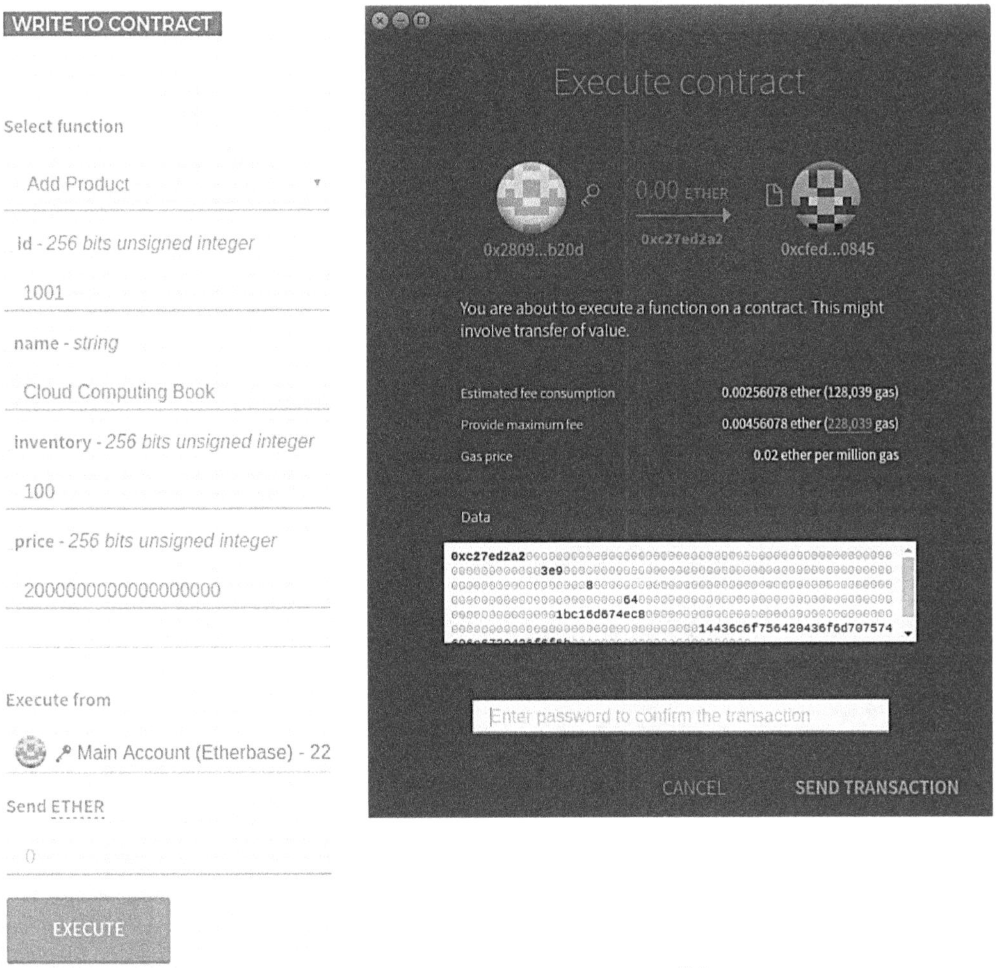

Figure 5.3: Sending a transaction to the ProductSales contract

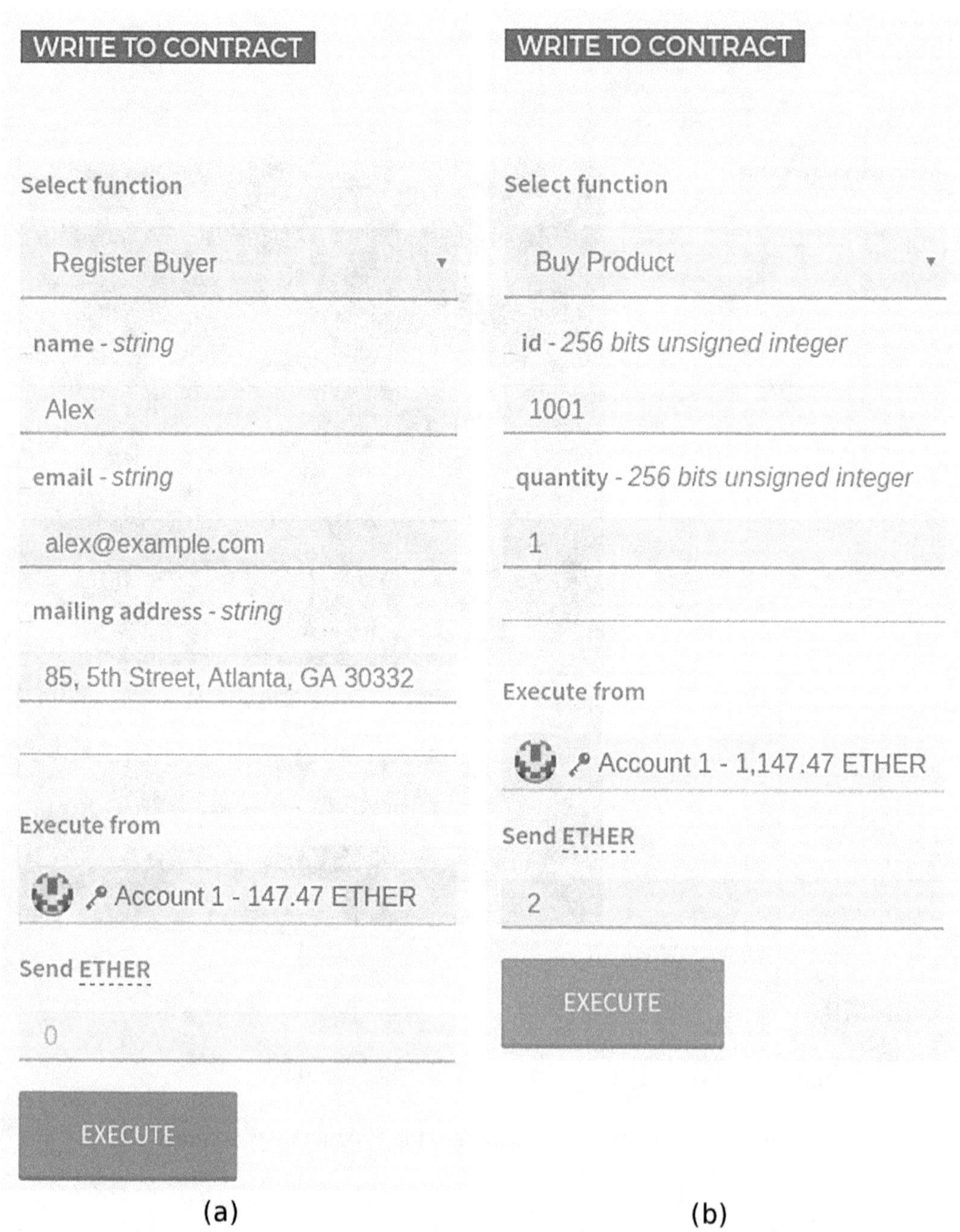

WRITE TO CONTRACT

Select function

Register Buyer ▾

name - *string*

Alex

email - *string*

alex@example.com

mailing address - *string*

85, 5th Street, Atlanta, GA 30332

Execute from

🔑 Account 1 - 147.47 ETHER

Send ETHER

0

EXECUTE

(a)

WRITE TO CONTRACT

Select function

Buy Product ▾

id - *256 bits unsigned integer*

1001

quantity - *256 bits unsigned integer*

1

Execute from

🔑 Account 1 - 1,147.47 ETHER

Send ETHER

2

EXECUTE

(b)

Figure 5.4: Sending transactions to *registerBuyer* and *buyProduct* functions

Figures 5.5 and 5.6 show the contract's state variables (which are declared as public) as viewed in contract details page.

READ FROM CONTRACT

Num buyers

1

Num orders

1

Products

256 bits unsigned integer

1001

Id
1001

Name
Cloud Computing Book

Inventory
99

Price
2000000000000000000

Owner

Main account (Etherbase)

Figure 5.5: Viewing contract's state variables

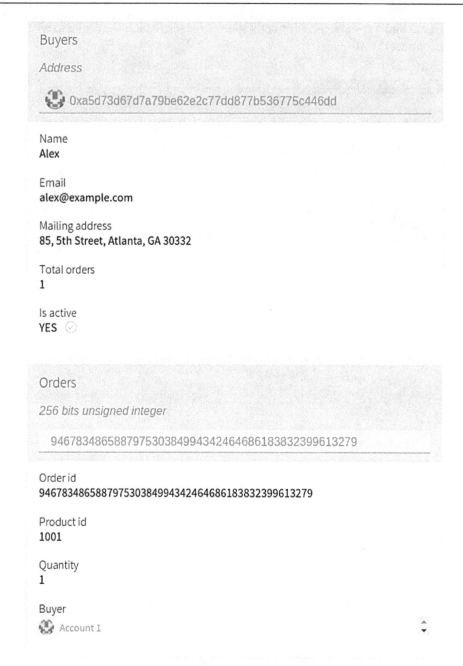

Figure 5.6: Viewing contract's state variables

Figure 5.7 shows the contract events triggered by the execution of the transactions. Figure 5.8 shows the details of the *NewProduct* event which is triggered when the transaction for adding a new product is processed. Figure 5.9 shows the details of the *NewBuyer* event which is triggered when the transaction for registering a new buyer is processed. Figure 5.10 shows the details of the *NewOrder* event which is triggered when the transaction for ordering a product is processed. Figure 5.11 shows the structure of the ProductSales contract and the transactions sent to the contract.

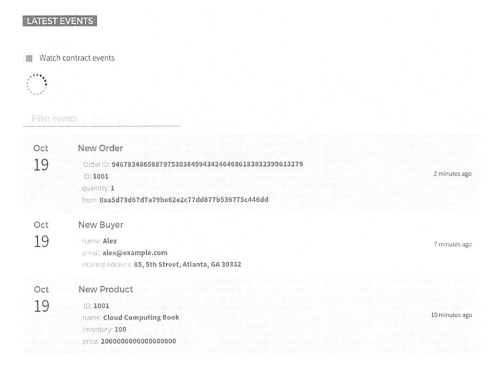

Figure 5.7: Viewing contract events

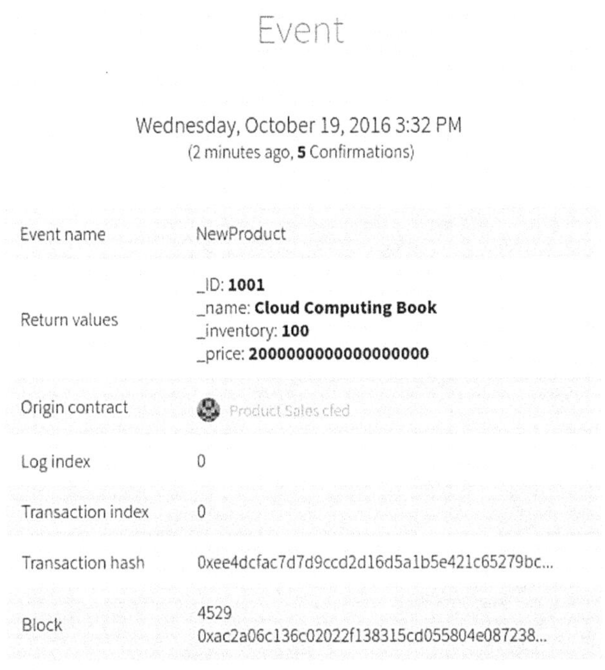

Figure 5.8: Viewing details of *NewProduct* event

Event

Wednesday, October 19, 2016 3:34 PM
(6 minutes ago, **21** Confirmations)

Event name	NewBuyer
Return values	_name: **Alex** _email: **alex@example.com** _mailingAddress: **85, 5th Street, Atlanta, GA 30332**
Origin contract	Product Sales cfed
Log index	0
Transaction index	0
Transaction hash	0xbd238ae99e0c26556ee5b5cc429ab323ed437d...
Block	4535 0x9358e234b1910dc56c759908be32e0c32c80da...

Figure 5.9: Viewing details of *NewBuyer* event

Event

Wednesday, October 19, 2016 3:40 PM
(a minute ago, **1** Confirmations)

Event name	NewOrder
Return values	_OrderID: **9467834865887975303849943424646861838323996132 79** _ID: **1001** _quantity: **1** _from: **0xa5d73d67d7a79be62e2c77dd877b536775c446dd**
Origin contract	Product Sales cfed
Log index	0
Transaction index	0
Transaction hash	0xe30bafecc2bfdc7d8e4b49c24d4952e5aacaa1...
Block	4555 0x8aec15b44bad99255202846c6fcfe29c5f9d89...

Figure 5.10: Viewing details of *NewOrder* event

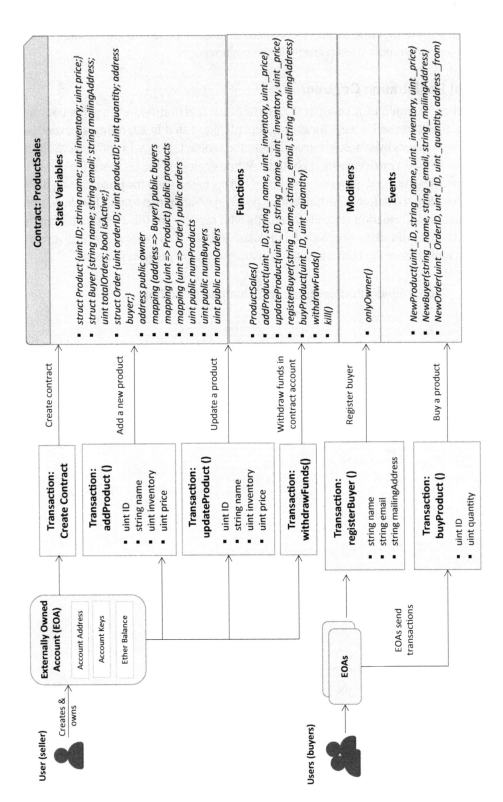

Figure 5.11: ProductSales contract structure and transactions

5.5   Smart Contract Examples

In this section, we will describe examples of smart contracts. Based on these examples we will identify some commonly used patterns in the contracts.

5.5.1   Event Registration Contract

Let us look at an example of a smart contract for event registration. Using this contract, the event organizers can sell tickets for events. People interested in attending an event can purchase the event tickets by sending transactions to the contract. Box 5.14 shows the Solidity implementation of the *EventRegistration* contract. While deploying the contract, the owner of the contract specifies the event quota (or number of tickets to sell) and the price of each ticket. In the smart contract, we define a custom data type to represent a registrant. The *Registrant* structure maintains information related to persons who register for the event including the amount paid, number of tickets purchased and email address. The *registrantsPaid* variable maintains a mapping from the address of the registrant to the *Registrant* structure.

■ **Box 5.14: Event registration contract implemented in Solidity**

```
contract EventRegistration {
  struct Registrant {
        uint amount;
        uint numTickets;
        string email;
    }

  address public owner;
  uint public numTicketsSold;
  uint public quota;
  uint public price;
  mapping (address => Registrant) registrantsPaid;

  event Deposit(address _from, uint _amount);
  event Refund(address _to, uint _amount);

  modifier onlyOwner()
    {
        if (msg.sender != owner) throw;
        _
    }

  modifier soldOut()
    {
        if (numTicketsSold >= quota) throw;
        _
    }

  function EventRegistration(uint _quota, uint _price) {
    owner = msg.sender;
    numTicketsSold = 0;
    quota = _quota;
    price = _price;
```

```
}

function buyTicket(string email, uint numTickets) soldOut {
     // Check if amount paid is not less than the total cost of tickets
     uint totalAmount = price*numTickets;
     if(msg.value<totalAmount){
          throw;
     }

  if(registrantsPaid[msg.sender].amount>0){
    //Already registered
    registrantsPaid[msg.sender].amount += totalAmount;
    registrantsPaid[msg.sender].email = email;
    registrantsPaid[msg.sender].numTickets += numTickets;
  }else{
    Registrant r = registrantsPaid[msg.sender];
        r.amount = totalAmount;
        r.email = email;
        r.numTickets=numTickets;
    }

  numTicketsSold = numTicketsSold+numTickets;

     // Refund balance remaining to buyer
     if(msg.value>totalAmount){
          uint refundAmount = msg.value - totalAmount;
          if (!msg.sender.send(refundAmount))
             throw;
     }

  Deposit(msg.sender, msg.value);

}

function refundTicket(address buyer) onlyOwner {
  if (registrantsPaid[buyer].amount >0) {
    if (this.balance >= registrantsPaid[buyer].amount) {
             registrantsPaid[buyer].amount = 0;
             numTicketsSold = numTicketsSold -
                             registrantsPaid[buyer].numTickets;
      if(!buyer.send(registrantsPaid[buyer].amount)) throw;
      Refund(buyer, registrantsPaid[buyer].amount);
    }
  }
}

  function withdrawFunds() onlyOwner{
     if (!owner.send(this.balance))
         throw;
  }

function getRegistrantAmountPaid(address buyer) returns(uint){
  return registrantsPaid[buyer].amount;
}
```

```
function kill() onlyOwner{
   suicide(owner);
}
}
```

Box 5.15 shows the commands for interacting with the *EventRegistration* contract from the *geth* console. To buy tickets for the event, a user can send a transaction to the *buyTicket* function of the contract along with the user's email address and number of tickets to buy. The user also sends a value equal to the total cost of the tickets along with the transaction. The *buyTicket* function has a function modifier, *soldOut*, which is used to check if the event is sold out. Within the *buyTicket* function, we check if the user is already registered with the event. If already registered, we update the number of tickets purchased by the user and the total amount paid. If not registered, we add the user's address to the *registrantsPaid* list and store the user's email address, the amount paid, and number of tickets purchased. If the value sent by the user is more than the total cost of the tickets, the balance is refunded.

The amount paid by all the users for the tickets purchased is held in the contract account. The contract owner (or beneficiary) can withdraw the amount from the contract account by sending a transaction to the *withdrawFunds* function. This function has a modifier, *onlyOwner*, to check if the transaction is sent by the owner. Figure 5.12 shows the structure of the EventRegistration contract and the transactions sent to the contract.

■ **Box 5.15: Working with event registration contract**

```
//Contract source converted to a string
var contractSource = "contract EventRegistration {...}";

//Compile contract
var contractCompiled = eth.compile.solidity(contractSource);

//Set event quota and ticket price
var quota = 1000;
var price = 10000000000000000000;

//Create contract
var myContract =
web3.eth.contract(contractCompiled.EventRegistration.info.abiDefinition);

//Deploy contract
var myContractInstance = myContract.new(
    quota,
    price,
    {
        from:web3.eth.accounts[0],
        data:contractCompiled.EventRegistration.code,
        gas: 1000000
    }, function(e, contract){
    if(!e) {
      if(!contract.address) {
        console.log("Contract transaction send: TransactionHash: " +
```

```
                       contract.transactionHash + " waiting to be mined...");
         } else {
           console.log("Contract mined! Address: " + contract.address);
         }
      }
   }
});

//Contract transaction send:
//TransactionHash: 0x41a3fdd60c6ec796db16dcae28d7908d534
               990893d7e5e1fc0e3295f9b36b049 waiting to be mined...

//Contract mined! Address: 0xf0e5c493d414ee17e6b18298c167ca6641dd39d1

// Send a call to check contract's state variable
> myContractInstance.quota.call();
1000

> myContractInstance.price.call();
10000000000000000000

// Send transaction to contract to buy ticket
> myContractInstance.buyTicket.sendTransaction("abc@example.com", 1,
      {from: eth.accounts[1], value: web3.toWei(10, "ether"),
       gas: 2000000})

// Check number of tickets sold
> myContractInstance.numTicketsSold.call();
1

// Check amount paid by a registrant
> myContractInstance.getRegistrantAmountPaid.call(eth.accounts[1])
10000000000000000000

// Send transaction to contract to refund ticket
> myContractInstance.refundTicket.sendTransaction(
         "0xa5d73d67d7a79be62e2c77dd877b536775c446dd",
         {from: eth.accounts[0],  gas: 2000000})

// Check number of tickets sold after refund transaction is processed
> myContractInstance.numTicketsSold.call();
0
```

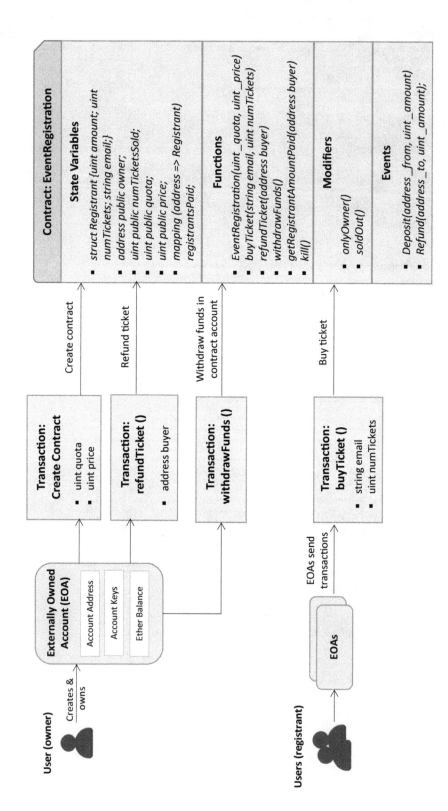

Figure 5.12: EventRegistration contract structure and transactions

5.5.2 Voting Contract

Let us look at an example of a smart contract for voting. To prevent voter fraud and manipulation in the voting process, the voting smart contract can be used, which ensures that voting can be accomplished in a secure and verifiable manner. Box 5.16 shows the Solidity implementation of the *Voting* contract. While deploying the voting contract, the creator of the contract (called the chairperson), provides a list of proposal names on which voting is to be done and the time (in seconds) for which the voting will be open. In the contract's constructor, the voting time, voting start timestamp, chairperson address and proposals list are updated.

■ **Box 5.16: Voting contract implemented in Solidity**

```
contract Voting {
    // Declare a complex type to reresent a single voter.
    struct Voter {
        bool voted;  // if true, that person already voted
        uint vote;   // index of the voted proposal
        bool rightToVote; // if true, that person has right to vote
    }

    // Declare a complex type to reresent a single proposal.
    struct Proposal
    {
        bytes32 name;   // short name
        uint voteCount; // number of accumulated votes
    }

    address public chairperson;
    uint public votingStart;
    uint public votingTime;
    uint public numProposals;
    mapping(address => Voter) public voters;
    mapping (uint => Proposal) public proposals;

    function Voting(bytes32[] proposalNames, uint _votingTime) {
        chairperson = msg.sender;
        voters[chairperson].rightToVote = true;
        votingStart = now;
        votingTime = _votingTime;
        numProposals=proposalNames.length;

        // For each of the provided proposal names, create a new
        // proposal object and add it to the end of the array.
        for (uint i = 0; i < proposalNames.length; i++) {
            Proposal p = proposals[i];
            p.name = proposalNames[i];
            p.voteCount = 0;
        }
    }

    function giveRightToVote(address voter) {
        if (msg.sender != chairperson || voters[voter].voted) {
```

```
                // `throw` terminates and reverts all changes to the state
                throw;
        }
        voters[voter].rightToVote = true;
    }


    function vote(uint proposal) {
        if (now > votingStart + votingTime) {
            // Revert the call if the voting period is over
            throw;
        }

        Voter sender = voters[msg.sender];

        if (sender.voted)
            throw;
        sender.voted = true;
        sender.vote = proposal;

        proposals[proposal].voteCount += 1;
    }

    function winningProposal() constant
            returns (uint winningProposal, bytes32 proposalName)
    {
        if (now <= votingStart + votingTime)
            throw; // voting did not yet end

        uint winningVoteCount = 0;
        for (uint p = 0; p < numProposals; p++) {
            if (proposals[p].voteCount > winningVoteCount) {
                winningVoteCount = proposals[p].voteCount;
                winningProposal = p;
                proposalName = proposals[p].name;
            }
        }
    }
}
```

Box 5.17 shows the commands for interacting with the *Voting* contract from the *geth* console. Once the contract is deployed, the chairperson can assign voting rights to the voters by sending transactions to the *giveRightToVote* function with the voter address. Voters can then vote for a proposal by sending a transaction to the *vote* function and passing the index of the proposal to vote for. Within the vote function, we check if the voting period is not over and then record the vote of the voter for the proposal specified. Upon completion of the voting period, a constant function, *winningProposal*, can be called to get the index and name of the winning proposal. Note that we send a call to the constant function *winningProposal* instead of a transaction, as the function does not change the state of the network, and is only executed to read data from the blockchain. Figure 5.13 shows the structure of the Voting contract and the transactions sent to the contract.

■ Box 5.17: Working with voting contract

```
//Contract source converted to a string
var contractSource = "contract Voting {...}";

//Compile contract
var contractCompiled = eth.compile.solidity(contractSource);

//Set event quota and ticket price
var proposalNames = ["Alpha", "Beta", "Gamma", "Delta"];
var votingTime = 86400 //in seconds

//Create contract
var myContract =
  web3.eth.contract(contractCompiled.Voting.info.abiDefinition);

//Deploy contract
var myContractInstance = myContract.new(proposalNames,
    votingTime,{from:web3.eth.accounts[0],
        data:contractCompiled.Voting.code, gas: 1000000
    }, function(e, contract){
    if(!e) {
      if(!contract.address) {
        console.log("Contract transaction send: TransactionHash: " +
            contract.transactionHash + " waiting to be mined...");
      } else {
        console.log("Contract mined! Address: " + contract.address);
    }}});

//Contract transaction send:
//TransactionHash: 0x41a3fdd60c6ec796db16dcae28d7908d534
                990893d7e5e1fc0e3295f9b36b049 waiting to be mined...

//Contract mined! Address: 0xf0e5c493d414ee17e6b18298c167ca6641dd39d1

// Send a call to check contract's state variable
> myContractInstance.numProposals.call();
4

> myContractInstance.votingTime.call();
86400

// Send transaction to give right of voting
> myContractInstance.giveRightToVote.sendTransaction(eth.accounts[1],
        {from: eth.accounts[0], gas: 2000000})

// Send transaction to give vote
> myContractInstance.vote.sendTransaction(2,
        {from: eth.accounts[1], gas: 2000000})

// Check winning proposal
> myContractInstance.winningProposal.call()
[2, "0x47616d6d610000000000000000000000000000000000000000000000000000000"]
```

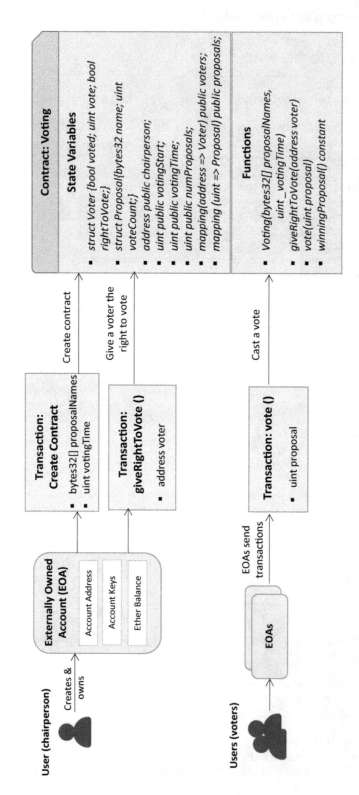

Figure 5.13: Voting contract structure and transactions

5.5.3 Name Registry Contract

A name registry can be used to associate names to addresses, for example, to assign
user-friendly names to smart contracts. Box 5.18 shows the Solidity implementation of
the *NameRegistrar* contract. In this contract, a custom defined type (*struct RegistryEntry*) is
used to store the registry entries. A registry includes the address of the owner of the registry,
a contract address and some content (such as contract description). The registry entry records
are stored in a mapping data type, which maps a byte array (for name) to a *RegistryEntry*
object.

■ **Box 5.18: NameRegistrar contract implemented in Solidity**

```
contract NameRegistrar {

    struct RegistryEntry {
        address owner;
        address addr;
        bytes32 content;
    }

    mapping ( bytes32 => RegistryEntry ) public records;
    uint public numRecords;

    event Registered(bytes32 name, address account);
    event Deregistered(bytes32 name, address account);

    function NameRegistrar(){
        numRecords=0;
    }

    function register(bytes32 name) returns (bool success) {
        if (records[name].owner == 0) {
            RegistryEntry r = records[name];
            r.owner = msg.sender;
            numRecords++;
            Registered(name, msg.sender);
            success = true;
        }

        else success = false;
    }

    function unregister(bytes32 name) returns (bool success) {
        if (records[name].owner == msg.sender) {
            records[name].owner = 0;
            success = true;
            numRecords--;
            Deregistered(name, msg.sender);
        }

        else success = false;
    }
```

```
    function transferOwnership(bytes32 name, address newOwner) {
        if (records[name].owner == msg.sender) {
            records[name].owner = newOwner;
        }
    }

    function getOwner(bytes32 name) returns (address addr) {
        return records[name].owner;
    }

    function setAddr(bytes32 name, address addr) {
        if (records[name].owner == msg.sender) {
            records[name].addr = addr;
        }
    }

    function getAddr(bytes32 name) returns (address addr) {
        return records[name].addr;
    }

    function setContent(bytes32 name, bytes32 content) {
        if (records[name].owner == msg.sender) {
            records[name].content = content;
        }
    }

    function getContent(bytes32 name) returns (bytes32 content) {
        return records[name].content;
    }
}
```

Box 5.19 shows the commands for interacting with the *NameRegistrar* contract from the *geth* console. To register a name, the user can send a transaction to the *register* function of the contract and pass the name to register. Once a name is registered, the user can set the address and content for the name by sending transactions to the *setAddr* and *setContent* functions respectively. The owner of a name can transfer the ownership to another user by sending a transaction to the *transferOwnership* function. To get details of a registered name, we can send a call to the *records* state variable as shown in Box 5.19. Figure 5.14 shows the structure of the *NameRegistrar* contract and the transactions sent to the contract.

■ Box 5.19: Working with NameRegistrar contract

```
//Contract source converted to a string
var contractSource = "contract NameRegistrar {...}";

//Compile contract
var contractCompiled = eth.compile.solidity(contractSource);

/Create contract
var myContract =
  web3.eth.contract(contractCompiled.NameRegistrar.info.abiDefinition);
```

```
//Deploy contract
var myContractInstance = myContract.new(
    {
        from:web3.eth.accounts[0],
        data:contractCompiled.NameRegistrar.code,
        gas: 1000000
    }, function(e, contract){
    if(!e) {
      if(!contract.address) {
        console.log("Contract transaction send: TransactionHash: " +
            contract.transactionHash + " waiting to be mined...");
      } else {
        console.log("Contract mined! Address: " + contract.address);
      }
    }
});


// Send transaction to contract to register a name
> myContractInstance.register.sendTransaction("CrowdFunding",
                    {from: eth.accounts[0], gas: 2000000})

// Send transaction to contract to set an address for a name
> myContractInstance.setAddr.sendTransaction("CrowdFunding",
        "0xc79d0f151f6c7f51772a4d9f488c90f5177fee4e",
        {from: eth.accounts[0], gas: 2000000})

// Send transaction to contract to set content for a name
> myContractInstance.setContent.sendTransaction("CrowdFunding",
      "Crowd funding contract", {from: eth.accounts[0], gas: 2000000})

// Send a call to check number of records
> myContractInstance.numRecords.call()
1

// Send a call to get details of a name
> myContractInstance.records.call("CrowdFunding")
["0x2809d4cb12b8bcaca9e4b805e474ad984c84b20d",
"0xc79d0f151f6c7f51772a4d9f488c90f5177fee4e",
"0x43726f77642066756e64696e6720636f6e747261637400000000000000000000"]
```

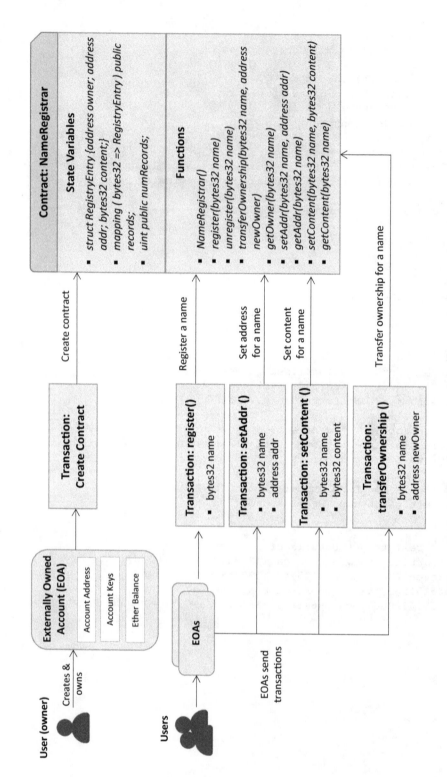

Figure 5.14: NameRegistrar contract structure and transactions

5.5.4 IoT Smart Switch Contract

Let us look at an example of using a smart contract for an IoT smart switch device. Users can turn a switch "on" or "off" for a certain duration by sending a transaction with a value to the smart contract associated with the switch. Box 5.20 shows the Solidity implementation of a *SmartSwitch* contract. The contract acts as an agreement between the user and the switch to turn on the switch on for a certain duration based on the amount of cryptocurrency (Ether) sent by the user to the *SmartSwitch* contract account. For example, a user can pay 1 Ether to turn the switch on for 1 hour. Such a contract can be used for automating solar charging stations, for example, where a user can connect their devices to a charging station and then send a transaction to the smart contract associated with the charging station to activate it.

> ■ **Box 5.20: SmartSwitch contract implemented in Solidity**

```
contract SmartSwitch {

    address public owner;
    mapping (address => uint) public usersPaid;
    uint public numUsers;

    event Deposit(address _from, uint _amount);
    event Refund(address _to, uint _amount);

    modifier onlyOwner()
    {
        if (msg.sender != owner) throw;
        _
    }

    function SmartSwitch() {
        owner = msg.sender;
        numUsers = 0;
    }

    function payToSwitch() {
        usersPaid[msg.sender] = msg.value;
        numUsers++;
        Deposit(msg.sender, msg.value);
    }

    function refundUser(address recipient, uint amount) onlyOwner {
        if (usersPaid[recipient] == amount) {
            if (this.balance >= amount) {
                if (!recipient.send(amount))
                    throw;
                Refund(recipient, amount);
                usersPaid[recipient] = 0;
                numUsers--;
            }
        }
    }

    function withdrawFunds() onlyOwner{
```

```
            if (!owner.send(this.balance))
                throw;
        }

    function kill() onlyOwner{
            suicide(owner);
        }
}
```

Box 5.21 shows the commands for interacting with the *SmartSwitch* contract from the *geth* console. Figure 5.15 shows the structure of the SmartSwitch contract and the transactions sent to the contract.

■ **Box 5.21: Working with smart switch contract**

```
//Contract source converted to a string
var contractSource = "contract SmartSwitch {...}";

//Compile contract
var contractCompiled = eth.compile.solidity(contractSource);

//Create contract
var myContract =
  web3.eth.contract(contractCompiled.SmartSwitch.info.abiDefinition);

//Deploy contract
var myContractInstance = myContract.new(
    {
        from:web3.eth.accounts[0],
        data:contractCompiled.SmartSwitch.code,
        gas: 1000000
    }, function(e, contract){
    if(!e) {
      if(!contract.address) {
        console.log("Contract transaction send: TransactionHash: " +
            contract.transactionHash + " waiting to be mined...");
      } else {
        console.log("Contract mined! Address: " + contract.address);
      }
    }
});

//Contract transaction send:
//TransactionHash: 0x0f558188e67cd96daae7cf63a8a4813756
1a1fce9616148e0e817db1746aac08 waiting to be mined...
//Contract mined! Address:
//0x0cafd203ca406bb39985d0f70d55b44b78d756eb

// Send transaction to pay an amount to contract account
> myContractInstance.payToSwitch.sendTransaction({from: eth.accounts[1],
            value: web3.toWei(0.1, "ether"), gas: 2000000})

> web3.fromWei(eth.getBalance(myContractInstance.address), "ether")
```

```
0.1

// Call contract to check number of users
> myContractInstance.numUsers.call()
1

// Call contract to check amount paid by a user
> myContractInstance.usersPaid.call(eth.accounts[1])
100000000000000000

// Send transaction to withdraw funds from
//contract account to owner's account
> myContractInstance.withdrawFunds.sendTransaction(
                        {from: eth.accounts[0], gas: 2000000})
```

For this case study, we use the Raspberry Pi single board computer (SBC). A relay module is connected to the GPIO pins of the Raspberry Pi board to control the switch. Box 5.22 shows the Python implementation of the controller service that runs on the IoT device. For this implementation, we use the EthJsonRpc Python client for Ethereum. We watch the account balance of the SmartSwitch contract every 2 seconds. If a change in balance is found, the switch is activated for 60 seconds.

■ **Box 5.22: Python controller component that runs on IoT smart switch device**

```python
from ethjsonrpc import EthJsonRpc
import time
import datetime
import RPi.GPIO as GPIO ## Import GPIO library

## Use board pin numbering
GPIO.setmode(GPIO.BOARD)

## Setup GPIO Pin 7 to OUT
GPIO.setup(7, GPIO.OUT)

# Connect to Blockchain network
c = EthJsonRpc('192.168.1.20', 8101)

# Device account address to watch
account_to_watch = "0x0cafd203ca406bb39985d0f70d55b44b78d756eb"

# Get balance in the device account
balance = c.eth_getBalance(account_to_watch)
print "Starting Balance = " + str(balance)

# Switch is off initially
onStatus=False
GPIO.output(7,False) ## Turn off GPIO pin 7

while True:
    newbalance = c.eth_getBalance(account_to_watch)
    if onStatus==True:
```

```
        nowTime = datetime.datetime.now()
        timeElapsed = nowTime - onTime
        #print "Switch ON, Elapsed Time: " + str(timeElapsed.seconds)
        if timeElapsed.seconds >= 60:
            print "Switching OFF"
            onStatus=False
            GPIO.output(7,False) ## Turn off GPIO pin 7

    elif (newbalance > balance):
        #print "New Balance = " + str(newbalance)
        balance=newbalance
        #print "Switching ON"
        onStatus=True
        GPIO.output(7,True) ## Turn on GPIO pin 7
        onTime = datetime.datetime.now()

time.sleep(2)
```

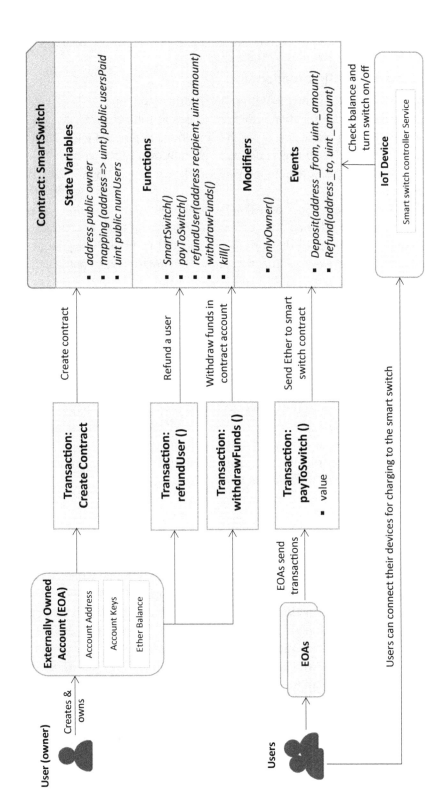

Figure 5.15: SmartSwitch contract structure and transactions

5.6   Smart Contract Patterns

In this section we will describe some commonly used design patterns for smart contracts.

5.6.1   Conditions-Effects-Interaction

When a function in a contract interacts with other contracts or sends Ether, it is a good practice to structure the contract function into three phases as follows:

1. **Conditions**: In the first phase, check for the conditions to proceed with the execution of the function, and if a condition is not valid, then throw an exception.
2. **Effects**: In the second phase, actions are performed such as updating the state variables (or the conditions).
3. **Interaction**: Interactions are performed in the final phase. An interaction can either be a call to a function in another contract or sending Ether to an EOA or contract account.

To understand the importance of the correct ordering of the three phases, let us look at two implementations of the *refundTicket* function of the *EventRegistration* contract, described earlier in this chapter.

Box 5.23 shows an incorrect ordering of the conditions, effects and interaction phases. In this case, the interaction phase comes before the effects phase. The *refundTicket* function is used by the owner of the contract (event organizer) to issue refunds to the event registrants who request for ticket cancellation. In the conditions phase of this function, we check if the amount paid by the registrant is not zero and the tickets purchased by the registrant is not zero. Next, we check if the contract has enough balance to refund the registrant. In this incorrect implementation, after performing the conditions phase, we perform the interactions. The interaction here is to send Ether to the registrant. We check the return status of this transfer and if it fails, we throw an exception. After performing this interaction, we perform the effects phase where we set the amount paid and number of tickets purchased by the registrant to zero and also update the total number of tickets sold.

Re-Entrancy Problem

Now let us look into the problem with the ordering of the Conditions, Effects and Interaction phases as shown in Box 5.23. This *refundTicket* function is vulnerable to "re-entrancy", described as follows. Let us say the registrant to whom we are sending Ether is a contract account. For any contract, when a transaction is sent to the contract with an Ether value and without any data (i.e., without a function being called), a fallback function in the contract is executed. If there is no fallback function, the Ether transfer is rejected. However, if there is a fallback function in the called contract, and a call is made from the fallback function to the calling contract (the contract which sent the Ether transfer call) the called contract can get multiple refunds. The called contract can call back into the *refundTicket* function of the calling contract before the send Ether interaction is completed and since the effects phase has not yet been executed (conditions are not updated), the conditions would still be true. This is called "re-entrancy". Due to the re-entrancy vulnerability of the *refundTicket* function, a registrant (which is a contract account) can get multiple refunds and even retrieve all the Ether in the contract.

■ Box 5.23: Incorrect ordering of the Conditions, Effects and Interaction phases

```
//Incorrect ordering of phases

function refundTicket(address buyer) onlyOwner {
    // Conditions phase
    // Check if the amount paid by registrant is not zero
    if (registrantsPaid[buyer].amount == 0)
        throw;

    // Check if the number of tickets purchased by
    // the registrant is not zero
    if (registrantsPaid[buyer].numTickets==0)
        throw;

    // Check if the contract has enough balance to refund the registrant
    if (this.balance < registrantsPaid[buyer].amount)
        throw;

    // Interaction phase
    // Refund the amount to the buyer
    if(!buyer.send(registrantsPaid[buyer].amount))
        throw;
    Refund(buyer, registrantsPaid[buyer].amount);

    // Effects phase
    // Update the state variables
    numTicketsSold = numTicketsSold - registrantsPaid[buyer].numTickets;
    registrantsPaid[buyer].amount = 0;
    registrantsPaid[buyer].numTickets=0;

}
```

Box 5.24 shows the correct ordering of the conditions, effects and interaction phases. In this case, the effects phase comes before the interaction phase. In the effects phase, we update the conditions, i.e., the amount paid and number of tickets purchased by the registrant are set to zero and the total number of tickets sold is updated. In this implementation, even if the interaction results in a re-entrancy, multiple refunds would not be issued because the condition has already been updated, and will throw an exception the next time the *refundTicket* function is called.

■ Box 5.24: Correct ordering of the Conditions, Effects and Interaction phases

```
//Correct ordering of phases

function refundTicket(address buyer) onlyOwner {
    // Phase-1:  Conditions
    // Check if the amount paid by registrant is not zero
    if (registrantsPaid[buyer].amount == 0)
        throw;

    // Check if the number of tickets purchased by
```

```
    // the registrant is not zero
    if (registrantsPaid[buyer].numTickets==0)
        throw;

    // Check if the contract has enough balance to refund the registrant
    if (this.balance < registrantsPaid[buyer].amount)
        throw;

    // Phase-2:  Effects
    // Update the state variables
    numTicketsSold = numTicketsSold - registrantsPaid[buyer].numTickets;
    registrantsPaid[buyer].amount = 0;
    registrantsPaid[buyer].numTickets=0;

    // Phase-3: Interaction
    // Refund the amount to the buyer
    if(!buyer.send(registrantsPaid[buyer].amount))
        throw;
    Refund(buyer, registrantsPaid[buyer].amount);

}
```

5.6.2   Withdrawal

While the Conditions-Effects-Interaction pattern can be used to prevent re-entrancy, however, if the interaction is to send Ether, the withdrawal pattern is recommended. Let us look at two implementations of the *checkGoalReached* function of the *CrowdFunding* contract, described earlier in this chapter. This function is called by the owner of the crowdfunding campaign upon completion of the campaign to withdraw the funds to the beneficiary account, if the campaign succeeds, or issue refunds to the campaign backers. Box 5.25 shows an implementation of the *checkGoalReached* function, which has the correct ordering of the conditions, effects and interaction phases. The interaction here is either to transfer the contract balance to the campaign beneficiary or refund the campaign backers. Let us say if one of the backers is a contract which has a fallback function. When the interaction to refund Ether to this backer takes place, the fallback function in the contract is called. There is limited gas available for the execution of the fallback function (a gas stipend of 2300 gas). If the fallback function performs computations that consume more than the gas stipend, an out-of-gas exception is raised. This exception will cause the Ether transfer interaction to fail. When the Ether transfer interaction fails, an exception will be thrown in the *checkGoalReached* function. Thus a malicious backer which is a contract account instead of an EOA, can block the progress of the *checkGoalReached* function by consuming more than the gas stipend in the fallback function. To prevent this problem, the withdrawal pattern can be used. In the withdrawal pattern, the recipients (or backers) are allowed to withdraw Ether themselves by calling a withdraw function implemented in the contract. Thus instead of the contract sending Ether to each recipient, the recipients themselves can call the withdraw function to get the refunds.

■ Box 5.25: checkGoalReached function of CrowdFunding contract without using the withdrawal pattern

```
function checkGoalReached () onlyOwner returns (bool ended){
    // Phase-1:  Conditions
    if (ended)
        throw; // this function has already been called

    if(block.timestamp<deadline)
        throw;

    if (amountRaised >= goal) {
        // Phase-2:  Effects
        campaignStatus = "Campaign Succeeded";
        ended = true;

        // Phase-3: Interaction
        if (!owner.send(this.balance))
            throw; // If anything fails,
                   // this will revert the changes above
    }else{
        // Phase-2:  Effects
        campaignStatus = "Campaign Failed";
        ended = true;
        uint i = 0;
        while (i <= numBackers){
            backers[i].amount = 0;

            // Phase-3: Interaction
            if (!backers[i].addr.send(backers[i].amount))
                throw; // If anything fails,
                       // this will revert the changes above

            Refund(backers[i].addr, backers[i].amount);
            i++;
        }
    }
}
```

Let us look at a more secure implementation as shown Box 5.26 which uses the withdrawal pattern. In this implementation, *checkGoalReached* function of the *CrowdFunding* contract has been replaced by two withdrawal functions, one for the owner and other for the backers. The *withdrawOwner* function is called by the owner (or beneficiary of the campaign). In this function, we perform the conditions, effects and interaction phases. In the conditions phase, we check if the campaign has ended. Next, we check if the campaign goal has been reached. Next, we check if the owner has already been paid the contract balance. If these conditions are true, the effects phase is executed. In the effects phase, we update the condition *ownerPaid* to true, to indicate that the owner has been paid. Finally, in the interaction phase, we send all the Ether in the contract to the owner. We check the status of this interaction and if the Ether transfer fails, we set *ownerPaid* to false, to indicate that the owner has not been paid.

The *withdrawBacker* function is called by each backer of the crowdfunding campaign separately, to get back the amount contributed to the campaign. In this function, we perform the conditions, effects and interaction phases. In the conditions phase, we check if the campaign has ended. Next, we check if the campaign goal has not been reached. The campaign backers can withdraw only if the campaign ends and fails to reach its goal. Next, we iterate through the list of backers and get the amount paid by the backer and the backer index. In the effects phase, we set the amount paid by backer to zero. Finally, in the interaction phase, we refund the amount paid by the backer. We check the status of this interaction and if the Ether transfer fails, we set the amount paid by backer to its original value to indicate that the backer has not been refunded.

■ **Box 5.26: Using withdrawal pattern for CrowdFunding contract**

```
function withdrawOwner () onlyOwner returns (bool ownerPaid){
    // Phase-1:  Conditions
    // Check if campaign ended
    if(block.timestamp<deadline)
        throw;

    // Check if campaign succeeded
    if (amountRaised < goal)
        throw;

    // Check if the campaign owner has already been paid
    if (ownerPaid)
        throw;

    // Phase-2:  Effects
    ownerPaid = true; // set to true to prevent re-entrancy attack

    // Phase-3: Interaction
    if (!owner.send(this.balance)){
        ownerPaid = false; // set to false if transfer to owner failed
    }
}

function withdrawBacker (address backerAddress) returns (bool){
    // Phase-1:  Conditions
    // Check if campaign ended
    if(block.timestamp<deadline)
        throw;

    // Check if campaign failed
    // Refund is issued only when campaign fails
    if (amountRaised > goal)
        throw;

    // Get the amount paid by the backer and the backer index
    uint amount;
    uint index;
    uint i=0;
    while (i <= numBackers){
```

```
                    if(backers[i].addr == backerAddress){
                        amount = backers[i].amount;
                        index = i;
                        break;
                    }
                    i++;
                }

                // Check if backer has already been redunded
                if (amount==0)
                    throw;

                // Phase-2:  Effects
                // Set the amount paid by backer to zero
                backers[index].amount = 0;

                // Phase-3: Interaction
                // Refund the bàcker
                if (backerAddress.send(amount)){
                    Refund(backers[index].addr, backers[index].amount);
                    return true;
                }else {
                    // Reset the amount pending to the backer if transfer fails
                    backers[index].amount = amount;
                    return false;
                }
            }
}
```

5.6.3 Access Restriction

The access restriction pattern can be used to restrict access to the functions of a contract. For example, we may want to restrict access to certain functions to only the owner of the contract. Box 5.27 shows an example of access restriction pattern. We use a function modifier, *onlyOwner*, which checks if the sender of the transaction is the owner of the contract. The *onlyOwner* modifier is added to the *withdrawFunds* function, as we want only the owner to withdraw funds in the contract.

■ **Box 5.27: Sample contract showing access restriction pattern**

```
contract MyContract {
    address owner;

    function MyContract() {
        owner = msg.sender;
    }

    modifier onlyOwner(){
    if (msg.sender != owner) throw;
    _
    }

    function withdrawFunds() onlyOwner{
```

```
        if (!owner.send(this.balance))
            throw;
    }
}
```

Box 5.28 shows an alternative approach for access restriction, where we create a separate contract named *Owned* with a function modifier. Other contracts which want to use the access restriction can inherit this contract. In this example, *MyContract* inherits the *Owned* contract. In the constructor of the *MyContract*, the constructor of the *Owned* contract is called which initializes the address of the owner to the account which creates the contract.

■ Box 5.28: Access restriction with a contract

```
contract Owned  {
  address owner;

  modifier onlyOwner() {
    if (msg.sender==owner) _
  }

  function owned() {
    owner = msg.sender;
  }

  function changeOwner(address newOwner) onlyOwner {
    owner = newOwner;
  }

  function getOwner() constant returns (address){
    return owner;
  }
}


contract MyContract is Owned{

  function MyContract(){
      owned();
  }

  function withdrawFunds() onlyOwner{
    if (!owner.send(this.balance))
      throw;
  }

}
```

5.6.4 Mortal

Mortal pattern helps in preventing the funds getting locked in a contract account. Box 5.29 shows an example of the mortal pattern. In this example, a *kill* function is added the contract. When the owner of the contracts sends a transaction to the *kill* function, the *suicide* function is executed, to which we pass the address of the owner. In Ethereum, *suicide* is an EVM level operation (or OPCODE). When *suicide* is called with an address from a contract, all of the contract's current balance is sent to the address. Using the *suicide* function is preferred when you are finished with a contract, because it consumes much less gas as compared to a send Ether transaction.

■ **Box 5.29: Sample contract showing mortal pattern**

```
contract MyContract {
    address public owner;

    function MyContract() {
        owner = msg.sender;
    }

    function kill() {
        if (msg.sender == owner) {
            suicide(owner);
        }
    }
}
```

Box 5.30 shows an alternative approach for using the mortal pattern, where we create a separate contract named *Mortal*. Other contracts which want to use the mortal pattern can inherit this contract.

■ **Box 5.30: Sample contract showing mortal pattern**

```
contract Mortal {
  function kill() {
    if (msg.sender == owner) suicide(owner);
  }
}


contract MyContract is Mortal{
   :
   :
}
```

5.6.5   Automatic Expiration

The automatic expiration pattern allows a contract to automatically expire after a certain duration. Box 5.31 shows an example of the automatic expiration pattern used for the *Voting* contract. In this example, we create a contract, *AutoExpires*, which is inherited by the *Voting* contract. When the voting contract is initialized, the constructor for the *AutoExpires* contract is called, and an expiry duration (in seconds) is set. The *AutoExpires* contract has function modifiers to check if the contract has expired or not. We use these function modifiers within the *Voting* contract. For the *giveRightToVote* and *vote* functions, we use the *notExpired* function modifier, which throws an exception if the contract is expired. For the *winningProposal* function, we use the *isExpired* function modifier, which throws an exception if the contract is not expired. The automatic expiration pattern in the voting contract allows voting to be done only while the contract has not expired. When the voting period expires (current time is greater than the voting duration), the winning proposal can be checked using the *winningProposal* function.

■ Box 5.31: Voting contract using automatic expiration pattern

```
contract AutoExpires {
    uint expires;

    function AutoExpires(uint t) {
        expires = now + t;
    }

    function expired() returns (bool) {
        return now > expires ? true : false;
    }

    modifier isExpired() {
        if (!expired()) throw;
        _
    }

    modifier notExpired() {
        if (expired()) throw;
        _
    }
}

contract Voting is AutoExpires{
    // Declare a complex type to reresent a single voter.
    struct Voter {
        bool voted;  // if true, that person already voted
        uint vote;    // index of the voted proposal
        bool rightToVote; // if true, that person has right to vote
    }

    // This is a type for a single proposal.
    struct Proposal
    {
        bytes32 name;   // short name
        uint voteCount; // number of accumulated votes
    }

    address public chairperson;

    uint public numProposals;

    mapping(address => Voter) public voters;
    mapping (uint => Proposal) public proposals;

    function Voting(bytes32[] proposalNames, uint _votingTime) {
        chairperson = msg.sender;
        voters[chairperson].rightToVote = true;
        AutoExpires(_votingTime);
```

```
        numProposals=proposalNames.length;

        // For each of the provided proposal names,
        // create a new proposal object and add it
        // to the end of the array.
        for (uint i = 0; i < proposalNames.length; i++) {
            Proposal p = proposals[i];
            p.name = proposalNames[i];
            p.voteCount = 0;
        }
    }

    function giveRightToVote(address voter) notExpired {
        if (msg.sender != chairperson || voters[voter].voted) {
            // `throw` terminates and reverts all changes to the state
            throw;
        }
        voters[voter].rightToVote = true;
    }

    function vote(uint proposal)  notExpired {
        Voter sender = voters[msg.sender];

        if (sender.voted)
            throw;
        sender.voted = true;
        sender.vote = proposal;

        proposals[proposal].voteCount += 1;
    }

    function winningProposal() constant isExpired
            returns (uint winningProposal, bytes32 proposalName)
    {
        uint winningVoteCount = 0;
        for (uint p = 0; p < numProposals; p++) {
            if (proposals[p].voteCount > winningVoteCount) {
                winningVoteCount = proposals[p].voteCount;
                winningProposal = p;
                proposalName = proposals[p].name;
            }
        }
    }
}
```

5.6.6 Rejector

The rejector pattern can be used within a contract to reject all Ether sent directly to the contract (i.e., without a function being called). For any contract, when a transaction is sent to the contract with an Ether value and without any data, a fallback function in the contract is executed. By throwing an exception in the fallback function, we can reject all Ether sent directly to the contract. Box 5.32 shows an example of the rejector pattern. An excerpt from CrowdFunding contract described earlier in this chapter is shown.

■ **Box 5.32: Excerpt from CrowdFunding contract showing rejector pattern**

```
contract Crowdfunding {

    // Rejector
    function () {
        // This function gets executed if a
        // transaction with invalid data is sent to
        // the contract or just ether without data.
        // We revert the send so that no-one
        // accidentally loses money when using the
        // contract.
        throw;
    }

    // Backers have to call fund function to send Ether to the contract
    function fund() {
        Backer b = backers[numBackers++];
        b.addr = msg.sender;
        b.amount = msg.value;
        amountRaised += b.amount;
        Deposit(msg.sender, msg.value);
    }

}
```

5.6.7 Circuit Breaker

The circuit breaker pattern allows the contract to be stopped or started again. Box 5.33 shows an example of the circuit breaker pattern used for the CrowdFunding contract, described earlier in this chapter. In this example, we create a contract *CircuitBreaker*, which is inherited by the *CrowdFunding* contract. The *CircuitBreaker* contract maintains a flag (*stopped*), whose value can be set to true or false. Function modifiers are used to check if the contract is in stopped state or not. To toggle the contract between stopped or started state, the owner can send a transaction to the *toggleCircuit* function. The function modifier, *notStopped*, is applied to the *fund* function of the CrowdFunding contract so that the contract can accept funds only when the contract is not in the stopped state. The owner of the contract can temporarily stop the crowdfunding campaign by toggling the state of the contract using the circuit breaker.

■ **Box 5.33: CrowdFunding contract using circuit breaker pattern**

```
contract Owned  {
  address owner;

  modifier onlyOwner() {
    if (msg.sender==owner) _
  }

  function owned() {
    owner = msg.sender;
  }
```

```
  function changeOwner(address newOwner) onlyOwner {
    owner = newOwner;
  }

  function getOwner() constant returns (address){
    return owner;
  }
}


contract CircuitBreaker is Owned {
    bool stopped;

    function circuitBreaker() {
        stopped = false;
        owned();
    }

    function toggleCircuit() onlyOwner public {
        stopped = !stopped;
    }

    modifier isStopped() {
        if (!stopped) throw;
        _
    }

    modifier notStopped() {
        if (stopped) throw;
        _
    }

}

contract Crowdfunding is CircuitBreaker{
    struct Backer {
        address addr;
        uint amount;
    }

    uint public numBackers;
    uint public deadline;
    string public campaignStatus;
    bool ended;
    uint public goal;
    uint public amountRaised;
    mapping (uint => Backer) backers;

    event Deposit(address _from, uint _amount);
    event Refund(address _to, uint _amount);


    function Crowdfunding(uint _deadline, uint _goal) {
```

```
        owner = msg.sender;
        deadline = _deadline;
        goal = _goal;
        campaignStatus = "Funding";
        numBackers = 0;
        amountRaised = 0;
        ended = false;
        circuitBreaker();
    }

    function fund() notStopped{
        Backer b = backers[numBackers++];
        b.addr = msg.sender;
        b.amount = msg.value;
        amountRaised += b.amount;
        Deposit(msg.sender, msg.value);
    }

    function checkGoalReached () onlyOwner returns (bool ended){
        if (ended)
            throw; // this function has already been called

        if(block.timestamp<deadline)
            throw;

        if (amountRaised >= goal) {
            campaignStatus = "Campaign Succeeded";
            ended = true;
            if (!owner.send(this.balance))
                throw; // If anything fails,
                       // this will revert the changes above
        }else{
            uint i = 0;
            campaignStatus = "Campaign Failed";
            ended = true;
            while (i <= numBackers){
                backers[i].amount = 0;
                if (!backers[i].addr.send(backers[i].amount))
                    throw; // If anything fails,
                           // this will revert the changes above
                Refund(backers[i].addr, backers[i].amount);
                i++;
            }
        }
    }

    function kill() {
        if (msg.sender == owner) {
            suicide(owner);
        }
    }
}
```

5.6.8 Allow Once per Account

The 'allow once per account' pattern allows a function of a contract to be executed only once per account. This pattern can be used to prevent repeated or duplicate transactions to a function from one account. Box 5.34 shows an example of a *Registration* contract that uses the 'allow once per account' pattern. In this example, a user can send a transaction to the *register* function to register with the contract. Every time a user registers, the total number of participants are incremented by one. A function modifier, *onlyOnce*, is applied to the *register* function to limit duplicate registrations. A mapping of participants is maintained which maps the participant address to a custom data-type (*struct Participant*) for a participant. The *Participant* struct has a flag to check if the participant is already registered. The *onlyOnce* function modifier checks this flag and throws an exception if the participant is already registered. This pattern is also used in the voting contract, described earlier in the chapter, to allow a voter to vote only once.

▪ **Box 5.34: Example of allow once per account pattern**

```
contract Registration {
    struct Participant {
        bool registered;   // if true, that person already registered
    }

    mapping(address => Participant) public participants;
    uint public numParticipants;

    modifier onlyOnce() {
        if (participants[msg.sender].registered) throw;
        _
    }

    function Registration() {
        numParticipants = 0;
    }

    function register() onlyOnce{
        Participant p = participants[msg.sender];
        p.registered = true;
        numParticipants++;
    }
}
```

Summary

In this chapter, we described the structure of a smart contract and how to implement, compile, deploy and interact with smart contracts. A smart contract is a piece of code that resides on a blockchain and is identified by a unique address. A smart contract includes a set of executable functions, state variables, events, and modifiers. Contracts can be written in various high-level languages (such as Solidity or Serpent), and then compiled into Ethereum-specific binary format (EVM bytecode) using language-specific compilers. After compiling, the contract is deployed to the blockchain network using Ethereum clients such as *geth* or the Ethereum

Mist Wallet. Users interact with the contracts by sending transactions. When a transaction is sent to a contract account, the transaction data payload is used to provide input to the contract function to be executed. While transactions change the state of the network, you can use calls to get the state of a contract. The difference between a transaction and a call is that, while a transaction is submitted to the network for inclusion in the blockchain, whereas, a call runs locally. Ethereum uses a concept of a crypto-fuel called Gas, which is consumed for performing the operations on a blockchain network. All the transactions on the network are charged a certain amount of gas. When a transaction sent to a contract is executed, a series of log entries are generated and incorporated into the block. Events can be added in contracts to track the execution of the transactions sent to the contract. Whenever an event is called in a contract, the arguments to the event are stored in the transaction log. We described various design patterns which can be used within smart contracts. The Conditions-Effects-Interaction pattern is useful for contracts which interact with other contracts. When this pattern is used within a contract function, the function is structured into conditions, effects and interaction phases. We described the importance of a correct ordering of these three phases and how an incorrect ordering can make a contract function vulnerable to "re-entrancy". Next, we described the withdrawal pattern, which makes use of a 'withdraw' function in a contract to allow the contract stakeholders to withdraw Ether themselves by calling a withdraw function, instead of the contract sending Ether to each stakeholder. The access restriction pattern can be used to restrict access to functions of a contract by using function modifiers. The mortal pattern makes use of a modifier to help prevent the funds in a contract getting locked in the contract account. The automatic expiration pattern allows a contract to automatically expire after a certain duration. The circuit breaker pattern allows the contract to be stopped or started again. The 'allow once per account' pattern allows a function of a contract to be executed only once per account.

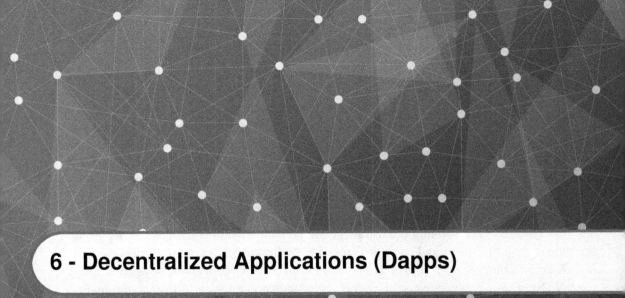

6 - Decentralized Applications (Dapps)

This chapter covers

- Implementing Dapps
- Case Studies
    - Crowdfunding
    - Event Registration
    - Document Verification
    - Call Option
    - Interest Rate Swap
    - Industrial IoT - Machine Maintenance
    - Solar Charging Stations

A Decentralized Application (or Dapp) is an application that is backed by one or more smart contracts, which are in turn deployed on a blockchain network. Dapps provide a user-friendly web-based interface to smart contracts. Figure 6.1 lists the difference between a cloud/web application and a Dapp. Most cloud or web applications are centralized in nature and are deployed on one or more server instances under the control of a single organization or cloud platform. While the cloud applications can be distributed in nature with different services within the application running on separate server instances within one or more data centers, the cloud infrastructure is usually under the control of one organization. Dapps, in contrast to cloud or web applications, are decentralized in nature with no single entity or organization controlling the infrastructure on which the applications are deployed. In the context of Ethereum, Dapps are backed by smart contracts which are deployed on the Ethereum blockchain platform that is maintained by Ethereum nodes or peers worldwide. A Dapp itself is deployed on a central server which is either a full Ethereum node or a server which can communicate with an Ethereum node. However, the server only serves the Dapp's web interface. The Dapp logic is controlled by the associated smart contracts which are deployed on the blockchain platform. Dapps provide user-friendly interfaces to smart contracts, where the users can submit transactions to the contracts from a web interface. A Dapp's web interface forwards the transactions to the blockchain platform and displays the transaction receipts or state information in the smart contracts in the web interface.

Category	Cloud/Web Application	Dapp
Logic	Web app code (e.g. model, view, controller implementation)	Contract and Dapp JavaScript
Data	Database or local storage	Blockchain
Presentation	HTML, CSS, JavaScript	HTML, CSS, JavaScript
Static Storage	Server or cloud storage	Swarm or IPFS
Interaction/ Communication	HTTP, HTTPS	Whisper

Figure 6.1: Difference between a cloud/web application and a Dapp

A Dapp can be accessed in a browser using the URL or the address of the server from which it is served. The standard way of interacting with Dapps is through the Ethereum Mist Browser as shown in Figure 6.2. The Mist browser allows Ethereum users (running a full Ethereum node) to connect their wallets to the Dapps and send transactions to the Dapps. However, users who do not want to install the Mist Browser and download the entire blockchain can use the MetaMask Chrome extension as shown in Figure 6.3. MetaMask allows you to run Ethereum Dapps in your browser without running a full Ethereum node [31].

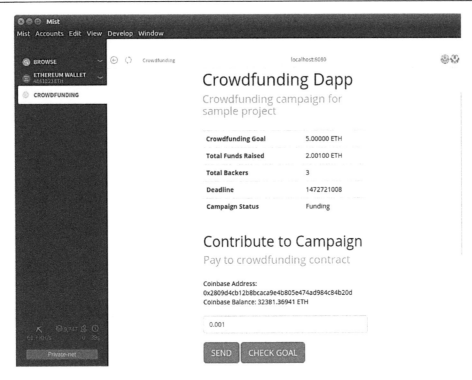

Figure 6.2: Accessing a Dapp from Ethereum Mist browser

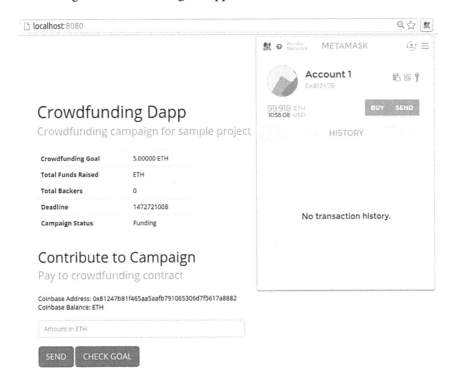

Figure 6.3: Accessing a Dapp from Chrome browser with MetaMask extension

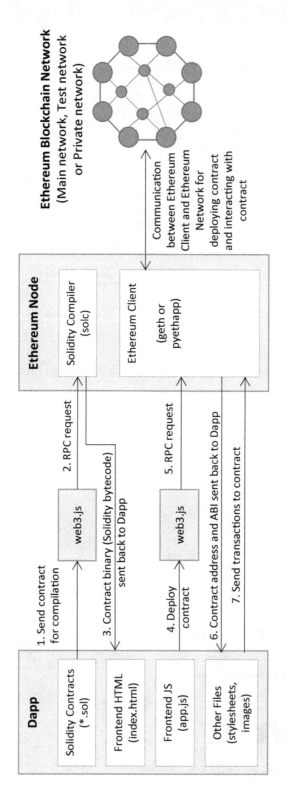

Figure 6.4: Dapp creation workflow

6.1 Implementing Dapps

In Chapter-3, we described how to setup and work with the Truffle Dapp framework. In this section, we describe the steps involved in building a Dapp using the Truffle framework. Figure 6.4 shows the workflow for Dapp creation. Building a Dapp with Truffle involves the following steps:

1. Implement smart contracts in a high-level language such as Solidity.
2. Implement the web interface for the Dapp using HTML, CSS and JavaScript.
3. Implement a Dapp JavaScript for interacting with smart contracts using the Web3 JavaScript API.
4. Build the Dapp.
5. Deploy the Dapp contracts on the Ethereum blockchain network.
6. Serve the Dapp.

   Let us take the example of a Dapp for sharing revenue among shareholders. Assuming the shareholders of a company already have their accounts on the Ethereum network, the company can use the revenue sharing Dapp to disburse the revenue equally among the shareholders.

   To initialize new Dapp project, run the *truffle init* command from within a new directory. This will create the Dapp directory structure including example contracts and tests.

   For the Dapps examples in this chapter, we will use the TestRPC Ethereum client which creates an in-memory blockchain and processes the transactions instantly. Once you are confident that your contracts and Dapps work as expected, you can connect your Truffle Dapp to the Ethereum main network or test network using a full Ethereum client such as *geth*. Box 6.1 shows an example of a Truffle project configuration file that we will use for the Dapps in this chapter. When using TestRPC with Truffle the default value for host is "localhost" and port is 8545.

■ Box 6.1: Truffle project configuration file

```
module.exports = {
  build: {
    "index.html": "index.html",
    "app.js": [
      "javascripts/app.js",
    ],
    "app.css": [
      "stylesheets/app.css"
    ],
    "images/": "images/"
  },
  rpc: {
    host: "localhost",
    port: 8545
  }
};
```

   After initializing a new Dapp project and editing the Truffle project configuration file, the next step is to implement the smart contracts within the "contracts" directory. Implement a smart contract for revenue sharing as shown in Box 6.2.

■ **Box 6.2: Revenue Sharing contract (RevenueShare.sol)**

```solidity
contract RevenueShare {
  address public creator;
  mapping(uint => address) public shareholders;
  uint public numShareholders;

  event Disburse(uint _amount, uint _numShareholders);

  function RevenueShare(address[] addresses) {
    creator = msg.sender;
    numShareholders = addresses.length;

    for (uint i = 0; i < addresses.length; i++) {
          shareholders[i] = addresses[i];
      }
  }

  function shareRevenue() returns (bool success) {
    uint amount = msg.value / numShareholders;

    for (uint i = 0; i < numShareholders; i++) {
      if (!shareholders[i].send(amount)) throw;
    }

    Disburse(msg.value, numShareholders);

    return true;
  }

  function kill() {
    if (msg.sender == creator) suicide(creator);
  }
}
```

You will now have a directory structure as shown in Box 6.3. Next, add the contracts to the "2_deploy_contracts.js" migration file within the "migrations" directory.

■ **Box 6.3: Directory structure for a Dapp created with Truffle**

```
.
|-- app
|   |-- images
|   |-- index.html
|   |-- javascripts
|   |   `-- app.js
|   `-- stylesheets
|       `-- app.css
|-- contracts
|   |-- RevenueShare.sol
|   `-- Migrations.sol
|-- migrations
|   |-- 1_initial_migration.js
```

```
|    '-- 2_deploy_contracts.js
'-- truffle.js
```

Next, implement the web interface for the Dapp (index.html) using HTML as shown in Box 6.4. For the web interface, we also use the jQuery JavaScript library and Bootstrap CSS. In this web interface, we display the address of the deployed revenue sharing contract and addresses of the shareholders. We also provide an input text box for the contract owner to specify the amount to pay to the contract and a send button to submit the transaction.

■ **Box 6.4: HTML source code for the Revenue Sharing Dapp web interface (index.html)**

```html
<!DOCTYPE html>
<html lang="en">
<head>
  <title>RevShare - Simple Revenue Sharing</title>
  <meta name="viewport" content="width=device-width, initial-scale=1">
  <link rel="stylesheet" href="./bootstrap.min.css">
  <link href="./app.css" rel='stylesheet' type='text/css'>
  <script src="./app.js"></script>
</head>
<body>
  <div class="container-fluid">
    <h1>Revenue Sharing Contract</h1>
    <h3 style="margin-top: 0px; margin-bottom: 30px;">
    Share revenue between shareholders</h3>

    <table class="table table-fluid">
      <tr>
        <th></th>
        <th>Address</th>
        <th>Balance</th>
      </tr>
      <tr>
        <th>Contract</th>
        <td><span class="black">
        <span id="c_address" class="c_address"></span></span>
        </td>
        <td>
        <span class="black"><span id="c_balance"></span> ETH</span>
        </td>
      </tr>
       <tr>
        <th>Coinbase</th>
        <td>
        <span class="black">
        <span id="cb_address" class="c_address"></span>
        </span>
        </td>
        <td>
        <span class="black"><span id="cb_balance"></span> ETH</span>
        </td>
      </tr>
```

```
            <tr>
              <th>Shareholder A</th>
              <td>
              <span class="black"><span id="a_address"></span></span></td>
              <td><span class="black"><span id="a_balance"></span> ETH</span>
              </td>
            </tr>
            <tr>
              <th>Shareholder B</th>
              <td>
              <span class="black"><span id="b_address"></span></span>
              </td>
              <td>
              <span class="black"><span id="b_balance"></span> ETH</span>
              </td>
            </tr>
          </table>


          <h2 style="padding-top: 20px;">Pay Contract</h2>
          <h3 style="margin-top: 0px; margin-bottom: 30px;">
          Pay to contract from Coinbase account</h3>

            <input style="height: 38px;" type="text"
            class="form-control" id="amount" placeholder="Amount in ETH"/>
            <br>
          <button class="btn btn-primary btn-lg" onclick="send();">
          SEND</button><br><br>
      <div id="status"></div>
        </div>
        <script src="./jquery.min.js"></script>
    <script src="./bootstrap.min.js"></script>
    </body>
    </html>
```

Next, implement the Dapp JavaScript (app.js) as shown in Box 6.5. This JavaScript file is included in the Dapp's web page (index.html) and has functions for interacting with the smart contract. When the Dapp's web page loads, the *initializeContract()* function is executed in which we create an instance of the deployed contract associated with the Dapp. The contract can be accessed with the contract name as follows: *RevenueShare.deployed()*. The contract's instance, *myContractInstance*, is used to send calls to the contract to fetch the values of the state variables, and also to send transactions to the contract's functions.

■ Box 6.5: Revenue Sharing Dapp JavaScript (app.js)

```
var accounts;
var account;
var balance;


var myContractInstance;

// Initialize
function initializeContract() {
```

```
  myContractInstance = RevenueShare.deployed();
  $("#c_address").html(myContractInstance.address);
  $("#cb_address").html(account);
  $("#a_address").html(accounts[1]);
  $("#b_address").html(accounts[2]);

  myContractInstance.setShareholders(accounts[1],
      accounts[2], {from: account}).then(function() {
    refreshBalances();
  }).catch(function(e) {
    console.log(e);
  });
```

```
}

function setStatus(message) {
  $("#status").html(message);
};

function refreshBalances() {
  $("#c_balance").html(web3.fromWei(
      web3.eth.getBalance(myContractInstance.address),
                        "ether").toFixed(5));
  $("#a_balance").html(web3.fromWei(
      web3.eth.getBalance(accounts[1]), "ether").toFixed(5));
  $("#b_balance").html(web3.fromWei(
      web3.eth.getBalance(accounts[2]), "ether").toFixed(5));
  $("#cb_balance").html(web3.fromWei(
      web3.eth.getBalance(web3.eth.coinbase), "ether").toFixed(5));
};

function send() {

  var amount = web3.toWei(parseFloat($("#amount").val()), "ether");

  setStatus("Initiating transaction... (please wait)");

  web3.eth.sendTransaction({from: web3.eth.coinbase,
      to: myContractInstance.address, value: amount},
          function(error, result) {
    if(error) {
      console.log(error);
      setStatus(error);
    }
    else {
      web3.eth.getTransactionReceiptMined(result).then(function(receipt){
        setStatus("Transaction complete!");
        refreshBalances();
      }).catch(function(e) {
        console.log(e);
        setStatus(e);
      });
    }
  });
```

```
};

window.onload = function() {
  web3.eth.getAccounts(function(err, accs) {
    if (err != null) {
      alert("There was an error fetching your accounts.");
      return;
    }

    if (accs.length == 0) {
      alert("Couldn't get any accounts!");
      return;
    }

    accounts = accs;
    account = accounts[0];
    initializeContract();
  });

  web3.eth.getTransactionReceiptMined = function (txnHash, interval) {
    var transactionReceiptAsync;
    interval |= 500;
    transactionReceiptAsync = function(txnHash, resolve, reject) {
        try {
            var receipt = web3.eth.getTransactionReceipt(txnHash);
            if (receipt == null) {
                setTimeout(function () {
                    transactionReceiptAsync(txnHash, resolve, reject);
                }, interval);
            } else {
                resolve(receipt);
            }
        } catch(e) {
            reject(e);
        }
    };

    return new Promise(function (resolve, reject) {
        transactionReceiptAsync(txnHash, resolve, reject);
    });
  };
}
```

Next, to build the Truffle project, run the *truffle build* command. Once the project is built, run the *truffle migrate* command to deploy the contracts on the blockchain network. Finally, run the *truffle serve* command to serve the Dapp on "localhost" port 8080. Box 6.6 shows the commands for building, deploying and serving the Dapp.

■ **Box 6.6: Building, deploying and serving Truffle Dapp**

```
$ truffle build
Compiling Migrations.sol...
Compiling RevenueShare.sol...
```

```
Writing artifacts to ./build/contracts

$ truffle migrate
Running migration: 1_initial_migration.js
  Deploying Migrations...
  Migrations: 0x71c596dd5eaf8c9998ec07d0e64a18908bcbd7bb
Saving successful migration to network...
Saving artifacts...
Running migration: 2_deploy_contracts.js
  Deploying RevenueShare...
  RevenueShare: 0x9f7e94eba71e28c66ab8d212ec0c1a076fa9b297
Saving successful migration to network...
Saving artifacts...

$ truffle serve
Serving app on port 8080...
```

Figure 6.5 shows a screenshot of the revenue sharing Dapp.

Revenue Sharing Contract
Share revenue between shareholders

	Address	Balance
Contract	0xab3bfd9c305821ce2e0f47ef375990d7d9ba6d5f	1.00000 ETH
Coinbase	0x67764e6ea2e15d056dda5efd6d9745480a5ce34d	99.00000 ETH
Shareholder A	0x6812e393a50fb575f4aff97b69fa8839ba499ee4	100.00000 ETH
Shareholder B	0x1dc046441b850490cbaa7d382b259a9d52612383	100.00000 ETH

Pay Contract
Pay to contract from Coinbase account

Figure 6.5: Screenshot of Revenue Sharing Dapp

6.2　Case Studies

In the previous section, we described in detail all the steps involved in developing a Dapp with the Truffle framework. In this section, we will describe more elaborate Dapp case studies. For each Dapp, we provide an implementation of the smart contract associated with the Dapp, the Dapp's web page (index.html) and the Dapp JavaScript (app.js).

6.2.1　Crowdfunding

Let us look at a Dapp for a crowdfunding campaign. Box 6.7 shows the Solidity implementation of a CrowdFunding contract. With this contract, a crowdfunding campaign can be setup by specifying a campaign goal and deadline. In the smart contract, we define a custom data type to represent a backer. The *Backer* structure maintains information related to a backer of a campaign including the address of the backer and the amount contributed to the campaign. The *backers* variable maintains a mapping from the backer index to the *Backer* structure. A backer interested in supporting the funding campaign, can send a transaction to the *fund* function of the contract along with the value (in Ether) to contribute to the campaign. The funds raised are held in the contract account. When the campaign ends, the owner of the campaign can check if the campaign goal has been reached by sending a transaction to the *checkGoalReached* function. If the campaign succeeds, the funds are released to the campaign beneficiary (or the owner of the contract). However, if the campaign fails, the backers are issued refunds.

■ **Box 6.7:　CrowdFunding contract**

```
contract CrowdFunding {
    struct Backer {
        address addr;
        uint amount;
    }

    address public owner;
    uint public numBackers;
    uint public deadline;
    string public campaignStatus;
    bool ended;
    uint public goal;
    uint public amountRaised;
    mapping (uint => Backer) backers;

    event Deposit(address _from, uint _amount);
    event Refund(address _to, uint _amount);

    modifier onlyOwner(){
        if (msg.sender != owner) throw;
        _
    }

    function CrowdFunding(uint _deadline, uint _goal) {
        owner = msg.sender;
        deadline = _deadline;
```

```
        goal = _goal;
        campaignStatus = "Funding";
        numBackers = 0;
        amountRaised = 0;
        ended = false;
}

function fund() {
    Backer b = backers[numBackers++];
    b.addr = msg.sender;
    b.amount = msg.value;
    amountRaised += b.amount;
    Deposit(msg.sender, msg.value);
}

function checkGoalReached () onlyOwner returns (bool ended){
    if (ended)
        throw; // this function has already been called

    if(block.timestamp<deadline)
        throw;

    if (amountRaised >= goal) {
        campaignStatus = "Campaign Succeeded";
        ended = true;
        if (!owner.send(this.balance))
            throw; // If anything fails,
                    // this will revert the changes above
    }else{
        uint i = 0;
        campaignStatus = "Campaign Failed";
        ended = true;
        while (i <= numBackers){
            backers[i].amount = 0;
            if (!backers[i].addr.send(backers[i].amount))
                throw; // If anything fails,
                        // this will revert the changes above
            Refund(backers[i].addr, backers[i].amount);
            i++;
        }
    }
}

function destroy() {
    if (msg.sender == owner) {
        suicide(owner);
    }
}

function () {
    // This function gets executed if a transaction with
    // invalid data is sent to the contract or just ether
    // without data. We revert the send so that no-one
    // accidentally loses money.
```

```
                throw;
        }
}
```

Box 6.8 shows the HTML implementation of the web interface for the Dapp (index.html).

■ **Box 6.8: HTML source code for the CrowdFunding Dapp web interface**

```html
<!DOCTYPE html>
<html lang="en">
<head>
  <title>Crowdfunding</title>
  <meta name="viewport" content="width=device-width, initial-scale=1">
  <link rel="stylesheet" href="./bootstrap.min.css" >
  <link href="./app.css" rel='stylesheet' type='text/css'>
  <script src="./app.js"></script>
</head>
<body>
  <div class="container-fluid">
    <h1>Crowdfunding Dapp</h1>
    <h3 style="margin-top: 0px; margin-bottom: 30px;">
    Crowdfunding campaign for sample project</h3>

<div class="row">
  <div class="col-md-6">
<table class="table table-fluid">
    <tr>
       <th>Crowdfunding Goal</th>
       <td><span class="black">
       <span id="cf_goal"></span> ETH</span></td>
    </tr>
    <tr>
       <th>Total Funds Raised</th>
       <td><span class="black">
       <span id="cf_balance"></span> ETH</span></td>
    </tr>
    <tr>
       <th>Total Backers</th>
       <td><span class="black">
       <span id="cf_backers"></span></span></td>
    </tr>
    <tr>
       <th>Deadline</th>
       <td><span class="black">
       <span id="cf_days"></span> </span></td>
    </tr>
    <tr>
       <th>Campaign Status</th>
       <td><span class="black">
       <span id="cf_status"></span> </span></td>
    </tr>
  </table>
  </div>
```

```
</div>

<div class="row">
  <div class="col-md-8">
      <h2 style="padding-top: 20px;">Contribute to Campaign</h2>
      <h3 style="margin-top: 0px; margin-bottom: 30px;">
      Pay to crowdfunding contract</h3>

      <span class="black">Coinbase Address:
      <span id="cb_address" class="c_address"></span></span><br>
      <span class="black">Coinbase Balance:
      <span id="cb_balance"></span> ETH</span><br><br>
       <input style="height: 38px;"
       type="text" class="form-control" id="amount"
       placeholder="Amount in ETH"/><br>
     <button class="btn btn-primary btn-lg"
     onclick="contribute();">SEND</button>
     <button class="btn btn-primary btn-lg"
     onclick="checkGoalReached();">CHECK GOAL</button>
     <br><br>
 <div id="status"></div>
     </div>
     <div class="col-md-4">
     <center>
   <h3>Send Ether to</h3>
<span class="black"><span id="cf_address"></span></span><br>
<div id="qrcode"></div>
</center>
  </div>
</div>
  </div>
<script src="./jquery.min.js"></script>
<script src="./bootstrap.min.js"></script>

</body>
</html>
```

Box 6.9 shows the Dapp JavaScript (app.js). This JavaScript file is included in the Dapp's web page (index.html) and has functions for interacting with the smart contract. When the Dapp's web page loads, the *initializeContract* function is executed in which we create an instance of the deployed contract associated with the Dapp. The contract can be accessed with the contract name as follows: *Crowdfunding.deployed()*. The contract's instance, *myContractInstance*, is used to send calls to the contract to fetch the values of the state variables, and also to send transactions to the contract's functions. The *contribute* function in the JavaScript is called when a user clicks the *SEND* button in the Dapp's web interface. In this function, we parse the value entered by the user in the input field for the amount to contribute, and then send a transaction to the *fund* function of the contract.

■ Box 6.9: CrowdFunding Dapp JavaScript

```javascript
var accounts;
var account;
var balance;
var myContractInstance;

function initializeContract() {
  myContractInstance = Crowdfunding.deployed();
  $("#cf_address").html(myContractInstance.address);
  $("#cb_address").html(account);
  $("#qrcode").html("<img src=
    \"https://chart.googleapis.com/chart?cht=qr&chs=350&chl="+
    myContractInstance.address+"\" height=\"350\"/>");

  myContractInstance.numBackers.call().then(
    function(numBackers) {
      console.log(numBackers.toNumber());
      $("#cf_backers").html(numBackers.toNumber());
      return myContractInstance.goal.call();
  }).then(
    function(goal) {
      console.log(goal.toNumber());
      $("#cf_goal").html(web3.fromWei(goal, "ether").toFixed(5));
      return myContractInstance.campaignStatus.call();
  }).then(
    function(campaignStatus) {
      console.log(campaignStatus);
      $("#cf_status").html(campaignStatus);
      return myContractInstance.deadline.call();
  }).then(
    function(deadline) {
      console.log(deadline.toNumber());
      $("#cf_days").html(deadline.toNumber());
      refreshBalances();
  });

}

function setStatus(message) {
  $("#status").html(message);
};

function checkGoalReached() {
  myContractInstance.checkGoalReached({from: account}).then(
    function() {
    return myContractInstance.goal.call();
  }).then(
    function(goal) {
      $("#cf_goal").html(web3.fromWei(goal, "ether").toFixed(5));
      return myContractInstance.campaignStatus.call();
  }).then(
    function(campaignStatus) {
      console.log(campaignStatus);
```

```
          $("#cf_status").html(campaignStatus);
      });
  }

  function refreshBalances() {
    $("#cb_balance").html(
      web3.fromWei(web3.eth.getBalance(web3.eth.coinbase),
                                    "ether").toFixed(5));

    myContractInstance.numBackers.call().then(
      function(numBackers) {
        console.log(numBackers.toNumber());
        $("#cf_backers").html(numBackers.toNumber());
        return myContractInstance.amountRaised.call();
    }).then(
      function(amountRaised) {
        $("#cf_balance").html(web3.fromWei(amountRaised,
                            "ether").toFixed(5));
    });
  };

  function contribute() {
    var amount = web3.toWei(parseFloat($("#amount").val()), "ether");
    setStatus("Initiating transaction... (please wait)");

    myContractInstance.fund({from: account, value: amount}).then(
      function(result) {
      web3.eth.getTransactionReceiptMined(result).then(function(receipt) {
          setStatus("Transaction complete!");
          refreshData();
      }).catch(function(e) {
          console.log(e);
          setStatus(e);
      });
    });

  };

  window.onload = function() {
    web3.eth.getAccounts(function(err, accs) {
      if (err != null) {
        alert("There was an error fetching your accounts.");
        return;
      }

      if (accs.length == 0) {
        alert("Couldn't get any accounts!");
        return;
      }

      accounts = accs;
      account = accounts[0];
      initializeContract();
    });
```

```
web3.eth.getTransactionReceiptMined = function (txnHash, interval){
  var transactionReceiptAsync;
  interval |= 500;
  transactionReceiptAsync = function(txnHash, resolve, reject){
      try {
          var receipt = web3.eth.getTransactionReceipt(txnHash);
          if (receipt == null) {
              setTimeout(function () {
                  transactionReceiptAsync(txnHash, resolve, reject);
              }, interval);
          } else {
              resolve(receipt);
          }
      } catch(e) {
          reject(e);
      }
  };

  return new Promise(function (resolve, reject) {
      transactionReceiptAsync(txnHash, resolve, reject);
  });
};
}
```

Crowdfunding Dapp

Crowdfunding campaign for sample project

Crowdfunding Goal	5.00000 ETH
Total Funds Raised	6.00000 ETH
Total Backers	1
Deadline	1472721008
Campaign Status	Campaign Succeeded

Contribute to Campaign

Pay to crowdfunding contract

Coinbase Address: 0x2a0733b20fff250f04e23be05f558298c9a98dc8
Coinbase Balance: 99.75685 ETH

Amount in ETH

SEND   CHECK GOAL

Send Ether to
0x2773c6f32156f541b6cb00d0df185f149b970947

Figure 6.6: Screenshot of CrowdFunding Dapp

Figure 6.6 shows a screenshot of the crowdfunding Dapp. Backers interested in supporting the funding campaign can connect their Ethereum wallets to the Dapp, and send transactions to the contract account associated with the Dapp, with the value (in Ether) to contribute to the campaign. The funds raised from the backers are held in the contract account associated with the Dapp. When the campaign ends, the owner of the campaign can check if the campaign goal has been reached.

6.2.2 Event Registration

Let us look at an example of a Dapp for event registration. Using this Dapp, the event organizers can sell tickets for events. People interested in attending the event can purchase the event tickets by sending transactions to the contract. Box 6.10 shows the Solidity implementation of the *EventRegistration* contract. While deploying the contract, the owner of the contract specifies the event quota (or number of tickets to sell) and the price of each ticket. In the smart contract, we define a custom data type to represent a registrant. The *Registrant* structure maintains information related to persons who register for the event including the amount paid, number of tickets purchased and email address. The *registrantsPaid* variable maintains a mapping from the address of the registrant to the *Registrant* structure.

■ **Box 6.10: Event Registration contract**

```
contract EventRegistration {
  struct Registrant {
        uint amount;
        uint numTickets;
        string email;
    }

  address public owner;
  uint public numTicketsSold;
  uint public quota;
  uint public price;
  mapping (address => Registrant) registrantsPaid;

  event Deposit(address _from, uint _amount);
  event Refund(address _to, uint _amount);

  modifier onlyOwner()
    {
        if (msg.sender != owner) throw;

        _
    }

    modifier soldOut()
    {
        if (numTicketsSold >= quota) throw;

        _
    }

    function EventRegistration(uint _quota, uint _price) {
      owner = msg.sender;
```

```
      numTicketsSold = 0;
      quota = _quota;
      price = _price;
  }

  function buyTicket(string email, uint numTickets) soldOut {
        // Check if amount paid is not less than the total cost of tickets
        uint totalAmount = price*numTickets;
        if(msg.value<totalAmount){
            throw;
        }

  if(registrantsPaid[msg.sender].amount>0){
    //Already registered
    registrantsPaid[msg.sender].amount += totalAmount;
    registrantsPaid[msg.sender].email = email;
    registrantsPaid[msg.sender].numTickets += numTickets;
  }else{
    Registrant r = registrantsPaid[msg.sender];
        r.amount = totalAmount;
        r.email = email;
        r.numTickets=numTickets;
    }

  numTicketsSold = numTicketsSold+numTickets;

        // Refund balance remaining to buyer
        if(msg.value>totalAmount){
            uint refundAmount = msg.value - totalAmount;
            if (!msg.sender.send(refundAmount))
                throw;
        }

  Deposit(msg.sender, msg.value);

  }

  function refundTicket(address buyer) onlyOwner {
    if (registrantsPaid[buyer].amount >0) {
      if (this.balance >= registrantsPaid[buyer].amount) {
                registrantsPaid[buyer].amount = 0;
                numTicketsSold = numTicketsSold -
                                 registrantsPaid[buyer].numTickets;
        if(!buyer.send(registrantsPaid[buyer].amount)) throw;
        Refund(buyer, registrantsPaid[buyer].amount);
      }
    }
  }

  function withdrawFunds() onlyOwner{
      if (!owner.send(this.balance))
          throw;
  }
```

```
  function getRegistrantAmountPaid(address buyer) returns(uint){
    return registrantsPaid[buyer].amount;
  }

  function kill() onlyOwner{
    suicide(owner);
  }
}
```

Box 6.11 shows the HTML implementation of the web interface for the Dapp (index.html).

■ **Box 6.11: HTML source code for the Event Registration Dapp web interface**

```
<!DOCTYPE html>
<html lang="en">
<head>
  <title>Event Registration</title>
  <meta name="viewport" content="width=device-width, initial-scale=1">
  <link rel="stylesheet" href="./bootstrap.min.css">
  <link href="./app.css" rel='stylesheet' type='text/css'>
  <script src="./app.js"></script>
</head>
<body>
  <div class="container-fluid">
    <h1>Event Registration Dapp</h1>
    <h3 style="margin-top: 0px; margin-bottom: 30px;"></h3>

<div class="row">
  <div class="col-md-6">

<table class="table table-fluid">
    <tr>
      <th>Event Details</th>
      <td><span class="black">
      <span id="cf_date">Food Festival, Atlanta, GA</span></span></td>
    </tr>
    <tr>
      <th>Date</th>
      <td><span class="black">
      <span id="cf_date">Nov 2, 2016</span></span></td>
    </tr>
    <tr>
      <th>Ticket Price</th>
      <td><span class="black">
      <span id="cf_price">4</span> ETH</span></td>
    </tr>
     <tr>
      <th>Quota</th>
      <td><span class="black">
      <span id="cf_quota"></span></span></td>
    </tr>
    <tr>
      <th>Registrants</th>
```

```
            <td><span class="black">
            <span id="cf_registrants"></span></span></td>
        </tr>
    </table>
  </div>
</div>


<div class="row">
  <div class="col-md-8">

      <h2 style="padding-top: 20px;">Register for Event</h2>
      <h3 style="margin-top: 0px; margin-bottom: 30px;"></h3>

      <span class="black">Coinbase Address:
      <span id="cb_address" class="c_address"></span></span><br>
      <span class="black">Coinbase Balance:
      <span id="cb_balance"></span> ETH</span><br><br>

       <input type="email" class="form-control" id="email"
                  placeholder="Email"/><br>
        <br>
      <select class="form-control" id="numTickets"
                  onclick="showTotal();">
      <option value="0">Select number of tickets to buy</option>
      <option value="1">1</option>
      <option value="2">2</option>
      <option value="3">3</option>
      <option value="4">4</option>
      <option value="5">5</option>
      </select>
      <br><br>
         <span class="black">Total:
         <span id="ticketsTotal">0</span> ETH</span><br><br>
      <button class="btn btn-primary btn-lg"
      onclick="buyTicket();">BUY TICKET</button>
      <button class="btn btn-primary btn-lg"
      onclick="cancelTicket();">CANCEL TICKET</button>
      <br><br>
 <div id="status"> </div>
      </div>
      <div class="col-md-4">
  </div>
</div>

  </div>
  <script src="./jquery.min.js"></script>
<script src="./bootstrap.min.js"></script>

</body>
</html>
```

Box 6.12 shows the Dapp JavaScript (app.js). The *buyTicket* function in the JavaScript is called when a user clicks the *BUY TICKET* button in the Dapp's web interface. In this function, we compute the total amount to be paid by the user based on the number of tickets to purchase and then send a transaction to the *buyTicket* function of the contract. Similarly, the *cancelTicket* function is called when the user clicks the *CANCEL TICKET* button in the Dapp's web interface.

■ Box 6.12: Event Registration Dapp JavaScript

```
var accounts;
var account;
var balance;
var ticketPrice;
var myContractInstance;

function initializeContract() {
  myContractInstance = Event.deployed();
  $("#cf_address").html(myContractInstance.address);
  $("#cb_address").html(account);

  myContractInstance.numRegistrants.call().then(
    function(numRegistrants) {
      $("#cf_registrants").html(numRegistrants.toNumber());
      return myContractInstance.quota.call();
  }).then(
    function(quota) {
      $("#cf_quota").html(quota.toNumber());
      return myContractInstance.price.call();
  }).then(
    function(price) {
      ticketPrice = web3.fromWei(price, "ether").toFixed(5);
      $("#cf_price").html(ticketPrice);
      refreshBalance();
  });
}

function setStatus(message) {
  $("#status").html(message);
};

function showTotal() {
   var numTickets = $("#numTickets").val();
   var ticketAmount = numTickets*ticketPrice;
  $("#ticketsTotal").html(ticketAmount);
};

function refreshBalance() {
  $("#cb_balance").html(web3.fromWei(
    web3.eth.getBalance(web3.eth.coinbase), "ether").toFixed(5));
}


function buyTicket() {
  var numTickets = parseFloat($("#numTickets").val());
  var ticketAmount = numTickets*ticketPrice;
```

```
    var ticketAmountWei = web3.toWei(ticketAmount, "ether");
    var email = $("#email").val();
    var amountAlreadyPaid;
    var amountPaidNow;

    setStatus("Initiating transaction... (please wait)");

    myContractInstance.getRegistrantAmountPaid.call(account).then(
      function(result) {
      amountAlreadyPaid = result.toNumber();
      return myContractInstance.buyTicket(email,
      numTickets, { from: web3.eth.coinbase, value: ticketAmountWei});
      }).then(
      function(result) {
        return myContractInstance.numRegistrants.call();
      }).then(
      function(numRegistrants) {
        $("#cf_registrants").html(numRegistrants.toNumber());
        return myContractInstance.getRegistrantAmountPaid.call(account);
      }).then(
      function(valuePaid) {
        amountPaidNow = valuePaid.toNumber() - amountAlreadyPaid;
        if (amountPaidNow == ticketAmountWei) {
          setStatus("Purchase successful");
        } else {
          setStatus("Purchase failed");
        }
        refreshBalance();
      });
}

function cancelTicket() {
    setStatus("Initiating transaction... (please wait)");
    myContractInstance.getRegistrantAmountPaid.call(account).then(
    function(result) {
      if (result.toNumber() == 0) {
        setStatus("Buyer is not registered - no refund!");
      } else {
        myContractInstance.refundTicket(account,
                        {from: accounts[0]}).then(
          function() {
            return myContractInstance.numRegistrants.call();
          }).then(
          function(numRegistrants) {
            $("#cf_registrants").html(numRegistrants.toNumber());
            return myContractInstance.getRegistrantAmountPaid.call(
                                                  account);
          }).then(
          function(valuePaid) {
            if (valuePaid.toNumber() == 0) {
              setStatus("Refund successful");
            } else {
              setStatus("Refund failed");
            }
```

```
                refreshBalance();
            });
        }
    });
}

window.onload = function() {
  web3.eth.getAccounts(function(err, accs) {
    if (err != null) {
      alert("There was an error fetching your accounts.");
      return;
    }
    if (accs.length == 0) {
      alert("Couldn't get any accounts!");
      return;
    }
    accounts = accs;
    account = accounts[0];
    initializeContract();
  });
}
```

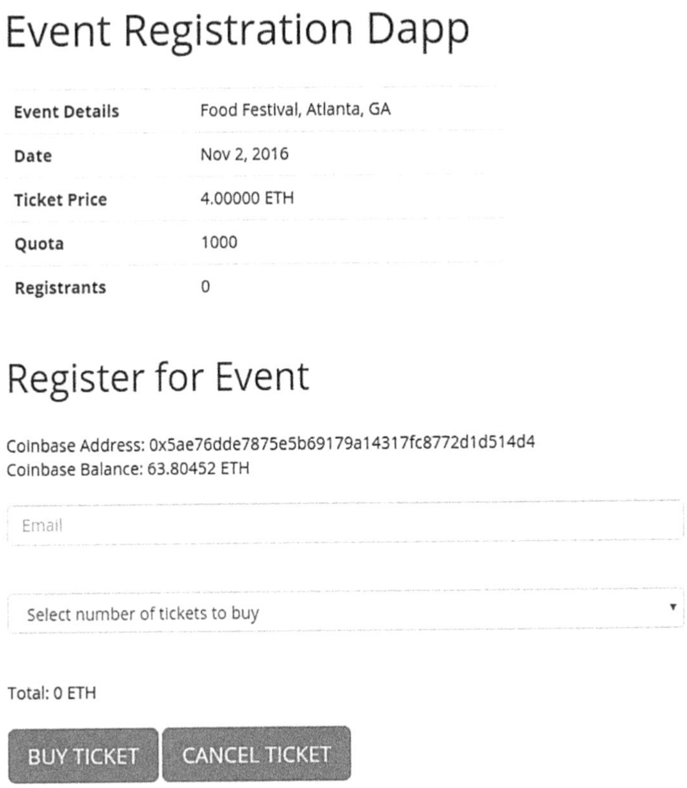

Event Registration Dapp

Event Details	Food Festival, Atlanta, GA
Date	Nov 2, 2016
Ticket Price	4.00000 ETH
Quota	1000
Registrants	0

Register for Event

Coinbase Address: 0x5ae76dde7875e5b69179a14317fc8772d1d514d4
Coinbase Balance: 63.80452 ETH

Email

Select number of tickets to buy ▼

Total: 0 ETH

[BUY TICKET] [CANCEL TICKET]

Figure 6.7: Screenshot of Event Registration Dapp

Figure 6.7 shows a screenshot of the event registration Dapp. The details of the event such as event location, ticket price, quota and number of registrants are displayed. To buy tickets for the event, users can connect their Ethereum wallets to the Dapp and send transactions to the *buyTicket* function of the contract from the Dapp's web interface. To register for the event and buy one or more tickets, the user provides an email address and the number of tickets to purchase. The user also sends a value equal to the total cost of the tickets along with the transaction. A user who has already purchased a ticket can cancel the ticket and get a refund using the Dapp's web interface. The amount paid by all the users for the tickets purchased are held in the contract account. The contract owner (or beneficiary) can withdraw the amount from the contract account by sending a transaction to the *withdrawFunds* function.

6.2.3   Document Verification

The document verification Dapp can be used to store a cryptographic hash of any document on the Ethereum blockchain. Users can verify the existence and validity of a document whose hash is stored on the blockchain. The Dapp does not store the documents anywhere. While adding a new document, its cryptographic hash is computed on the client side. The document hash along with a timestamp is then submitted to the smart contract associated with the Dapp. Box 6.13 shows the Solidity implementation of the *DocVerify* contract for this Dapp. In this contract, for each document, we store the document hash, a timestamp when the document is added and the address of the owner of the document or the user who submitted the document. Once these details for a document are added to the contract, any Ethereum user can later verify if the document existed at that time. The cryptographic hash of a document depends on the document's content. Any changes in the document will change its hash. Thus users can securely verify the existence of a document and be assured that the same document existed at a particular moment in time. The benefit of using such a Dapp is that it acts as a decentralized proof of existence, without the need for a centralized authority to certify a document.

■ **Box 6.13: Document Verification contract**

```
contract DocVerify {
    struct Document {
        address owner;
        uint blockTimestamp;
    }

    address public creator;
    uint public numDocuments;
    mapping(bytes32 => Document) public documentHashMap;

    function DocVerify(){
        creator = msg.sender;
        numDocuments=0;
    }

    function newDocument(bytes32 hash) returns (bool success){
        if (documentExists(hash)) {
            success = false;
```

```
        }else{
            Document d = documentHashMap[hash];
            //d.hash = hash;
            d.owner = msg.sender;
            d.blockTimestamp = block.timestamp;
            numDocuments++;
            success = true;
        }
        return success;
    }

    function documentExists(bytes32 hash) constant
                            returns (bool exists){
        if (documentHashMap[hash].blockTimestamp>0) {
            exists = true;
        }else{
            exists= false;
        }
        return exists;
    }

    function getDocument(bytes32 hash) constant
            returns (uint blockTimestamp, address owner){
        blockTimestamp = documentHashMap[hash].blockTimestamp;
        owner = documentHashMap[hash].owner;
    }

    function destroy() {
        if (msg.sender == creator) {
            suicide(creator);
        }
    }
}
```

Box 6.14 shows the HTML implementation of the web interface for the Dapp (index.html).

■ **Box 6.14: HTML source code for the Document Verification Dapp web interface**

```
<!DOCTYPE html>
<html lang="en">
<head>
  <title>Document Verification</title>
  <meta name="viewport" content="width=device-width, initial-scale=1">
  <link rel="stylesheet" href="./bootstrap.min.css" >
  <link href="./app.css" rel='stylesheet' type='text/css'>
  <script src="./app.js"></script>
  <script src="./crypto.js"></script>
</head>
<body>
  <div class="container-fluid">
    <h1>Document Verification Dapp</h1>
    <h3 style="margin-top: 0px; margin-bottom: 30px;"></h3>
```

```
<div class="row">
  <div class="col-md-8">

<table class="table table-fluid">
      <tr>
         <th>Contract Address</th>
         <td><span class="black">
         <span id="cf_address"></span></span></td>
      </tr>
      <tr>
         <th>Documents Submitted</th>
         <td><span class="black">
         <span id="cf_documents"></span></span></td>
      </tr>
    </table>
  </div>
</div>

<div class="row">
  <div class="col-md-12">

      <h2 style="padding-top: 20px;">Add/Verify Document</h2>
      <h3 style="margin-top: 0px; margin-bottom: 30px;">
      Calculate document hash and submit to
      blockchain or verify existing document </h3>

 <span class="black">Coinbase Address:
 <span id="cb_address" class="c_address"></span></span><br>
      <span class="black">Coinbase Balance:
      <span id="cb_balance"></span> ETH</span><br><br>

        <input class="form-control" type="file"
        name="fileUpload" id="fileUpload" /><br>
       <button class="btn btn-primary btn-lg"
       onclick="calculateHash();">Calculate Hash</button>
           <br><br>
         <span class="black">Hash: <span id="docHash"></span></span><br>
      <button class="btn btn-primary btn-lg"
      onclick="submitDocument();">Submit Document</button>
       <button class="btn btn-primary btn-lg"
       onclick="verifyDocument();">Verify Document</button>
      <br><br>
      <div id="status"> </div>
      </div>
</div>
  </div>
  <script src="/jquery.min.js"></script>
<script src="/bootstrap.min.js" ></script>
</body>
</html>
```

Box 6.15 shows the Dapp JavaScript (app.js).

■ Box 6.15: Document Verification Dapp JavaScript

```javascript
var accounts;
var account;
var myContractInstance;
var docHash;
function initializeContract() {
  myContractInstance = DocVerify.deployed();
  $("#cf_address").html(myContractInstance.address);
  $("#cb_address").html(account);

  myContractInstance.numDocuments.call().then(
    function(numDocuments) {
      $("#cf_documents").html(numDocuments.toNumber());
      refreshBalance();
  });
}

function setStatus(message) {
  $("#status").html(message);
};

function showTotal() {
   var numTickets = $("#numTickets").val();
   var ticketAmount = numTickets*ticketPrice;
  $("#ticketsTotal").html(ticketAmount);
};

function refreshBalance() {
  $("#cb_balance").html(web3.fromWei(
    web3.eth.getBalance(web3.eth.coinbase), "ether").toFixed(5));
}

function progress (p) {
  var w = ((p*100).toFixed(0));
}

function finished(result) {
  console.log(result.toString(CryptoJSH.enc.Hex))
  docHash = result.toString(CryptoJSH.enc.Hex);
  $("#docHash").html(docHash);
  setStatus("Hash calculaton done");
}

function calculateHash() {
  setStatus("Calculating Hash");
    var file = document.getElementById('fileUpload').files[0]
    var reader = new FileReader();
    reader.onload = function(e) {
        var data = e.target.result;
        var res = CryptoJSH.SHA256(data,progress,finished);
      };
    reader.readAsBinaryString(file)
}
```

```
function submitDocument() {
  setStatus("Submitting document... (please wait)");

  myContractInstance.newDocument(docHash,
             { from: web3.eth.coinbase}).then(
    function(result) {
      return myContractInstance.numDocuments.call();
    }).then(
    function(numDocuments) {
      $("#cf_documents").html(numDocuments.toNumber());
      return myContractInstance.documentExists.call(docHash);
    }).then(
    function(exists) {
      if (exists) {
        setStatus("Document hash submitted");
      } else {
        setStatus("Error in submitting document hash");
      }
      refreshBalance();
    });
}

function verifyDocument() {
  setStatus("Verifying document... (please wait)");

  myContractInstance.documentExists.call(docHash).then(
    function(exists) {
      if (exists) {
        myContractInstance.getDocument.call(docHash).then(
          function(result) {
            var theDate = new Date(result[0].toNumber() * 1000);
            dateString = theDate.toGMTString();

            var res = "Document Registered: " +
                dateString + "<br>Document Owner: " +  result[1];
            setStatus(res);
          });

      } else {
        setStatus("Document cannot be verified");
      }
      refreshBalance();
    });
}

window.onload = function() {
  web3.eth.getAccounts(function(err, accs) {
    if (err != null) {
      alert("There was an error fetching your accounts.");
      return;
    }
    if (accs.length == 0) {
      alert("Couldn't get any accounts!");
```

```
      return;
    }
    accounts = accs;
    account = accounts[0];
    initializeContract();
  });
}
```

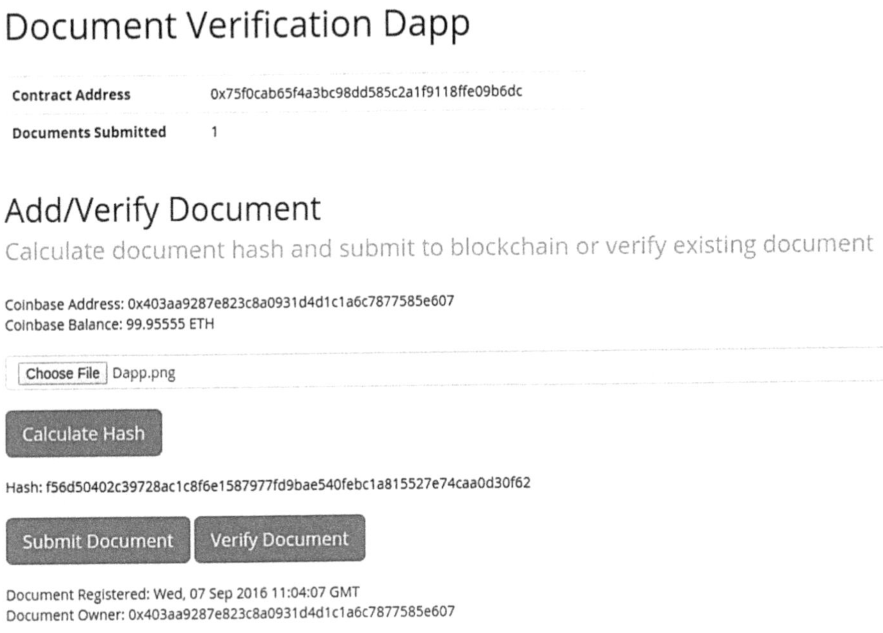

Document Verification Dapp

Contract Address	0x75f0cab65f4a3bc98dd585c2a1f9118ffe09b6dc
Documents Submitted	1

Add/Verify Document

Calculate document hash and submit to blockchain or verify existing document

Coinbase Address: 0x403aa9287e823c8a0931d4d1c1a6c7877585e607
Coinbase Balance: 99.95555 ETH

| Choose File | Dapp.png |

Calculate Hash

Hash: f56d50402c39728ac1c8f6e1587977fd9bae540febc1a815527e74caa0d30f62

Submit Document   Verify Document

Document Registered: Wed, 07 Sep 2016 11:04:07 GMT
Document Owner: 0x403aa9287e823c8a0931d4d1c1a6c7877585e607

Figure 6.8: Screenshot of Document Verification Dapp

Figure 6.8 shows a screenshot of the document verification Dapp. To add a new document, a user first connects her Ethereum wallet to the Dapp. Next, the user browses for the document on the local machine from the Dapp's web interface and then clicks the 'Calculate Hash' button. For computing the hash we use the CryptoJS [36] JavaScript library which provides implementations of various cryptographic algorithms. We compute the SHA256 digest of the document. Next, the user clicks the 'Submit Document' button to add the document's details (hash, timestamp and user's Ethereum address) to the contract. To verify the existence of a document, any user who has the same document can use the Dapp in a similar manner, i.e., by browsing the document from the Dapp, computing its hash and then clicking the 'Verify Document' button. If the document is the same document which was previously added to the contract, its hash would be the same. The document's details are fetched from the contract and displayed in the Dapp.

6.2.4   Call Option

A Call Option is a financial derivative instrument that specifies a financial contract between a buyer and a seller. The financial contract gives the right, but not the obligation, to buy a certain asset or financial instrument (the underlying) from the seller at a certain time (the expiration date) for a certain price (the strike price). The buyer pays a fee (premium) for this right. A call option contract includes the following elements:

- **Seller**: Seller is the party which issues the call option contract and has the obligation to sell the asset or financial instrument if the option is exercised by the buyer.
- **Buyer**: Buyer is the party which gains the right, but not the obligation, to the asset or financial instrument.
- **Underlying**: The underlying asset or financial instrument associated with the call option.
- **Strike Price**: The price at which the asset or financial instrument can be traded.
- **Premium**: Premium is the price which the buyer pays to the seller while purchasing the call option.
- **Expiration Date**: Date on which the call option contract expires. A call option contract can be exercised by the buyer any time before its expiry.

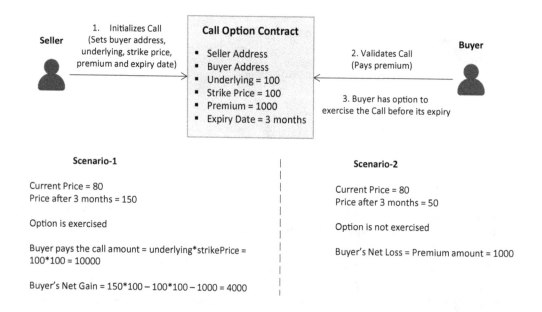

Figure 6.9: Call Option contract structure and example

Figure 6.9 shows the structure of a call option contract. Also shown are two scenarios, one in which the buyer exercises the call and the other in which the call is not exercised. Let us say the seller creates a call option for 100 units of an asset (e.g. 100 shares of a stock), with an expiry date 3 months later. The buyer purchases the option by paying a premium of 1000 (say in USD). The current price of each share is 80 and at the end of 3 months, the price of each share becomes 150. In this case, the buyer exercises the call and pays the strike price of 100 for each share. The buyer's net gain, in this case, is 4000. In the second scenario, let us say if the price of each share becomes 50 at the end of 3 months. In this case, the buyer doesn't exercise the call. The buyer's net loss is equal to the premium paid.

Box 6.16 shows the Solidity implementation of a call option contract. With this contract, a seller can initialize a call option by providing details such as the address of the buyer, underlying, strike price, premium and time to expiry. The buyer can then validate the call and purchase the option by paying the premium. After the buyer and seller enter into the contract, the buyer can exercise the call option any time before its expiry by paying for the assets (or shares) at the strike price.

■ Box 6.16: Call Option contract

```
contract owned {
  address public owner;
  function owned() {
    owner = msg.sender;
  }
  modifier onlyowner() {
    if (msg.sender == owner) _
  }
}

contract mortal is owned {
  function kill() onlyowner {
    if (msg.sender == owner) suicide(owner);
  }
}

contract CallOption is owned, mortal {
    bool public   isActive;
    bool public   isComplete;
    address public buyer;
    address public seller;
    uint public   strikePrice;
    uint public premium;
    string public underlyingName;
    uint public underlying;
    uint public timeToExpiry;
    uint public startTime;

    function CallOption() {
        isActive = false;
        isComplete = false;
        seller = msg.sender;
    }

    // Seller initializes the contract
    function initialize(
        address _buyer,
        uint    _strikePrice,
        string  _underlyingName,
        uint    _underlying,
        uint    _premium,
```

```
            uint     _timeToExpiry) {

        // Can only be initialized by seller
        if(msg.sender != seller){
            throw;
        }

        buyer = _buyer;
        strikePrice = _strikePrice;
        premium = _premium;
        underlyingName = _underlyingName;
        underlying = _underlying;
        timeToExpiry = _timeToExpiry;
        startTime = now;
    }

    // Buyer validates the contract in order to activate it
    function validate() {
        if (isActive) {
            throw;
        }

        if (isExpired()) {
            throw;
        }

        if(msg.sender != buyer){
            throw;
        }

        if(msg.value<premium){
            throw;
        }

        // Pay premium to seller and refund balance if any to buyer
        if(msg.value==premium){
            if (!seller.send(premium)) throw;
        }else if(msg.value>premium){
            if (!seller.send(premium)) throw;
            if (!buyer.send(msg.value - premium)) throw;
        }

        isActive = true;
    }

function exercise() returns (bool) {
        // Can only be exercised by buyer
        if(msg.sender != buyer){
            throw;
        }

        // Can only be exercised is active
        if(!isActive){
            throw;
```

```
        }

        // Call can only be exercised if it is not expired
        if (isExpired()) {
            throw;
        }

        uint amount = strikePrice * underlying;

        if(msg.value < amount){
            throw;
        }

        // Pay the amount to seller to exercise the option
        // and refund the balance, if any, to buyer
        if(msg.value==amount){
            if (!seller.send(amount)) throw;
        }else if(msg.value>premium){
            if (!seller.send(amount)) throw;
            if (!buyer.send(msg.value - amount)) throw;
        }

        isActive = false;
        isComplete = true;
    }

    function isExpired() constant returns (bool) {
        if (now > startTime + timeToExpiry) {
            return true;
        } else {
            return false;
        }
    }
}
```

Box 6.17 shows the HTML implementation of the web interface for the Dapp (index.html).

■ Box 6.17: HTML source code for the Call Option Dapp web interface

```
<!DOCTYPE html>
<html lang="en">
<head>
  <title>Call Option</title>
  <meta name="viewport" content="width=device-width, initial-scale=1">
  <link rel="stylesheet" href="/bootstrap.min.css" >
  <link rel="stylesheet" href="/jquery-ui.css">
  <link href="./app.css" rel='stylesheet' type='text/css'>
  <script src="./app.js"></script>
</head>
<body>
  <div class="container-fluid">
    <h1>Call Options Dapp</h1>
    <h3 style="margin-top: 0px; margin-bottom: 30px;"></h3>
```

```
<div id="tabs">
  <ul>
    <li><a href="#tabs-1">Seller: Initialize Call</a></li>
    <li><a href="#tabs-2">Buyer: Validate Call</a></li>
    <li><a href="#tabs-3">Buyer: Exercise Call</a></li>
  </ul>
  <div id="tabs-1">
    <div class="row">
  <div class="col-md-8">
      <h2 style="padding-top: 20px;">Initialize Call Option </h2>
      <h3 style="margin-top: 0px; margin-bottom: 30px;">
                Seller initializes the call option</h3>

      <span class="black">Coinbase Address:
          <span id="cb_address" class="c_address"></span></span>
      <span class="black">Coinbase Balance:
          <span id="cb_balance"></span> ETH</span><br><br>

      <input type="text" class="form-control"
          id="buyer" placeholder="Buyer"/><br>
      <input type="text" class="form-control"
          id="strikePrice" placeholder="Strike Price"/><br>
      <input type="text" class="form-control"
          id="underlyingName" placeholder="Underlying"/><br>
      <input type="text" class="form-control"
          id="underlying" placeholder="Underlying Units"/><br>
      <input type="text" class="form-control"
          id="premium" placeholder="Premium"/><br>
      <input type="text" class="form-control"
          id="timeToExpiry" placeholder="Time To Expiry (in seconds)"/>
    <button class="btn btn-primary btn-lg"
        onclick="initialize();">INITIALIZE CALL OPTION</button>
    <br><br>
 <div id="status"> </div>
    </div>
    <div class="col-md-4">
  </div>

</div>
  </div>
  <div id="tabs-2">
    <div class="row">
  <div class="col-md-8">
      <h2 style="padding-top: 20px;">Validate Call Option</h2>
      <h3 style="margin-top: 0px; margin-bottom: 30px;">
        Buyer validates the call option</h3>
      <span class="black">Coinbase Address:
      <span id="cb_address1" class="c_address"></span></span><br>
      <span class="black">Coinbase Balance:
      <span id="cb_balance1"></span> ETH</span><br><br>
      <input style="height: 38px;" type="text"
      class="form-control" id="premiumAmount"
      placeholder="Pay premium amount in Wei"/><br>
    <button class="btn btn-primary btn-lg"
```

```
         onclick="validate();">VALIDATE CALL OPTION</button>
  <div id="status1"> </div>
        </div>
        <div class="col-md-4">
   </div>
</div>
   </div>
   <div id="tabs-3">
    <div class="row">
   <div class="col-md-8">
        <h2 style="padding-top: 20px;">Exercise Call Option</h2>
        <h3 style="margin-top: 0px; margin-bottom: 30px;">
        Buyer executes the call option</h3>
        <span class="black">Coinbase Address:
        <span id="cb_address2" class="c_address"></span></span><br>
        <span class="black">Coinbase Balance:
        <span id="cb_balance2"></span> ETH</span><br><br>
        <input style="height: 38px;" type="text"
        class="form-control" id="callAmount"
        placeholder="Pay call amount in Wei"/><br>
      <button class="btn btn-primary btn-lg"
      onclick="exercise();">EXERCISE CALL OPTION</button>
  <div id="status2"> </div>
        </div>
        <div class="col-md-4">
   </div>

</div>
   </div>
</div>

<div class="row">
   <div class="col-md-6">
<h2 style="padding-top: 20px;">Call Option Contract</h2>
        <h3 style="margin-top: 0px; margin-bottom: 30px;"></h3>
<table class="table table-fluid">
        <tr>
          <th>Seller</th>
          <td><span class="black">
          <span id="cf_seller"></span></span></td>
        </tr>
        <tr>
          <th>Buyer</th>
          <td><span class="black">
          <span id="cf_buyer"></span></span></td>
        </tr>
        <tr>
          <th>Underlying</th>
          <td><span class="black">
          <span id="cf_underlyingName"></span></span></td>
        </tr>
        <tr>
          <th>Underlying Units</th>
          <td><span class="black">
```

```
                <span id="cf_underlying"></span></span></td>
            </tr>
             <tr>
              <th>StrikePrice</th>
              <td><span class="black">
              <span id="cf_strikePrice"></span></span></td>
            </tr>
            <tr>
              <th>Premium</th>
              <td><span class="black">
              <span id="cf_premium"></span></span></td>
            </tr>
            <tr>
              <th>Start Time</th>
              <td><span class="black">
              <span id="cf_startTime"></span></span></td>
            </tr>
            <tr>
              <th>Time to Expiry</th>
              <td><span class="black">
              <span id="cf_timeToExpiry"></span></span></td>
            </tr>
            <tr>
              <th>Is Active</th>
              <td><span class="black">
              <span id="cf_isActive"></span></span></td>
            </tr>
            <tr>
              <th>Is Complete</th>
              <td><span class="black">
              <span id="cf_isComplete"></span></span></td>
            </tr>
        </table>
     </div>

     <div class="col-md-4">
         <center>
       <h3>Contract Address</h3>
<span class="black"><span id="cf_address">

</span></span><br>
<div id="qrcode"></div>
</center>
     </div>
</div>
     </div>
     <script src="./jquery.min.js"></script>
<script src="/bootstrap.min.js"></script>
 <script src="./jquery-1.12.4.js"></script>
   <script src="./jquery-ui.js"></script>
</body>
</html>
```

Box 6.18 shows the Dapp JavaScript (app.js). The *initialize* function in the JavaScript is called when the *INITIALIZE CALL OPTION* button in the Dapp web interface is clicked.

In this function, a transaction is sent to the *initialize* function of the CallOption contract. The *validate* function is called when the *VALIDATE CALL OPTION* button in the Dapp web interface is clicked. In this function, a transaction is sent to the *validate* function of the CallOption contract. The *exercise* function is called when the *EXERCISE CALL OPTION* button in the Dapp web interface is clicked. In this function, a transaction is sent to the *exercise* function of the CallOption contract.

■ **Box 6.18: Call Option Dapp JavaScript**

```
var accounts;
var account;
var balance;
var ticketPrice;
var myContractInstance;

function initializeContract() {
  myContractInstance = CallOption.deployed();
  $("#cf_address").html(myContractInstance.address);
  $("#cb_address").html(account);
  $("#cb_address1").html(account);
  $("#cb_address2").html(account);
  $("#qrcode").html("<img src=
    \"https://chart.googleapis.com/chart?cht=qr&chs=350&chl="+
    myContractInstance.address+"\" height=\"350\"/>");
  refreshVars();
}

function setStatus(message) {
  $("#status").html(message);
};

function setStatus1(message) {
  $("#status1").html(message);
};

function setStatus2(message) {
  $("#status2").html(message);
};

function refreshVars(){
  myContractInstance.buyer.call().then(
      function(buyer) {
        $("#cf_buyer").html(buyer);
        return myContractInstance.seller.call();
      }).then(
      function(seller) {
        $("#cf_seller").html(seller);
        return myContractInstance.strikePrice.call();
      }).then(
      function(strikePrice) {
        $("#cf_strikePrice").html(strikePrice.toNumber());
        return myContractInstance.premium.call();
      }).then(
```

```
        function(premium) {
          $("#cf_premium").html(premium.toNumber());
          return myContractInstance.underlyingName.call();
        }).then(
        function(underlyingName) {
          $("#cf_underlyingName").html(underlyingName);
          return myContractInstance.underlying.call();
        }).then(
        function(underlying) {
          $("#cf_underlying").html(underlying.toNumber());
          return myContractInstance.startTime.call();
        }).then(
        function(startTime) {
          $("#cf_startTime").html(startTime.toNumber());
          return myContractInstance.timeToExpiry.call();
        }).then(
        function(timeToExpiry) {
          $("#cf_timeToExpiry").html(timeToExpiry.toNumber());
          return myContractInstance.isActive.call();
        }).then(
        function(isActive) {
          if(isActive){
            $("#cf_isActive").html("True");
          }else{
            $("#cf_isActive").html("False");
          }
          return myContractInstance.isComplete.call();
        }).then(
        function(isComplete) {
          if(isComplete){
            $("#cf_isComplete").html("True");
          }else{
            $("#cf_isComplete").html("False");
          }
          setStatus("");
          setStatus1("");
          setStatus2("");
          refreshBalance();
        });
}

function refreshBalance() {
  var balance = web3.fromWei(web3.eth.getBalance(web3.eth.coinbase),
                             "ether").toFixed(5);
  $("#cb_balance").html(balance);
  $("#cb_balance1").html(balance);
  $("#cb_balance2").html(balance);
}


function initialize() {
  var buyer = $("#buyer").val();
  var strikePrice = parseFloat($("#strikePrice").val());
  var underlyingName = $("#underlyingName").val();
```

```javascript
  var underlying = parseFloat($("#underlying").val());
  var premium = parseFloat($("#premium").val());
  var timeToExpiry = parseFloat($("#timeToExpiry").val());

  setStatus("Initiating transaction... (please wait)");

  myContractInstance.initialize(buyer, strikePrice,
      underlyingName, underlying, premium, timeToExpiry,
       {from: accounts[0]}).then(
           function() {
             refreshVars();
           });
}

function validate() {
  var amount = parseFloat($("#premiumAmount").val());
  console.log(amount);

  setStatus1("Initiating transaction... (please wait)");

   myContractInstance.validate({from: accounts[0],
                                value: amount}).then(
       function() {
         refreshVars();
       });
}

function exercise() {

  var amount = parseFloat($("#callAmount").val());
  console.log(amount);

  setStatus2("Initiating transaction... (please wait)");

   myContractInstance.exercise({from: accounts[0],
                                value: amount}).then(
           function() {
             refreshVars();
           });
}

window.onload = function() {
  $( "#tabs" ).tabs();
  web3.eth.getAccounts(function(err, accs) {
    if (err != null) {
      alert("There was an error fetching your accounts.");
      return;
    }

    if (accs.length == 0) {
      alert("Couldn't get any accounts! ");
      return;
    }
```

```
    accounts = accs;
    account = accounts[0];
    initializeContract();
  });
}
```

Figure 6.10 shows a screenshot of the call option Dapp. In this Dapp we have three tabs. In the first tab, the seller can initialize the call option by providing the required information. Once the call option is initialized, its details can be viewed at the bottom half of the Dapp web page. In the second tab, as shown in Figure 6.11, the buyer can validate the option by paying the premium. In the third tab, as shown in Figure 6.12, the buyer can exercise the call option by paying for the total value of the underlying at the strike price.

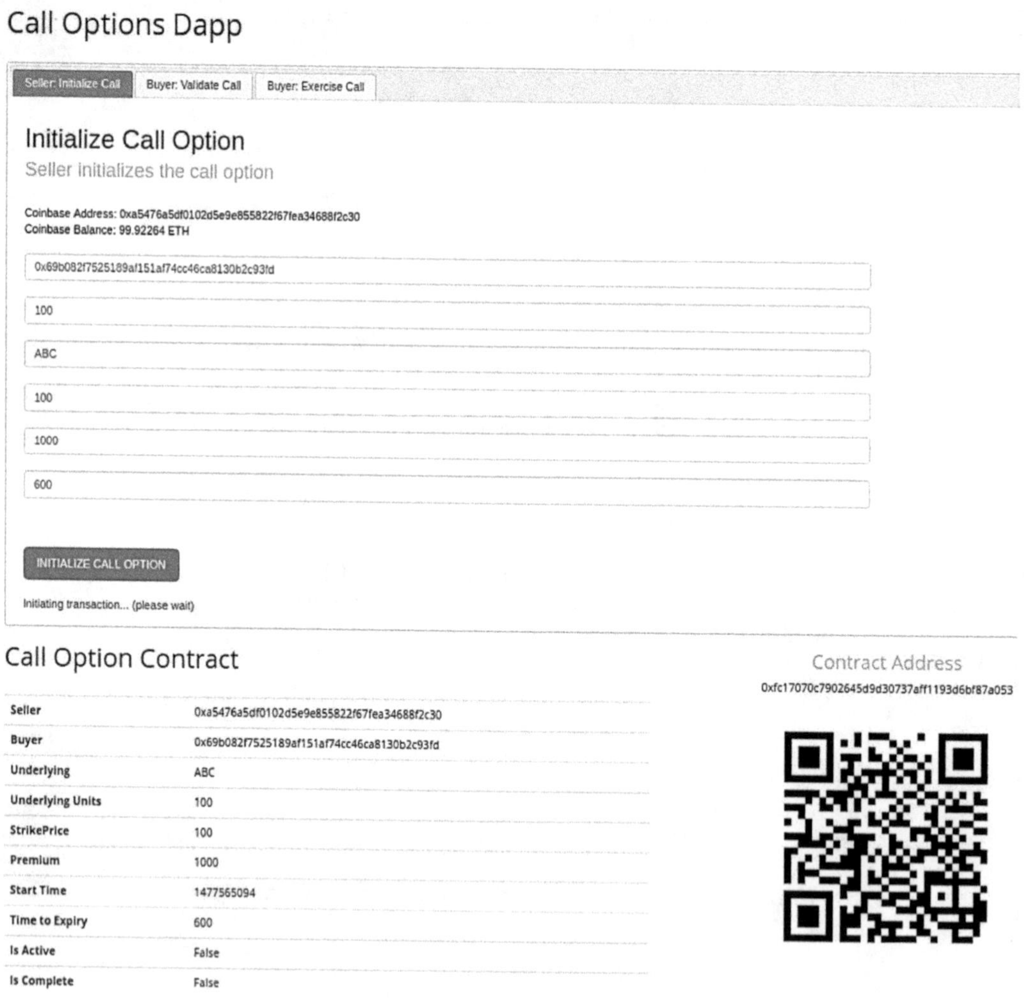

Figure 6.10: Screenshot of Call Option Dapp - initializing the call option

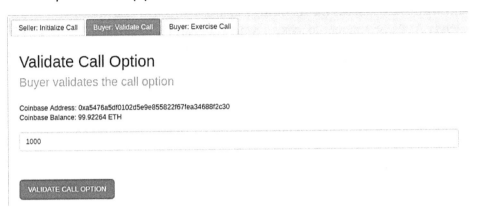

Figure 6.11: Screenshot of Call Option Dapp - validating the call option

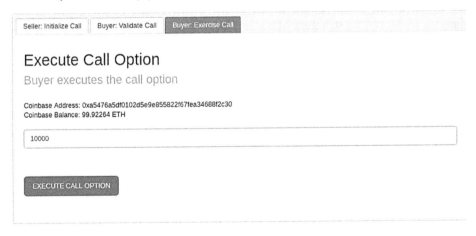

Figure 6.12: Screenshot of Call Option Dapp - exercising the call option

6.2.5 Interest Rate Swap

An Interest Rate Swap is a financial derivative instrument in which two parties agree to exchange interest rate cash flows based on a notional amount. The swap can either be from a fixed rate to a floating rate or from one floating rate to another floating rate. In this section, we describe a case study of a Dapp that allows fixed for floating rate swap. The interest rate swap (IRS) contract includes the following elements:

- **Party A**: Party A agrees to make payments to Party B based on a fixed interest rate.
- **Party B**: Party B agrees to make payments to Party A based on a floating interest rate.
- **Fixed Rate**: Fixed Rate paid by Party A to Party B.
- **Floating Rate**: Floating Rate paid by Party B to Party A.
- **Reference Rate**: The floating rate is indexed to a reference rate such as the London Inter bank Offered Rate (LIBOR).
- **Notional**: Notional is the amount by which the fixed and floating rates are multiplied, to determine the amount each party needs to pay to the other. When both the fixed and floating legs of the IRS contract are in the same currency, only the net amount due (difference of the amounts each party owes to the other) is paid to the party.
- **Schedule**: The schedule for exercising the swap, for example monthly, quarterly, or yearly.
- **Expiration Date**: Date on which the IRS contract expires.

Let us consider an example of an interest rate swap contract with 100000 notional, a monthly schedule and 10-year maturity. Let the fixed leg pay 1.5% monthly, and the floating leg pay (LIBOR + 1%) monthly. Let us say if the LIBOR rate is 0.30% at the end of a particular month. Now Party A needs to pay (1.5% * 100000) to Party B, and, Party B needs to pay (1.3% * 100000) to Party A. The net amount due in this case is 20000 to be paid by Party A to Party B. Now let's say the LIBOR rate increases to 0.60% at the end of a particular month. Now Party A needs to pay (1.5% * 100000) to Party B, and, Party B needs to pay (1.6% * 100000) to Party A. The net amount due in this case is 10000 to be paid by Party B to Party A.

Figure 6.13 shows the structure of the interest rate swap contract and the related smart contracts. For this Dapp we have a smart contract for interest rate swap, a smart contract for the trading accounts of the two parties and a smart contract for the rate provider which provides the current reference rate. Box 6.19 shows the Solidity implementation of an IRS contract. With this contract, the contract owner (either of the two parties) can initialize a contract by providing details such as the addresses of the trading accounts of the two parties, fixed rate, floating rate margin, schedule and time to expiry. The other party can then validate the contract. After the two parties enter into the contract, the contract is exercised as per the schedule (e.g. every month) till it expires.

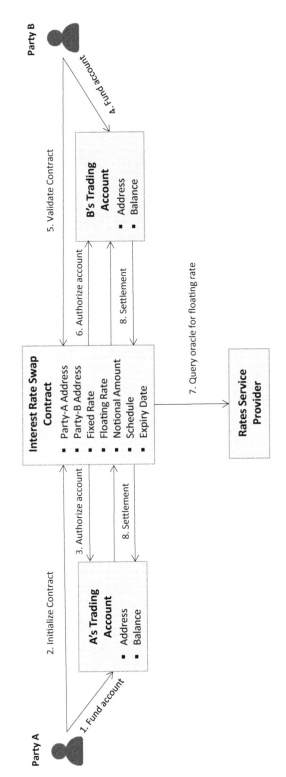

Figure 6.13: Interest Rate Swap contract structure

■ Box 6.19: Interest Rate Swap contract

```
contract owned {
  address public owner;
  function owned() {
    owner = msg.sender;
  }
  modifier onlyowner() {
    if (msg.sender == owner) _
  }
}

contract mortal is owned {
  function kill() onlyowner {
    if (msg.sender == owner) suicide(owner);
  }
}

contract InterestRateSwap is owned, mortal {
    bool public  isActive;
    address public       partyA;
    address public       partyB;
    TradingAccount  public    partyATradingAcct;
    TradingAccount  public    partyBTradingAcct;
    uint public  fixedRate;
    uint public floatingRateMargin;
    uint public notional;
    uint public schedule; // every X minutes
    RateProvider public rateFeed;
    string public feedName;
    uint public timeToExpiry;
    uint public startTime;
    uint public lastAmountPaid;

    function InterestRateSwap() {
        isActive = false;
    }

    // partyB initializes the contract
    function initialize(
        address _partyATradingAcct,
        address _partyBTradingAcct,
        uint    _fixedRate,
        uint    _floatingRateMargin,
        uint    _notional,
        uint    _schedule,
        string  _feedName,
        address _rateProvider,
        uint    _timeToExpiry) {

        // Trading accounts
        partyATradingAcct = TradingAccount(_partyATradingAcct);
        partyA = partyATradingAcct.owner();
        partyBTradingAcct = TradingAccount(_partyBTradingAcct);
```

```
        partyB = partyBTradingAcct.owner();

        fixedRate = _fixedRate;
        floatingRateMargin = _floatingRateMargin;
        notional = _notional;
        schedule = _schedule;
        feedName = _feedName;
        rateFeed = RateProvider(_rateProvider);

        timeToExpiry = _timeToExpiry;
        startTime = now;
        lastAmountPaid = 0;
        // Authorize trading account of caller
        authorizeTradingAccounts();
    }

    // partyA validates the contract in order to activate it
    function validate() {
        if (isActive) {
            throw;
        }

        if (isExpired()) {
            throw;
        }

        // Need authorized trading accounts
        if (!(partyATradingAcct.isAuthorized(this) ||
            partyBTradingAcct.isAuthorized(this))) {
            throw;
        }

        // Authorize trading account of caller
        authorizeTradingAccounts();

        isActive = true;
    }

    function exercise() {
        // Can only be exercised if active
        if(!(isActive)){
            throw;
        }

        // Call can only be exercised if it is not expired
        if (isExpired()) {
            throw;
        }

        // Get current rate from the rate provider
        uint currentRate = getRate();
        uint floatingRate = currentRate + floatingRateMargin;

        //Calculate amount each party owes to the other
```

```
    uint amountAowesB = (notional * floatingRate)/100;
    uint amountBowesA = (notional * fixedRate)/100;

    // Settle the difference in the amount owed
    if (amountAowesB>amountBowesA){
        lastAmountPaid = amountAowesB-amountBowesA;
        partyATradingAcct.withdraw(lastAmountPaid);
        partyBTradingAcct.deposit.value(lastAmountPaid)();
    }else{
        lastAmountPaid = amountBowesA-amountAowesB;
        partyBTradingAcct.withdraw(lastAmountPaid);
        partyATradingAcct.deposit.value(lastAmountPaid)();
    }
}


// Authorize trading accounts
function authorizeTradingAccounts() {
    if (msg.sender == partyA) {
        partyATradingAcct.authorize(this, timeToExpiry);
    }
    if (msg.sender == partyB) {
        partyBTradingAcct.authorize(this, timeToExpiry);
    }
}

function isExpired() constant returns (bool) {
    if (now > startTime + timeToExpiry) {
        return true;
    } else {
        return false;
    }
}

function getRate() returns (uint) {
    return rateFeed.getPrice(feedName);
}
```

Box 6.20 shows the Solidity implementation of the trading account contract. Instead of directly using the Ethereum accounts of the two parties for the swap payments, separate trading contract accounts are setup by each party. Each party maintains a sufficient balance in their trading account to facilitate the swap payments, every time the IRS contract is exercised. Each party authorizes the IRS contract to deposit/withdraw money to/from their trading account. Thus, when the IRS contract is exercised, the contract itself can automatically deposit or withdraw money to/from trading accounts without additional permissions from the two parties. The IRS contract is authorized to operate the trading accounts only till the expiry of the IRS contract.

■ **Box 6.20: Trading Account contract**

```
contract TradingAccount  {
    struct AuthPeriod {
        uint         duration; // in minutes
        uint         startTime;
    }

    mapping(address => AuthPeriod)  public authorized;
    address[]  public addresses;
    address public owner;

    function TradingAccount() {
        owner = msg.sender;
    }

    function deposit() returns (bool) {
        if (isOwner(msg.sender) || isAuthorized(msg.sender)) {
            return true; // Accept the deposit
        } else {
            throw;
        }

        return false;
    }

    function withdraw(uint amount) returns (bool) {
        if (amount > this.balance) {
            throw;
        }

        if (isOwner(msg.sender) || isAuthorized(msg.sender)) {
            if(!msg.sender.send(amount)){throw;}
            return true;
        }

        return false;
    }

    function authorize(address accountAddr,
                    uint duration) returns (bool) {
        if (duration == 0) {
            return false;
        }

        AuthPeriod period = authorized[accountAddr];
        if (period.duration == 0) {
            // Add this account to the list of authorized accounts
            authorized[accountAddr] = AuthPeriod(duration,
                                        block.timestamp);
            addresses.push(accountAddr);
        } else if (timeRemaining(accountAddr) < duration) {
            // Extend the authorized duration for this account
            authorized[accountAddr] = AuthPeriod(duration,
```

```
                                                       block.timestamp);
        }

        return true;
    }

    function isAuthorized(address accountAddr) returns (bool) {
        // Check if address is authorized and
        // authorization hasn't expired
        if (authorized[accountAddr].duration > 0 &&
            timeRemaining(accountAddr) >= 0){
            return true;
        }else{
            return false;
        }
    }

    function isOwner(address accountAddr) returns (bool) {
        // Check if address is authorized and
        // authorization hasn't expired
        if (accountAddr==owner){
            return true;
        }else{
            return false;
        }
    }

    function timeRemaining(address accountAddr) private returns (uint) {
        uint timeElapsed = (block.timestamp -
                            authorized[accountAddr].startTime) / 60;
        return authorized[accountAddr].duration - timeElapsed;
    }

    function kill() {
        if (msg.sender == owner) suicide(owner);
    }
}
```

Box 6.21 shows the Solidity implementation of the rate provider contract which provides the current reference rate which is used for computing the floating rate within the IRS contract. A rate provider contract can be used by a market data publisher to provide external market data and reference rates. To get the current rate for a symbol, any contract can send a transaction to the *getPrice()* function of the rate provider contract along with the symbol name. The data publisher can update the current rate of a symbol using the *updateRate()* function.

■ **Box 6.21:** **Rate Provider contract**

```
contract RateProvider {
    mapping(bytes32 => uint) public  rates;
    mapping(bytes32 => uint) public  timestamps;

    function RateProvider() {
        rates['XIBOR']  = 50;
        rates['VIBOR']  = 80;

        timestamps['XIBOR']  = block.timestamp;
        timestamps['YIBOR']  = block.timestamp;
    }

    // Returns the rate of a symbol
    function getPrice(string _symbol) constant returns(uint) {
        bytes32 symbol = stringToBytes(_symbol);
        return rates[symbol];
    }

    // Returns the timestamp of the latest rate for a symbol.
    function getTimestamp(string _symbol) constant returns (uint) {
        bytes32 symbol = stringToBytes(_symbol);
        return timestamps[symbol];
    }

    // Update rate for a given symbol.
    function updateRate(string _symbol, uint _rate) returns(bool) {
        bytes32 symbol = stringToBytes(_symbol);

        rates[symbol] = _rate;
        timestamps[symbol] = block.timestamp;
        return true;
    }

    // Converts 'string' to 'bytes32'
    function stringToBytes(string s) returns (bytes32) {
      bytes memory b = bytes(s);
      uint r = 0;
      for (uint i = 0; i < 32; i++) {
          if (i < b.length) {
              r = r | uint(b[i]);
          }
          if (i < 31) r = r * 256;
      }
      return bytes32(r);
    }
}
```

Box 6.22 shows the HTML implementation of the web interface for the Dapp (index.html).

■ Box 6.22: HTML source code for the Interest Rate Swap Dapp web interface

```html
<!DOCTYPE html>
<html lang="en">
<head>
  <title>Interest Rate Swap</title>
  <meta name="viewport" content="width=device-width, initial-scale=1">
  <link rel="stylesheet" href="./bootstrap.min.css">
  <link rel="stylesheet" href="h./jquery-ui.css">
  <link href="./app.css" rel='stylesheet' type='text/css'>
  <script src="./app.js"></script>
</head>
<body>

  <div class="container-fluid">
    <h1>Interest Rate Swap Dapp</h1>
    <h3 style="margin-top: 0px; margin-bottom: 30px;"></h3>

<div id="tabs">
  <ul>
    <li><a href="#tabs-1">Party-A: Initialize Contract</a></li>
    <li><a href="#tabs-2">Party-B: Validate Contract</a></li>
    <li><a href="#tabs-3">Exercise</a></li>
  </ul>
  <div id="tabs-1">
    <div class="row">
  <div class="col-md-8">

      <h2 style="padding-top: 20px;">Initialize Contract </h2>
      <h3 style="margin-top: 0px; margin-bottom: 30px;">
      Party-A initializes the contract</h3>

      <span class="black">Coinbase Address:
        <span id="cb_address" class="c_address"></span></span><br>
      <span class="black">Coinbase Balance:
        <span id="cb_balance"></span> ETH</span><br><br>

      <input type="text" class="form-control"
        id="partyATradingAcct" placeholder="Party-A Trading Account"/>
      <input type="text" class="form-control"
       id="partyBTradingAcct" placeholder="Party-B Trading Account"/>
      <input type="text" class="form-control"
       id="fixedRate" placeholder="Fixed Rate (*100)"/>
      <input type="text" class="form-control"
       id="floatingRateMargin" placeholder="Floating Rate Margin(*100)"/>
      <input type="text" class="form-control"
       id="notional" placeholder="Notional"/>
      <input type="text" class="form-control"
       id="schedule" placeholder="Schedule (in minutes)"/>
      <input type="text" class="form-control"
       id="rateFeed" placeholder="Address of Rate Provider"/>
      <input type="text" class="form-control"
```

```
            id="feedName" placeholder="Feed Name"/>
        <input type="text" class="form-control"
          id="timeToExpiry" placeholder="Time To Expiry(in minutes)"/>

        <button class="btn btn-primary btn-lg" onclick="initialize();">
        INITIALIZE CONTRACT</button>
        <br><br>
  <div id="status"> </div>
        </div>
        <div class="col-md-4">
    </div>

</div>
    </div>
    <div id="tabs-2">
      <div class="row">
    <div class="col-md-8">
        <h2 style="padding-top: 20px;">Validate Contract</h2>
        <h3 style="margin-top: 0px; margin-bottom: 30px;">
        Party-B validates the contract</h3>
        <span class="black">Coinbase Address:
        <span id="cb_address1" class="c_address"></span></span>
        <span class="black">Coinbase Balance:
        <span id="cb_balance1"></span> ETH</span><br><br>
        <br><br>
        <button class="btn btn-primary btn-lg" onclick="validate();">
        VALIDATE CONTRACT</button>
        <br><br>
  <div id="status1"> </div>
        </div>
        <div class="col-md-4">
    </div>

</div>
    </div>
    <div id="tabs-3">
     <div class="row">
    <div class="col-md-8">
        <h2 style="padding-top: 20px;">Exercise</h2>
        <h3 style="margin-top: 0px; margin-bottom: 30px;">
        Exercise the contract</h3>
        <span class="black">Coinbase Address:
        <span id="cb_address2" class="c_address"></span></span>
        <span class="black">Coinbase Balance:
        <span id="cb_balance2"></span> ETH</span><br><br>
        <br><br>
        <button class="btn btn-primary btn-lg"
        onclick="exercise();">EXERCISE</button>
        <br><br>
  <div id="status2"> </div>
        </div>
        <div class="col-md-4">
    </div>
</div>
```

```
    </div>
</div>

<div class="row">
  <div class="col-md-6">
<h2 style="padding-top: 20px;">Interest Rate Swap Contract</h2>
      <h3 style="margin-top: 0px; margin-bottom: 30px;"></h3>
<table class="table table-fluid">
      <tr>
        <th>Party-A</th>
        <td><span class="black">
        <span id="cf_partyA"></span></span></td>
      </tr>
      <tr>
        <th>Party-B</th>
        <td><span class="black">
        <span id="cf_partyB"></span></span></td>
      </tr>
      <tr>
        <th>Notional</th>
        <td><span class="black">
        <span id="cf_notional"></span></span></td>
      </tr>
      <tr>
        <th>Fixed Rate</th>
        <td><span class="black">
        <span id="cf_fixedRate"></span></span></td>
      </tr>
       <tr>
        <th>Floating Rate Margin</th>
        <td><span class="black">
        <span id="cf_floatingRateMargin"></span></span></td>
      </tr>
      <tr>
        <th>Last Amount Paid</th>
        <td><span class="black">
        <span id="cf_lastAmountPaid"></span></span></td>
      </tr>
      <tr>
        <th>Schedule</th>
        <td><span class="black">
        <span id="cf_schedule"></span></span></td>
      </tr>
      <tr>
        <th>Start Time</th>
        <td><span class="black">
        <span id="cf_startTime"></span></span></td>
      </tr>
      <tr>
        <th>Time to Expiry</th>
        <td><span class="black">
        <span id="cf_timeToExpiry"></span></span></td>
      </tr>
      <tr>
```

```
            <th>Is Active</th>
            <td><span class="black">
            <span id="cf_isActive"></span></span></td>
        </tr>
        <tr>
            <th>Is Expired</th>
            <td><span class="black">
            <span id="cf_isExpired"></span></span></td>
        </tr>
    </table>
  </div>
  <div class="col-md-4">
      <center>
    <h3>Contract Address</h3>
<span class="black"><span id="cf_address"></span></span><br>
<div id="qrcode"></div>
</center>
  </div>
</div>
  </div>
  <script src="/jquery.min.js"></script>
<script src="/bootstrap.min.js"></script>
 <script src="/jquery-1.12.4.js"></script>
  <script src="/jquery-ui.js"></script>
</body>
</html>
```

Box 6.23 shows the Dapp JavaScript (app.js).

▪ Box 6.23: Interest Rate Swap Dapp JavaScript

```javascript
var accounts;
var account;
var balance;
var ticketPrice;
var myContractInstance;

function initializeContract() {
  myContractInstance = InterestRateSwap.deployed();
  $("#cf_address").html(myContractInstance.address);
  $("#cb_address").html(accounts[0]);
  $("#cb_address1").html(accounts[1]);
  $("#cb_address2").html(accounts[0]);
  $("#qrcode").html("<img src=
    \"https://chart.googleapis.com/chart?cht=qr&chs=350&chl="+
    myContractInstance.address+"\" height=\"350\"/>");

  refreshVars();
}

function setStatus(message) {
  $("#status").html(message);
};
```

```
function setStatus1(message) {
  $("#status1").html(message);
};

function setStatus2(message) {
  $("#status2").html(message);
};

function refreshVars(){
  myContractInstance.partyA.call().then(
      function(partyA) {
        $("#cf_partyA").html(partyA);
        return myContractInstance.partyB.call();
      }).then(
      function(partyB) {
        $("#cf_partyB").html(partyB);
        return myContractInstance.notional.call();
      }).then(
      function(notional) {
        $("#cf_notional").html(notional.toNumber());
        return myContractInstance.fixedRate.call();
      }).then(
      function(fixedRate) {
        $("#cf_fixedRate").html(fixedRate.toNumber());
        return myContractInstance.floatingRateMargin.call();
      }).then(
      function(floatingRateMargin) {
        $("#cf_floatingRateMargin").html(floatingRateMargin.toNumber());
        return myContractInstance.lastAmountPaid.call();
      }).then(
      function(lastAmountPaid) {
        $("#cf_lastAmountPaid").html(lastAmountPaid.toNumber());
        return myContractInstance.schedule.call();
      }).then(
      function(schedule) {
        $("#cf_schedule").html(schedule.toNumber());
        return myContractInstance.startTime.call();
      }).then(
      function(startTime) {
        $("#cf_startTime").html(startTime.toNumber());
        return myContractInstance.timeToExpiry.call();
      }).then(
      function(timeToExpiry) {
        $("#cf_timeToExpiry").html(timeToExpiry.toNumber());
        return myContractInstance.isActive.call();
      }).then(
      function(isActive) {
        if(isActive){
          $("#cf_isActive").html("True");
        }else{
          $("#cf_isActive").html("False");
        }
        return myContractInstance.isExpired.call();
```

```
        }).then(
        function(isExpired) {
          if(isExpired){
            $("#cf_isExpired").html("True");
          }else{
            $("#cf_isExpired").html("False");
          }
          setStatus("");
          setStatus1("");
          setStatus2("");
          refreshBalance();
        });
}

function refreshBalance() {
  var balance = web3.fromWei(web3.eth.getBalance(web3.eth.accounts[0]),
                             "ether").toFixed(5);
  $("#cb_balance").html(balance);
  $("#cb_balance2").html(balance);
  var balance1 = web3.fromWei(web3.eth.getBalance(web3.eth.accounts[1]),
                              "ether").toFixed(5);
  $("#cb_balance1").html(balance1);
}

function initialize() {
  var partyATradingAcct = $("#partyATradingAcct").val();
  var partyBTradingAcct = $("#partyBTradingAcct").val();
  var fixedRate = parseFloat($("#fixedRate").val());
  var floatingRateMargin = parseFloat($("#floatingRateMargin").val());
  var notional = parseFloat($("#notional").val());
  var schedule = parseFloat($("#schedule").val());
  var rateFeed = $("#rateFeed").val();
  var feedName = $("#feedName").val();
  var timeToExpiry = parseFloat($("#timeToExpiry").val());

  setStatus("Initiating transaction... (please wait)");

  myContractInstance.initialize(partyATradingAcct, partyBTradingAcct,
          fixedRate, floatingRateMargin, notional, schedule, feedName,
          rateFeed, timeToExpiry,
          {from: web3.eth.accounts[0], gas: 2000000}).then(
          function() {
            refreshVars();
          });
}

function validate() {
  setStatus1("Initiating transaction... (please wait)");
  myContractInstance.validate({from: web3.eth.accounts[1],
                               gas: 2000000}).then(
          function() {
            refreshVars();
          });
}
```

```
function exercise() {
  setStatus2("Initiating transaction... (please wait)");
  myContractInstance.exercise({from: web3.eth.accounts[0],
                                gas: 2000000}).then(
        function() {
          refreshVars();
        });
}

window.onload = function() {
  $( "#tabs" ).tabs();
  web3.eth.getAccounts(function(err, accs) {
    if (err != null) {
      alert("There was an error fetching your accounts.");
      return;
    }
    if (accs.length == 0) {
      alert("Couldn't get any accounts!");
      return;
    }
    accounts = accs;
    account = accounts[0];
    initializeContract();
  });
}
```

Figure 6.14 shows a screenshot of the IRS Dapp. In this Dapp we have three tabs. In the first tab, Party A can initialize the interest rate swap contract by providing the addresses of the trading accounts of the two parties, fixed rate, floating rate margin, notional amount, schedule, address of the rate provider contract, feed name (required for querying the rate provider) and time to expiry. Once the contract is initialized, its details can be viewed at the bottom half of the Dapp web page.

In the second tab, as shown in Figure 6.15, Party-B can validate the contract. In the third tab, as shown in Figure 6.16, the contract can be exercised. Currently, there is no direct way of scheduling the execution of a contract in Ethereum. Hence the option to manually exercise the IRS contract is provided in the Dapp. Additional checks can be added in the IRS contract to ensure that the contract is only exercised as per the schedule.

This Dapp demonstrates a design pattern that can be used for other FinTech applications as well. The key elements of this pattern are the smart contract for the trading accounts of the two parties, a smart contract for the financial instrument and a smart contract for the rate provider.

Interest Rate Swap Dapp

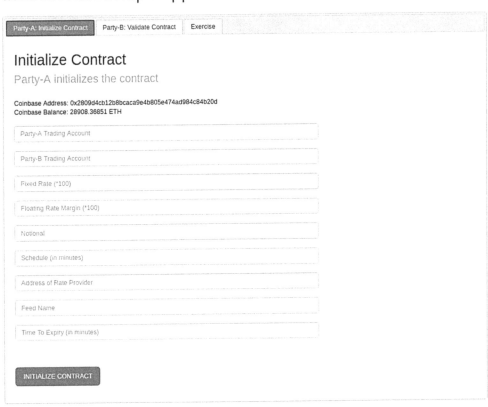

Interest Rate Swap Contract

Party-A	0x2809d4cb12b8bcaca9e4b805e474ad984c84b20d
Party-B	0xa5d73d67d7a79be62e2c77dd877b536775c446dd
Notional	1000
Fixed Rate	500
Floating Rate Margin	100
Last Amount Paid	0
Schedule	300
Start Time	1478601746
Time to Expiry	3000
Is Active	False
Is Expired	False

Contract Address
0x7aa1b233b9bba550f32b428fa04437c66c0b6ebf

Figure 6.14: Screenshot of Interest Rate Swap Dapp - initializing the contract

Figure 6.15: Screenshot of Interest Rate Swap Dapp - validating the contract

Figure 6.16: Screenshot of Interest Rate Swap Dapp - exercising the contract

6.2.6   Industrial IoT - Machine Maintenance

In Chapter-1, we described various industrial and manufacturing applications for which blockchain can be used. In this section, we describe a case study of a Dapp for Industrial Internet of Things (IIoT).

To enable existing machines to communicate with the blockchain network, an IoT device can be used as shown in Figure 6.17. The IoT device is a 'plug and play' solution that allows machines to exchange data on their operations, send transactions to the associated smart contracts and receive transactions from the peers on the blockchain network. The IoT device includes an interface board (based on Arduino) and a single-board computer (based on Beaglebone Black or Raspberry Pi). The interface board is equipped with sensors to monitor the temperature and vibration levels of different parts of a machine. The interface board makes use of digital, analog, serial and USB interfaces to capture data from a variety of sensors and systems. While modern industrial machines can directly communicate with the interface board (over digital, analog, serial or USB interfaces), many legacy machines make use of controllers that are either impractical to access, or the digital communication is nonexistent. Therefore, the interface board makes use of sensors which are external to the legacy machines' control box.

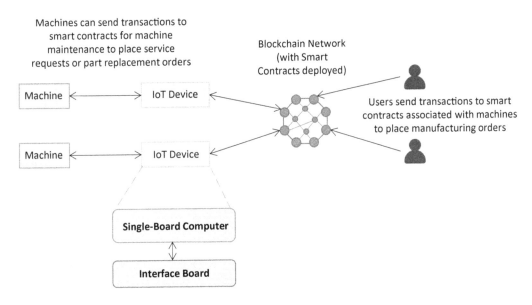

Figure 6.17: Using Blockchain for Industrial Internet of Things

Let us look at a specific example of an industrial application that can leverage the Blockchain and IoT technologies. We describe a machine maintenance application where a machine can automatically monitor its state and place service requests if any problem is detected. Box 6.24 shows the Solidity implementation of the smart contract for the machine maintenance Dapp. The smart contract acts an agreement between the machine and the service vendor to schedule a service request for the machine. In the smart contract, we define custom data types to represent machines and service requests. The *Machine* structure maintains information related to machines including the machine name, purchase date, address of the machine owner and manufacturer name. The *machines* variable maintains a mapping from the machine-ID to the *Machine* structure. The *ServiceRequest* structure maintains information related to service requests including the request timestamp, remarks and the address of the requester. The *serviceRequests* variable maintains a mapping from the machine-ID to the *ServiceRequest* structure.

■ Box 6.24: Machine Maintenance contract

```
contract Maintenance {
    struct Machine {
        string machineName;
        uint purchaseDate;
        address owner;
        string manufacturer;
    }

    struct ServiceRequest {
        uint timestamp;
        string remarks;
        address requester;
    }

    address public creator;
    uint public numMachines;
    uint public numServiceRequests;
    mapping (uint => ServiceRequest) serviceRequests;
    mapping (uint => Machine) machines;
    bool public result;

    event ServiceRequested(address requester,
            uint timestamp, uint machineID, string remarks);

    function Maintenance() {
        creator = msg.sender;
        numMachines = 0;
        numServiceRequests = 0;
    }

    function registerMachine(uint machineID,
        string machineName, uint purchaseDate,
        string manufacturer) public {
        Machine m = machines[machineID];
        m.machineName = machineName;
        m.purchaseDate = purchaseDate;
        m.owner = msg.sender;
        m.manufacturer = manufacturer;
        numMachines++;
    }

    function getMachineDetails(uint machineID)
        returns(string machineName, uint purchaseDate,
        address owner, string manufacturer){
        machineName = machines[machineID].machineName;
        purchaseDate = machines[machineID].purchaseDate;
```

```
            owner = machines[machineID].owner;
            manufacturer = machines[machineID].manufacturer;
        }

    function getServiceRequest(uint machineID)
            returns(uint timestamp, string remarks, address requester){
        timestamp = serviceRequests[machineID].timestamp;
        remarks = serviceRequests[machineID].remarks;
        requester = serviceRequests[machineID].requester;
    }

    function requestService(uint timestamp,
                uint machineID, string remarks) public {
        ServiceRequest s = serviceRequests[machineID];
        s.timestamp = timestamp;
        s.requester = msg.sender;
        s.remarks = remarks;
        numServiceRequests++;
        ServiceRequested(msg.sender, timestamp, machineID, remarks);
    }

    function destroy() {
        if (msg.sender == creator) {
            suicide(creator);
        }
    }
}
```

Box 6.25 shows the Python implementation of a controller service that runs on the IoT device (single-board computer, SBC). The controller service constantly monitors the temperature and vibration levels of different parts of the machine (as sensed by the sensors on the interface board which is connected to SBC over the serial port). Within the controller service, different rules are defined to determine if machine service request or part replacement order needs to be placed. For example, if the vibration levels of the machine go beyond a pre-defined threshold for a certain number of times, the controller service sends a machine service request. For sending the service request, a transaction is sent to the *requestService* function of the *Maintenance* smart contract between the machine and the service vendor. To register a machine with the smart contract, the machine owner sends a transaction to the *registerMachine* function of the contract with the machineID, machine name, purchase date, and manufacturer as input arguments.

▪ Box 6.25: Python controller component that runs on IoT device

```
from ethjsonrpc import EthJsonRpc
import time
import datetime
import time
import serial

ser = serial.Serial('/dev/ttyACM0', 38400)
```

```
contract_addr = '0xc421d5e214ddb07a41d28cf89ee37495aa5edba7'
machineID = 123

#Wait for sometime to initialize serial port
time.sleep(10)

# Connect to Blockchain network
c = EthJsonRpc('192.168.1.20', 8101)

tempCount = 0
vibrationCount = 0
tempThreshold = 200
vibrationThreshold = 100
tempCountThreshold = 1000
vibrationCountThreshold = 1000

while True:
  line = serialTTL.readline()
  data = line.split(',')
  vibration = data[0]
  temperature = data[1]

  if(vibration>vibrationThreshold):
    vibrationCount = vibrationCount+1

  if(temperature>tempThreshold):
    tempCount = tempCount+1

  ts = int(time.time())
  if(vibrationCount>vibrationCountThreshold):
    #Send a transaction to requestService function of
    #MachineService contract with Machine-ID
    c.call_with_transaction(c.eth_coinbase(),
    contract_addr, 'requestService(uint256,uint256,string)',
    [ts, machineID, 'High vibrations'])
    vibrationCount = 0

  if(tempCount>tempCountThreshold):
    c.call_with_transaction(c.eth_coinbase(),
    contract_addr, 'requestService(uint256,uint256,string)',
    [ts, machineID, 'High temperature'])
    tempCount = 0

  time.sleep(1)
```

Box 6.26 shows the HTML implementation of the web interface for the Dapp (index.html).

■ Box 6.26: HTML source code for the Machine Maintenance Dapp web interface

```
<!DOCTYPE html>
<html lang="en">
<head>
  <title>Machine Maintenance</title>
```

```html
    <meta name="viewport" content="width=device-width, initial-scale=1">
    <link rel="stylesheet" href="./bootstrap.min.css">
    <link href="./app.css" rel='stylesheet' type='text/css'>
    <script src="./app.js"></script>
      <script src="./jquery.min.js"></script>
<script src="./bootstrap.min.js"></script>
</head>
<body>
   <div class="container-fluid">
      <h1>Machine Maintenance Dapp</h1>
      <h3 style="margin-top: 0px; margin-bottom: 30px;"></h3>

<div class="row">
   <div class="col-md-8">
<table class="table table-fluid">
      <tr>
        <th>Contract Address</th>
        <td><span class="black">
        <span id="cf_address"></span></span></td>
      </tr>
      <tr>
        <th>Machines Registered</th>
        <td><span class="black">
        <span id="cf_machines"></span></span></td>
      </tr>
      <tr>
        <th>Service Requests</th>
        <td><span class="black">
        <span id="cf_servicerequests"></span></span></td>
      </tr>
    </table>
  </div>
</div>

<div class="row">
 <h2 style="padding-top: 20px;">Service Requests</h2>
      <h3 style="margin-top: 0px; margin-bottom: 30px;">
      View recent service requests.
      Click on a machine-ID to view machine details.</h3>
  <div class="col-md-7">
 <div id="serviceTable"></div>
 <br><br>
 <div id="status"> </div>
      </div>
      <div class="col-md-5">
     <table class="table table-fluid">
       <tr>
         <th>Machine-ID</th>
         <td><span class="black">
         <span id="cf_machineID"></span></span></td>
       </tr>
       <tr>
         <th>Machine Name</th>
         <td><span class="black">
```

```
        <span id="cf_machineName"></span></span></td>
    </tr>
    <tr>
      <th>Purchase Date</th>
      <td><span class="black">
      <span id="cf_purchaseDate"></span></span></td>
    </tr>
    <tr>
      <th>Owner</th>
      <td><span class="black">
      <span id="cf_owner"></span></span></td>
    </tr>
    <tr>
      <th>Manufacturer</th>
      <td><span class="black">
      <span id="cf_manufacturer"></span></span></td>
    </tr>
   </table>
  </div>
 </div>
  </div>
</body>
</html>
```

Box 6.27 shows the Dapp JavaScript (app.js). In this implementation we provide examples of registering a machine (*registerMachine* function) and requesting a service (*requestService* function). The *getServiceRequests* function gets called when the Dapp's web page is loaded. In this function, we watch for the *ServiceRequested* events of the Maintenance smart contract. Whenever a new service is requested, the *ServiceRequested* event is triggered in the smart contract. These events are displayed in the Dapp's web interface. A hyperlink is created for each machine-ID in the service requests table, displayed in the Dapp. When the hyperlink for a machine-ID is clicked, the *getMachineDetails* function is called, which retrieves the machine details from the smart contract and displays it in the Dapp.

■ Box 6.27: Machine Maintenance Dapp JavaScript

```
var accounts;
var account;
var myContractInstance;

function initializeContract() {
  myContractInstance = Maintenance.deployed();
  $("#cf_address").html(myContractInstance.address);
  $("#cb_address").html(account);

  myContractInstance.numMachines.call().then(
    function(numMachines) {
      $("#cf_machines").html(numMachines.toNumber());
      return myContractInstance.numServiceRequests.call();
  }).then(
    function(numServiceRequests) {
      $("#cf_servicerequests").html(numServiceRequests.toNumber());
```

```
        getServiceRequests();
   });
}

function setStatus(message) {
  $("#status").html(message);
};

function showTotal() {
   var numTickets = $("#numTickets").val();
   var ticketAmount = numTickets*ticketPrice;
  $("#ticketsTotal").html(ticketAmount);
};

function refreshBalance() {
  $("#cb_balance").html(web3.fromWei(web3.eth.getBalance(
      web3.eth.coinbase), "ether").toFixed(5));
}

function registerMachine(){
  var machineID=987655;
  var machineName="CNC";
  var purchaseDate = "1472721009";
  var manufacturer = "XYZ Corp";

  myContractInstance.registerMachine(machineID, machineName,
      purchaseDate, manufacturer, { from: web3.eth.coinbase}).then(
    function(result) {
      return myContractInstance.getMachineDetails.call(machineID);
    }
  ).then(
          function(result) {
            console.log(result);
            if (result[1].toNumber() >0) {
              console.log("Machine registered");
            } else {
              console.log("Registration failed");
            }
          });
}

function getMachineDetails(machineID){
      return myContractInstance.getMachineDetails.call(machineID).then(
          function(result) {
            console.log(result);
            $('#cf_machineID').html(machineID);
            $('#cf_machineName').html(result[0]);
            $('#cf_purchaseDate').html(result[1].toNumber());
            $('#cf_owner').html(result[2]);
            $('#cf_manufacturer').html(result[3]);
          });
}

function requestService(){
```

```
    var machineID=987655;
    var timestamp = "1472721012";
    var remarks = "Valve issue";

    myContractInstance.requestService(timestamp, machineID,
                remarks, { from: web3.eth.coinbase}).then(
        function(result) {
          return myContractInstance.getServiceRequest.call(machineID);
        }
    ).then(
            function(result) {
              console.log(result);
              if (result[0].toNumber() >0) {
                setStatus("Service request successful");
              } else {
                setStatus("Service request failed");
              }
            });
}

function getServiceRequests(){
    var serviceRequested = myContractInstance.ServiceRequested(
                        {fromBlock: 0, toBlock: 'latest'});
    serviceRequested.watch(function(error, result) {
    });

    var events = myContractInstance.allEvents({fromBlock: 0,
                toBlock: 'latest', event: 'ServiceRequested'});

    events.get(function(error, result) {
      var htmlString='<table class="table"><tr><th>Timestamp</th>\
                    <th>Machine-ID</th><th>Remarks</th></tr>';
      for(var i=0; i<result.length; i++){
          htmlString += '<tr>' +
                        '<td>'+ result[i].args.timestamp.toNumber()+'</td>'+
                        '<td><a href="#" onclick=getMachineDetails('+
                        result[i].args.machineID.toNumber()+');>'+
                        result[i].args.machineID.toNumber()+ '</a></td>'+
                        '<td>'+ result[i].args.remarks+'</td>'+
                        '</tr>'
      }

      htmlString +='</table>';

      $("#serviceTable").html(htmlString);
    });
}

window.onload = function() {
  web3.eth.getAccounts(function(err, accs) {
    if (err != null) {
      alert("There was an error fetching your accounts.");
      return;
    }
```

```
    if (accs.length == 0) {
      alert("Couldn't get any accounts! ");
      return;
    }

    accounts = accs;
    account = accounts[0];
    initializeContract();
  });
}
```

Figure 6.18 shows a screenshot of the machine maintenance Dapp. From the web interface of this Dapp, you can view the machines registered with the Dapp and the recent service requests.

Machine Maintenance Dapp

Contract Address	0xd1619cb112c859d57910ea809c7e7a8f09d21582
Machines Registered	2
Service Requests	2

Service Requests

View recent service requests. Click on a machine-ID to view machine details.

Timestamp	Machine-ID	Remarks
1472721010	987654	Heating Issue
1472721012	987655	Valve issue

Machine-ID	987655
Machine Name	CNC
Purchase Date	1472721009
Owner	0xa1ab84a233417b3723a38298da264d4294207095
Manufacturer	XYZ Corp

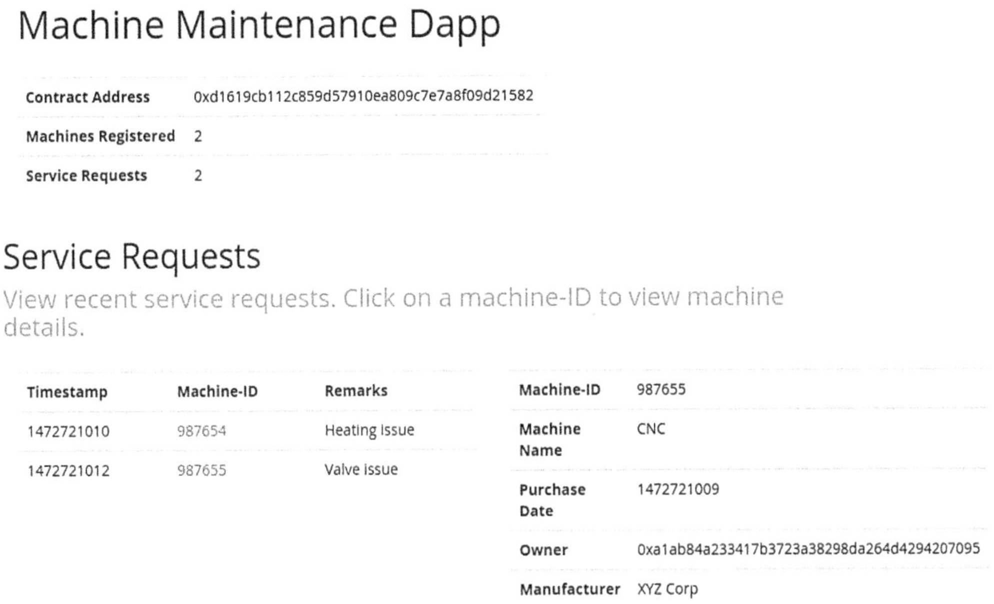

Figure 6.18: Screenshot of Machine Maintenance Dapp

6.2.7 Solar Charging Stations

The Dapp examples described till now in this Chapter, have user-friendly web interfaces that allow the users to send transactions to the associated smart contracts and view the state information in the contract. These Dapps are accessed by users either through the Ethereum Mist browser or through the Chrome browser with the MetaMask extension. In this section, we describe an implementation case study of a hybrid of a Dapp and a Web-app for a system of solar charging stations, which we have named as SolarCharge.

The SolarCharge system comprises a network of solar charging stations deployed in various locations. Figure 6.19 shows the key entities in the SolarCharge system, described as follows:

- **Server**: The server runs a full Ethereum node and also a REST web API which is used by the SolarCharge mobile application. The server translates the REST API requests received from the mobile application to blockchain transactions.
- **Mobile Application**: The mobile application allows users to send transactions to the solar charging stations. Mobile application uses the SolarCharge REST API and doesn't need to know how to transact directly with the blockchain network.
- **IoT Device**: Each SolarCharge station has an IoT device that controls the station.

Figure 6.20 shows the architecture of a SolarCharge station. Each charging station has an IoT device comprising a Beaglebone black single board computer (SBC), a relay module and a universal plug. A controller service running on the SBC, polls the SolarCharge smart contract at regular intervals and checks the status of the station. If the station state in the smart contract is updated (activated or de-activated) the SBC toggles the state of the relay module. Each station has a unique ID associated with it. A user who wishes to charge a device at the station can activate the station using the SolarCharge mobile application.

Box 6.28 shows the Solidity implementation of the SolarCharge smart contract. For the SolarCharge system, we define coins called *SolarCoins*, which can be used by the users to activate the charging stations for specific durations. Users can purchase SolarCoins through the SolarCharge Dapp by paying Ether. The rate of SolarCoins, in Ether, is defined in the smart contract as the *coinRate* state variable. In the smart contract, we define custom data types to represent users and charging stations. The *Station* structure maintains information related to the charging stations including the charging rate (SolarCoins per minute), location, station balance (in SolarCoins), timestamp of last activation, and duration of last activation. The *stations* variable maintains a mapping of the station-ID to the *Station* structure. The *User* structure maintains information related to users who have registered with the SolarCharge Dapp, including user name, user's Ethereum address, the amount paid by a user (in Ether) and user's SolarCoin balance. The *users* variable maintains a mapping of the user email to the *User* structure. A user can register with SolarCharge smart contract by sending a transaction to the *registerUser* function with the username and email as the input arguments. A registered user can buy SolarCoins by sending a transaction to the *buyCoins* function with email as the input argument and a value (in Ether) accompanying the transaction. The number of SolarCoins issued depend on the coin rate set in *coinRate* state variable. For user registration and purchase of SolarCoins, we also provide an implementation of a Dapp, which is described later in this section.

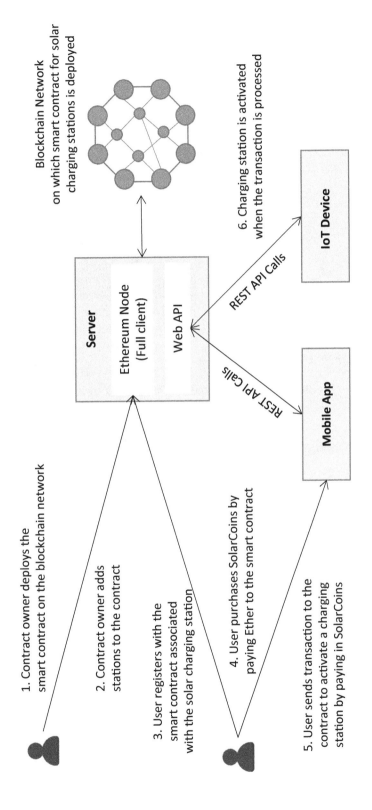

Figure 6.19: SolarCharge system

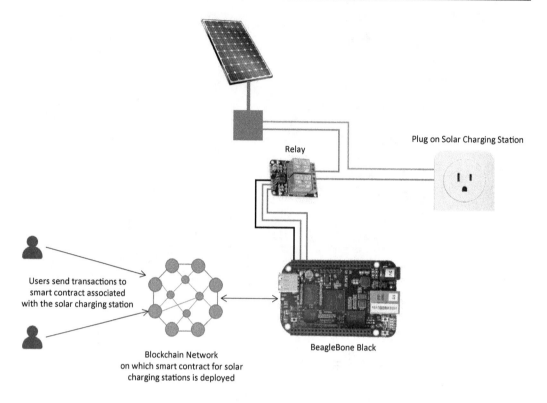

Figure 6.20: SolarCharge station architecture

■ Box 6.28: SolarCharge smart contract

```
contract SolarCharge {
  struct User {
    string name;
      address userAccount;
        uint amountPaid;
        uint solcoins;
  }

  mapping (bytes32 => User) public users;

  struct Station {
      uint rate;
      string location;
      uint coinBalance;
      uint lastActivated;
      uint lastDuration;
  }

  mapping (uint => Station) public stations;

 address public owner;
 uint public numUsers;
```

```
uint public numStations;
uint public coinRate; // coins per ether

function SolarCharger() {
  owner = msg.sender;
  numUsers = 0;
  numStations = 0;
  coinRate = 1000000000000000000;
}

function registerUser(string _email, string _name) public {
  bytes32 email = stringToBytes(_email);

  if(users[email].userAccount>0){
    throw;
  }

  User u = users[email];
      u.userAccount = msg.sender;
      u.name = _name;
      u.amountPaid = 0;
      u.solcoins =0;
  numUsers += 1;
}

function buyCoins(string _email) public {
  bytes32 email = stringToBytes(_email);

  if(users[email].userAccount!=msg.sender){
    throw;
  }
      users[email].amountPaid += msg.value;
      users[email].solcoins += msg.value*coinRate;
}

function addStation(uint ID, uint _rate, string _location) public {
  if(msg.sender!=owner){
    throw;
  }
  if(stations[ID].rate!=0){
    throw;
  }

  Station s = stations[ID];
      s.coinBalance = 0;
      s.lastActivated = 0;
      s.lastDuration = 0;
      s.location = _location;
      s.rate = _rate;
      numStations += 1;
}

function activateStation(string _email, uint ID, uint duration) public {
  bytes32 email = stringToBytes(_email);
```

```
  // Station does not exist
  if(stations[ID].rate==0){
    throw;
  }

  // Station is busy
  if(now<(stations[ID].lastActivated+stations[ID].lastDuration)){
    throw;
  }

  uint coinsRequired = stations[ID].rate*duration;

  // User has insufficient coins
  if (users[email].solcoins<coinsRequired){
    throw;
  }

      users[email].solcoins -= coinsRequired;
      stations[ID].coinBalance += coinsRequired;
      stations[ID].lastActivated = now;
      stations[ID].lastDuration = duration;
}

function getStationState(uint ID) constant returns (bool){
  if(now<(stations[ID].lastActivated+stations[ID].lastDuration)){
    return true;
  }else{
    return false;
  }
}

function getUser(string _email) constant returns (string name,
      address userAccount, uint amountPaid, uint solcoins){
  bytes32 email = stringToBytes(_email);
  name = users[email].name;
  userAccount = users[email].userAccount;
      amountPaid = users[email].amountPaid;
      solcoins = users[email].solcoins;
}

function getStation(uint ID) constant returns (uint rate,
          string location, uint coinBalance,
          uint lastActivated, uint lastDuration){
  rate = stations[ID].rate;
      location = stations[ID].location;
      coinBalance = stations[ID].coinBalance;
      lastActivated = stations[ID].lastActivated;
      lastDuration = stations[ID].lastDuration;
}

// Converts 'string' to 'bytes32'
function stringToBytes(string s) returns (bytes32) {
  bytes memory b = bytes(s);
```

```
    uint r = 0;
    for (uint i = 0; i < 32; i++) {
        if (i < b.length) {
            r = r | uint(b[i]);
        }
        if (i < 31) r = r * 256;
    }
    return bytes32(r);
}

function destroy() {
    if (msg.sender == owner) {
        suicide(owner);
    }
}
}
```

The owner of the SolarCharge smart contract can add stations to the contract by sending a transaction to the *addStation* function with the station ID, rate and location as input arguments. Figure 6.21 shows how to add a station using the Ethereum Mist Wallet application.

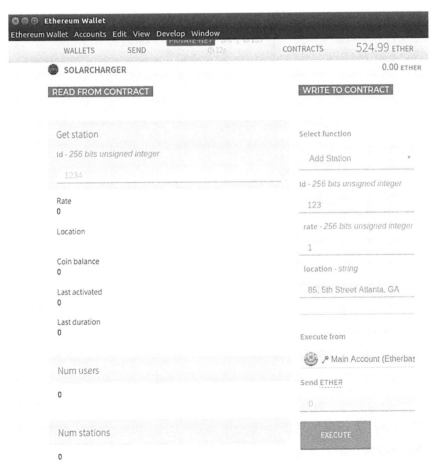

Figure 6.21: Adding a SolarCharge station using Ethereum Mist Wallet

While the contract owner can use either the geth console or Mist Wallet application to interact with the contract, for the end users, we provide an implementation of a Dapp. Through this Dapp, the users can register with the SolarCharge contract and purchase SolarCoins. Box 6.29 shows the HTML implementation of the web interface for the Dapp (index.html).

■ **Box 6.29: HTML source code for the SolarCharge Dapp web interface**

```html
<!DOCTYPE html>
<html lang="en">

<head>
  <title>SolarCharger Dapp</title>
  <link rel="stylesheet" href="bootstrap.min.css">
  <link href="./app.css" rel='stylesheet' type='text/css'>
  <script src="./app.js"></script>
</head>

<body>
  <div class="container-fluid">
    <h1>SolarCharger Dapp</h1>
    <h3 style="margin-top: 0px; margin-bottom: 30px;"></h3>

    <div class="row">
      <div class="col-md-6">

        <table class="table table-fluid">
          <tr>
            <th>Contract Address</th>
            <td><span class="black">
            <span id="cf_address"></span></span>
            </td>
          </tr>
          <tr>
            <th>Number of Stations</th>
            <td><span class="black">
            <span id="cf_stations"></span></span>
            </td>
          </tr>
          <tr>
            <th>Number of Users</th>
            <td><span class="black">
            <span id="cf_users"></span></span>
            </td>
          </tr>
          <tr>
            <th>Coin Rate</th>
            <td><span class="black">
            <span id="cf_rate"></span> Coins/ETH</span>
            </td>
          </tr>
        </table>
      </div>
    </div>
```

```
      </div>

    <div class="row">
      <div class="col-md-6">
        <h2 style="padding-top: 20px;">User Registration</h2>
        <input type="email" class="form-control"
                 id="email" placeholder="Email" /><br>

        <input type="text" class="form-control"
                 id="name" placeholder="Name" /><br><br><br>

        <button class="btn btn-primary btn-lg"
              onclick="registerUser();">REGISTER</button>
        <br><br>
      </div>
      <div class="col-md-6">
        <h2 style="padding-top: 20px;">Buy SolarCoins</h2>

        <span class="black">Coinbase Address:
        <span id="cb_address" class="c_address"></span></span><br>
        <span class="black">Coinbase Balance:
        <span id="cb_balance"></span> ETH</span><br><br>

        <input type="email" class="form-control"
                 id="email1" placeholder="Email" /><br>

        <input type="text" class="form-control"
                 id="amount" placeholder="Amount" /><br>
        <br><br>

        <button class="btn btn-primary btn-lg"
              onclick="buyCoins();">BUY COINS</button>
        <br><br>
      </div>
      <div id="status"> </div>
    </div>
  </div>
  <script src="jquery.min.js"></script>
  <script src="bootstrap.min.js"></script>
</body>

</html>
```

Box 6.30 shows the Dapp JavaScript (app.js).

■ Box 6.30: SolarCharge Dapp JavaScript

```
var accounts;
var account;
var balance;
var ticketPrice;
var myContractInstance;
```

```
function initializeContract() {
  myContractInstance = SolarCharger.deployed();
  $("#cf_address").html(myContractInstance.address);
  $("#cb_address").html(account);
  refreshVars();
}

function setStatus(message) {
  $("#status").html(message);
};

function refreshBalance() {
  $("#cb_balance").html(web3.fromWei(
      web3.eth.getBalance(web3.eth.coinbase), "ether").toFixed(5));
}

function refreshVars(){
  myContractInstance.numUsers.call().then(
    function(numUsers) {
      $("#cf_users").html(numUsers.toNumber());
      return myContractInstance.numStations.call();
  }).then(
    function(numStations) {
      $("#cf_stations").html(numStations.toNumber());
      return myContractInstance.coinRate.call();
  }).then(
    function(coinRate) {
      $("#cf_rate").html(coinRate.toNumber());
      refreshBalance();
  });
}

function registerUser() {
  var name = $("#name").val();
  var email = $("#email").val();
  setStatus("Initiating transaction... (please wait)");

  myContractInstance.registerUser(email, name,
    { from: web3.eth.coinbase, gas: 2000000}).then(
    function(result) {
      setStatus("Done!");
      refreshVars();
    });
}

function buyCoins() {
  var amount = parseFloat($("#amount").val());
  var email = $("#email1").val();

  setStatus("Initiating transaction... (please wait)");

  myContractInstance.buyCoins(email,
    { from: web3.eth.coinbase, value: amount, gas: 2000000}).then(
    function(result) {
```

```
      setStatus("Done!");
      refreshVars();
    });
  }

  window.onload = function() {
    web3.eth.getAccounts(function(err, accs) {
      if (err != null) {
        alert("There was an error fetching your accounts.");
        return;
      }

      if (accs.length == 0) {
        alert("Couldn't get any accounts!");
        return;
      }
      accounts = accs;
      account = accounts[0];
      initializeContract();
    });
  }
```

Figure 6.22 shows a screenshot of the SolarCharge Dapp.

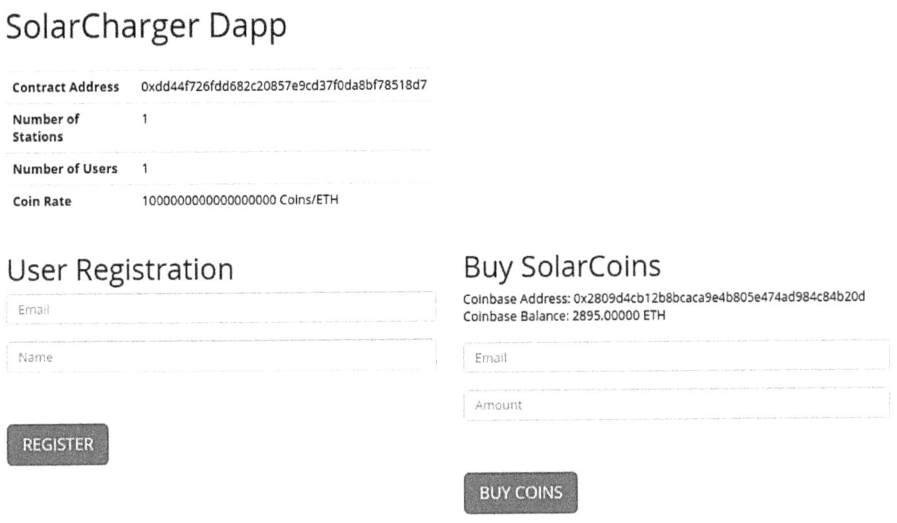

SolarCharger Dapp

Contract Address	0xdd44f726fdd682c20857e9cd37f0da8bf78518d7
Number of Stations	1
Number of Users	1
Coin Rate	1000000000000000000 Coins/ETH

User Registration

Email

Name

REGISTER

Buy SolarCoins

Coinbase Address: 0x2809d4cb12b8bcaca9e4b805e474ad984c84b20d
Coinbase Balance: 2895.00000 ETH

Email

Amount

BUY COINS

Figure 6.22: Screenshot of SolarCharge Dapp

Once a user has registered with SolarCharge contract and purchased SolarCoins, the SolarCharge mobile application can be used to activate a charging station. The user can login into the mobile application with the same email which was used to register with the SolarCharge contract as shown in Figure 6.23(a). Once logged in, the mobile application will show the user details such as name, email, amount paid and SolarCoin balance as shown in Figure 6.23(b).

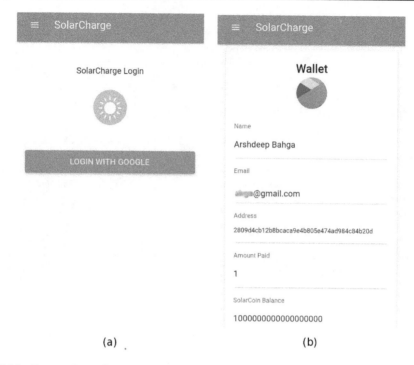

(a)   (b)

Figure 6.23: Screenshot of SolarCharge mobile app: (a) Login page (b) User details page

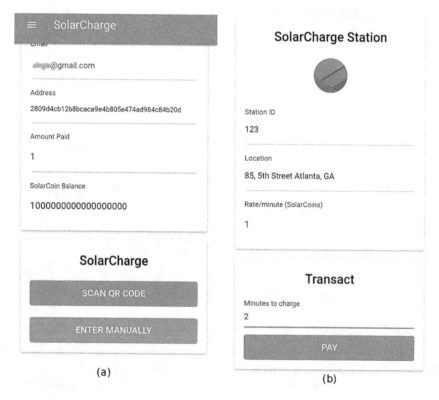

(a)   (b)

Figure 6.24: Screenshot of SolarCharge mobile app: (a) Scanning QR code of station (b) Station details page

Confirm Transaction

SolarCharge

Minutes to charge

2

SolarCoins to Pay

2

CONFIRM TRANSACTION

SolarCharge

Transaction Sent

Transaction ID
'0x228f659da72b6b068451707cdecdbcfaf30d05be561b035cefb8f75dd27c35

Minutes to charge

2

SolarCoins Paid

2

Connect your device to the plug on the charging station. The charging station will activate in a moment.

(a)   (b)

Figure 6.25: Screenshot of SolarCharge mobile app: (a) Confirm transaction page (b) Transaction details page

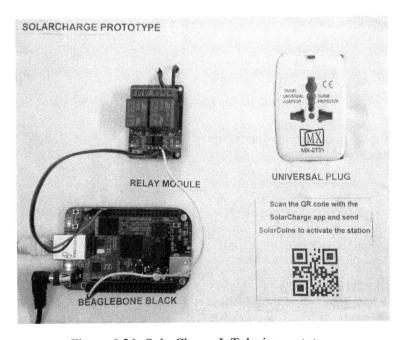

Figure 6.26: SolarCharge IoT device prototype

After logging into the mobile application, the user can scan the QR code of a station (generated from the station ID) or enter the station ID manually as shown in Figure 6.24(a). Next, the user will see the station details page showing station information such as station ID, location, and rate as shown in Figure 6.24(b). From this page, the user can send a transaction to activate the station by specifying the number of minutes. Figure 6.25(a) shows the transaction confirmation page and Figure 6.25(b) shows the transaction details page.

Figure 6.26 shows a picture of the actual SolarCharge prototype device based on Beaglebone black SBC. Box 6.31 shows the python implementation of a controller service that runs on the Beaglebone black SBC in a solar charging station. The controller service periodically polls the '/api/stationstate/' endpoint of the SolarCharge REST web service which returns True if the station is activated or False if the station is deactivated. Based on the return value, the controller toggles the state of the relay module by sending high or low output to the GPIO pin connected to the relay.

■ **Box 6.31: Python controller component that runs on IoT device**

```python
import Adafruit_BBIO.GPIO as GPIO
import time
import requests
import json

stationID='123'
url='http://192.168.1.79:5000/api/stationstate/'+stationID

GPIO.setup("P8_10", GPIO.OUT) #GPIO - 68

onStatus=False

while True:
    r = requests.get(url)
    r = str(r.text)
    result = json.loads(r)

    if (onStatus==False):
        if(result[0]==True):
            print "Switch ON"
            onStatus=True
            GPIO.output("P8_10", GPIO.LOW)
    elif (onStatus==True):
        if(result[0]==False):
            print "Switch OFF"
            onStatus=False
            GPIO.output("P8_10", GPIO.HIGH)

    time.sleep(2)
```

The mobile application and the IoT device make use of the SolarCharge REST web service to obtain user and station information and to activate a station. Box 6.32 shows the Python implementation of REST web service. The web service exposes endpoints to (1) get user information, (2) get station information, (3) get station state, (4) activate a station. While the first three endpoints accept HTTP GET requests, the fourth endpoint for activating a station accepts HTTP POST request. For implementing the web service, we used the Python Flask web framework and EthJsonRpc Python client for Ethereum.

■ Box 6.32: Python implementation of REST web service

```
#!flask/bin/python
from flask import Flask, jsonify, abort,
        request, make_response, url_for

from ethjsonrpc import EthJsonRpc
import time
import datetime

c = EthJsonRpc('127.0.0.1', 8101)

contract_addr = "0xdd44F726FDd682c20857e9CD37F0dA8bf78518D7"
stationID = [123]
balance = c.eth_getBalance(contract_addr)
print "Starting Balance = " + str(balance)


app = Flask(__name__, static_url_path="")

#curl -i http://localhost:5000/api/stationstate/123
@app.route('/api/stationstate/<int:id>', methods=['GET'])
def getStationState(id):
    result = c.call(contract_addr, 'getStationState(uint256)',
                [id], ['bool'])
    return jsonify(result)

#curl -i http://localhost:5000/api/station/123
@app.route('/api/station/<int:id>', methods=['GET'])
def getStation(id):
    result = c.call(contract_addr, 'stations(uint256)',
            [id], ['uint256','string','uint256','uint256','uint256'])
    return jsonify(result)

#curl -i http://localhost:5000/api/user/abc@gmail.com
@app.route('/api/user/<string:email>', methods=['GET'])
def getUser(email):
    result = c.call(contract_addr, 'getUser(string)', [email],
            ['string','address','uint256','uint256'])
    return jsonify(result)


#curl -i -H "Content-Type: application/json" -X POST -d
#'{"email": "abc@gmail.com", "ID": 123, "duration": 30}'
#http://localhost:5000/api/activateStation
@app.route('/api/activateStation', methods=['POST'])
def activateStation():
    if not request.json:
        abort(400)

    print request.json
```

```
     email = request.json['email']
     ID = request.json['ID']
     duration = request.json['duration']

     result = c.call_with_transaction(c.eth_coinbase(),
              contract_addr, 'activateStation(string,uint256,uint256)',
              [email,ID,duration], gas=300000)

     return jsonify(result)

if __name__ == '__main__':
    app.run(debug=True, host="0.0.0.0", port=5000)
```

The mobile application is implemented using the Apache Cordova framework [37]. Cordova is an open-source mobile development framework that allows you to use standard web technologies such as HTML5, CSS3, and JavaScript for cross-platform mobile application development. Boxes 6.33, 6.34, 6.35, 6.36, 6.37 show the HTML source code for the login page, user details page, contract details page, confirmation page, and transaction details page respectively.

■ **Box 6.33: SolarCharge mobile app - login page HTML**

```
<html>
<head>
  <title>SolarCharge</title>
  <link rel="stylesheet" href="./css/font-awesome.min.css" />
  <link rel="stylesheet" href="./css/jquery.mobile.min.css" />
  <link rel="stylesheet" href="./css/nativedroid2.css" />
</head>

<body>
  <div data-role="page" class="nd2-no-menu-swipe">
    <nd2-include data-src="panel.left.html"></nd2-include>

    <div data-role="header" data-position="fixed" class="wow fadeIn">
      <a href="#leftpanel" class="ui-btn ui-btn-left wow fadeIn"
          data-wow-delay='0.8s'><i class="zmdi zmdi-menu"></i></a>
      <h1 class="wow fadeIn" data-wow-delay='0.4s'>SolarCharge</h1>
    </div>

    <div role="main" class="ui-content wow fadeIn"
        data-inset="false" data-wow-delay="0.2s">
    <form>
      <div class="row">
        <div class="col-xs-12 col-sm-6 col-md-4">
          <div class="box">
            <center>
              <h5>SolarCharge Login</h5>
              <img class="profile-thumbnail"
              src="./img/icon.png" width="20%" />
```

```
                    <h4 class="clr-red" id="loginmessage"></h4>
                    <br>
                </center>
                <a href="#" id="loginwithgoogle"
                    class="ui-btn ui-btn-raised clr-primary">
                    Login with Google</a>
            </div>
        </div>
    </div>
    </form>
    </div>
</div>
<script src="./js/jquery.min.js"></script>
<script src="./js/jquery-ui.min.js"></script>
<script src="./js/jquery.mobile.min.js"></script>
<script src="./js/nativedroid2.js"></script>
<script src="nd2settings.js"></script>
<script type="text/javascript" src="cordova.js"></script>
</body>
</html>
```

■ **Box 6.34: SolarCharge mobile app - user details page HTML**

```
<html>
<head>
  <title>SolarCharge</title>
  <link rel="stylesheet" href="./css/font-awesome.min.css" />
  <link rel="stylesheet" href="./css/jquery.mobile.min.css" />
  <link rel="stylesheet" href="./css/nativedroid2.css" />
  <script src="cordova.js"></script>
</head>

<body>
  <div data-role="page">
    <nd2-include data-src="panel.left.html"></nd2-include>
    <div data-role="header" data-position="fixed">
      <a href="#leftpanel" class="ui-btn ui-btn-left">
      <i class="zmdi zmdi-menu"></i></a>
      <h1>SolarCharge</h1>
    </div>

    <div role="main" class="ui-content" data-inset="false">
      <div class="nd2-card">
        <div class="card-title has-supporting-text">
          <center>
            <h4 class="card-primary-title clr-black">Wallet</h4>
            <img class="profile-thumbnail" id="profileimg"
                src="./img/profile.png" width="20%" />
          </center>
          <br>
          <label>Name</label>
          <p id="username"></p>
```

```html
        <center>
          <hr width="98%">
        </center>
        <label>Email</label>
        <p id="useremail"></p>
        <center>
          <hr width="98%">
        </center>
        <label>Address</label>
        <p id="address" style="font-size:12px"></p>
        <center>
          <hr width="98%">
        </center>
        <label>Amount Paid</label>
        <p id="amountpaid"></p>
        <center>
          <hr width="98%">
        </center>
        <label>SolarCoin Balance</label>
        <p id="balance"></p>
      </div>
    </div>

    <div class="nd2-card">
      <div class="card-title has-supporting-text">
        <center>
          <h4 class="card-primary-title clr-black">SolarCharge</h4>
        </center>
        <br>
        <a href="#" id="btnbarcode"
           class="ui-btn clr-btn-blue">Scan QR Code</a><br>
        <a href="#" id="btnmanual"
           class="ui-btn clr-btn-green">Enter Manually</a>

      </div>
    </div>

  </div>

</div>

<script src="./js/jquery.min.js"></script>
<script src="./js/jquery.mobile.min.js"></script>
<script src="./js/nativedroid2.js"></script>
<script src="nd2settings.js"></script>

<script>
  $(document).on('pagebeforecreate', '[data-role="page"]', function() {
    setTimeout(function() {
      $.mobile.loading('show');
    }, 1);
  });

  $(document).on('pageshow', '[data-role="page"]', function() {
```

```
        setTimeout(function() {
          $.mobile.loading('hide');
        }, 1);
      });
  </script>

  <script>
    $(document).ready(function() {
      var useremail = sessionStorage.getItem('useremail');
      var username = sessionStorage.getItem('username');
      var userimg = sessionStorage.getItem('userimg');
      var userdata = JSON.parse(sessionStorage.getItem('userdata'));
      $('#useremail').html(useremail);
      $('#username').html(userdata[0]);
      $('#address').html(userdata[1]);
      $('#amountpaid').html(userdata[2]);
      $('#balance').html(userdata[3]);
    });
  </script>
</body>

</html>
```

■ **Box 6.35: SolarCharge mobile app - contract details page HTML**

```
<html>
<head>
  <title>SolarCharge</title>
  <link rel="stylesheet" href="./css/font-awesome.min.css" />
  <link rel="stylesheet" href="./css/jquery.mobile.min.css" />
  <link rel="stylesheet" href="./css/nativedroid2.css" />
  <script src="cordova.js"></script>
</head>

<body>
  <div data-role="page">
    <nd2-include data-src="panel.left.html"></nd2-include>
    <div data-role="header" data-position="fixed">
      <a href="#leftpanel" class="ui-btn ui-btn-left">
      <i class="zmdi zmdi-menu"></i></a>
      <h1>SolarCharge</h1>
    </div>

    <div role="main" class="ui-content" data-inset="false">
      <div class="nd2-card">
        <div class="card-title has-supporting-text">
          <center>
            <h4 class="card-primary-title clr-black">
                SolarCharge Station</h4><br>
            <img class="profile-thumbnail"
                src="./img/profile1.png" width="20%" />
```

```
          </center>
          <br>
          <label>Station ID</label>
          <p id="stationID" style="font-size:14px"></p>
          <center>
            <hr width="98%">
          </center>
          <label>Location</label>
          <p id="location" style="font-size:14px"></p>
          <center>
            <hr width="98%">
          </center>
          <label>Rate/minute (SolarCoins)</label>
          <p id="rate"></p>
        </div>
      </div>


      <div class="nd2-card">
        <div class="card-title has-supporting-text">
          <center>
            <h4 class="card-primary-title clr-black">Transact</h4>
          </center>
          <br>
          <label>Minutes to charge</label>
          <input type="text" name="minutes" id="minutes" value=""
              data-clear-btn="true" placeholder="">
          <a href="#" id="btnpay" class="ui-btn clr-btn-blue">Pay</a>

        </div>
      </div>

    </div>

</div>
<script src="./js/jquery.min.js"></script>
<script src="./js/jquery.mobile.min.js"></script>
<script src="./js/nativedroid2.js"></script>
<script src="nd2settings.js"></script>

<script>
  $(document).on('pagebeforecreate', '[data-role="page"]', function() {
    setTimeout(function() {
      $.mobile.loading('show');
    }, 1);
  });

  $(document).on('pageshow', '[data-role="page"]', function() {
    setTimeout(function() {
      $.mobile.loading('hide');
    }, 1);
  });
</script>

<script>
```

```
    $(document).ready(function() {
      var address = sessionStorage.getItem('qrcode');
      var stationdata = JSON.parse(sessionStorage.getItem('stationdata'));
      $('#stationID').html(address);
      $('#rate').html(stationdata[0]);
      $('#location').html(stationdata[1]);
    });
  </script>
</body>
</html>
```

■ Box 6.36: SolarCharge mobile app - transaction confirmation page HTML

```
<html>
<head>
  <title>SolarCharge</title>
  <link rel="stylesheet" href="./css/font-awesome.min.css" />
  <link rel="stylesheet" href="./css/jquery.mobile.min.css" />
  <link rel="stylesheet" href="./css/nativedroid2.css" />
  <script src="cordova.js"></script>
</head>

<body>
  <div data-role="page">
    <nd2-include data-src="panel.left.html"></nd2-include>
    <div data-role="header" data-position="fixed">
      <a href="#leftpanel" class="ui-btn ui-btn-left">
      <i class="zmdi zmdi-menu"></i></a>
      <h1>SolarCharge</h1>
    </div>

    <div role="main" class="ui-content" data-inset="false">
      <div class="nd2-card">
        <div class="card-title has-supporting-text">
          <center>
            <h4 class="card-primary-title clr-black">Confirm
            Transaction</h4>
            <br>
            <img class="profile-thumbnail"
              src="./img/profile.png" width="20%" />
            <img class="profile-thumbnail"
              src="./img/arrow.png" width="20%" />
            <img class="profile-thumbnail"
              src="./img/profile1.png" width="20%" />

          </center>
          <br>
          <label>Minutes to charge</label>
          <p id="minutes"></p>
          <center>
            <hr width="98%">
          </center>
```

```
              <label>SolarCoins to Pay</label>
              <p id="amount"></p>
              <center>
                <hr width="98%">
              </center>
              <br>
              <a href="#" id="btnconfirm" class="ui-btn clr-btn-blue">Confirm
              Transaction</a>
          </div>
        </div>
      </div>
    </div>

    <script src="./js/jquery.min.js"></script>
    <script src="./js/jquery.mobile.min.js"></script>
    <script src="./js/nativedroid2.js"></script>
    <script src="nd2settings.js"></script>

    <script>
      $(document).on('pagebeforecreate', '[data-role="page"]', function() {
        setTimeout(function() {
          $.mobile.loading('show');
        }, 1);
      });

      $(document).on('pageshow', '[data-role="page"]', function() {
        setTimeout(function() {
          $.mobile.loading('hide');
        }, 1);
      });
    </script>

    <script>
      $(document).ready(function() {
        var amount = sessionStorage.getItem('amount');
        $('#amount').html(amount);
        var minutes = sessionStorage.getItem('minutes');
        $('#minutes').html(minutes);
      });
    </script>
  </body>
</html>
```

■ **Box 6.37: SolarCharge mobile app - transaction details page HTML**

```
<html>
<head>
  <title>SolarCharge</title>
  <link rel="stylesheet" href="./css/font-awesome.min.css" />
  <link rel="stylesheet" href="./css/jquery.mobile.min.css" />
  <link rel="stylesheet" href="./css/nativedroid2.css" />
  <script src="cordova.js"></script>
```

```
</head>

<body>
  <div data-role="page">
    <nd2-include data-src="panel.left.html"></nd2-include>
    <div data-role="header" data-position="fixed">
      <a href="#leftpanel" class="ui-btn ui-btn-left">
      <i class="zmdi zmdi-menu"></i></a>
      <h1>SolarCharge</h1>
    </div>

    <div role="main" class="ui-content" data-inset="false">
      <div class="nd2-card">
        <div class="card-title has-supporting-text">
          <center>
            <h4 class="card-primary-title clr-black">
              Transaction Sent</h4>
            <br>
            <img class="profile-thumbnail"
                src="./img/tick.png" width="30%" />

          </center>

          <label>Transaction ID</label>
          <p id="txdata" style="font-size:9px"></p>
          <center>
            <hr width="98%">
          </center>
          <label>Minutes to charge</label>
          <p id="minutes"></p>
          <center>
            <hr width="98%">
          </center>
          <label>SolarCoins Paid</label>
          <p id="amount"></p>
          <center>
            <hr width="98%">
          </center>

          <p>Connect your device to the plug on the charging station.
          The charging station will activate in a moment. </p>
          <br>
          <center>
            <img class="profile-thumbnail"
              src="./img/switch.png" width="20%" />
            <img class="profile-thumbnail"
              src="./img/arrow.png" width="20%" />
            <img class="profile-thumbnail"
              src="./img/plug.png" width="20%" />
          </center>
          <br>

        </div>
      </div>
```

```
      </div>

   </div>

   <script src="./js/jquery.min.js"></script>
   <script src="./js/jquery.mobile.min.js"></script>
   <script src="./js/nativedroid2.js"></script>
   <script src="nd2settings.js"></script>

   <script>
     $(document).on('pagebeforecreate', '[data-role="page"]', function() {
       setTimeout(function() {
         $.mobile.loading('show');
       }, 1);
     });

     $(document).on('pageshow', '[data-role="page"]', function() {
       setTimeout(function() {
         $.mobile.loading('hide');
       }, 1);
     });
   </script>

   <script>
     $(document).ready(function() {
       var amount = sessionStorage.getItem('amount');
       $('#amount').html(amount);
       var minutes = sessionStorage.getItem('minutes');
       $('#minutes').html(minutes);
       var txdata = sessionStorage.getItem('txdata');
       $('#txdata').html(txdata);
     });
   </script>
</body>

</html>
```

Box 6.38 shows the JavaScript code for the mobile application. For the mobile application, we use the jQuery Mobile JavaScript library and *nativeDroid2* which is a material design theme for jQuery Mobile. In the JavaScript code, we use *jQuery.ajax()* method to send asynchronous HTTP requests to the SolarCharge REST web service. To enable the 'Login with Google' feature, we use the Cordova plugin *cordova-plugin-googleplus*. To enable scanning of QR code we use the *cordova-plugin-barcodeScanner* plugin.

■ **Box 6.38: SolarCharge mobile app JavaScript**

```
var postURL = 'http://192.168.1.79:5000';

function scanBarcode() {
  cordova.plugins.barcodeScanner.scan(
    function(result) {
```

```
      if (result.cancelled == false) {
         sessionStorage.setItem('qrcode', result.text);
         var stationID = result.text;
         $.ajax({
           url: postURL + '/api/station/' + stationID,
           method: 'GET',
           crossDomain: true,
           dataType: 'json',
           contentType: "application/json; charset=utf-8",
           success: function(data) {
             sessionStorage.setItem('stationdata', JSON.stringify(data));
             var stationdata = JSON.parse(
                             sessionStorage.getItem('stationdata'));
             sessionStorage.setItem('rate', stationdata[0]);
             sessionStorage.setItem('location', stationdata[1]);

             console.log(data);
             location.href = 'contract.html';
           },
           error: function() {
             console.log("Error");
           }
         });
      }
   },
   function(error) {
     $('#blemessage').html('QR code scanning failed: ' + error);
   }, {
     "preferFrontCamera": false,
     "showFlipCameraButton": true,
     "prompt": "Place a QR inside the scan area",
     "formats": "QR_CODE",
     "orientation": "portrait"
   }
 );
}

function transactionConfirm() {

  location.href = 'confirm.html';
}

function transactPage() {
  var minutes = parseFloat($('#minutes').val());
  var rate = sessionStorage.getItem('rate');
  var amount = minutes * rate;
  sessionStorage.setItem('amount', amount);
  sessionStorage.setItem('minutes', minutes);

  location.href = 'transact.html';
}

function onDeviceReady() {
  window.StatusBar.backgroundColorByHexString("#ff5722");
```

```
}

function transactionConfirm() {
  var email = sessionStorage.getItem('useremail');
  var ID = parseFloat(sessionStorage.getItem('qrcode'));
  var duration = parseFloat(sessionStorage.getItem('minutes')) * 60;
  var datadir = {
    email: email,
    ID: ID,
    duration: duration
  };
  console.log(datadir);
  $.ajax({
    url: postURL + '/api/activateStation',
    method: 'POST',
    crossDomain: true,
    dataType: 'json',
    contentType: "application/json; charset=utf-8",
    success: function(data) {
      sessionStorage.setItem('txdict', JSON.stringify(datadir));
      sessionStorage.setItem('txdata', JSON.stringify(data));
      location.href = 'confirm.html';
    },
    error: function() {
      console.log("Failed");
    },
    data: JSON.stringify(datadir)
  });
}

function isAvailable() {
  window.plugins.googleplus.isAvailable(function(avail) {
    alert(avail)
  });
}

function login() {
  $('#loginmessage').html("Logging in...");
  window.plugins.googleplus.login({},
    function(obj) {
      $('#loginmessage').html(obj.email + ' - ' + obj.displayName);
      sessionStorage.setItem('userimg', obj.imageUrl);
      sessionStorage.setItem('username', obj.displayName);
      sessionStorage.setItem('useremail', obj.email);
      var emailid = obj.email;
      $.ajax({
        url: postURL + '/api/user/' + emailid,
        method: 'GET',
        crossDomain: true,
        dataType: 'json',
        contentType: "application/json; charset=utf-8",
        success: function(data) {
          sessionStorage.setItem('userdata', JSON.stringify(data));
          //console.log(data);
```

```
            $('#loginmessage').html("Success");
            location.href = 'home.html';
        },
        error: function() {
          $('#loginmessage').html("Error");
        }
      });
    },
    function(msg) {
      $('#loginmessage').html(msg);
    }
  );
}

function trySilentLogin() {
  window.plugins.googleplus.trySilentLogin({},
    function(obj) {
      //console.log(obj.email);
    },
    function(msg) {
      //console.log(msg);
    }
  );
}

function logout() {
  window.plugins.googleplus.logout(
    function(msg) {
      //console.log(msg);
    },
    function(msg) {
      //console.log(msg);
    }
  );
}

$(document).ready(function() {
  document.addEventListener('deviceready', onDeviceReady, false);

  $("#btnbarcode").on('click', function(e) {
    e.preventDefault();
    scanBarcode();
  });

  $("#btnpay").on('click', function(e) {
    e.preventDefault();
    transactPage();
  });

  $("#btnconfirm").on('click', function(e) {
    e.preventDefault();
    transactionConfirm();
  });
```

```
  $("#loginwithgoogle").on('click', function(e) {
    e.preventDefault();
    login();
  });

  $("#logout").on('click', function(e) {
    e.preventDefault();
    logout();
  });
});


$(document).on('pagebeforecreate', '[data-role="page"]', function() {
  setTimeout(function() {
    $.mobile.loading('show');
  }, 1);
});

$(document).on('pageshow', '[data-role="page"]', function() {
  setTimeout(function() {
    $.mobile.loading('hide');
  }, 1);
});
```

Box 6.39 shows the commands for setting up Cordova, installing the required libraries and plugins, creating mobile application project, and building the mobile application for the Android platform.

■ Box 6.39: Working with Codova

```
#Install Cordova
sudo npm install -g cordova

#Install jQuery Mobile
sudo npm install -g jquery-mobile

#Install nativeDroid2
sudo npm install -g bower
bower install nativeDroid2

#Create Cordova app project
cordova create solarcharge
cd solarcharge

#Add Android platform to the project
cordova platform add android --save

#Install cordova plugins
cordova plugin add cordova-plugin-googleplus
cordova plugin add cordova-plugin-barcodescanner

#Build application
cordova build android
```

Summary

In this chapter, we described the structure of a Decentralized Application (Dapp) and how to implement and deploy Dapps. The difference between Dapps and cloud applications is that unlike cloud applications, Dapps are decentralized in nature with no single entity or organization controlling the infrastructure on which the applications are deployed. The Dapp logic is controlled by the associated smart contracts which are deployed on the blockchain platform. Dapps provide user-friendly interfaces to smart contracts, where the users can submit transactions to the contracts from a web interface. A Dapp can be accessed in a browser using the URL or the address of the server from which it is served. Next, we described the Dapp creation workflow and how frameworks such as Truffle can be used to simplify the steps involved in implementing, deploying and serving Dapps. Next, we described various Dapp case studies. For each Dapp case study we described the implementation of the associated smart contracts (implemented in Solidity), web interface (implemented using HTML, CSS and JavaScript) and the Dapp JavaScript for interacting with smart contracts (implemented using the Web3 JavaScript API).

Summary

7 - Mining

This chapter covers

- Consensus on Blockchain Network
- Mining Steps
  - Determine Uncles
  - Determine and Process Transactions
  - Apply Mining Rewards
  - Compute Mining Proof of Work
- Block Validation
- Setting up Mining Node
- State Storage in Ethereum
  - World State
  - Transactions List
  - Transaction Receipts
  - Modified Merkle Patricia Tree

In Ethereum-based blockchain networks, mining is a process in which new blocks are produced and added to the blockchain. In the previous chapters, we looked at two types of transactions that can be sent on the Ethereum network: (1) transactions to transfer Ether from one externally owned account to another and (2) transactions sent to smart contracts. When a transaction is sent on the blockchain network, it is combined with other pending transactions into a block. The peers in the blockchain network who perform the mining operations are called miners. The miners validate the transactions and reach a consensus on the block that should be added next to the blockchain. The newly mined block (called the winning block) is then broadcast to the entire network. Miners are given incentives, in the form of Ether, for performing the mining operations. Miners compete to do a complex mathematical computation, and the node that wins, earns a reward in Ether. Miners produce blocks which are verified by other miners for validity. A valid block is one which contains a proof-of-work (PoW) of a given difficulty. In this chapter, you will learn about the concepts related to mining on the Ethereum blockchain network and how to setup your own mining node.

7.1   Consensus on Blockchain Network

Ethereum blockchain network is a distributed environment, in which no trusted central authority or service is needed to establish consensus among the participating nodes in the network. The nodes, themselves, need to agree on the transactions and the order in which they are processed. In the absence of a consensus mechanism, the nodes can have different views of the state of the network. Ethereum uses a distributed and decentralized consensus mechanism in which the nodes assemble the transactions into blocks and compete with each other (by performing computationally expensive calculations) to get their blocks added next to the blockchain. The consensus is based on choosing a block that has the most computation done upon it (i.e., the block with the highest total difficulty). The blocks produced by the miners are checked by other participating nodes for validity.

7.2   Mining

Miners produce blocks which are checked for validity by other participating nodes. The process of finalizing a block during mining involves the following stages:

7.2.1   Stage-1: Determine Uncles

Uncles are stale blocks which are descendants of the current block's ancestors (up to Nth-generation, where $N \leq 6$). In other words, uncles are blocks whose parents are ancestors of the current block. Ethereum allows a maximum of two uncles per block. Uncles are included in a block to increase network security as described in Chapter-10.

7.2.2   Stage-2: Determine and Process Transactions

When the process for mining the next block on the chain is initiated by the Ethereum network, all the transactions received since the last block was mined are collected and added to a list of pending transactions for the next block. Next, a new block is initialized based on a parent block. While initializing the block, the block header is created with the following fields:

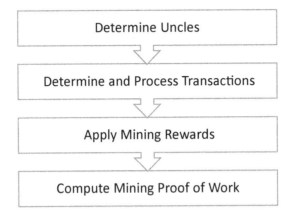

Figure 7.1: Steps involved in mining on Ethereum network

- **Block Number** *(number)*: This is a scalar value equal to the number of ancestors of the block. For genesis block, the block number is zero.
- **Timestamp** *(timestamp)*: This is the UNIX timestamp value at the creation of the block.
- **Nonce** *(nonce)*: The nonce field is a 64-bit hash, which along with mixhash field is used to verify that a sufficient amount of computation has been carried out on this block, and the block contains a valid proof-of-work (PoW).
- **Mix Hash** *(mixhash)*: The mixhash field is a 256-bit hash, which along with nonce field is used to verify that the block contains a valid proof-of-work.
- **Parent Hash** *(prevhash)*: Each block in a blockchain is linked to its parent through the parentHash, which is the hash of the parent block header.
- **Coinbase Address** *(coinbase)*: This is a 20-byte address of the account to which all the rewards for mining of the block and the execution of contracts are transferred.
- **Block Difficulty** *(difficulty)*: This field specifies a difficulty value for mining. A block is valid only if it contains a valid proof-of-work (PoW) of a given difficulty.
- **Gas Limit** *(gas_limit)*: The gas limit value is the limit of gas expenditure for the block.
- **Gas Used** *(gas_used)*: This is the total gas used for all the transactions in the block.
- **Extra Data** *(extra_data)*: Optional 32-byte extra data can be provided in the block.
- **Uncles Hash** *(uncles_hash)*: This is the 32 byte hash of the RLP encoded list of uncle headers.
- **State Root** *(state_root)*: This is the 32 byte hash of the root of the block's state trie after the transactions are executed.
- **Transactions List Root** *(tx_list_root)*: This is the 32 byte hash of the root of the block's transaction trie which is populated with the transactions in the block.
- **Receipts Root** *(receipts_root)*: This is the 32 byte hash of the root of the block's receipts trie which is populated with the receipts of the transaction in the transactions list of the block.
- **Bloom Filter** *(bloom)*: Bloom filter composed from the set of logs created through execution of the transactions in the block.

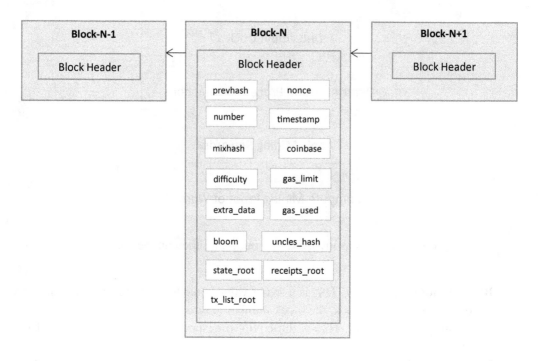

Figure 7.2: A blockchain showing three blocks. Also shown are the fields in the block header.

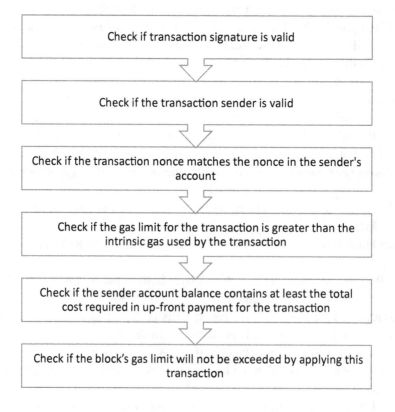

Figure 7.3: Steps involved in transaction validation

Box 7.1 shows the Python function for initializing a block based on its parent (excerpt taken from the pyethereum source).

■ Box 7.1: Python function for initializing a block based on its parent (code excerpt from pyethereum file - block.py)

```
def init_from_parent(cls, parent, coinbase, nonce=b'', extra_data=b'',
                     timestamp=int(time.time()), uncles=[], env=None):
    """Create a new block based on a parent block.

    The block will not include any transactions and will not be finalized.
    """
    header = BlockHeader(prevhash=parent.hash,
                         uncles_hash=utils.sha3(rlp.encode(uncles)),
                         coinbase=coinbase,
                         state_root=parent.state_root,
                         tx_list_root=trie.BLANK_ROOT,
                         receipts_root=trie.BLANK_ROOT,
                         bloom=0,
                         difficulty=calc_difficulty(parent, timestamp),
                         mixhash='',
                         number=parent.number + 1,
                         gas_limit=calc_gaslimit(parent),
                         gas_used=0,
                         timestamp=timestamp,
                         extra_data=extra_data,
                         nonce=nonce)
    block = Block(header, [], uncles, env=env or parent.env,
                  parent=parent, making=True)
    block.ancestor_hashes = [parent.hash] + parent.ancestor_hashes
    block.log_listeners = parent.log_listeners
    return block
```

Figure 7.2 shows the fields in the block header. At this step, the block does not include any transactions and the state of the block is not yet finalized. The *nonce* and *mixhash* fields are set to blank at this stage. Next, the list of transactions for this block is validated and added to the transaction trie of the block. For validating the transactions, various checks are performed as follows:

1. Check if the transaction signature is valid.
2. Check if the transaction sender is valid.
3. Check if the transaction *nonce* matches the *nonce* in the sender's account.
4. Check if the gas limit for the transaction is greater than the intrinsic gas used by the transaction
5. Check if the sender account balance contains at least the total cost required in up-front payment for the transaction (*startgas * gasprice*).
6. Check if the block's gas limit will not be exceeded by applying this transaction.

Box 7.2 shows the Python function for transaction validation (excerpt taken from the pyethereum source).

**■ Box 7.2: Python function for transaction validation
(code excerpt from pyethereum file - processblock.py)**

```python
def validate_transaction(block, tx):

  def rp(what, actual, target):
    return '%r: %r actual:%r target:%r' % (tx, what, actual, target)

  # (1) The transaction signature is valid;
  # sender is set and validated on Transaction initialization
  if not tx.sender:
    if block.number >= config.default_config["METROPOLIS_FORK_BLKNUM"]:
      tx._sender = normalize_address(
                   config.default_config["METROPOLIS_ENTRY_POINT"])
    else:
      raise UnsignedTransaction(tx)
  if block.number >= config.default_config["HOMESTEAD_FORK_BLKNUM"]:
      tx.check_low_s()

  # (2) the transaction nonce is valid (equivalent to the
  #   sender account's current nonce);
  acctnonce = block.get_nonce(tx.sender)
  if acctnonce != tx.nonce:
    raise InvalidNonce(rp('nonce', tx.nonce, acctnonce))

  # (3) the gas limit is no smaller than the intrinsic gas,
  # g0, used by the transaction;
  if tx.startgas < tx.intrinsic_gas_used:
    raise InsufficientStartGas(rp('startgas',
              tx.startgas, tx.intrinsic_gas_used))

  # (4) the sender account balance contains at least the
  # cost, v0, required in up-front payment.
  total_cost = tx.value + tx.gasprice * tx.startgas
  if block.get_balance(tx.sender) < total_cost:
    raise InsufficientBalance(rp('balance',
              block.get_balance(tx.sender), total_cost))

  # check block gas limit
  if block.gas_used + tx.startgas > block.gas_limit:
    raise BlockGasLimitReached(rp('gaslimit',
              block.gas_used + tx.startgas, block.gas_limit))

  return True
```

Next, the state transition function is executed, where the pending transactions are applied to the current state, to determine the new state of the network. The state transition function performs the following tasks:

1. Validate transactions as described above.
2. Calculate the total fee for the transaction (*=startgas * gasprice*) and subtract the fee

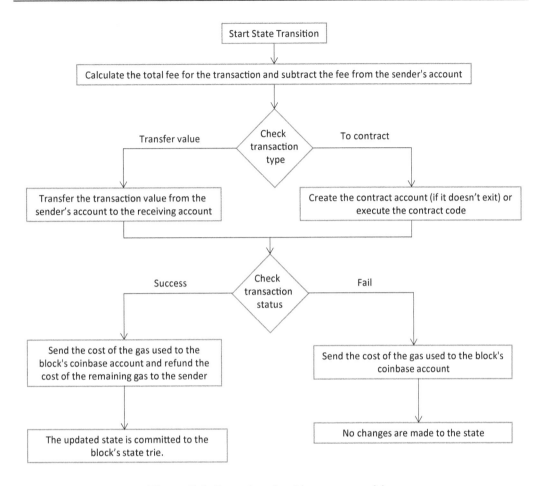

Figure 7.4: Steps involved in state transition

from the sender's account.

3. If the transaction is to transfer value from the sender account to another account, then transfer the transaction value from the sender's account to the receiving account. If the receiving account does not exist then create the account (as this is a contract creation transaction). If the transaction is sent to a contract account then, execute the contract code.

4. If the transaction succeeds, send the cost of the gas used (*gasprice * gas_used*) to the block's coinbase account and refund the cost of the remaining gas (*gasprice * gas_remained*) to the sender. However, if the transaction fails (or runs out of gas), send the cost of the gas used (*gasprice * gas_used*) to the block's coinbase account.

5. If the transaction fails, no changes are made to the state. If the transaction succeeds, the updated state is committed to the block's state trie.

Box 7.3 shows the Python function for performing a state transition (excerpt taken from the pyethereum source).

■ Box 7.3: Python function for state transition (code excerpt from pyethereum file - processblock.py)

```python
def apply_transaction(block, tx):
  validate_transaction(block, tx)

  # print(block.get_nonce(tx.sender), '@@@')

  def rp(what, actual, target):
    return '%r: %r actual:%r target:%r' % (tx, what, actual, target)

  intrinsic_gas = tx.intrinsic_gas_used
  if block.number >= block.config['HOMESTEAD_FORK_BLKNUM']:
    assert tx.s * 2 < transactions.secpk1n
    if not tx.to or tx.to == CREATE_CONTRACT_ADDRESS:
      intrinsic_gas += opcodes.CREATE[3]
      if tx.startgas < intrinsic_gas:
        raise InsufficientStartGas(rp('startgas',
              tx.startgas, intrinsic_gas))

  log_tx.debug('TX NEW', tx_dict=tx.log_dict())
  # start transacting #################
  block.increment_nonce(tx.sender)

  # buy startgas
  assert block.get_balance(tx.sender) >= tx.startgas * tx.gasprice
  block.delta_balance(tx.sender, -tx.startgas * tx.gasprice)
  message_gas = tx.startgas - intrinsic_gas
  message_data = vm.CallData([safe_ord(x) for x in tx.data],
                             0, len(tx.data))
  message = vm.Message(tx.sender, tx.to, tx.value, message_gas,
                       message_data, code_address=tx.to)

  # MESSAGE
  ext = VMExt(block, tx)
  if tx.to and tx.to != CREATE_CONTRACT_ADDRESS:
    result, gas_remained, data = apply_msg(ext, message)
    log_tx.debug('_res_', result=result, gas_remained=gas_remained,
              data=lazy_safe_encode(data))
  else:  # CREATE
    result, gas_remained, data = create_contract(ext, message)
    assert utils.is_numeric(gas_remained)
    log_tx.debug('_create_', result=result, gas_remained=gas_remained,
              data=lazy_safe_encode(data))

  assert gas_remained >= 0

  log_tx.debug("TX APPLIED", result=result, gas_remained=gas_remained,
        data=lazy_safe_encode(data))

  if not result:  # 0 = OOG failure in both cases
```

```
    log_tx.debug('TX FAILED', reason='out of gas',
            startgas=tx.startgas, gas_remained=gas_remained)
    block.gas_used += tx.startgas
    block.delta_balance(block.coinbase, tx.gasprice * tx.startgas)
    output = b''
    success = 0
else:
    log_tx.debug('TX SUCCESS', data=lazy_safe_encode(data))
    gas_used = tx.startgas - gas_remained
    block.refunds += len(set(block.suicides)) * opcodes.GSUICIDEREFUND
    if block.refunds > 0:
        log_tx.debug('Refunding', gas_refunded=min(block.refunds,
                                          gas_used // 2))
        gas_remained += min(block.refunds, gas_used // 2)
        gas_used -= min(block.refunds, gas_used // 2)
        block.refunds = 0
    # sell remaining gas
    block.delta_balance(tx.sender, tx.gasprice * gas_remained)
    block.delta_balance(block.coinbase, tx.gasprice * gas_used)
    block.gas_used += gas_used
    if tx.to:
        output = b''.join(map(ascii_chr, data))
    else:
        output = data
    success = 1
block.commit_state()
suicides = block.suicides
block.suicides = []
for s in suicides:
    block.ether_delta -= block.get_balance(s)
    block.set_balance(s, 0)
    block.del_account(s)
block.add_transaction_to_list(tx)
block.logs = []
return success, output
```

Next, the block is finalized and the mining rewards are applied.

7.2.3 Stage-3: Apply Mining Rewards

Miners in the Ethereum network are rewarded for dedicating their computational resources for maintaining the network and mining new blocks. A successful miner, whose block is selected to be added next on the blockchain, is rewarded with a static block reward ($R_b =$ 5 Ether). In addition to the static reward, the miner also gets the cost of the gas consumed within the block (where *gasCost = gasPrice * gasConsumed*). For every uncle (stale block) included a block, the miner of the block gets an extra reward of 1/32 per uncle (or 3.125% of the static reward). The mining rewards are the only mechanism by which the wealth is distributed (in the form of Ether) post the launch of Ethereum. Box 7.4 shows the Python function for applying mining rewards (excerpt taken from the pyethereum source).

■ **Box 7.4: Python function for applying mining rewards (code excerpt from pyethereum file - block.py)**

```python
def finalize(self):
    """Apply rewards and commit."""
    delta = int(self.config['BLOCK_REWARD'] +
        self.config['NEPHEW_REWARD'] * len(self.uncles))

    self.delta_balance(self.coinbase, delta)
    self.ether_delta += delta

    br = self.config['BLOCK_REWARD']
    udpf = self.config['UNCLE_DEPTH_PENALTY_FACTOR']

    for uncle in self.uncles:
        r = int(br * (udpf + uncle.number - self.number) // udpf)

        self.delta_balance(uncle.coinbase, r)
        self.ether_delta += r
    self.commit_state()
```

7.2.4 Stage-4: Compute Mining Proof-of-Work

In Ethereum, the mining proof-of-work (PoW) is a cryptographically secure *nonce* that proves that a certain amount of work was done to find the *nonce* input to the PoW algorithm. The PoW algorithm used in Ethereum is called Ethash.

Ethash: Mining Proof-of-Work Algorithm

Ethash is the mining proof-of-work (PoW) algorithm used in Ethereum. Ethash finds an *nonce* input to the algorithm so that the result is below a certain difficulty threshold. Ethash builds on two key algorithms: (1) Dagger [39] algorithm (introduced by Vitalik Buterin) and (2) Hashimoto [40] algorithm (introduced by Thaddeus Dryja). Though originally called the Dagger-Hashimoto algorithm, the Ethereum PoW algorithm is no longer called so because many features of both algorithms have been changed.

Before going into the details of the Ethash algorithm, let us first look at the key design considerations for a PoW algorithm.

1. **ASIC resistance**: The PoW algorithm should be resistant to application-specific integrated circuits (ASICs). ASICs are specialized hardware designed to perform a specific task. ASICs can be thousands of times more efficient than general purpose hardware. One of the limitations of the Bitcoin cryptocurrency network has been the use of ASICs by miners. A PoW algorithm that benefits from the use of ASICs can compromise the network security, as a powerful group of miners can make use of ASICs to gain a significant amount of the network's total mining power. The Ethereum PoW algorithm was designed to minimize the rewards from specialized hardware so that the network is accessible to as many people as possible, thus increasing the network security. To achieve ASIC resistance, the Ethereum PoW algorithm has been designed to be sequential memory-hard, such that it consumes the nearly the entire available memory access bandwidth. This ensures that it is not possible to use memory in parallel to find multiple *nonces* simultaneously. Furthermore, to limit the benefits

of ASICs, the type of computation required for the algorithm has been chosen to be general-purpose. Therefore, even if the specialized hardware is used to perform the general-purpose computation, there would be negligible (if not none) benefits as compared to commodity hardware.

2. **Verifiable on Light Clients**: The verification of the proof-of-work should have low CPU and memory requirements so that the verification can be done on a light client, within a few milliseconds. Furthermore, the light clients should be able to become fully operational to verify blocks within a few seconds.

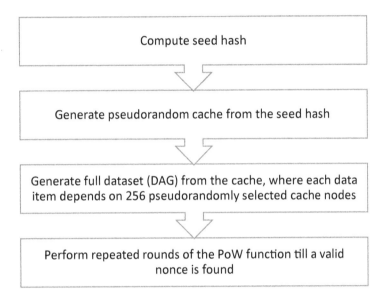

Figure 7.5: Steps involved in Ethash

The Ethash mining proof-of-work (PoW) algorithm works as follows:

1. **Seed-Hash**: A *seed* hash is used for generating a pseudorandom cache. The seed hash changes after every epoch (where each epoch has 30000 blocks). For the first epoch, the seed hash is the Keccak-256 hash of a series of 32 bytes of zeros ([b'\x00' * 32]). For successive epochs, the seed hash is the Keccak-256 hash of the previous seed hash.

2. **Cache**: A pseudorandom cache is generated from the seed hash. The size of the cache (c_{size}) is initially 2^{24} bytes or 16MB at genesis. The cache size grows 2^{17} per epoch. Thus the size of the cache depends on the block number. To generate the cache, first the c_{size} bytes of memory are filled sequentially (by computing Keccak-512 hash of the seed hash) and then two rounds of the RandMemoHash algorithm [41] are performed. The light clients store the cache which is used in the PoW verification. Box 7.5 shows the Python implementation of the cache generation function (excerpt taken from the pyethereum source).

■ **Box 7.5: Cache generation function
(code excerpt from pyethereum file - ethash.py)**

```
# Size of the dataset relative to the cache
CACHE_BYTES_INIT = 2**24
# Size of the dataset relative to the cache
CACHE_BYTES_GROWTH = 2**17
# blocks per epoch
EPOCH_LENGTH = 30000
# hash length in bytes
HASH_BYTES = 64
# number of rounds in cache production
CACHE_ROUNDS = 3

cache_seeds = [b'\x00' * 32]

def mkcache(block_number):
  while len(cache_seeds) <= block_number // EPOCH_LENGTH:
    cache_seeds.append(sha3.sha3_256(cache_seeds[-1]).digest())

  seed = cache_seeds[block_number // EPOCH_LENGTH]

  n = get_cache_size(block_number) // HASH_BYTES
  return _get_cache(seed, n)


@lru_cache(5)
def _get_cache(seed, n):
  # Sequentially produce the initial dataset
  o = [sha3_512(seed)]
  for i in range(1, n):
    o.append(sha3_512(o[-1]))

  for _ in range(CACHE_ROUNDS):
    for i in range(n):
      v = o[i][0] % n
      o[i] = sha3_512(list(map(xor, o[(i - 1 + n) % n], o[v])))

  return o
```

3. **Full Dataset (DAG):** From the cache, we generate a dataset whose initial size is 2^{30} bytes or 1GB at genesis. The dataset size grows by 2^{23} bytes per epoch. The dataset has a property that each item in the dataset depends on only a small number of items from the cache. Each item in the dataset is 64 bytes in size. To generate a dataset item, 256 items are pseudorandomly selected from the cache and then hashed. Full clients store the dataset which is used for generating the mining PoW. The full dataset is called a DAG. A new dataset is generated after every epoch (every 30000 blocks). Box 7.6 shows the Python implementation of the full dataset generation function (excerpt taken from the pyethereum source).

■ Box 7.6: Full dataset generation function (code excerpt from pyethereum file - ethash.py)

```python
# bytes in word
WORD_BYTES = 4
# bytes in dataset at genesis
DATASET_BYTES_INIT = 2**30
# growth per epoch (~7 GB per year)
DATASET_BYTES_GROWTH = 2**23
# hash length in bytes
HASH_BYTES = 64
# number of parents of each dataset element
DATASET_PARENTS = 256

def calc_dataset_item(cache, i):
    n = len(cache)
    r = HASH_BYTES // WORD_BYTES
    mix = copy.copy(cache[i % n])
    mix[0] ^= i
    mix = sha3_512(mix)
    for j in range(DATASET_PARENTS):
        cache_index = fnv(i ^ j, mix[j % r])
        mix = list(map(fnv, mix, cache[cache_index % n]))
    return sha3_512(mix)

def calc_dataset(full_size, cache):
    o = []
    percent = (full_size // HASH_BYTES) // 100
    for i in range(full_size // HASH_BYTES):
        if i % percent == 0:
            sys.stderr.write("Completed %d items,
                %d percent\n" % (i, i // percent))
        o.append(calc_dataset_item(cache, i))
    return o
```

4. **Proof-of-Work function**: The PoW function takes as input the following parameters: (1) a *header* which is the Keccak-256 hash of the RLP representation of the block header excluding the *mixHash* and *nonce*, (2) a 64-bit *nonce* value which is initialized to a pseudorandomly selected integer value in the range $(0, 2^{64})$, (3) The full dataset computed in the previous step. With these input parameters, the PoW function computes two items as follows: (1) a compressed mix (*cmix*), and (2) the Keccak-256 hash of the concatenation of the compressed mix with a seed hash (*sha3_256(s+cmix)*). The seed hash used here is the Keccak-512 hash of the *header* and *nonce* input parameters to the PoW function. To compute the compressed mix (*cmix*), the PoW function maintains a (*mix*) which is 128 bytes wide. The *mix* is initialized by replicating the seed hash and filling an array 128 bytes wide. Next, we sequentially fetch 128 bytes from the full dataset and use the FNV function (which is a non-associative substitute for XOR) to combine it with the mix. The algorithm has been designed such that, for sequentially fetching data from the full dataset, the entire available memory access bandwidth is consumed (to make it ASIC resistant). Box 7.7 shows the Python implementation of the PoW function (excerpt taken from the pyethereum source).

■ **Box 7.7: PoW function implementation
(code excerpt from pyethereum file - ethash.py)**

```python
 # bytes in word
WORD_BYTES = 4
# width of mix
MIX_BYTES = 128
# hash length in bytes
HASH_BYTES = 64
# number of accesses in hashimoto loop
ACCESSES = 64

def hashimoto(header, nonce, full_size, dataset_lookup):
    n = full_size // HASH_BYTES
    w = MIX_BYTES // WORD_BYTES
    mixhashes = MIX_BYTES // HASH_BYTES
    s = sha3_512(header + nonce[::-1])
    mix = []
    for _ in range(MIX_BYTES // HASH_BYTES):
        mix.extend(s)
    for i in range(ACCESSES):
        p = fnv(i ^ s[0], mix[i % w]) % (n // mixhashes) * mixhashes
        newdata = []
        for j in range(mixhashes):
            newdata.extend(dataset_lookup(p + j))
        mix = list(map(fnv, mix, newdata))
    cmix = []
    for i in range(0, len(mix), 4):
        cmix.append(fnv(fnv(fnv(mix[i], mix[i + 1]),
                    mix[i + 2]), mix[i + 3]))
    return {
        "mix digest": serialize_hash(cmix),
        "result": serialize_hash(sha3_256(s + cmix))
    }


def hashimoto_light(block_number, cache, header, nonce):
    return hashimoto(header, nonce, get_full_size(block_number),
                lambda x: calc_dataset_item(cache, x))


def hashimoto_full(dataset, header, nonce):
    return hashimoto(header, nonce, len(dataset) * HASH_BYTES,
                lambda x: dataset[x])
```

5. **Mining**: The mining function performs repeated rounds of the PoW function described in the previous step, till the output of the PoW algorithm is below the desired target and a valid *nonce* is found. In each round, a new value of *nonce* is passed to the PoW function. The *nonce* value is initialized to a pseudorandomly selected integer value in the range $(0, 2^{64})$. In successive rounds, the *nonce* is incremented by one. A valid *nonce* is the one, for which the output of the PoW algorithm is below the desired target *nonce ≤ target*. The target value is related to difficulty as: *target* $= 2^{256}/difficulty$. For finding a valid *nonce*, there is no better strategy than to enumerate all the possible

options. By running successive rounds of the PoW algorithm and incrementing *nonce* by one after each round, we eventually find a valid *nonce*. The time for finding a new block can be controlled by manipulating the difficulty. A successful PoW miner is one whose block is selected to be added next to the blockchain. Once a winning block is selected all other nodes update to that new block. Box 7.8 shows the Python implementation of the mining function (excerpt taken from the pyethereum source).

■ **Box 7.8: Mining function implementation (code excerpt from pyethereum file - ethash.py)**

```
def mine(full_size, dataset, header, difficulty):
    from random import randint
    nonce = randint(0, 2**64)
    while decode_int(hashimoto_full(full_size,
            dataset, header, nonce)) < difficulty:
        nonce += 1
        nonce %= 2**64
    return nonce
```

7.3 Block Validation

Blocks mined by miners are checked for validity by other participating nodes in the network. Block validation can be done with low CPU and small memory by using the cache to regenerate the specific pieces of the dataset required for verification. Therefore, light clients only need to store the cache.

The block validation algorithm in Ethereum is as follows:

1. Check if the block's *prevhash* and the parent's hash match. In other words, the previous block which is referenced by a block should be valid.
2. Check if the block's number is the successor of its parent block's number.
3. Check if the block's *gaslimit* and *difficulty* is consistent with its parent's *gaslimit* and *difficulty*.
4. Check if the total gas used within the block is less than the block's *gaslimit*.
5. Check if the block's transaction root and uncle root are valid.
6. Check if the timestamp of the block is greater than the timestamp of its parent and less than 15 minutes into the future.
7. Check if the proof-of-work on the block is valid, i.e., the block *nonce* has been cryptographically generated as described in the previous section. Box 7.9 shows a Python function for checking if the proof-of-work of the block is valid (code excerpt from pyethereum).
8. Check if the final state root provided in the block header is valid. For checking the state, start with the state of the block's parent. Then apply all the transactions in the block's transaction list to the parent's state and determine the new state. Then apply the mining rewards to determine the final state. Check if the Merkle tree root of this final state is equal to the final state root included in the block header.

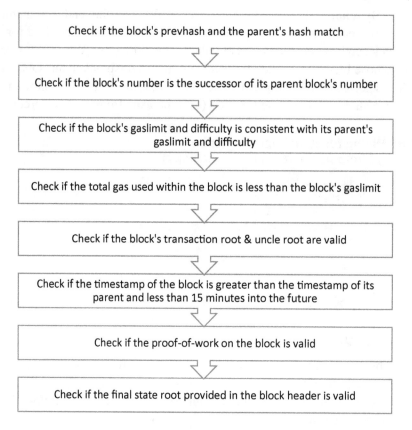

Figure 7.6: Steps involved in block validation

**■ Box 7.9: Python function for checking if the proof-of-work of the block is valid
(code excerpt from pyethereum file - ethpow.py)**

```python
def check_pow(block_number, header_hash, mixhash, nonce, difficulty):
    """Check if the proof-of-work of the block is valid.
    :param nonce: if given the proof of work function will be evaluated
            with this nonce instead of the one already present in
            the header
    :returns: `True` or `False`"""
    log.debug('checking pow', block_number=block_number)
    if len(mixhash) != 32 or len(header_hash) != 32 or len(nonce) != 8:
        return False

    # Grab current cache
    cache = get_cache(block_number)
    mining_output = hashimoto_light(block_number, cache,
                                    header_hash, nonce)
    if mining_output[b'mix digest'] != mixhash:
        return False
    return utils.big_endian_to_int(mining_output[b'result']) <=
                                   2**256 // (difficulty or 1)
```

7.4   Setting up Mining Node

In Chapter-3, we described how to setup various Ethereum clients. Let us now look at how to start mining on the Ethereum network with the *geth* Ethereum client. To start mining, you can use the '–mine' option with *geth* as follows:

■ **Run Miners**
```
geth –mine –minerthreads 4
```

The *minerthreads* option is used to specify the number of threads to do mining in parallel. This is usually set equal to the number of CPU cores in the system. The full command to mine on a private blockchain network would look as follows:

■ **Create Private Blockchain**
```
geth –datadir "/home/ubuntu/ethchain" –dev –unlock 0,1 –mine
 –minerthreads 4 –rpc –rpcaddr 0.0.0.0
 –rpccorsdomain "*" –rpcport 8101
```

When you start mining with *geth*, you will see an output as shown in the box below:

■ **Mining with geth client**
```
miner/miner.go:119] Starting mining operation (CPU=2 TOT=3)
miner/worker.go:555] commit new work on block 1216 with 0 txs & 0 uncles.
Took 930.600027ms

ethash.go:259] Generating DAG for epoch 0 (size 32768)
ethash.go:291] Generating DAG: 0%
ethash.go:291] Generating DAG: 1%
:
:
I1003 16:21:14.328891 ethash.go:291] Generating DAG: 100%

I1003 16:21:14.328932 ethash.go:276] Done generating DAG for epoch 0, it
took 151.051905ms
```

Note that the full dataset (DAG) is generated prior to mining. Alternatively, you can use *miner.start()* function in the *geth* console to start mining. When a transaction is sent on the network, you will see a notification as shown in the box below. The box also shows the mining notification for a block and the time taken to mine the block (on a private blockchain network).

■ **Output of geth client showing mining notifications**
```
Tx(0xef48c316a516504f5ef7430d6ef83e806b7e177dd8d37ae0e95f4fae7ff244f9)
to:   0xc421d5e214ddb07a41d28cf89ee37495aa5edba7

Mined block (#1219 / 2f65e595). Wait 5 blocks for confirmation
commit new work on block 1220 with 1 txs & 0 uncles.  Took 9.88836ms
commit new work on block 1220 with 1 txs & 0 uncles.  Took 348.84μs
```

7.5   State Storage in Ethereum

In this section, we describe how Ethereum stores the world state, transactions list and the transaction receipts within the blocks.

7.5.1   World State

The world state in Ethereum is a mapping between the account addresses and the account states. The account state comprises the following fields:

- **Nonce**: The account *nonce* is a scalar value which is equal to the number of transactions sent from the account (for an externally-owned account) or the number of contract creations made by the account (in case of a contract account).
- **Balance**: The *balance* in Wei associated with the account.
- **Storage Root**: The *storageRoot* field is the 32 byte hash of the root of the trie structure that encodes the storage contents of the account.
- **Code Hash**: The *codeHash* field is the hash of the EVM code associated with the account (in case of a contract account).

Ethereum stores the world state in a special tree structure called a Merkle Patricia Tree (also called a Trie in Ethereum). While describing the block header in Section 7.2.2, we mentioned the *state_root* field which is the 32 byte hash of the root of the block's state trie after the transactions are executed.

7.5.2   Transactions List

The list of transactions in a block is stored in a trie structure. While describing the block header, we mentioned the *tx_list_root* field which is the 32 byte hash of the root of the block's transaction trie populated with the transactions in the block.

7.5.3   Transaction Receipts

A receipt of each transaction which contains information related to the transaction execution is stored in a trie structure. While describing the block header, we mentioned the *receipts_root* field which is the 32 byte hash of the root of the block's receipts trie populated with the receipts of the transactions in a block. A transaction receipt is a tuple of four items as follows:

- **Post-transaction state**: The Ethereum state after the transaction is executed.
- **Cumulative Gas used**: The cumulative gas used in the block immediately after the transaction has been executed.
- **Transaction Logs**: Set of logs created from the execution of the transaction.
- **Bloom Filter**: Bloom filter created from information in the transaction logs. Bloom filters allow searching logs in an efficient and secure way.

7.5.4   Modified Merkle Patricia Tree

A Merkle tree is a type of binary tree in which the leaf nodes store the data. Each non-leaf node in a Merkle tree is labeled with the hash of its two child nodes. Any change made to any of the leaf nodes in a Merkle tree results in change of the node above (as the parent node's hash depends on its child nodes) and the changes propagate upward to the root node. Merkle Trees are often used in peer-to-peer networks where the data can be delivered in parts from different peers. The hashing mechanism used for labeling the nodes ensures that the data can be received from different peers while still being sure that the tree structure remains unaltered.

A Patricia tree is a kind of radix tree (or trie) which is optimized for space [43]. PATRICIA is an acronym which stands for "Practical Algorithm To Retrieve Information Coded In Alphanumeric". A trie is typically used for storing strings. The position of a node in a trie defines the key associated with the node. The key for a node can be obtained by traversing from the root of the trie to that node. All strings which share a prefix are descendants of a common node. The problem with trie structure is that when the keys are sparse, many of the nodes in a trie may have only one descendant leading to high space complexity. Patricia tree is a space-optimized trie in which each node, that is the only child, is merged with its parent.

Ethereum uses a special tree structure called the Modified Merkle Patricia Tree for storing information related to the world state, transactions and their receipts within the block. A Merkle Patricia tree is a cryptographically authenticated data structure which stores key-value pairs. In a normal radix tree, the key corresponding to a value is obtained by traversing through the tree from the root node to the leaf node which stores the value. A Merkle Patricia tree defines two optimizing nodes (extension node and branch node) for reducing the space complexity. There are three kinds of nodes in a Merkle Patricia Tree:

- **Leaf Node**: A leaf node has two items (key, value). The first item (key) includes the remaining nibbles (where 1 nibble = 4 bits) in the full-key which not already included while traversing the Trie from the root to the leaf node.
- **Extension Node**: An extension node has two items (key, value). The first item (key) includes the remaining nibbles in the Key which not already included while traversing the Trie from the root to the leaf node, and are shared by two distinct full-keys.
- **Branch Node**: A branch node is a list of 17 items, where the first 16 items are the 16 possible nibble values (0-9 and a-f). The last item has a value which is used if a full-key terminates in this branch node.

For encoding an arbitrary number of nibbles (in the keys of the leaf and extension nodes) as a byte array, Hex-prefix encoding is used. Hex-prefix encoding uses two nibbles (in the first byte of the hex-prefix encoded key) which are used to differentiate between the type of nodes and the oddness of the length of the key.

The leaf node's key is hex-prefix encoded, such that the first byte of the encoded key is 20 if the key has an even number of nibbles, and $(3+x[0])$ if the key has an odd number of nibbles (where $x[0]$ is the first nibble in the key). For example, if the leaf key is 1332 (even in length), then the hex-prefix encoded key will be 201332. If the leaf key is 7 (odd in length) then the hex-prefix key will be 37.

The extension node's key is hex-prefix encoded, such that the first byte of the encoded key is 00 if the key has an even number of nibbles, and $(1+x[0])$ if the key has an odd number of nibbles (where $x[0]$ is the first nibble in the key). For example, if the extension node's key is *b2* (even in length), then the hex-prefix encoded key will be *00b2*. If the key is 9 (odd in length) then the hex-prefix key will be 19.

Instead of the storing the entire trie structure within the block, which would be highly inefficient, Ethereum stores the hash of the root node of the trie. The trie structure has a special property that the hash of the root node of the trie is cryptographically dependent on all data stored in the trie nodes. Any attempt to change the data stored in any of the internal nodes in the trie changes the root node hash. The block header stores the root hash of the

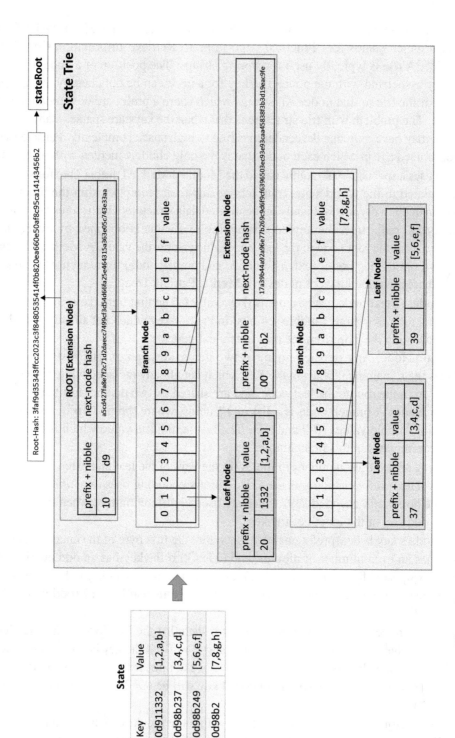

Figure 7.7: Example of a Merkle Patricia Tree (Trie) used in Ethereum for state storage

trie structures (*stateRoot*, *tx_list_root* and *receipts_root*). This is a more efficient approach than storing an entire trie structure in the block, because the 32 byte hash of the root of a trie gives a single value that identifies the set of key-value pairs stored in the nodes in the trie. Moreover, from one block to the next block, only a small portion of the trie needs to be updated and the majority of the trie remains the same. The individual nodes can be referenced using the node hashes.

For understanding the working of Merkle Patricia Tree, we extracted the Trie specific implementation files from the pyethereum repository and developed an example (adapted from [42]), as shown in Box 7.10. The trie generated from this example is shown in Figure 7.7.

■ Box 7.10: Merkle Patricia Tree example

```
>>> import trie, utils, rlp

>>> state = trie.Trie('triedb', trie.BLANK_ROOT)
>>> state.update('\x0d\x91\x13\x32', rlp.encode(['1,2,a,b']))
>>> state.update('\x0d\x98\xb2\x37', rlp.encode(['3,4,c,d']))
>>> state.update('\x0d\x98\xb2\x49', rlp.encode(['5,6,e,f']))
>>> state.update('\x0d\x98\xb2', rlp.encode(['7,8,g,h']))

>>> state.to_dict()
{'\r\x98\xb2I': '\xc8\x875,6,e,f', '\r\x98\xb2': '\xc8\x877,8,g,h',
'\r\x91\x132': '\xc8\x871,2,a,b', '\r\x98\xb27': '\xc8\x873,4,c,d'}

>>> state.root_hash.encode('hex')
'3faf9d35343ffcc2023c3f8480535414f0b820ea660e50af8c95ca14143456b2'

>>> state.root_node[1].encode('hex')
'a5cd427fa8e7f2c71d2daecc7499cf3d54d66fa25e464315a363e05c743e33aa'

>>> b=state._decode_to_node(state.root_node[1])
>>> b
['', [' \x132', '\xc8\x871,2,a,b'], '', '', '', '', '', '',
'\x17\xa3\x9bD\xa9*\x96\xe7{&\x9c\x9do\x9c\xf69e\x03
\xec\x93\xe9<\xaaE\x83\x8f;=\x19\xea\xc9\xfe',
'', '', '', '', '', '', '', '']

>>> b[1][0].encode('hex')
'201332'

>>> b[8].encode('hex')
'17a39b44a92a96e77b269c9d6f9cf6396503ec93e93caa45838f3b3d19eac9fe'

>>> c=state._decode_to_node(b[8])
>>> c
['\x00\xb2', '\xc5)\xadu\xbe\xfe\xf3\x08\x8d\x19j\x9a\x1d
\xdaW>\x1f\xd0K\xd4\xe0\x1b\xd7\xf9\xcaee\xec\xdf\xc2X4']

>>> c[0].encode('hex')
'00b2'
```

```
>>> d=state._decode_to_node(c[1])
>>> d
['', '', '', ['7', '\xc8\x873,4,c,d'], ['9', '\xc8\x875,6,e,f'],
'', '', '', '', '', '', '', '', '', '', '', '\xc8\x877,8,g,h']

>>> d[3][0].encode('hex')
'37'

>>> d[4][0].encode('hex')
'39'

>>> d[16]
'\xc8\x877,8,g,h'
```

Summary

In this chapter, we described the mining process in Ethereum which produces new blocks that are added to the blockchain. When a transaction is sent on the blockchain network, it is combined with other pending transactions into a block. The peers in the blockchain network that perform the mining operations are called miners. The miners validate the transactions and reach a consensus on the block that should be added next to the blockchain. The newly mined block (called the winning block) is then broadcast to the entire network. Ethereum uses a distributed and decentralized consensus mechanism in which the nodes assemble the transactions into blocks and compete with each other (by performing computationally expensive calculations), to get their blocks added next to the blockchain. The process of finalizing a block during mining involves determining the uncles (or stale blocks), determining and processing the transactions, applying the mining rewards and computing the mining proof-of-work. Miners in Ethereum network are rewarded for dedicating their computational resources for maintaining the network and mining new blocks. We described the mining proof-of-work (PoW) algorithm used in Ethereum, called Ethash. Next, we described the block validation algorithm in Ethereum. Next, we described how to start mining on the Ethereum network with the *geth* Ethereum client. Finally, we described how Ethereum stores state information. Ethereum uses a special tree structure called the Modified Merkle Patricia Tree for storing information related to the world state, transactions and their receipts within the block.

8 - Whisper

This chapter covers

- Whisper Protocol
- Whisper Routing Approaches
- Whisper API
- Case Study: Smart Switch Dapp

8.1 Whisper Protocol

Whisper is a communication protocol that allows decentralized applications (Dapps) on a blockchain network to communicate with each other. With Whisper, Dapps can publish messages to each other. Whisper messages are transient in nature and have a time-to-live (TTL) set. Each message has one or more topics associated with it. The Dapps running on a node inform the node about the topics to which they want to subscribe. Whisper uses topic-based routing where the nodes advertise their topics of interest to their peers. Topics are used for filtering the messages which are delivered to a node, which are then distributed to the Dapps running on the node.

While transactions to the smart contracts associated with the Dapps can be used to signal the Dapps and update their state, the transactions are processed on the blockchain which requires transaction fees (in the form of gas) to be paid by the senders of the transactions. Whisper is useful for pure communication between Dapps, where consensus on the blockchain is not required. Unlike transactions, Whisper messages do not require gas to be paid by the sender. Dapps can use Whisper messages to send small amounts of information to each other. Dapps can also use Whisper messages to signal each other and collaborate on a transaction. Whisper protects the privacy of the messages and also of the sender and receiver. Whisper provides 'dark' communication where the messages are forwarded in a probabilistic manner and the intermediate nodes have no information about the sender or the receiver.

Whisper has been designed to provide efficient unicast (1-1), multi-cast (1-N) and broadcast communication (1-all). Unicast and multicast messages have lower latency as compared to broadcast messages. Also, messages with lower TTLs are prioritized. Whisper is not designed for high-bandwidth and low latency applications.

8.1.1 Whisper Envelope and Message

Whisper can be considered as a hybrid of a distributed hash table (DHT) and a datagram messaging system. Like in a DHT, Whisper has keys and values, however, each key can have multiple values (multi-value keys) and each value can have multiple keys (multi-key values). Topics play the role of keys in Whisper. Each message in Whisper has one or more topics associated with it. There can be multiple messages sharing the same topic. Figure 8.1 shows the structure of Whisper Envelope and Message, which are the key entities in Whisper. An envelope includes the following fields:

- **Expiry**: The absolute time of expiry of the message within the envelope.
- **TTL**: Time to Live (in seconds) for the message.
- **Topics**: List of topics which the receiver can use to identify and filter messages.
- **Data**: A series of bytes which form the encrypted message.
- **Nonce**: An integer value which can be used to prove that a given amount of work was done in composing the message.
- **Hash**: SHA3 hash of the envelope.

A message includes the following fields:

- **Flags**: A series of bytes where the first bit is used to specify if the message has a signature. The rest of the bits reserved for future use.
- **Signature**: Signature of the sender of the message. If a signature is present in a message, the first bit of the flag field is set to 1.

- **payload**: The payload of the message.
- **From/Sent**: The identity of the sender. If provided, the whisper message is signed with the sender's private key.
- **To**: The identity of the receiver. If provided, the whisper message is encrypted with the receiver's public key.

If Whisper is considered as a DHT, then Envelope plays the role of an item/value, which has associated keys or topics. If Whisper is considered as a datagram messaging system then Envelope plays the role of a packet which contains an encrypted datagram. Whisper communication is asynchronous in nature and the envelopes have a time-to-live (TTL). Envelopes are not encrypted and can be comprehended by any node. However, messages are encrypted and can be decrypted only by the intended recipients.

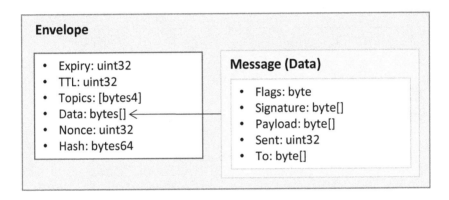

Figure 8.1: Structure of Whisper Envelope and Message

8.1.2 Configurable Privacy and Efficiency

In Whisper, the routing privacy and routing efficiency of a message can be configured by the user. A sender while posting a Whisper message can decide the amount of information that the sender wants to disclose to the intermediate nodes who route the message to the recipient. A tradeoff exists between privacy and efficiency. Messages with higher privacy are less efficient (i.e. they take more time to reach) whereas messages with less privacy are more efficient (i.e. they are delivered faster). If the 'From' option is provided for a message, the message is signed with the sender's private key. If the 'To' option is provided for a message, the message is encrypted with the receiver's public key. In this case, only the intended recipient can decrypt the message with its private key.

8.1.3 Whisper Communication Patterns

The user-configurable routing privacy and routing efficiency in Whisper results in four different communication patterns as shown in Figure 8.2. The patterns are described as follows:

- **Anonymous broadcast**: In this type of communication, the message is neither signed (no 'From' option is provided) nor encrypted (no 'To' option is provided). The identity of the sender is not known and the message can be comprehended by any node which receives the message.

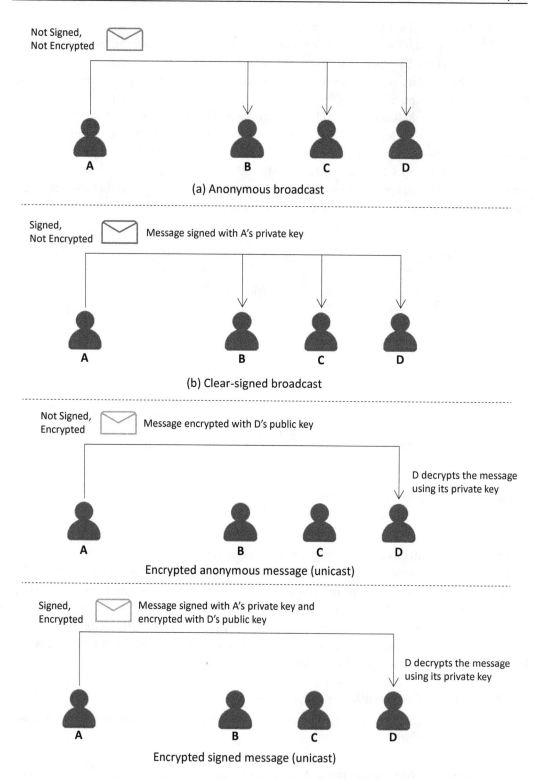

Figure 8.2: Whisper communication patterns

- **Clear-signed broadcast**: In this type of communication, the message is signed by the sender ('From' option is provided) however it is not encrypted (no 'To' option is provided). The message can be comprehended by any node which receives the message and the recipient knows the identity of the sender.
- **Encrypted anonymous message (unicast)**: In this type of communication, the message is not signed (no 'From' option is provided) but encrypted ('To' option is provided) by the recipient's public key. In this case, only the intended recipient can decrypt the message with its private key and the recipient doesn't know who the sender is.
- **Encrypted signed message (unicast)**: In this type of communication, the message is both signed ('From' option is provided) and encrypted ('To' option is provided). In this case, only the intended recipient can decrypt the message with its private key and the recipient knows who the sender is.

8.1.4 Whisper Wire Protocol

Whisper uses the DEVp2p wire protocol for peer-to-peer communications between nodes. Whisper wire protocol includes three types of messages as shown in Figure 8.3. The *Status* message (denoted by 0x00 message code) is sent after the initial handshake happens between peers and is used to inform about the Whisper status to the peers. The *Messages* (denoted by 0x01 message code) contain one or more envelopes or packets. The *TopicFilter* message (denoted by 0x02 message code) is used to specify the bloom filter of the topics which the node is interested in.

Status

Code	Protocol Version
0x00	uint64

Messages

Code	Expiry	TTL	Topics	Data	Nonce
0x01	uint32	uint32	[bytes4,...]	byte[]	uint32

TopicFilter

Code	Bloom
0x02	bytes64

Figure 8.3: Whisper Wire Protocol

8.1.5 Posting a Message

Figure 8.4 lists the steps involved in posting a Whisper message. The user provides arguments for posting a new message into Whisper network to the Whisper's post method as a JSON object. These include the *topics*, *payload*, *ttl*, *priority/workToProve* and optional *from* and *to* fields. A new message object is created from the payload. If the 'from' option is provided, the message is signed with the sender's private key. If the 'to' the option is provided, the message is encrypted with the receiver's public key. Next, the message is wrapped into an envelope and the TTL, Expiry, Topics and Data fields of the envelope are set. The data field includes a series of bytes which form the message flags, signature, and payload. Next, the envelope is sealed and closed by spending the requested amount of time as a proof of work on hashing the data and, Nonce field of the envelope is set. Finally, the message is injected into the Whisper send queue to be distributed in the network.

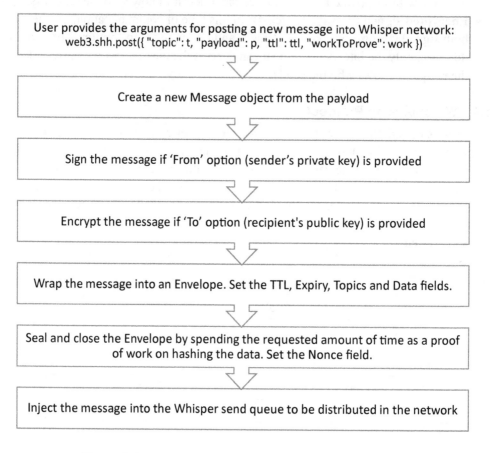

Figure 8.4: Steps involved in posting a Whisper message

8.1.6 Topics, Abridged Topics & Bloomed Topics

A *topic* is a cryptographically secure probabilistic partial-classification of a message determined by the 32-bytes SHA3 hash of the topic string given by the author of the message. The *abridged topic* is the first 4 bytes of the *topic*. The message envelope contains only the abridged topics. Whereas the full topics are stored along with the payload field which is encrypted and forms the Data field of the envelope. The payload field of a message is encrypted either using the public key of the recipient (if 'to' option is provided) or using a randomly generated key. This randomly generated key is XORed with each of the full topics to form a salted topic. The salted topic is stored along with the encrypted data in the Data field of the envelope. The peer nodes which route the Whisper messages can comprehend only the envelope and not the encrypted message in the envelope which is part of the Data field. Thus, these peer nodes only know about the abridged topics and do not know about the full topics. Routing is done via abridged topics only, whereas, the full topics are used for encrypting the message payloads. This ensures that the intermediate nodes which route the messages cannot read the contents of the messages.

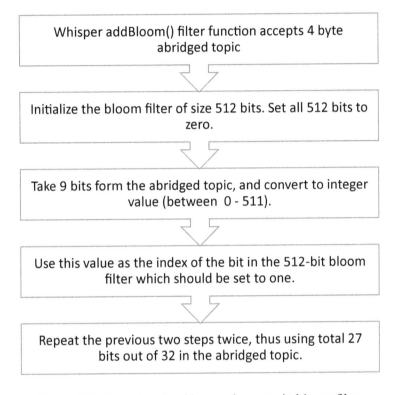

Figure 8.5: Steps involved in creating a topic bloom filter

A topic can be viewed either as a DHT multi-key (if we consider Whisper as a DHT) or a secure and probabilistic routing endpoint (if we consider Whisper as a datagram messaging system). The Dapps on a node inform the node about the topics in which they are interested. The node advertises the topics to its peers. Instead of advertising the actual topics themselves (which can leak information about the node and its Dapps), the node advertises a topic mask by creating a bloom filter of the topics. Figure 8.5 shows the steps involved in creating a topic bloom filter. The topic bloom filter is used in the *TopicFilter* message type in the Whisper wire protocol to inform the peers about the topics which a node is interested in without disclosing the full topics. Whisper's addBloom() filter function takes as input, a 4-byte abridged topic and creates a bloom filter of size 512-bits. To set the bits of the bloom filter, 9 bits are taken from the abridged topic and converted to an integer value (between 0 - 511). This integer value gives the index of the bit in the 512-bit bloom filter which should be set to one. The steps for setting the bits in the bloom filter are then repeated twice. Thus in total 27 bits from the abridged topic (9-bits in three rounds) are used to set the bits of the bloom filter.

8.2   Whisper Routing Approaches

Whisper has been designed to protect the routing privacy of the sender and receiver. While the existing communication protocols use encryption to prevent unauthorized parties from sniffing the messages, however, encryption alone doesn't protect the privacy of the sender and receiver. The meta-data (e.g., IP addresses) sent along with an encrypted message, which is required for routing the message from the sender to the receiver, can reveal the location and identity of the sender. Thus, even if the messages are encrypted, the meta-data alone can compromise the privacy of the communicating parties. By knowing the IP addresses of the sender and receiver, and by examining the IP address logs collected over a period of time, an attacker who sniffs the network traffic can identify which party is communicating with whom.

Whisper's routing approach is *dark* in nature where the identity of the sender and receiver is not known to the intermediate routing nodes in the network. Earlier in this chapter, we described how the routing privacy and routing efficiency of a Whisper message can be configured by the user. In the most secure mode (where the message is signed by the sender and encrypted by the public key of the receiver), no meta-data about the sender and receiver is leaked to the intermediate routing nodes. Thus Whisper is 100% dark in this mode. Whisper uses probabilistic message forwarding where minimal routing information is revealed. Whisper uses passive and active routing approaches to route messages probabilistically.

8.2.1   Passive Routing - Peer Steering

The passive routing approach is based on the ability of Whisper to rate peers, over time. The nodes rate their peers such that the peers which forward useful messages (which a node is interested in) are rated higher. Also, peers which forward messages with low TTLs and high proofs-of-work are rated higher than the nodes which forward expired messages or low proof-of-work messages. Using the rating system for peers, each node can probabilistically alter the set of peers with which it communicates. This approach is called peer-steering. Peer-steering approach allows a node to rotate out the peers which do not forward useful messages in the favor of other peers. Thus, over time, the network evolves as the nodes alter their set of peers. Peer-steering also serves as an incentive mechanism where the nodes are incentivised to provide useful messages to their peers or risk disconnection. The peers prioritize the messages in which their peers have expressed interest. Also, messages with lower TTLs and higher proof-of-work are prioritized.

8.2.2   Active Routing - Topic Filtering

The active routing approach is based on the ability of the nodes to advertise the topics of their interest. Whisper uses abridged-topics to determine how the envelopes should be forwarded. Nodes advertise the topics of their interest in the form of topic bloom filters. The nodes receive Whisper envelopes continuously. Each node maintains a map of the envelopes which is indexed by expiry time. Nodes use the topic bloom filters to determine which envelopes to forward to their peers. The benefit of using topic bloom filters (or topic masks) is that the nodes do not need to reveal the actual topics in which they are interested. Also, the information that a node shares can be customized per-peer or per-Dapp running on the node. Thus, the peers which a node trusts more can be better informed than other peers, and the Dapps which exchange sensitive information can have greater privacy (i.e. less topic advertising can be used for sensitive Dapps).

8.3 Whisper API

In Chapter-3, we described the Web3 JavaScript API which provides methods for interacting with the Ethereum network [32]. Web3 provides a JavaScript object, *web3*, which includes various sub-objects. The *shh* sub-object provides methods for Whisper interaction. In this section, we will describe the Whisper API and how to work with Whisper using *web3.shh* JavaScript API.

8.3.1 NewIdentity

The *newIdentity* method generates a new cryptographic identity for the client, and injects it into the known identities for message decryption. The box below shows an example of the *newIdentity* method.

```
■ Whisper newIdentity method
> var identity = web3.shh.newIdentity();
> identity
"0x049d21eb458d3da76f393d01a909af7932d5d4acc9
9fe46bdd72ad854fe179dc80605d1c1c7e3685c746007
fd5d532327f36ebcf090f20f8715585a77b5b7f1623"
```

8.3.2 HasIdentity

The *hasIdentity* method checks if the Whisper node is configured with the private key of the specified public-private keypair. The box below shows an example of the *hasIdentity* method.

```
■ Whisper hasIdentity method
> web3.shh.hasIdentity(identity);
true
```

8.3.3 Post

The *post* method injects a message into the Whisper network for distribution. The *post* method accepts the following parameters:
- **from**: The identity of the sender. If provided, the whisper message is signed with the sender's private key.
- **to**: The identity of the receiver. If provided, the whisper message is encrypted with the receiver's public key.
- **topics**: List of topics which the receiver can use to identify and filter messages.
- **payload**: The payload of the message.
- **ttl**: Time to Live (in seconds) for the message.
- **workToProve/priority**: An integer which specifies the amount of work that must be done in composing the message. Messages with a higher amount of work have higher priority.

The box below shows an example of the *post* method.

■ **Whisper post method**

```
web3.shh.post({
  "from": identity,
  "topics": [web3.fromAscii("example")],
  "payload": web3.fromAscii("Test"),
  "ttl": 100,
  "workToProve": 1000
});
```

8.3.4 Filter

The *filter* method creates and registers a new message filter to watch for inbound Whisper messages. The *filter* method accepts the following parameters:
- **from**: This option is used to filter messages by the identity of the sender.
- **to**: This option is used to filter messages by the identity of the receiver.
- **topics**: List of topics to be used for filtering messages.

The box below shows an example of the *filter* method.

■ **Whisper filter method**

```
var options = {
  from: identity,
  topics: [web3.fromAscii("example")]
};

var myfilter = web3.shh.filter(options).watch(function(err, msg) {
  if(err){
    console.log("Error:", JSON.stringify(err));
  }else{
    console.log("Message:", JSON.stringify(msg));
    console.log("Payload:", web3.toAscii(msg.payload));
  }
});
```

8.3.5 Working with Whisper

Box 8.1 shows a complete example of working with Whisper. In this example, we create a new identity for the sender and then check if the identity exists. Next, we create a new filter. Finally, we post a message. The filter's callback function is executed when the message is received. The callback function logs the message to the console.

■ Box 8.1: Working with Whisper

```javascript
// Create a new identity
var identity = web3.shh.newIdentity();

// Check identity
var result = web3.shh.hasIdentity(identity);
console.log(result); // true

// Filter options
var options = {
  from: identity,
  topics: [web3.fromAscii("example")]
};

// Create a filter and watch for incoming whisper messages
var myfilter = web3.shh.filter(options).watch(
  function(err, msg) {
  if(err){
    console.log("Error:",  JSON.stringify(err));
  }else{
    console.log("Message:",  JSON.stringify(msg));
    console.log("Payload:",  web3.toAscii(msg.payload));
  }
});

// Create a new message
var message = {
  from: identity,
  topics: [web3.fromAscii("example")],
  payload: web3.fromAscii("Test"),
  ttl: 100,
  workToProve: 1000
};

// Post whisper message
web3.shh.post(message);

//-----Output-------
//Message: {"expiry":0,"from":"0x0487a3a8f738e8bab596ed33db2
//         fc36a90c42aa889982c6c1bc1760e78e7600e19ca69ae279b
//         fb1c5abb299d6ca159cdc25b689c2f56e9da14ac9fe67842fc11b1",
//         "hash":"0xf9f63c04928fffd2d6465565a838e1e4f7b0b92
//               00accf55a2d3c4ec326bce82e",
//         "payload":"0x54657374","sent":1478863242,"to":"0x0",
//         "topics":[],"ttl":100,"workProved":0}
//Payload: Test
```

8.4 Case Study: Smart Switch Dapp

Let us look at a case study of a Smart Switch Dapp from which the users can subscribe to use a solar charging station. Figure 8.6 shows the block diagram of the solar charging station and the Smart Switch Dapp. Box 8.2 shows the Solidity implementation of the smart contract for the Dapp.

■ Box 8.2: Smart Switch contract

```
contract SmartSwitch {
  struct User {
      uint amountPaid;
      uint authorizedTill;
  }

  address public owner;
  uint public numUsers;
  uint public rate;
  mapping (address => User) public users;

  function SmartSwitch() {
    owner = msg.sender;
    numUsers = 0;
    rate = 1000000000000; //in Wei per second
  }

  function buySubscription() public {
    uint duration = (msg.value/rate); //in seconds
    if(users[msg.sender].amountPaid>0){
      //Already registered, extend the authorization
      users[msg.sender].amountPaid += msg.value;
      users[msg.sender].authorizedTill += duration;
    }else{
      User u = users[msg.sender];
          u.amountPaid = msg.value;
          u.authorizedTill = now+duration;
          numUsers = numUsers+1;
    }
  }

  function isUserAuthorized(address userAddr) returns(bool){
    if(users[userAddr].authorizedTill>now){
      return true;
    }
    else{
      return false;
    }
  }

  function destroy() {
    if (msg.sender == owner)
      suicide(owner);
  }
}
```

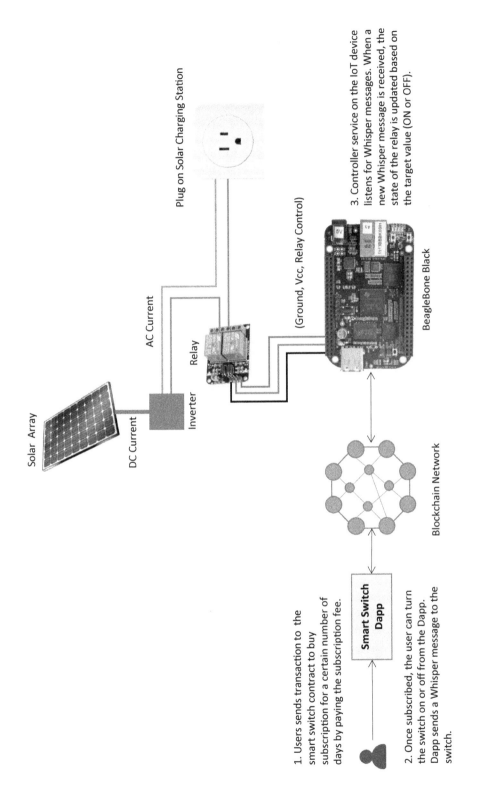

Figure 8.6: Solar charging station and Smart Switch Dapp

The solar charging station has an IoT device (Beaglebone Black), a relay switch module and a universal plug. The relay switch is connected to the GPIO pins of the IoT device. Users can subscribe to use the solar charging station for a certain period (1 day, 1 week or 1 month) by paying the subscription fee (in Ether). Once subscribed, the user can control the switch on the charging station from the Dapp itself. The Dapp sends a Whisper message when the user toggles the state of the switch from the Dapp. A controller service running on the IoT device watches for the Whisper message and updates the state of the relay based on the target value set in the Whisper message.

When the contract is initialized we set a rate for the charging station (in Wei/seconds). In the contract, we maintain a mapping from the addresses of the subscribed users to a custom *User* data type which stores the amount paid by the user and the UNIX timestamp till when the subscription is active. Users can subscribe by sending a transaction to the *buySubscription()* function along with the value (in Ether).

Box 8.3 shows the HTML implementation of the web interface for the Dapp (index.html).

■ Box 8.3: Smart Switch Dapp HTML

```
<!DOCTYPE html>
<html lang="en">

<head>
  <title>Smart Switch</title>
  <meta name="viewport" content="width=device-width, initial-scale=1">
  <link rel="stylesheet" href="./bootstrap.min.css">
  <link href="./bootstrap-toggle.min.css" rel="stylesheet">
  <link href="./app.css" rel='stylesheet' type='text/css'>
  <script src="./app.js"></script>
</head>

<body>
  <div class="container-fluid">
    <h1>Smart Switch Dapp</h1>
    <h3 style="margin-top: 0px; margin-bottom: 30px;"></h3>

    <div class="row">
      <div class="col-md-6">

        <table class="table table-fluid">
          <tr>
            <th>Switch Contract Address</th>
            <td><span class="black">
            <span id="cf_address"></span></span>
            </td>
          </tr>
          <tr>
            <th>Rate</th>
            <td><span class="black">
            <span id="cf_rate"></span> (Wei/sec)</span>
            </td>
          </tr>
          <tr>
```

```
            <th>Number of Users</th>
            <td><span class="black">
            <span id="cf_numUsers"></span></span>
            </td>
        </tr>
      </table>
    </div>
  </div>

  <div class="row">
    <div class="col-md-6">

      <h2 style="padding-top: 20px;">Subscribe to use switch</h2>

      <span class="black">Coinbase Address:
      <span id="cb_address" class="c_address"></span></span><br>
      <span class="black">Coinbase Balance:
      <span id="cb_balance"></span> ETH</span><br><br>

    <select class="form-control" id="numDays" onclick="showTotal();">
    <option value="0">Select number of days</option>
    <option value="1">1</option>
    <option value="7">7</option>
    <option value="30">30</option>
    </select>
      <br>
      <span class="black">Total:
      <span id="subscriptionTotal">0</span> ETH</span><br><br>

      <button class="btn btn-primary btn-lg"
        onclick="buySubscription();">BUY SUBSCRIPTION</button>
      <br><br>
      <div id="status"> </div>
    </div>

    <div class="col-md-6">
      <h2 style="padding-top: 20px;">Use switch</h2>
      <span class="black">User Address:
      <span id="cf_userAddress"></span></span><br>
      <span class="black">User Amount Paid:
      <span id="cf_userAmountPaid"></span></span><br>
      <span class="black">Authorized Till:
      <span id="cf_usersAuthorizedTill"></span></span><br>
      <span class="black">Authorization Status:
      <span id="cf_authStatus"></span></span><br>
      <br>

      <input id="toggle-event" type="checkbox"
            data-toggle="toggle" disabled>
      <div id="switchStatus"> </div>
    </div>
  </div>
</div>
<script src="./jquery.min.js"></script>
```

```
  <script src="./bootstrap.min.js"></script>
  <script src="./bootstrap-toggle.min.js"></script>
</body>
</html>
```

Box 8.4 shows the Dapp JavaScript (app.js).

■ **Box 8.4: Smart Switch Dapp JavaScript**

```
var accounts;
var account;
var balance;
var switchRate = 10;
var myContractInstance;

var options = {
  from: '0x0',
  to: '0x0',
  target: 'OFF' // or 'ON'
}

function initializeContract() {
  myContractInstance = SmartSwitch.deployed();
  $("#cf_address").html(myContractInstance.address);
  $("#cb_address").html(account);
  $("#cf_userAddress").html(account);
  options.from = account;
  options.to = myContractInstance.address;

  myContractInstance.numUsers.call().then(
    function(numUsers) {
      $("#cf_numUsers").html(numUsers.toNumber());
      return myContractInstance.rate.call();
    }).then(
    function(rate) {
      switchRate = rate.toNumber();
      $("#cf_rate").html(rate.toNumber());
      return myContractInstance.users.call(account);
    }).then(
    function(user) {
      console.log(user);
      $("#cf_userAmountPaid").html(user[0].toNumber());
      $("#cf_usersAuthorizedTill").html(user[1].toNumber());
      return myContractInstance.isUserAuthorized.call(account);
    }).then(
    function(result) {
      console.log(result);
      if (result == true) {
        $("#cf_authStatus").html('Active');
        $('#toggle-event').removeAttr('disabled');
      } else {
        $("#cf_authStatus").html('Inactive');
        $('#toggle-event').attr('disabled');
```

```
      }
      refreshBalance();
    });
}

function setStatus(message) {
  $("#status").html(message);
};

function showTotal() {
  var numDays = $("#numDays").val();
  var subscriptionTotal = numDays * switchRate * 86400;
  var subscriptionTotalEth = web3.fromWei(subscriptionTotal, "ether");
  $("#subscriptionTotal").html(subscriptionTotalEth);
};

function refreshBalance() {
  $("#cb_balance").html(web3.fromWei(
        web3.eth.getBalance(web3.eth.coinbase), "ether").toFixed(5));
}


function buySubscription() {
  var numDays = parseFloat($("#numDays").val());
  var subscriptionTotal = numDays * switchRate * 86400;

  setStatus("Initiating transaction... (please wait)");

  myContractInstance.buySubscription({
    from: web3.eth.coinbase,
    value: subscriptionTotal
  }).then(
    function() {
      return myContractInstance.numUsers.call();
    }).then(
    function(numUsers) {
      $("#cf_numUsers").html(numUsers.toNumber());
      return myContractInstance.users.call(account);
    }).then(
    function(user) {
      console.log(user);
      setStatus('');
      $("#cf_userAmountPaid").html(user[0].toNumber());
      $("#cf_usersAuthorizedTill").html(user[1].toNumber());
      return myContractInstance.isUserAuthorized.call(account);
    }).then(
    function(result) {
      console.log(result);
      if (result == true) {
        $("#cf_authStatus").html('Active');
        $('#toggle-event').removeAttr('disabled');
      } else {
        $("#cf_authStatus").html('Inactive');
        $('#toggle-event').attr('disabled');
```

```
      }

      refreshBalance();
   });
}

function sendMessage(options) {
  var data = {
    from: options.from,
    target: options.target
  };

  var message = {
    topics: [web3.fromAscii(options.to)],
    payload: web3.fromAscii(JSON.stringify(data)),
    ttl: 50,
    workToProve: 100
  };

  console.log(message);
  web3.shh.post(message);
}

function turnON() {
  options.target = 'ON';
  $('#switchStatus').html('Switch ON');
  sendMessage(options);
}

function turnOFF() {
  options.target = 'OFF';
  $('#switchStatus').html('Switch OFF');
  sendMessage(options);
}

window.onload = function() {
  $('#toggle-event').change(function() {
    if ($(this).prop('checked') == true) {
      turnON();
    } else {
      turnOFF();
    }
  });

  web3.eth.getAccounts(function(err, accs) {
    if (err != null) {
      alert("There was an error fetching your accounts.");
      return;
    }
    if (accs.length == 0) {
      alert("Couldn't get any accounts!");
      return;
    }
    accounts = accs;
```

```
   account = accounts[0];
   initializeContract();
 });
}
```

Figure 8.7 shows a screenshot of the Smart Switch Dapp. From the web interface of this Dapp, a user can subscribe to use the solar charging station for a certain number of days by paying the subscription fee. The subscription fee is calculated using the rate (in Wei/sec) provided in the contract. The toggle switch in the web interface is initially disabled. When the transaction to buy a subscription is processed, the toggle switch becomes enabled. The user can then activate the switch on the charging station using the toggle switch in the Dapp's web interface as shown in Figure 8.8. When the state of the toggle switch in the web interface changes, a Whisper message is sent. The topic of the Whisper message is set to the address of the contract associated with the Dapp. The message payload is a JSON object which includes the address of the sender and the target value for the switch (ON or OFF).

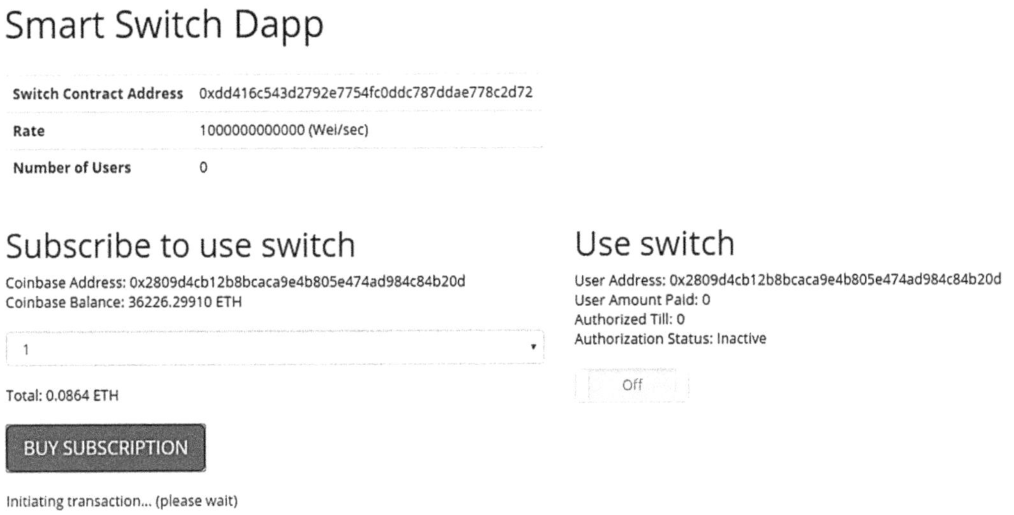

Smart Switch Dapp

Switch Contract Address	0xdd416c543d2792e7754fc0ddc787ddae778c2d72
Rate	1000000000000 (Wei/sec)
Number of Users	0

Subscribe to use switch

Coinbase Address: 0x2809d4cb12b8bcaca9e4b805e474ad984c84b20d
Coinbase Balance: 36226.29910 ETH

1	▾

Total: 0.0864 ETH

BUY SUBSCRIPTION

Initiating transaction... (please wait)

Use switch

User Address: 0x2809d4cb12b8bcaca9e4b805e474ad984c84b20d
User Amount Paid: 0
Authorized Till: 0
Authorization Status: Inactive

Off

Figure 8.7: Screenshot of Smart Switch Dapp - buying subscription

Box 8.5 shows the NodeJS implementation of a controller service that runs on the IoT device (Beaglebone Black). In the controller service, we instantiate the smart contract using the contract address and ABI. Next, we create a Whisper filter and start watching for Whisper messages which have the topic set to the address of the contract associated with the Dapp. When a new Whisper message is received from the Dapp, the payload is parsed and we extract the address of the sender and the target value (ON or OFF). Next, we check if the sender is a valid subscriber, and is authorized to use the switch by sending a call to the *isUserAuthorized()* function of the contract. If the sender is authorized, the state of the relay is changed based on the target value. For controlling the relay switch through the GPIO pins on the IoT device we use the *mraa* NodeJS library.

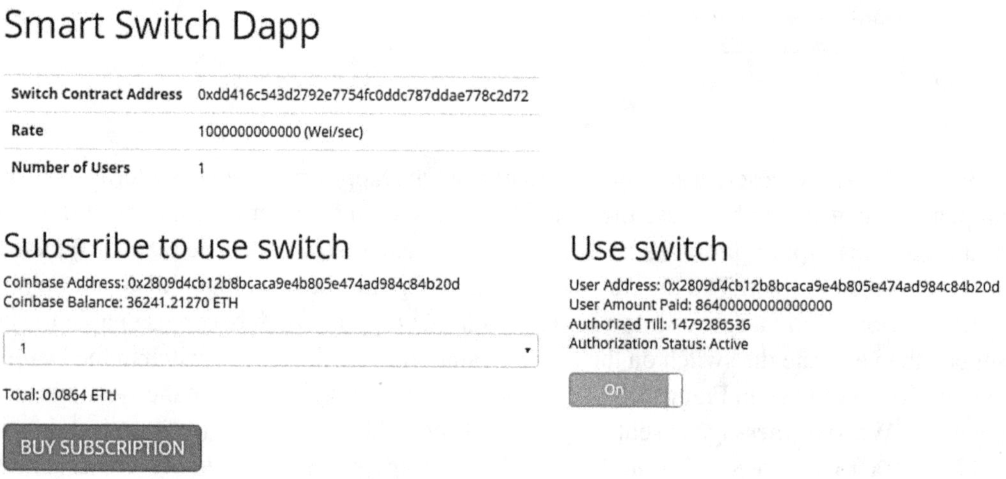

Smart Switch Dapp

Switch Contract Address	0xdd416c543d2792e7754fc0ddc787ddae778c2d72
Rate	1000000000000 (Wei/sec)
Number of Users	1

Subscribe to use switch

Coinbase Address: 0x2809d4cb12b8bcaca9e4b805e474ad984c84b20d
Coinbase Balance: 36241.21270 ETH

1	▾

Total: 0.0864 ETH

BUY SUBSCRIPTION

Use switch

User Address: 0x2809d4cb12b8bcaca9e4b805e474ad984c84b20d
User Amount Paid: 86400000000000000
Authorized Till: 1479286536
Authorization Status: Active

On

Figure 8.8: Screenshot of Smart Switch Dapp - turning the switch ON

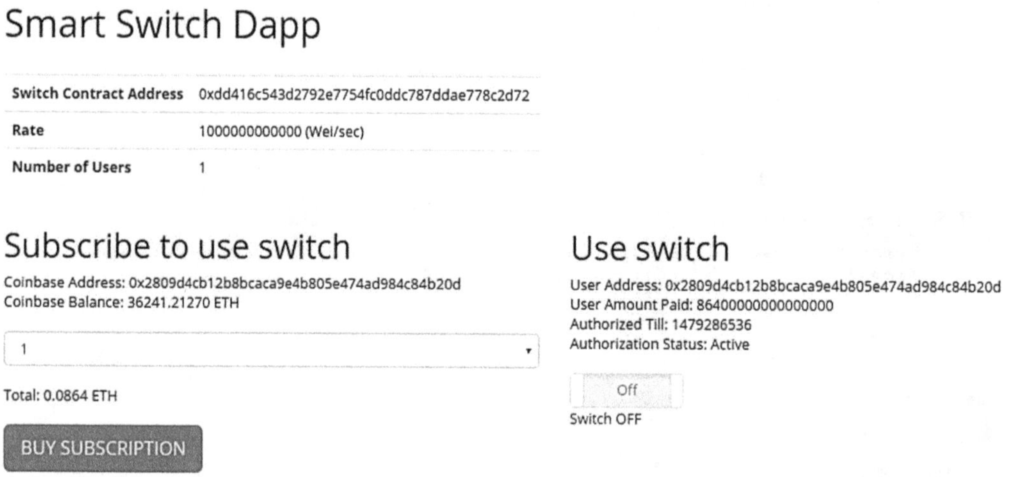

Smart Switch Dapp

Switch Contract Address	0xdd416c543d2792e7754fc0ddc787ddae778c2d72
Rate	1000000000000 (Wei/sec)
Number of Users	1

Subscribe to use switch

Coinbase Address: 0x2809d4cb12b8bcaca9e4b805e474ad984c84b20d
Coinbase Balance: 36241.21270 ETH

1	▾

Total: 0.0864 ETH

BUY SUBSCRIPTION

Use switch

User Address: 0x2809d4cb12b8bcaca9e4b805e474ad984c84b20d
User Amount Paid: 86400000000000000
Authorized Till: 1479286536
Authorization Status: Active

Off
Switch OFF

Figure 8.9: Screenshot of Smart Switch Dapp - turning the switch OFF

■ Box 8.5: NodeJS controller component that runs on the IoT device

```
var mraa     = require('mraa'); //npm install mraa
var Web3     = require('web3'); //npm install web3
var gethURL = 'http://127.0.0.1:8101';
var provider = new Web3.providers.HttpProvider(gethURL);
var web3 = new Web3(provider);
var switchStatus='OFF';
var turnedON=false;
var relayPin    = new mraa.Gpio(67);

// Contract ABI
var abi = [{"constant":true,"inputs":[],"name":"numUsers",
```

```
"outputs":[{"name":"","type":"uint256"}],"type":"function"},
{"constant":false,"inputs":[],"name":"buySubscription","outputs":[],
"type":"function"},{"constant":true,"inputs":[],"name":"rate",
"outputs":[{"name":"","type":"uint256"}],"type":"function"},
{"constant":false,"inputs":[],"name":"destroy","outputs":[],
"type":"function"},{"constant":false,"inputs":[{"name":"userAddr",
"type":"address"}],"name":"isUserAuthorized","outputs":[{"name":"",
"type":"bool"}],"type":"function"},{"constant":true,"inputs":[],
"name":"owner","outputs":[{"name":"","type":"address"}],
"type":"function"},{"constant":true,"inputs":[{"name":"",
"type":"address"}],"name":"users","outputs":[{"name":"amountPaid",
"type":"uint256"},{"name":"authorizedTill","type":"uint256"}],
"type":"function"},{"inputs":[{"name":"_rate","type":"uint256"}],
"type":"constructor"}];

// Contract address
var contractAddress = '0xdd416c543d2792e7754fc0ddc787ddae778c2d72';

// Create contract object
var MyContract = web3.eth.contract(abi);

// Instantiate contract for an address
var myContractInstance = MyContract.at(contractAddress);

function turnON(){
    console.log("Switching ON");
    switchStatus='ON';
    relayPin.write(0);
}

function turnOFF(){
    console.log("Switching OFF");
    switchStatus='OFF';
    relayPin.write(1);
}

function setup() {
    console.log("web3 version:", web3.version.api);
    console.log('MRAA Version: ' + mraa.getVersion());
    relayPin.dir(mraa.DIR_OUT);
    turnOFF();

    web3.shh.filter({
        "topics": [ web3.fromAscii(contractAddress) ]
    }).watch(function(err, message){
        console.log(message)
        var data = {};
        try {
            data = JSON.parse(web3.toAscii(message.payload));
        } catch(error) {
            return;
        }

        //Call contract to if user is authorized
```

```
            var result = myContractInstance.isUserAuthorized.call(data.from);

        if(result==true){
            //Toggle switch based on data.target
            if(data.target=='ON'){
                turnON();
            }else if(data.target=='OFF'){
                turnOFF();
            }
        }
    });

}

function loop(){
    if(switchStatus=='ON' && turnedON==false){
        console.log("Switch is now ON");
        turnedON=true;
    }else if(switchStatus=='OFF' && turnedON==true){
        console.log("Switch is now OFF");
        turnedON=false;
    }
}

// Run setup
setup();

// Run loop
setInterval(loop, 2000);
```

Box 8.6 shows the output of NodeJS controller component that runs on the IoT device. In the output, we can see the contents of the Whisper messages.

■ Box 8.6: Output of NodeJS controller component that runs on the IoT device

```
$ node controller.js
web3 version: 0.17.0-alpha
---------------------------
Message Received:
{ payload: '0x7b2266726f6d223a22307832383039643463636231326238626
           36163613965346238303565343734616439383463383462323230
           64222c22746172676574223a224f4e227d',
  to: '0x0',
  from: '0x0',
  sent: 1479200152,
  ttl: 50,
  hash: '0xca23b4879bb1cc05b8fbaa0901aa74d3bc3b0874
        ad9caf9e144a4a58e8177173',
  expiry: 0,
  workProved: 0,
  topics: [] }
---------------------------
Switching ON
```

```
Switch is now ON
--------------------------
Message Received:
{ payload: '0x7b2266726f6d223a2230783238303964346363623132623862636
            1636139653462383035653437346164393834633834623302306422
            2c22746172676574223a224f4646227d',
  to: '0x0',
  from: '0x0',
  sent: 1479200186,
  ttl: 50,
  hash: '0xc6b47dcdc58d9c5fc0fd52d31d24615ad110b74dd
         02aae691e37bc23483632f6',
  expiry: 0,
  workProved: 0,
  topics: [] }
--------------------------
Switching OFF
Switch is now OFF
```

Summary

In this chapter, we described the Whisper communication protocol that allows decentralized applications (Dapps) to communicate with each other. With Whisper, Dapps can publish messages to each other. Whisper messages are transient in nature and have a time-to-live (TTL) set. Each message has one or more topics associated with it. The Dapps running on a node inform the node about the topics to which they want to subscribe. Whisper uses topic-based routing where the nodes advertise their topics of interest to their peers. Topics are used for filtering the messages which are delivered to a node, which are then distributed to the Dapps running on the node. Whisper can be considered as a hybrid of a distributed hash table (DHT) and a datagram messaging system. If Whisper is considered as a DHT, then Envelope plays the role of an item/value, which has associated keys or topics. If Whisper is considered as a datagram messaging system then Envelope plays the role of a packet which contains an encrypted datagram. In Whisper, the routing privacy and routing efficiency of a message can be configured by the user. We described the Whisper communication patterns such as anonymous broadcast, clear-signed broadcast, encrypted anonymous message, and encrypted signed message. Next, we described the Whisper wire protocol and the steps involved in posting a new Whisper message. Next, we described the use of topics, abridged topics and bloomed topics in Whisper. We described the Whisper's routing approach which is 'dark' in nature where the identity of the sender and receiver is not known to the intermediate routing nodes in the network. Whisper uses passive and active routing approaches to route messages probabilistically. We described the Whisper's JavaScript API. Finally, we described an implementation case study of Smart Switch Dapp that makes use of Whisper messages.

9 - Swarm

This chapter covers

- Swarm Architecture and Concepts
  - Swarm Nodes
  - Storage Layer
  - Network Layer
- Incentive Mechanisms in Swarm
  - SWAP
  - SWEAR
  - SWINDLE
- Swarm Setup
- Working with Swarm
- Swarm Dapp Examples
- Case Study: Stock Photos Dapp

Swarm is a decentralized storage platform and content distribution service for Ethereum. Swarm forms the base layer of the Ethereum blockchain stack described in Chapter-1. Swarm has been designed to serve as a decentralized and redundant store of Ethereum's public record, and also to store and distribute Dapp code. Swarm is a peer-to-peer storage platform which is maintained by the peers who contribute their storage and bandwidth resources. Being a peer-to-peer system, Swarm has no single point of failure and is resistant to faults and distributed denial of service (DDoS) attacks. Swarm is also censorship-resistant as it is not controlled by any central authority. Swarm has a built-in incentive system for peers who pool in their storage and bandwidth resources. Swarm has been designed to dynamically scale up to serve popular content and has a mechanism to ensure the availability of the content which is not popular or frequently requested.

9.1 Swarm Architecture and Concepts

9.1.1 Swarm Nodes

Swarm is enabled by swarm nodes or peers who are connected to the Ethereum blockchain network. The nodes pool in their storage and bandwidth resources to offer distributed storage and content distribution services. Each swarm node has an address (called the *bzzkey*) which is derived from the Keccak 256-bit SHA3 hash of the Ethereum coinbase address of the node.

9.1.2 Storage Layer

Data Units

When a user uploads new content (e.g a document/file) to Swarm, it is broken up into fixed size uints (of max size 4096 bytes) called *chunks*. A chunk is a basic unit of storage in swarm. Each chunk is uniquely identified by a swarm-hash which also serves as an address of the chunk. Swarm defines a data structure called Manifest which allows URL-based access to content and collections of documents. A manifest defines a mapping between arbitrary paths and documents to handle document collections. Manifest includes metadata for each document in a collection (such as path, hash, and content-type). Swarm provides a high-level API for the manifests which allows users to upload and download a single document or a collection of documents.

LocalStore

The Swarm LocalStore provides local computing resources for a swarm node. The LocalStore comprises an in-memory fast cache (called MemStore) and a persistent disk storage (called DBStore). Both MemStore and DBStore are of the type ChunkStore implemented by swarm. LocalStore implements Get and Put methods for storing and retrieving chunks.

NetStore

The Swarm NetStore implements a distributed hash table (DHT). The Swarm DHT is 'strictly content addressed', meaning that the node (or nodes) which are closest to the address of a chunk actually host and serve the content. NetStore implements the shared logic of network served chunk store/retrieval requests. The store/retrieval requests can either be local (coming from DPA API) or remote (coming from peers via bzz protocol).

Distributed Preimage Archive

The Distributed Preimage Archive (DPA) is the local interface for storage and retrieval of documents. DPA provides the Store and Retrieve client API entry points. When a store request is received, the DPA calls the Chunker to segment the document or the input data stream into a Merkle hashed tree of chunks. The key of the root block of the Merkle tree is returned to the client. This key can be later used to retrieve the content. When a retrieve request is received along with the key of the root block of the content to retrieve, the DPA retrieves the block chunks and reconstructs the original data and passes it back as a *lazy reader*. The lazy reader is a reader which retrieves the relevant parts of the underlying document on-demand (i.e. only when they are actually read). Thus, the chunks which are needed to reconstruct a document, are only retrieved and processed if that particular part of the document is actually read.

Chunker

Chunker is the interface to a component that segments large data into fixed size data units called chunks. Chunker is a pluggable component and can support different data chunking approaches. The current implementation of Swarm, uses the *TreeChunker* which implements a Chunker based on a tree structure. The TreeChunker works as follows:

1. The TreeChunker builds a tree out of the document where each node in the tree including the root and other branching nodes are stored as a chunk.
2. A node can either be a leaf node or a branching non-leaf node. A leaf node encodes an actual subslice of the input data. A branching non-leaf node encodes data contents that include the size of the data slice covered by its entire subtree under the node as well as the hash keys of all its children.
3. The maximum chunk size is 4096 bytes. If the data size is less than maximum chunk size, the data is stored in a single chunk, where the key of the root block of the content is defined as: key = hash(int64(size) + data).
4. If the data size is more than the chunk-size, the data is split into slices where all the slices (except the last one) are of equal size. The key of the root block of the content is defined as: key = hash(int64(size) + key(slice0) + key(slice1) + ...).
5. The hash algorithm used is configurable. In the current implementation, Swarm uses the *bzzhash* algorithm.

When a store request is received, the DPA calls the split method of the chunker which splits the document into chunks and builds the tree. The resulting chunks are pushed to the DPA. The DPA then dispatches the chunk store requests to its ChunkStore (NetStore or LocalStore) and the root hash of the document tree is returned to the user.

Swarm Hash

Swarm uses a Merkle tree hash-based scheme as shown in Figure 9.1. Swarm-hash is the cryptographic hash of the data that serves as its unique identifier and address. The smallest unit of data that is identified by a swarm hash is a chunk. Swarm uses a hashing algorithm called *bzzhash*. A tree structure is generated by the Chunker when a document is uploaded to Swarm. The tree structure includes two types of nodes: leaf nodes and branching nodes. The leaf nodes store an actual subslice of the input data. Whereas the branching nodes store the hashes of all its children. For a leaf-node, the hash is computed for the concatenation of the 64-bit length of the subslice of the data, and the subslice itself. For a branching node, the hash is computed for the concatenation of the 64-bit length of the content hashed by the entire sub-tree rooted on that chunk and the hashes of its children. The hash function used by *bzzhash* is the Keccak 256-bit SHA3. The hash tree generated for a document must be balanced, i.e., all root to leaf branches should be of equal length. All the chunks in the tree are of 4096 bytes. The rightmost chunk can be of a smaller size. The hash of the root of the tree generated for some content (root-hash) uniquely identifies the content. The hashes are collision free and no two documents/files can have the same hash. The hash function used is deterministic in nature and the same content always leads to the same hash. This hashing scheme ensures that the content stored in Swarm is immutable and also guarantees data integrity. Any attempt to change the content will change the hash. Since the hash is dependent on the content, Swarm has a self-addressing scheme for content.

The addresses of the swarm nodes and the swarm-hashes of the content belong to the same address space. Thus it is possible to define a distance measure for the address space to compute the distance of a node from some content. Swarm stores the chunks on the nodes which are closest to the chunk addresses.

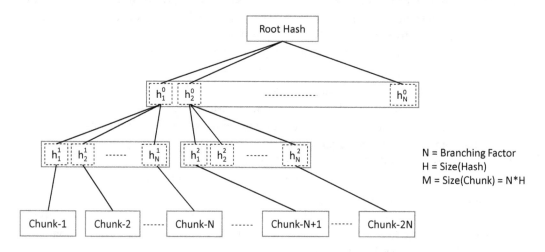

Figure 9.1: Swarm's Merkle tree structure

Syncing

Swarm uses a strictly content addressed distributed hash table (DHT), where the nodes closest to some content not only serve the content but also store the content. Swarm has a synchronization protocol (called *syncing*) that ensures that the chunks (generated from the content) are moved from the uploader to the nodes which are closest to the chunk addresses. When the DPA dispatches a new chunk to the swarm storage network, the syncing process propagates the chunk from node to node till the chunk ends up at the node whose address is closest to the chunk hash. This syncing process makes it easier for chunks to be located and retrieved later. Each Swarm node has a syncer agent which manages content distribution and forwarding of chunks. The syncer agents on a node forward all chunks to nodes whose address is closer to the chunk addresses. Syncing also handles the delivery of chunks for a retrieve request. For delivery, the chunks are forwarded from the nodes where they are stored to the node requesting the chunks.

Storing & Retrieving Data

Swarm makes use of content-addressed ChunkStores for storing the chunks. The chunk addresses and the node addresses come from the same value space, thus the same distance measure can be used to compute the distance between two chunks or two nodes or a chunk and a node. Since swarm makes use of an address-key based retrieval protocol, the probability of a given chunk being ever requested is inversely proportional to the distance of the chunk from the node. In other words, the closer a chunk is to a node, the higher is the probability of the chunk being requested by the node.

The syncing process propagates the chunks to the nodes which are closer to the chunks as shown in Figure 9.2. As new chunks reach the nodes closest to them, the chunks are stored on the nodes. When the storage capacity of a node is reached, the oldest requested chunks are deleted to make space for new chunks. Due to this mechanism of storing chunks based on their access counts, the content which is more frequently accessed is more likely to remain available, while the content which is rarely requested may get deleted. Swarm has an incentive mechanism to ensure availability of content, which is described later this chapter.

When a chunk is requested, the chunk retrieve requests are forwarded to nodes which are closer to the chunk, as shown in Figure 9.3. When a chunk request reaches the node which has the chunk, the chunk is delivered back to the requester along the same path from which the request came. When a chunk is served, the intermediate nodes in the request path store the chunk. Thus, repeated requests for a chunk can be served either from the local store of a node or the nearby nodes. This strategy of caching the forwarded chunks, ensures auto-scaling of the Swarm network to handle popular content. The more popular a content is (or more frequently the content is accessed), a more number of nodes will have that content and will be able to serve the retrieve requests for the content. This mechanism of auto-scaling also reduces the retrieve latency for popular content and reduces the network traffic.

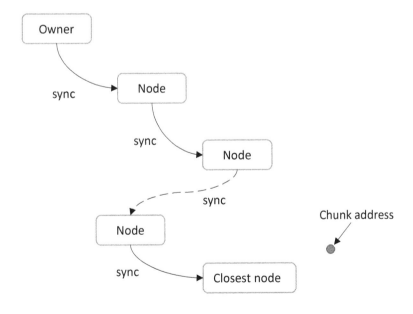

Figure 9.2: Storing a chunk

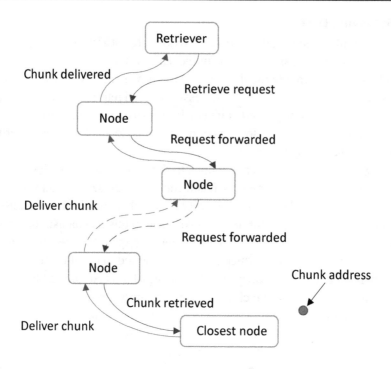

Figure 9.3: Retrieving a chunk

9.1.3 Network Layer

Kademlia Routing

Swarm uses a peer-to-peer distributed hash table (DHT) called Kademlia [44]. Kademlia offers very low and constant lookup times for nodes in a peer-to-peer network. Lookup time is logarithmic in the network size, i.e. O(log N), where N is the number of nodes in the network. Kademlia also has a low coordination overhead as it optimizes the number of control messages sent to other nodes.

Swarm uses Kademlia key-based routing for locating nodes and chunks in the network. The key for a chunk is the hash of the chunk. Similarly, the key for a node is the address of the node. Since the chunk hash and node addresses come from the same value space, a distance measure can be used to compute the distance between two chunks, two nodes or a chunk and a node. Kademlia uses XOR as the distance metric. The XOR distance metric satisfies the triangle inequality. To compute the distance between two nodes, the node addresses (which are 256-bits in length) are XORed bitwise and the resulting value is treated as a distance. Similarly, the distance between a node and chunk can be computed. The chunks are stored on the node(s) which are closest to the chunk addresses.

Each Swarm node maintains a Kademlia peer table or node table, which has a minimum of one row and a maximum of 255 rows. There is a row for each bit of the node address. Each row contains entries for nodes. A node entry contains all the information which is required for locating a node, such as the node address, node URL and last active time of a node. The row numbering starts from 0. The nth row contains all the nodes for which the first $n-1$ bits in the node address are the same. In other words, the nth row has entries for nodes which have the nth bit differing in their address. Each row can have at most k entries where k is called the *bucket size*.

Figure 9.4 shows an example of a Kademlia binary tree which shows 11 nodes. The addresses/IDs of the nodes are also shown. Since the node addresses are of 4-bits, the maximum network size in this example is $2^4 = 16$. There can be 4 rows in the Kademlia node table for each node. The figure shows the network partition for the node with the address 1110. The Kademlia table rows or k-buckets are represented by encircled nodes. The first row has the nodes which differ in bit-0 (node 1111). The second row has the nodes which differ in bit-1 (nodes 1100, 1101). The third row has the nodes which differ in bit-2 (nodes 1000, 1001, 1010). The fourth row has the nodes which differ in bit-3 (nodes 0000, 0001, 0010, 0100).

When a node wants to look up a chunk, it will first contact other nodes in the same row (k-bucket) of its Kademlia node table, which are closer to the target address, than the node itself. When these nodes receive a lookup request, they will look up the nodes in their respective rows (k-buckets) and return a list of best nodes which are closer to the target. Next, the nodes in this list are contacted. The search iterations continue in a similar manner till no other node is returned which is closer to the target, than the node previously returned. The chunk is retrieved from the node which is closest to the chunk address.

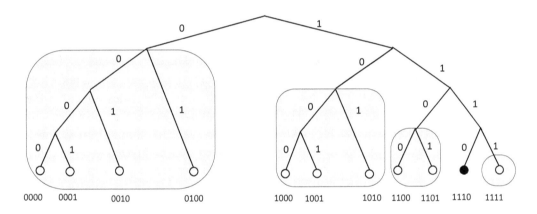

Figure 9.4: Example of a Kademlia binary tree

Hive

Hive is the logistic manager of Swarm. Hive maintains the Kademlia node table for each node, which has a list of active nodes in the network partitioned into rows or k-buckets. Hive provides methods for adding/removing peers to/from the Kademlia node table. Hive allows retrieving a list of live nodes that are closer to target than the current node itself. The search for content in Swarm proceeds with looking up nodes which are closer the to target than the current node.

Bzz Protocol

In Chapter-8, we described the Whisper sub-protocol called *shh* that runs on the Ethereum DEVp2p wire protocol. Similarly, Swarm also defines a sub-protocol called *bzz*. The bzz protocol instance runs on every Swarm node. The bzz protocol provides the following functionalities:

1. Handles protocol handshake.
2. Registers peers in the Kademlia table via the Hive logistic manager.
3. Dispatches to Hive for handling the DHT logic.
4. Encodes and decodes requests for storage and retrieval.
5. Handles sync protocol messages via the Syncer.
6. Talks the SWAP payment protocol.

9.2 Incentive Mechanisms in Swarm

In this section, we describe the incentive mechanisms in Swarm. The objective of these incentive mechanisms is to ensure that Swarm is self-sustaining and the nodes cooperate with each other. The incentive mechanisms reward nodes which play nicely and cooperate with other nodes and penalize nodes which do not cooperate, or try to hog the resources of other nodes. The incentive mechanisms are categorized into bandwidth or storage incentives, since these are the two types of resources which are contributed by the nodes to maintain Swarm.

9.2.1 SWAP

SWAP stands for Swarm Accounting Protocol. Swap is the Swarm's bandwidth incentive mechanism which keeps track of the number of chunks provided/received per peer. Swap is also called so because it keeps track of the information swapped between nodes. The basic unit of accounting is a chunk. When a node delivers a chunk to another node, it charges a fee for the service it provides. Swap is a pairwise accounting protocol, i.e., a node keeps a record of the chunks served to, and received from each node. The nodes can either trade chunk-for-chunk or chunk-for-payment. The basic idea behind Swap is that the nodes which serve content to its peers earn fees for making the content available. Similarly, nodes which download content, have to pay for it. With Swap, the nodes are incentivized to serve content. Nodes which serve popular content can earn more. Swap incentive mechanism also ensures that popular content will be widely distributed, and will have a more number of nodes serving the content. This makes Swam auto-scaling in nature, decreases the latency for popular content, and increases the available bandwidth.

In an ideal scenario, where the nodes serve each other well, the balance between any two nodes is close to zero. When a node serves more content than it receives from another, its balance increases. If the balance exceeds a certain threshold, the node can request a payment from the other node. However, if the balance of the serving node become too high and the served node becomes heavily indebted, the served node can be disconnected. Swarm defines the payment and disconnect thresholds. When the payment threshold is reached, the serving node can request a payment from the served node. When the disconnect threshold is reached, a heavily indebted node is disconnected. Thus, it is in the best interest of the nodes to keep their balance close to zero. When two nodes connect, they let each other know of their highest accepted chunk price and offered chunk price as a part of the protocol handshake. Exchange of chunks between nodes is possible only if the highest accepted chunk price of one node is less than the offered chunk price of the other.

For payments, Swarm makes use of a *chequebook* contract on the blockchain. Box 9.1 shows the Solidity implementation of the chequebook contract. The cheques are cumulative in nature and a node only has to cash the last cheque. To cash a cheque, a node sends a transaction with the signed cheque as the data to the *cash* method of the chequebook contract. The beneficiary node is paid the difference between the cumulative amount on the cheque and the cumulative amount on the last cashed cheque.

■ **Box 9.1: Solidity implementation of the chequebook contract**

```
import "mortal";

contract chequebook is mortal {
    // Cumulative paid amount in wei to each beneficiary
    mapping (address => uint256) public sent;

    event Overdraft(address deadbeat);

    /// Function to Cash cheque
    /// Parameters:
    /// beneficiary - beneficiary address
    /// amount - cumulative amount in wei
    /// sig_v - signature parameter v
    /// sig_r - signature parameter r
    /// sig_s - signature parameter s
    function cash(address beneficiary, uint256 amount,
        uint8 sig_v, bytes32 sig_r, bytes32 sig_s) {
        // Check if the cheque is old.
        // Only cheques that are more recent than the
        // last cashed one are considered.
        if(amount <= sent[beneficiary]) return;

        // Check the digital signature of the cheque.
        bytes32 hash = sha3(address(this), beneficiary, amount);
        if(owner != ecrecover(hash, sig_v, sig_r, sig_s)) return;

        // Attempt sending the difference between
        // the cumulative amount on the cheque
        // and the cumulative amount on the last
        // cashed cheque to beneficiary.
        if (amount - sent[beneficiary] >= this.balance) {
        // update the cumulative amount before sending
            sent[beneficiary] = amount;
            if (!beneficiary.send(amount - sent[beneficiary])) {
                // Upon failure to execute send, revert everything
                throw;
            }
        } else {
            // Upon failure, punish owner for writing a bounced cheque.
            Overdraft(owner);
            // Compensate beneficiary.
            suicide(beneficiary);
        }
    }
}
```

9.2.2 SWEAR

SWEAR stands for Storage With Enforced Archiving Rules or Swarm Enforcement And Registration. Swear is a storage incentive in Swarm to ensure that the data remains available. Swear is designed to address the "upload and disappear" problem, where a user uploads content only once, and then disappears from the network. Now if the user wants to make sure that the content remains available for a long time, even if the content is not popular, the user can pay other nodes to keep the data available. Swear mechanism allows the content owners to purchase storage promises from other nodes in the form of an insurance. A storage promise is valid for a certain period. The nodes that sell such 'promises-to-store' are registered with the Swear contract on the blockchain. The registered nodes pay a deposit to the Swear contract. When a registered node receives a request to store a chunk, it issues the storage promise in the form of a signed receipt. The deposit remains locked till the storage promise is active. When the storage promise expires, a registered node is entitled to receive its deposit back. If the registered node loses the content before the storage promise expires, the node loses its deposit. Thus registered nodes who 'swear' to keep the content available must fulfill their promises or lose their deposit.

9.2.3 SWINDLE

SWINDLE stands for Secured With INsurance Deposit Litigation and Escrow. Swindle is a mechanism to ensure that the registered nodes who 'swear' to keep the content available do not violate their promises. Swindle has auditing and litigation procedures to enforce the nodes to adhere to the rules. To check if the registered nodes are fulfilling their promises to keep the content, any node can issue a *challenge* for some specific chunk. The registered nodes who promised to keep that chunk, respond to the challenge with a *refutation*. To check the validity of a challenge and its refutation, the Swindle smart contract is used. A node can report the loss of some content by sending a challenge. The challenge is sent in the form of a transaction to the Swindle smart contract, with receipt(s) of the lost chunk as the data. The node who sends a challenge, has to pay an upfront deposit. This deposit is used to compensate the node who refutes the challenge, by uploading the chunk. The deposit requirement also prevents nodes from sending bogus challenges. To refute the challenge, the registered node which has the chunk presents the chunk to the contract. The contract validates the refutation of a challenge by checking if the hash of the presented chunk matches the receipt sent with the challenge. If the refutation is found to be valid, the node who refutes the challenge is compensated from the deposit of the challenge and the remaining amount is refunded.

If a challenge is not refuted and a chunk is indeed lost, a litigation is initiated. Nodes who promised to keep the chunk are punished if they are proven guilty of losing the chunk in the litigation process. The punishment is in the form of forfeit of deposit and cancellation of the node's registration.

9.3 Swarm Setup

As of writing this chapter, Swarm is in its early stages of development. The Swarm source code has been merged to the 'develop' branch of the go-ethereum repository on Github. To setup a Swarm node, download the latest go-ethereum source code from Github and build the go-ethereum client (*geth*) and Swarm tools as shown in Box 9.2. The Swarm tools include, the swarm daemon *bzzd*, swarm uploader *bzzup* and swarm hash calculator *bzzhash*.

■ Box 9.2: Setting up Swarm

```
# Prepare environment. Requires Go-Lang
export GOROOT=/usr/lib/go
export GOPATH="$HOME/go"

# Download go-ethereum source code
mkdir -p $GOPATH/src/github.com/ethereum
cd $GOPATH/src/github.com/ethereum
git clone https://github.com/ethereum/go-ethereum
cd go-ethereum
git checkout master
go get github.com/ethereum/go-ethereum

# Build go-ethereum and swarm tools
go build ./cmd/bzzd
go build ./cmd/bzzup
go build ./cmd/bzzhash
go build ./cmd/geth
```

Next, run the *geth* client and create one or more Ethereum accounts as described in Chapter-4. Note the Ethereum coinbase address or the address of the first account you create. Next, run the *geth* client to setup a private blockchain network and start mining. To start a Swarm node, run the *bzzd* daemon and connect the swarm daemon to the geth instance as shown in Box 9.3. Provide the address of the Ethereum coinbase account with *–bzzaccount* option while running the *bzzd* daemon. When the Swarm node is started, a Swarm HTTP proxy is setup on localhost:8500. You can also specify alternative proxy endpoints with the *–bzzapi* option.

■ Box 9.3: Starting a Swarm node

```
# Run Geth and start mining
./geth --datadir "$HOME/ethereum/datadir" --dev \
    --unlock 0,1 --mine --minerthreads 2 --rpc \
    --rpcaddr 0.0.0.0 --rpccorsdomain "*" --rpcport 8101 \
    --ipcpath "$HOME/ethereum/datadir/geth.ipc"

# Start Swarm node
./bzzd --bzzaccount "2809d4cb12b8bcaca9e4b805e474ad984c84b20d" \
    --datadir "$HOME/ethereum/datadir" \
    --ethapi "$HOME/ethereum/datadirgeth.ipc" \
    --maxpeers 0 \
```

9.4   Working with Swarm

When a Swarm node is started, a Swarm HTTP proxy is setup on localhost:8500. Swarm provides three distinct URL schemes for retrieving files, described as follows:

- **bzz**: The bzz URL scheme uses a manifest and a path. The manifest includes the manifest ID and one or more entries. Each entry includes a swarm hash and content-type of the document/file.

- **bzzi**: The bzzi URL scheme is the immutable scheme such that a given URL will always serve the same immutable content.
- **bzzr**: The bzzr URL scheme is the raw scheme which serves the content addressed by the URL directly without using a manifest. While the bzz and bzzi schemes are read-only schemes that support only GET requests, the bzzr scheme supports GET, POST and PUT requests.

Box 9.4 shows the commands for uploading a single file to Swarm using the *bzzup* swarm uploader. When the file is uploaded, the manifest is returned. In this case, the manifest contains the ID/address of the manifest (beginning with e124), and only one entry which includes the swarm hash (beginning with 12dd), and the content-type of the file. To retrieve the file from Swarm, you can either use the *wget* command line utility or simply point your browser to http://localhost:8500/bzz:/HASH, where HASH is the ID of a swarm manifest.

■ Box 9.4: Uploading a single file to Swarm and retrieving the file

```
# Uploading a single file to Swarm
$ ./bzzup /home/arshdeep/data.txt
uploading file /home/arshdeep/data.txt (12 bytes)
uploading manifest
{
  "hash": "e12494e670dc643b374c89975a88d08d42fc5e
          4e3bcb39a4219972ca3884ffc3",
  "entries": [
    {
      "hash": "12dd380c8a628e56a20ad6d69c748ff205
              b0c1c93e8734aad2c449ebc64e3388",
      "contentType": "text/plain; charset=utf-8"
    }
  ]
}


---


# Retrieving a file from Swarm
wget http://localhost:8500/bzz:/e12494e670dc643b37
     4c89975a88d08d42fc5e4e3bcb39a4219972ca3884ffc3
```

Box 9.5 shows the commands for uploading a directory to Swarm. When the directory is uploaded, the manifest is returned. In this case, the manifest contains the ID/address of the manifest and an entry for each file in the directory, along with their swarm hashes, content types, and paths within the directory. To retrieve a file within the directory from Swarm, you can either use the wget command line utility or simply point your browser to http://localhost:8500/bzz:/HASH/path, where HASH is the ID of a swarm manifest.

■ **Box 9.5: Uploading a directory to Swarm and retrieving a file from the directory**

```
# Uploading a directory to Swarm

$ ./bzzup --recursive /home/arshdeep/docs/
uploading file /home/arshdeep/docs/data.txt (12 bytes)
uploading file /home/arshdeep/docs/img.jpg (1998 bytes)
uploading file /home/arshdeep/docs/sample.pdf (2247 bytes)
uploading manifest
{
  "hash": "9dd0ebc5099fb9bad60fcf9feff14626e7bd4f
           27ed2e490806f0207fd806d8d7",
  "entries": [
    {
      "hash": "12dd380c8a628e56a20ad6d69c748ff205b
              0c1c93e8734aad2c449ebc64e3388",
      "contentType": "text/plain; charset=utf-8",
      "path": "data.txt"
    },
    {
      "hash": "4e87ccb50b6d284ea032bf2fe3521c7c61d5
              ad290152c7e4ec36bf3a08bf5225",
      "contentType": "image/jpeg",
      "path": "img.jpg"
    },
    {
      "hash": "e90d8050cdedbe2df078b6ed688efccf8caf3
              20d95633081fabd14121063aac6",
      "contentType": "application/pdf",
      "path": "sample.pdf"
    }
  ]
}

---

# Retrieving a file within the directory
wget http://localhost:8500/bzz:/9dd0ebc5099fb9bad60fcf9
      feff14626e7bd4f27ed2e490806f0207fd806d8d7/data.txt
```

Swarm provides an HTTP API for uploading and retrieving content. HTTP API works with the bzzr (raw) scheme and supports GET, POST and PUT request types. Box 9.6 shows the commands for uploading content to Swarm and retrieving the content using the HTTP interface. To upload new content to Swarm, we use the bzzr (raw) scheme and send a POST request with the content as the request payload. The Swarm hash of the content is returned in the response of the POST request. To retrieve the content, we send a GET request using the Swarm hash.

▪ Box 9.6: Uploading content to Swarm and retrieving the content using the HTTP interface

```
# Posting content to Swarm

$ curl -i -X POST -d "Hello World" http://localhost:8500/bzzr:/
HTTP/1.1 200 OK
Accept-Ranges: bytes
Content-Length: 64
Content-Type: text/plain
Last-Modified: Fri, 25 Nov 2016 10:11:12 GMT
Date: Fri, 25 Nov 2016 10:11:12 GMT

d85117d40c1b74239bf0b0c4f8201e2be7d85c36efbbddc77fb9b58ed3964287

--

# Retrieving content from Swarm

$ curl -i http://localhost:8500/bzzr:/d85117d40c1b74239bf0b0c4f8
                       201e2be7d85c36efbbddc77fb9b58ed3964287
HTTP/1.1 200 OK
Accept-Ranges: bytes
Content-Length: 11
Content-Type: application/octet-stream
Last-Modified: Fri, 25 Nov 2016 10:11:47 GMT
Date: Fri, 25 Nov 2016 10:11:47 GMT

Hello World
```

Box 9.7 shows the commands for uploading different types of files to Swarm and retrieving the files using the HTTP interface. To upload a file we use the *–data-binary* option of the CURL utility and provide the file path. To retrieve a file, you can point your browser to http://localhost:8500/bzzr:/HASH?content_type=<type>, where HASH is the Swarm hash of the file returned when the content is uploaded, and the *content_type* specifies the type of the file.

▪ Box 9.7: Uploading files to Swarm and retrieving the files using the HTTP interface

```
# Upload JPG image file to Swarm

curl -i -X POST --data-binary "@/home/ubuntu/img.jpg"
    http://localhost:8500/bzzr:/

--

# View JPG image file in browser
http://localhost:8500/bzzr:/4e87ccb50b6d284ea032bf2f
    e3521c7c61d5ad290152c7e4ec36bf3a08bf5225?content_type=image/jpeg

-----
```

```
# Upload PDF file to Swarm
curl -i -X POST --data-binary "@/home/ubuntu/data.pdf"
    http://localhost:8500/bzzr:/

--
# View PDF file in browser
http://localhost:8500/bzzr:/5b5570b68d5745e3f06536d585
    3a348b644fd404ebc519331daccd2255bf1d46?content_type=application/pdf
```

9.5 Case Study: Stock Photos Dapp

In this section, we describe a case study of a Dapp for stock photos. With this Dapp, users (who own original photos) can upload their photos to the Dapp and set a price for sale. Other users can browse through the stock photos from the Dapp and purchase the photos they like. This Dapp uses Swarm for storing the original photos and their watermarked/thumbnail versions. The swarm hashes of the photos are stored in the smart contract associated with the Dapp. Box 9.8 shows the Solidity implementation of the smart contract for the Dapp. In the contract, we have a custom *Photo* data type which stores the information related to a photo such as the address of the author, the swarm hashes of the original photo and its thumbnail, photo upload timestamp, number of downloads of the photo and the addresses of the users who have purchased the photo.

■ Box 9.8: Stock Photos contract

```
contract StockPhotos {
    struct Photo {
        address author;
        string title;
        string tags;
        string photoID;
        string thumbnailID;
        uint timestamp;
        uint price;
        uint downloads;
        mapping(address => uint) usersPaid;
    }

    address public owner;
    uint public numPhotos;
    mapping(bytes32 => Photo) photos;
    mapping (uint => bytes32) photosIndex;

    function StockPhotos(){
        owner = msg.sender;
        numPhotos=0;
    }

    function newPhoto(string _photoIDString, string _thumbnailIDString,
                string _title, string _tags, uint _price) returns (bool){
        bytes32 _photoID = stringToBytes(_photoIDString);
```

```
        bytes32 _thumbnailID = stringToBytes(_thumbnailIDString);
        if (photoExists(_thumbnailIDString)) {
            return false;
        }else{
            Photo p = photos[_thumbnailID];
            p.author = msg.sender;
            p.title = _title;
            p.tags = _tags;
            p.photoID = _photoIDString;
            p.thumbnailID = _thumbnailIDString;
            p.timestamp = block.timestamp;
            p.price = _price;
            p.downloads = 0;
            photosIndex[numPhotos] = _thumbnailID;

            numPhotos++;
            return true;
        }
    }

    function photoExists(string _thumbnailIDString) returns (bool){
        bytes32 _thumbnailID = stringToBytes(_thumbnailIDString);
        if (photos[_thumbnailID].timestamp>0) {
            return true;
        }else{
            return false;
        }
    }

    function getPhotoWithID(string _thumbnailIDString) returns (string){
        bytes32 _thumbnailID = stringToBytes(_thumbnailIDString);

        // User has not purchased the photo
        if(photos[_thumbnailID].usersPaid[msg.sender]==0){
            throw;
        }

        return photos[_thumbnailID].photoID;

    }

    function getPhotoWithIndex(uint index) returns (string thumbnailID,
                            address author, string title, string tags,
                            uint timestamp, uint price, uint downloads){
        thumbnailID = photos[photosIndex[index]].thumbnailID;
        author = photos[photosIndex[index]].author;
        title = photos[photosIndex[index]].title;
        tags = photos[photosIndex[index]].tags;
        timestamp = photos[photosIndex[index]].timestamp;
        price = photos[photosIndex[index]].price;
        downloads = photos[photosIndex[index]].downloads;
    }

    function buyPhoto(string _thumbnailIDString){
```

```
            bytes32 _thumbnailID = stringToBytes(_thumbnailIDString);

            if(msg.value<photos[_thumbnailID].price){
                throw;
            }

            photos[_thumbnailID].downloads +=1;
            photos[_thumbnailID].usersPaid[msg.sender] = msg.value;
        }

    function destroy() {
        if (msg.sender == owner) {
            suicide(owner);
        }
    }


    // Converts 'string' to 'bytes32'
    function stringToBytes(string s) returns (bytes32) {
      bytes memory b = bytes(s);
      uint r = 0;
      for (uint i = 0; i < 32; i++) {
          if (i < b.length) {
              r = r | uint(b[i]);
          }
          if (i < 31) r = r * 256;
      }
      return bytes32(r);
    }

}
```

Box 9.9 shows the HTML implementation of the web interface for the Dapp (index.html).

■ Box 9.9: Stock Photos Dapp HTML

```html
<!DOCTYPE html>
<html lang="en">

<head>
  <title>Stock Photos</title>
  <meta name="viewport" content="width=device-width, initial-scale=1">
  <!-- Latest compiled and minified CSS -->
  <link rel="stylesheet" href="bootstrap.min.css">
  <link rel="stylesheet" href="jquery-ui.css">
  <link href="./app.css" rel='stylesheet' type='text/css'>
  <script src="./app.js"></script>
</head>

<body>
  <iframe id="my_iframe" style="display:none;"></iframe>
  <a id="downloadContainer" download></a>
```

```
<div class="container-fluid">
  <h1>Stock Photos Dapp</h1>
  <h3 style="margin-top: 0px; margin-bottom: 30px;"></h3>

  <div id="tabs">
    <ul>
      <li><a href="#tabs-1">Upload</a></li>
      <li><a href="#tabs-2">View</a></li>
    </ul>
    <div id="tabs-1">
      <div class="row">
        <div class="col-md-8">

          <h2 style="padding-top: 20px;">Upload a Photo </h2>

          <span class="black">Coinbase Address:
  <span id="cb_address" class="c_address"></span></span><br>
          <span class="black">Coinbase Balance:
  <span id="cb_balance"></span> ETH</span><br><br>

          <input type="text" class="form-control"
          id="title" placeholder="Title" /><br>

          <input type="text" class="form-control"
          id="tags" placeholder="Tags" /><br>

          <input type="text" class="form-control"
          id="price" placeholder="Price (in Wei)" /><br>

          <span class="black">Photo Thumbnail:
  <input class="form-control" type="file"
    name="thumbnailUpload" id="thumbnailUpload" /><br>
  </span>
          <span class="black">Photo:
  <input class="form-control" type="file"
      name="fileUpload" id="fileUpload" /><br>
  </span>
          <br><br>

          <button class="btn btn-primary btn-lg"
          onclick="uploadPhoto();">UPLOAD</button>
          <br><br>
          <div id="status"> </div>
          <div id="uploadedPhoto"> </div>

        </div>
        <div class="col-md-4">

        </div>

      </div>
    </div>
    <div id="tabs-2">
      <div class="row">
```

```html
          <div class="col-md-8">

            <h2 style="padding-top: 20px;">View Photos</h2>
            <button class="btn btn-primary btn-lg"
            onclick="getPhotos();">VIEW</button>

            <br><br>
            <div id="photosContainer"></div>

          </div>

          <div class="col-md-4">
          </div>
        </div>
      </div>

      <div class="row">
        <div class="col-md-6">
          <h2 style="padding-top: 20px;">Stock Photos Contract</h2>
          <h3 style="margin-top: 0px; margin-bottom: 30px;"></h3>
          <table class="table table-fluid">

            <tr>
              <th>Contract Address</th>
              <td><span class="black"><span id="cf_address"></span>
              </span>
              </td>
            </tr>

            <tr>
              <th>Total Photos</th>
              <td><span class="black"><span id="cf_numPhotos"></span>
              </span>
              </td>
            </tr>

          </table>

        </div>

        <div class="col-md-4">
        </div>
      </div>
    </div>
    <script src="jquery.min.js"></script>
    <script src="bootstrap.min.js"></script>
    <script src="jquery-1.12.4.js"></script>
    <script src="jquery-ui.js"></script>

</body>
</html>
```

Box 9.10 shows the Dapp JavaScript (app.js).

■ Box 9.10: Stock Photos Dapp JavaScript

```javascript
var accounts;
var account;
var myContractInstance;
var photoContainerHTML;
var photosCount ;

function initializeContract() {
  myContractInstance = StockPhotos.deployed();
  $("#cf_address").html(myContractInstance.address);
  $("#cb_address").html(account);

  myContractInstance.numPhotos.call().then(
    function(numPhotos) {
      $("#cf_numPhotos").html(numPhotos.toNumber());
      photosCount = numPhotos.toNumber();
      refreshBalance();
  });
}

function setStatus(message) {
  $("#status").html(message);
};

function refreshBalance() {
  $("#cb_balance").html(web3.fromWei(
    web3.eth.getBalance(web3.eth.coinbase), "ether").toFixed(5));
}

function uploadPhoto() {
  setStatus("Uploading photo");
    var file = document.getElementById('fileUpload').files[0];

    $.ajax({
        url: "http://localhost:8500/bzzr:/",
        type: "POST",
        data: file,
        processData: false,
        success: function (result) {
          uploadThumbnail(result);
        },
        error: function (result) {
            console.log(result);
        }
    });
}

function uploadThumbnail(photoID) {
  var thumbFile = document.getElementById('thumbnailUpload').files[0];

  $.ajax({
```

```
          url: "http://localhost:8500/bzzr:/",
          type: "POST",
          data: thumbFile,
          processData: false,
          success: function (result) {
            setStatus("Uploaded Photo. Hash: "+result);
            var htmlStr = "<img src=\"http://localhost:8500/bzzr:/"+
                    result+"?content_type=image/jpeg\" width=\"300px\">";
            $("#uploadedPhoto").html(htmlStr);
            newPhoto(photoID, result);
          },
          error: function (result) {
              console.log(result);
          }
      });
}

function newPhoto(photoID, thumbnailID) {
  var title = $("#title").val();
  var tags = $("#tags").val();
  var price = parseFloat($("#price").val());

  myContractInstance.newPhoto(photoID.toString(),
          thumbnailID.toString(), title.toString(), tags.toString(),
          price, {from: web3.eth.accounts[0], gas: 2000000}).then(
      function(result) {
        console.log(result);
        return myContractInstance.numPhotos.call();
      }).then(
      function(numPhotos) {
        console.log(numPhotos);
        $("#cf_numPhotos").html(numPhotos.toNumber());
        photosCount = numPhotos.toNumber();
        return myContractInstance.photoExists.call(thumbnailID);
      }).then(
      function(exists) {
        console.log(exists);
        if (exists) {
          setStatus("Photo submitted");
        } else {
          setStatus("Error in submitting photo");
        }
        refreshBalance();
      });
}

function getPhotoWithIndex(index){
  myContractInstance.getPhotoWithIndex.call(index).then(
      function(result) {
        console.log(result);
        photoContainerHTML += "<img src=\"http://localhost:8500/bzzr:/"+
            result[0]+"?content_type=image/jpeg\" width=\"350px\" \
                style=\"float: left; margin: 0 20px 20px 0;\">";
```

```
            photoContainerHTML += "<h2>"+result[2]+"</h2>";
            photoContainerHTML += "<p>Tags: "+result[3]+"</p>";
            photoContainerHTML += "<p>Author address: "+result[1]+"</p>";
            photoContainerHTML += "<p>Upload timestamp: "+result[4]+"</p>";
            photoContainerHTML += "<p>Downloads: "+result[6]+"</p>";
            photoContainerHTML += "<p>Price: "+result[5]+" Wei</p>";

            photoContainerHTML += "<button class=\"btn btn-primary btn-lg\" \
                onclick=\"buyPhoto('"+result[0]+"','"+result[5]+"');\">\
                BUY</button>";

            photoContainerHTML += "<br><br><br><br>";
            console.log(photoContainerHTML);
            $("#photosContainer").html(photoContainerHTML);
    });
}

function buyPhoto(thumbnailID, price){
  console.log(thumbnailID);
  console.log(price);

  myContractInstance.buyPhoto(thumbnailID,
      {from: web3.eth.accounts[0], gas: 2000000,
      value: parseFloat(price)}).then(
    function(result) {
    return myContractInstance.getPhotoWithID.call(thumbnailID);
    }).then(
    function(result) {
    var photoURL = "http://localhost:8500/bzzr:/"+
                result+"?content_type=image/jpeg";
    console.log(photoURL);
    $("#downloadContainer").attr("href", photoURL);
    document.getElementById('downloadContainer').click();

    });
}

function getPhotos() {
  photoContainerHTML="";

  for(i=0;i<photosCount;i++){
    getPhotoWithIndex(i);
  }
}

window.onload = function() {
  $( "#tabs" ).tabs();
  web3.eth.getAccounts(function(err, accs) {
    if (err != null) {
      alert("There was an error fetching your accounts.");
      return;
    }

    if (accs.length == 0) {
```

```
        alert("Couldn't get any accounts! ");
        return;
    }

    accounts = accs;
    account = accounts[0];
    initializeContract();
  });
}
```

Stock Photos Dapp

| Upload | View | Search |

Upload a Photo

Coinbase Address: 0x2809d4cb12b8bcaca9e4b805e474ad984c84b20d
Coinbase Balance: 18889.99890 ETH

| Title |

| Tags |

| Price (in Wei) |

Photo Thumbnail:
| Choose File | No file chosen |

Photo:
| Choose File | No file chosen |

UPLOAD

Stock Photos Contract

Contract Address	0x3fe7b986e532e5576b7d412192d07b22893f1c77
Total Photos	2

Figure 9.5: Screenshot of Stock Photos Dapp - uploading a photo

Figure 9.5 shows a screenshot of the upload tab in the Stock Photos Dapp. To sell a photo through the Dapp, original content owners can upload their photos through the Dapp's

Stock Photos Dapp

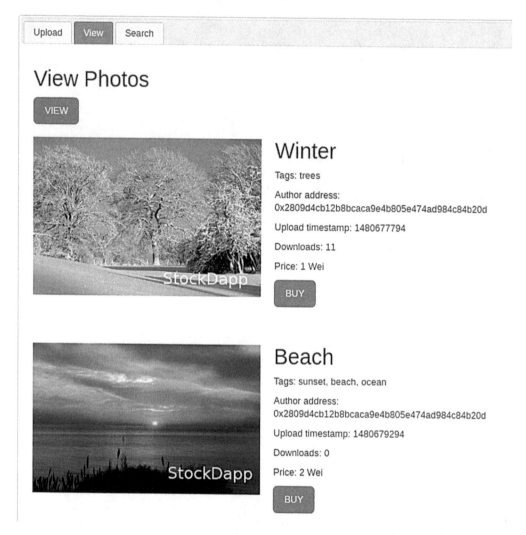

Figure 9.6: Screenshot of Stock Photos Dapp - buying a photo

web interface. While uploading a photo, the user specifies a title, tags, photo thumbnail, original photo and a price for the photo. When a user uploads a new photo, the photo and its thumbnail are uploaded to swarm. To upload a photo, a POST request is sent to swarm's HTTP interface from the Dapp's JavaScript. When the photo and its thumbnail is uploaded, their swarm hashes are returned. Next, the Dapp sends a transaction to the *newPhoto* method of the smart contract. The input parameters to the *newPhoto* method include the swarm hashes of the photo and its thumbnail, title, tags and price. Within the smart contract, we maintain a mapping from the swarm hash of the thumbnail to the photo object and another mapping from the index of the photo to the photo object. To retrieve the details of a photo, either the swarm hash of the thumbnail or the index of the photo is required.

Figure 9.6 shows a screenshot of the 'view photos' tab in the Stock Photos Dapp. Through this interface, users can browse for photos and purchase photos they like. To purchase a photo, users can connect their Ethereum wallets to the Dapp and then click on the 'Buy' button next to a photo. This sends a transaction to the *buyPhoto* method of the smart contract. In the *buyPhoto* method, we add the address of the user to the list of users who have purchased the photo and increment the download count of the photo. Next, the Dapp sends a call to the *getPhotoWithID* function of the smart contract. In this method, we check if the user has already purchased the photo and then return the swarm hash of the photo. Upon obtaining the swarm hash of the original photo, the Dapp sends a GET request to the swarm's HTTP interface to download the photo.

Summary

In this chapter, we described the Swarm decentralized storage platform and content distribution service for Ethereum. Swarm has been designed to serve as a decentralized and redundant store of Ethereum's public record, and also to store and distribute Dapp code. Swarm is a peer-to-peer storage platform which is maintained by the peers who contribute their storage and bandwidth resources. Being a peer-to-peer system, Swarm has no single point of failure and is resistant to faults and distributed denial of service (DDoS) attacks. Swarm is also censorship resistant as it is not controlled by any central authority. Swarm has a built-in incentive system for peers who pool in their storage and bandwidth resources. Swarm has been designed to dynamically scale up to serve popular content and has a mechanism to ensure the availability of the content which is not popular or frequently requested. Swarm is enabled by swarm nodes or peers who are connected to the Ethereum blockchain network. We described the Swarm's storage layer including data units, LocalStore, NetStore, Distributed Preimage Archive (DPA), Chunker, Swarm hash and Syncing. Next, we described the steps involved in storing and retrieving chunks. Next, we described the Swarm's networking layer. Swarm uses a peer-to-peer distributed hash table (DHT) called Kademlia. Hive is the logistic manager of the Swarm which maintains the Kademlia node table for each node, which has a list of active nodes in the network, partitioned into rows. Next, we described the Swarm Bzz protocol. We described the incentive mechanisms in Swarm which ensure that Swarm is self-sustaining and the nodes cooperate with each other. Swarm Accounting Protocol (SWAP) is the Swarm's bandwidth incentive mechanism which keeps track of the number of chunks provided/received per peer. Storage With Enforced Archiving Rules or Swarm Enforcement And Registration (SWEAR) is a storage incentive mechanism in Swarm to ensure that the data remains available. Secured With INsurance Deposit Litigation and Escrow (SWINDLE) is a mechanism to ensure that the registered nodes, who 'swear' to keep the content available, do not violate their promises. Next, we described how to setup and work with a Swarm node. Finally, we described an implementation case study of a Dapp for stock photos that makes use of Swarm.

Part III

ADVANCED TOPICS

10 - Advanced Topics on Blockchain

This chapter covers

- Double-Spending Problem
- Byzantine Fault Tolerance
- Proof-of-work vs Proof-of-Stake
- CAP Theorem
- Turing Completeness
- GHOST Protocol
- Sybil Attack
- Mining Pools and Centralization
- Smart Contracts Vulnerabilities
- Blockchain Scalability

In this chapter, we describe some advanced topics on blockchain and the security and scalability related challenges for the blockchain platforms.

10.1   Double-Spending Problem

Double-spending is a problem faced by peer-to-peer electronic cash systems and cryptocurrency networks. In such systems, due to the absence of a trusted central authority, a transacting party can try to spend the same digital token or currency twice as the digital assets can be duplicated (unlike physical currency). Double spending occurs when a party manages to spend the same money more than once. If the transactions were processed by a central authority that maintained a centralized ledger, double-spending would be easily detected and prevented. However, in peer-to-peer systems, where the peers do not trust each other, preventing double spending can be challenging. Bitcoin creator Satoshi Nakamoto proposed a solution to prevent double-spending. Nakamoto identified two key requirements: (1) publicly announcing all transactions, (2) having a system for the participants to agree on the transactions and their sequence. The first requirement led to the development of the blockchain structure which acts as a decentralized, public and immutable ledger of all transactions ever made on the network. The second requirement led to the development of a proof-of-work algorithm. We described the proof-of-work algorithm used by the Ethereum blockchain network in Chapter-7.

10.2   Byzantine Fault Tolerance

In distributed computing systems, a consensus mechanism is required to ensure that the components of the system (i.e. the participating nodes or peers) come to an agreement on the overall state of the network. Achieving consensus becomes more challenging when there is no trusted central authority present and the system components cannot trust each other. Lamport *et. al.* [15] named this consensus problem as the Byzantine Generals' Problem. In their original paper, Lamport *et. al.* formulated the problem with an example of a group of generals of the Byzantine army camped with their troops around an enemy city. These generals wish to formulate a plan for attacking the enemy city. To come to an agreement, the generals communicate their decision to attack or retreat as votes sent through a messenger. If all the generals are honest, they can come to a decision by communicating their decisions and come to an agreement based on the majority decision. However, the problem is complicated if one or more of the generals are traitors who try to confuse the others. The problem is further complicated if the messengers fail to deliver the votes or may forge false votes.

The Byzantine Generals' Problem is characterized by the idea that the peers do not trust each other and one or more of them can even lie, and the communication between the peers is also not reliable. A Byzantine fault tolerant system is one which can tolerate the class of failures known as the Byzantine Generals' Problem. This consensus problem in the field of computer science (and particularly in cryptography) had been long standing. Bitcoin creator Satoshi Nakamoto proposed a solution to Byzantine Generals' Problem by creating a blockchain and a proof-of-work algorithm. The proof-of-work chain is the key to achieve Byzantine fault tolerance and reach a consensus on the global state of the network.

10.3 **Proof-of-Work vs Proof-of-Stake**

Proof-of-work (PoW) is a transaction validation and consensus mechanism used in blockchain platforms. For example, Bitcoin platform uses a PoW algorithm based on SHA-256 and Ethereum uses a PoW algorithm called Ethash. Ethash is described in detail in Chapter-7.

Miners on the blockchain network create their own blocks by collecting the new transactions and then compute a proof-of-work for their blocks. Proof-of-work (PoW) is a cryptographically secure *nonce* that proves that a certain amount of work was done to find the *nonce* input to the PoW algorithm. While any miner can create its own block, only the block which contains a proof-of-work (PoW) of a given difficulty is added to the blockchain and only the longest chain which has the largest proof-of-work is accepted as the canonical chain.

While proof-of-work has a nice property that one can easily prove that a certain amount of work was done to produce a block, however, it is considered highly inefficient and expensive. The miners have to expend significant computational resources and energy to perform complex mathematical computations for computing the PoW *nonce*. Though miners are incentivized by providing mining rewards in the form of certain units of a cryptocurrency (e.g Ether), PoW has been criticized for consuming large amounts of electricity. This indirectly leads to environmental damage as many of the miners use electricity generated from dirty energy sources. Furthermore, since PoW relies on computer hardware to perform mathematical computations, miners with more powerful hardware have a higher probability of successfully mining blocks and receiving the mining rewards. This can lead to mining centralization as a group of powerful miners, who can invest large amounts of money on powerful computer hardware, can collude to control the network.

Proof-of-Stake (PoS) is an alternative to PoW for providing consensus and preventing double-spend on a blockchain platform. Unlike proof-of-work, in proof-of-stake, there is no mining involved. Instead, PoS involves validating the blocks and the peers who perform block validation are called validators. Each validator owns a 'stake' in the network in the form of a bond or security-deposit. The validators who post a bond, or in other words, make the security deposit, are called 'bonded validators'. Given a point of consensus (i.e. a block at a certain height), the PoS algorithm randomly selects a validator and assigns it the right to create the next block. The higher the security deposit made by a validator, higher is its probability of being chosen to create the next block. Other validators then vote for the block and broadcast their votes to others. The number of voting shares a validator gets is proportional to the security deposit made. As the validators receive the votes from other validators, they eventually come to a consensus about the next block. The incentive mechanism in PoS is such that the validators earn rewards for voting for the consensus and lose their deposit for voting against the consensus. Thus, any malicious validator who tries to cheat the network and vote for a block with invalid transactions loses its deposit and the right to vote.

Ethereum plans to transition from proof-of-work to proof-of-stake in a future release. A PoS algorithm called Casper [16] is most likely to be implemented in the Ethereum Serenity release. Casper is considered as an eventually-consistent and economic consensus protocol. Casper is based on the idea of 'consensus-by-bet'. The validators bet their deposit on what the consensus will be. The validators who bet correctly earn their deposit back with transaction fees and the validators who bet against the consensus earn back less of their deposit. For blocks at every height (i.e. every block number), the validators bet by assigning a probability to the block. The validators bet iteratively and eventually reach a consensus. A block is considered final when a supermajority of bonded validators bet with a very high probability for the block. The supermajority threshold is protocol dependent and may be chosen as some value between 60% to 90%.

The benefit of PoS over PoW is that in PoS there is no need to consume large amounts of electricity as there is no mining involved, hence PoS is considered as a much 'greener' consensus mechanism than PoW. Moreover, unlike PoW, PoS doesn't require powerful computer hardware, therefore even small nodes or light clients can participate in the network. For these reasons, PoS has lower centralization risks as compared to PoW. With PoS, the validators converge to a consensus in a timely manner.

10.4 Consistency, Availability & Partition Tolerance (CAP)

For distributed data systems, a trade-off exists between consistency and availability. These trade-offs are explained with the CAP Theorem, which states that under partitioning, a distributed data system can either be consistent or available but not both at the same time.

A consistent system is one in which all reads are guaranteed to incorporate the previous writes. In a consistent system, after an update operation is performed by a writer, it is seen by all the readers. Availability refers to the ability of the system to respond to all the queries without being unavailable. A distributed data system is called available when it can continue to perform its operations even in the event of failure of some of the nodes. Partition tolerance refers to the ability of the system to continue performing its operations in the event of network partitions. Network partitions can occur when two (or more) sets of nodes are unable to connect to each other.

The CAP theorem applies to blockchain networks as well. According to the CAP theorem the system can either favor consistency and partition tolerance over availability, or favor availability and partition tolerance over consistency. Blockchain gives up on consistency to be available and partition tolerant. Blockchain is a distributed ledger which is eventually consistent, i.e. all nodes eventually see the same ledger. When a network partition occurs in a blockchain network, the peers can attempt to double-spend. For example, in one partition a peer A can send an amount X to a peer B and in the other partition, the peer A can send the same amount X to a peer C. In such a case, the blockchain network can either choose to be available or consistent. If the system chooses to be available, it becomes inconsistent, as one partition of the network will see the first transaction completed and the other partition will see the second transaction completed. Whereas, if the system chooses to be consistent, it becomes unavailable as one or both of the transactions will not be processed.

The Casper proof-of-stake algorithm described in the previous section, for example, favors availability over consistency. This means that when Casper is used as a consensus protocol in a blockchain network, the network will always be available and eventually-consistent.

10.5   Turing Completeness

Turing Completeness is a concept related to computability theory. A computational system is called Turing-complete if it can do anything that a universal Turing machine can do. In other words, a Turing-complete system is one which can compute every Turing-computable function. Turing machine is an abstract machine invented by Alan Turing in 1936. The Turing machine could be implemented with a tape divided into cells and a head that moves left or right and positions itself over a cell to read or write symbols. Given a long enough tape and sufficient time, a universal Turing machine could solve any computable function. The concept of Turing completeness can be applied to any system (physical or virtual) that can manipulate data. For example, a physical machine like a computer or a programming language can be considered as Turing-complete if it can do any computation that a Turing machine can do, given enough memory and time.

In the context of a blockchain platform, Turing completeness refers to the ability of the platform to do any computation that a Turing machine can do. Ethereum, for example, is a programmable blockchain network which can be used to develop different types of applications, through smart contracts. The Ethereum Virtual Machine (EVM), which is the runtime environment for smart contracts in Ethereum, is considered as Turing complete. By using the programming languages for smart contracts such as Solidity and Serpent, it is possible to perform any computation including state storage, looping, and branching. The language-specific compilers are used to generate the EVM bytecode, and as EVM is Turing complete, these computations can be executed on the Ethereum blockchain platform.

Turing completeness for a blockchain network also means that if the network has unlimited compute, memory, and storage resources, then any computations can be performed on the network including infinite loops. Turing completeness for a blockchain platform comes at the cost of security, as any malicious user or an attacker can intentionally create and deploy contracts with infinite loops to prevent the miners from performing their operations and effectively forcing them to shut down. To address this security vulnerability, Ethereum uses the 'Gas' system where each transaction is required to set a gas limit. The gas limit provides a way to specify the maximum number of computational steps that it is allowed to take. If a transaction performs computations which consume more than the gas limit, the transaction is reverted. Due to the economic costs in performing computations on the Ethereum network and the limits on the compute, memory and storage resources available for smart contracts, Ethereum can be called a 'practically' Turing complete system instead of a 'truely universal' Turing complete system.

10.6   Greedy Heaviest-Observed Sub-Tree (GHOST)

The Bitcoin network has the block-time (time after which a new block is mined) of 10 minutes. This means that a user has to wait for 10 minutes for a transaction to be confirmed. Many blockchain applications require multiple confirmations for newly mined blocks to secure the transactions from double-spending. For such applications, it may take as long as an hour for a transaction to be confirmed.

However, in the case of Ethereum which has been designed as a general purpose programmable blockchain platform for decentralized applications, having a slow block-time will discourage the users who do not want to wait for too long for the transactions to be processed. Therefore, Ethereum chooses a fast block-time (roughly 17 seconds), which is much faster than the block-time in Bitcoin. A consequence of fast block-time is reduced security due to stale blocks being produced which are not added to the blockchain. Stale blocks are competing blocks produced by miners which do not contribute to the main chain. Stale blocks are produced because the blocks take a certain time to propagate through the network after they are mined. In [7] Decker and Wattenhofer, performed an analysis of the block propagation times and observed that it can take up to 6.5 seconds for 50% of the nodes to receive a newly mined block and up to 40 seconds for 90% of the nodes to receive the block. When new blocks are mined and added to the chain, the stale blocks are rejected by the network as a longer chain has already formed.

In [8] Vitalik Buterin has provided a detailed mathematical analysis of the effect of block propagation time on the stale rate. The stale rate is roughly $t/(T+t)$ where t is the transit time for a block to propagate through the network and T is the block interval. Therefore, assuming that we have a block-time of 12 seconds and the propagation delay is 12 seconds, we get a stale rate of $12/(12+12) = 50\%$. Such a high stale rate reduces the security of the main chain and the network becomes prone to '51%' attacks. The computing power of the network that goes into making the stale blocks does not contribute to the security of the blockchain network as these blocks do not make it to the chain. Thus due to high stale rate, the share of the network contributing to the main chain becomes smaller and the network could be attacked by a minority of miners (i.e. with less than 51% power).

Another consequence of the high stale rate is the centralization risk. To illustrate the centralization risk, let us assume we have a mining pool which has 30% hashpower of the network and all the miners in the pool are located in the same facility. Such a pool will produce a winning block which is added to the chain 30% of the time and the newly mined block will be instantly propagated to all the nodes in the pool. As a result, for 30% of the time, the pool will have a 0% stale rate, whereas all the other nodes in the network will still have to wait for the block to propagate to them and will have a higher stale rate. Due to lower stale rate, the mining pool will have a higher efficiency than the rest of the network. The mining pool becomes more efficient simply because of its size, which leads to a centralization risk as the pool can have a significant control over the mining process.

To counter the first problem of network security loss due to stale blocks, Sompolinsky and Zohar proposed the "Greedy Heaviest Observed Subtree" (GHOST) protocol [6]. In the original proof-of-work protocol, the stale blocks do not contribute to the security of the network. The longest chain which has the highest score (or the largest proof-of-work) is accepted as the canonical chain. The score of a chain is determined by summing up the scores of all the blocks in the chain going back from the current block all the way back to the genesis block. The stale blocks do not contribute to the score of the chain. The GHOST protocol solves the issue of network security loss by including stale blocks in calculating the score of the chain and determine which is the longest chain. Thus, when computing which chain has the largest total proof of work, the work of not just the parent and all the ancestors of a block but also the stale descendants of the block's ancestors are added to the calculation. The stale blocks can be considered as attaching to the side of the main chain forming a sort of a block-tree. In Ethereum, these stale blocks are called "uncles". An uncle is a block which has a valid header and which is the child of the parent of the parent of the block, but not the parent. According to the GHOST protocol, the blocks must specify 0 or more uncles. Ethereum adopts a limited version of the GHOST protocol where uncles up to 7th generation can be included in a block. Therefore an uncle included in a block must be the Nth generation ancestor of the block, where 2 <= N <= 7. Including uncles in the block, solves the first problem of reduced network security as the additional work done by the uncles also contributes to the network security.

To solve the second problem of centralization, Ethereum allows mining rewards for uncles. For every uncle, U included a block B, the miner of the block B gets an extra reward of 1/32 per uncle (or 3.125% of the static block reward) and the miner of the uncle U receives 93.75% of the static block reward. Rewarding the nodes for stale blocks or uncles ensures that even the high latency nodes have an incentive to mine on the main chain.

10.7 Sybil Attack

Sybil attack is an attack that can happen on a peer-to-peer network where an attacker can forge a large number of pseudonymous identities and then use them to gain a large influence on the network. Certain blockchain applications can be prone to Sybil attacks where the attacker can create multiple separate identities and influence the application in its favor. For example, a voting application on a blockchain can be vulnerable to Sybil attack as a user can create multiple blockchain accounts and cast multiple votes from separate accounts. Blockchain lacks identity management beyond the blockchain accounts and there is no way to know if two blockchain accounts belong to the same person. While the proof-of-work protocol protects the blockchain network itself from Sybil attacks, however, decentralized applications and smart contracts deployed on the blockchain network need additional mechanisms to prevent Sybil attacks. One approach is to authorize individual identities which can transact with the applications. For example, in a voting application, the chairperson who sets up a voting contract can assign the right to vote to individual blockchain accounts and make sure that each person has only one account which is authorized to vote. Another approach is to put an entry cost or stake which has to be paid before a user can interact with an application. A more advanced solution to prevent Sybil attack on blockchain applications is to use an identity and reputation system on the blockchain where a reputation (or a trust score) is attached to the public key of a blockchain account. Blockchain applications can require the users to have a certain reputation to be able to interact and transact with the applications.

10.8 Mining Pools and Centralization

Blockchain networks require the miners to perform complex mathematical computations for mining algorithms (such as proof-of-work algorithms). Proof-of-work algorithms require expensive computer hardware, consequently, miners with more powerful hardware have a higher probability of successfully mining blocks and receiving the mining rewards. Due to this reason, individual miners instead of mining for themselves, can mine for the pool and get a fixed reward proportional to their hashpower. Moreover, due to the requirement for powerful computer hardware, a group of powerful miners who can invest large amounts of money on computer hardware can form a mining pool. Mining pools pose a centralization risk to the blockchain networks because if a mining pool manages to get more than 50% of the processing power of the network, the pool can attempt a '51% attack'. In a 51% attack, the pool can rewrite the blockchain history and do double-spending to their advantage.

Another issue related to mining centralization is the performance gains that the miners can get by the use of application-specific integrated circuits (ASICs). ASICs are specialized hardware designed to perform a specific task and can be thousands of times more efficient than general purpose hardware. The proof-of-work algorithms in first generation blockchain networks (such as in Bitcoin) could benefit from the use of ASICs. This compromises the network security, as a powerful group of miners can make use of ASICs to gain a significant amount of the network's total mining power. PoW algorithms used in the second generation blockchain networks such as Ethereum have been designed to be ASIC resistant. We described ASIC resistance of the Ethereum's Ethash PoW algorithm in Chapter-7.

10.9   Smart Contracts Vulnerabilities

Smart contracts can have software vulnerabilities which can be exploited by hackers. For example, in Chapter-5, we described the "re-entrancy" problem where a contract which calls another contract can be tricked to call back into a function of the calling contract before the conditions in the calling contract are updated. Attackers can exploit re-entrancy problems with smart contracts to get multiple withdrawals or refunds from the contracts. A solution to the re-entrancy problem is to have the correct ordering of the conditions-effects-interaction phases in a smart contract.

In June 2016, an attacker managed to drain more than 3.6 million Ether from the Slock.it backed Decentralized Autonomous Organization (DAO) into a "child DAO". The attacker managed this by exploiting a "recursive call bug" vulnerability in the DAO smart contract. Since smart contracts are meant to be agreements between transacting parties on a blockchain and not legally enforceable outside the network, such attacks can put the organizations, miners and even the blockchain network at risk [5].

10.10   Blockchain Scalability

Scalability is an important concern faced by blockchain networks. The transaction validation and consensus mechanisms (such as proof-of-work) used in blockchain networks and the block-times determine how fast the network can process and confirm the transactions. While commercial payment networks can process thousands of transactions per second, for blockchain networks such as Ethereum where the block-time is roughly 17 seconds, a user has to wait for several seconds for a transaction to be confirmed. Furthermore, many blockchain applications require multiple confirmations for newly mined blocks to secure the transactions from double-spending. For such applications, it may take several minutes for a transaction to be confirmed.

While it is possible to make the block-times faster, so that the transactions can be processed faster, however, this would impact network security. Fast block times would make it impossible for average-sized miners to run as full nodes and only the powerful miners would be able to afford the resources required to mine successfully on the blockchain network. Thus fast block-times can lead to centralization risks. There exists a tradeoff between how fast the transactions can be processed on a blockchain network and the level of decentralization that can be maintained.

Another scalability concern for blockchain networks is the increasing size of the blockchain. The size of the Ethereum blockchain as of late 2016, is over 20GB and growing at the rate of a few GBs per month. As the size of the blockchain becomes larger, it can pose a centralization risk as it will make it difficult for small miners to function as full nodes. Only powerful miners would be able to afford the resources to download the blockchain and mine successfully.

Summary

In this chapter, we described the security and scalability related challenges for the blockchain platforms. Double-spending is a problem faced by blockchain and cryptocurrency networks and solution to the double-spending problem was proposed by Bitcoin creator Satoshi Nakamoto who identified two key requirements: (1) publicly announcing all transactions, (2) having a system for the participants to agree on the transactions and their sequence. Next, we described the Byzantine Generals' problem which is characterized by the idea that the peers do not trust each other, and one or more of them can even lie, and the communication between the peers is also not reliable. The proof-of-work chain is the key to achieve Byzantine fault tolerance and reach a consensus on the global state of the network. We described the difference between proof-of-work and proof-of-stake approaches for achieving consensus on a blockchain network. While proof-of-work involves miners who have to expend significant computational resources and energy to perform complex mathematical computations for computing the PoW nonce, in proof-of-stake, there is no mining involved. Instead, proof-of-stake involves 'bonded validators' who perform block validation. Ethereum plans to transition from the Ethash proof-of-work algorithm currently used in the network to the Casper proof-of-stake algorithm in a future release. Next, we described the applicability of the CAP Theorem to blockchain networks. According to the CAP theorem under partitioning, a distributed data system can either be consistent or available but not both at the same time. Blockchain gives up on consistency to be available and partition tolerant. Next, we described Turing completeness for the Ethereum blockchain platform. Ethereum is a programmable blockchain network which can be used to develop different types of applications, through smart contracts. Ethereum Virtual Machine (EVM), which is the runtime environment for smart contracts in Ethereum, is considered as Turing complete. Next, we described the challenges of having fast block-times on a blockchain network including the stale blocks problem and the centralization risk. The GHOST protocol solves the problem of network security loss due to stale blocks. The problem of centralization is solved by allowing mining rewards for stale blocks or uncles. Next, we described the centralization risks due to the requirement of having powerful hardware to mine successfully with high probability on a blockchain network and the importance of having ASIC resistance for proof-of-work algorithms. Next, we described smart contract vulnerabilities such as the "re-entrancy" problem. Finally, we described scalability concerns for blockchain networks due to fast block times and the growing size of the blockchain.

Solidity Language Tutorial

Solidity is a high-level JavaScript-like programming language for implementing smart contracts for Ethereum blockchain network. A smart contract implemented in Solidity comprises state variables, functions, modifiers, and events. The Solidity *solc* compiler is used to compile a contract into Ethereum Virtual Machine (EVM) bytecode. Once compiled the contracts are uploaded to the blockchain network which assigns a unique address to the contract. Any user on the blockchain network can trigger the functions in the contract by sending transactions to the contract.

Types

State information in a contract is stored in the state variables. Solidity is a statically typed language and the type of each variable must be specified. Types in Solidity can either be value types or reference types.

Value Types

Value types are the data types which are passed by value in function calls. Value types in Solidity include:

- **Boolean**: Boolean types are declared using the *bool* keyword and the possible values are *true* and *false*.
- **Integer**: Integer types are declared using the *int* keyword (for signed integers) or *uint* keyword (for unsigned integers). The size of the integer type can optionally be specified, in the range 8 to 256 in steps of 8. For example, *int256* for 256-bits signed integers and *uint256* for 256-bits unsigned integers.
- **Address**: Address types are used for storing 20 byte Ethereum addresses for externally owned accounts and contract accounts. Address types have two members: *balance* which is used to get the balance of the account with the given address and *send* which

is used to send Ether to the account with the given address.

```
■ Using address type

address a = '0x12345';

//Check balance
a.balance;

//Send Ether (in units of wei)
a.send(1);
```

- **Byte array**: Byte arrays can either be fixed-size or dynamically-sized. Fixed-size byte arrays are value types and have sizes in the range 1 to 32. For example, *bytes1*, *bytes2*, ..., *bytes32*. Dynamically-sized byte arrays are reference types (arrays) and described later in this section. Fixed-size byte arrays have a member - *length* which yields the fixed length of the byte array.

```
■ Using byte arrays

bytes a; // Same as bytes1
bytes32 b;

//Get length
b.length;

//Indexed access
b[1];
```

- **String**: The *string* type is similar to *bytes* but does not have the *length* member and doesn't allow index access.
- **Rational numbers and Integer Literals**: Rational numbers are of the type *ufixed* or *fixed* in Solidity where the fractional bits is as large as required, for example, 1/2 will receive the type *ufixed0x8*, whereas 1/3 will receive the type *ufixed0x256* as it is approximated with 256 fractional bits. An integer literal can be a decimal, octal, or hexadecimal. A prefix specifies the base or radix, for example, 0x for hexadecimal, O for octal, and no prefix for decimal.

Reference Types

Reference types are the complex types which do not always fit into 256 bits. Reference types are either stored in *memory* or the contract's *storage*. Memory storage is non-persisting and is used for function arguments and return parameters. Contract storage is persistent and is used for state variables. Reference types in Solidity include:

- **Array**: Arrays can either be fixed-size or dynamically sized. Arrays which are stored in the contract's storage can have any type. Whereas *memory* arrays cannot have a mapping type. Solidity also supports multi-dimensional arrays. Arrays have a member *length* which yields the length of the array. Dynamic storage arrays can be resized by changing the *length* of the array. Dynamic storage arrays have a member *push* to add an element at the end of the array.

```
■ Using arrays

//Fixed size array where each element is of type uint
uint[5] a;

//Dynamically sized array where each element is of type bytes32
bytes32[] b;

//Two-dimensional array
uint8[10][10] c;

// Multi-dimensional array having dynamic elements
uint d[][5];

//Add element
b.push('0x123');

// Check length
b.length;
```

- **Struct**: Complex types can be defined in Solidity using *struct*.

```
■ Using struct

struct User {
address addr;
string email;
uint amountPaid;
}
```

- **Mapping**: Mapping types are used to store key-value pairs. The key can have any type except for a mapping, dynamically sized array, an enum and a struct.

```
■ Using mapping

struct Backer {
address addr;
uint amount;
}
mapping (uint => Backer) backers;

Backer b = backers[0];
b.addr = '0x123';
b.amount = 1;
```

- **Enums**: Enums are used to create custom types with a finite set of values. Enum types can be explicitly converted to and from all integer types.

■ **Using enums**

```
enum State  Active, Inactive, Running ;

//Declare variable from enum
State s;
s = State.Created;

// enums can be explicitly converted to ints
uint index = uint(State.Active); // 0
```

Functions

Functions in a contract include the code which is executed when transactions are sent to the contract. A contract has a special function called a constructor, which is executed only once when the contract is deployed. Box A.1 shows an example of a simple contract with a few functions.

■ **A.1: A contract implemented in Solidity**

```
contract BalanceChecker {
    address owner;
    string name;

    function BalanceChecker(string _name) public
    {
        name = _name;
        owner = msg.sender;  // msg is a global variable
    }

    function getContractBalance() constant returns (uint)
    {
        return this.balance;
    }

    function getOwnerBalance() constant returns (uint)
    {
        return owner.balance;
    }

    //Standard kill() function to recover funds
    function kill()
    {
        if (msg.sender == owner)
            suicide(owner);  // kills this contract and
                             //  sends remaining funds back to owner
    }
}
```

Function Modifiers

Function modifiers can be used within a contract to change the behavior of functions in a declarative way. For example, a modifier can be used to check for a condition before executing a function. Let's look at an example of a function modifier that restricts access to certain functions to only the owner of the contract. Box A.2 shows an example of *onlyOwner* function modifier which checks if the sender of the transaction is the owner of the contract. The *onlyOwner* modifier is added to the *withdrawFunds* function, as we want only the owner to withdraw funds in the contract.

■ A.2: Sample contract showing access restriction pattern

```
contract MyContract {
    address owner;

    function MyContract() {
        owner = msg.sender;
    }

    modifier onlyOwner(){
    if (msg.sender != owner) throw;

        _
    }

    function withdrawFunds() onlyOwner{
        if (!owner.send(this.balance))
            throw;
    }
}
```

Visibility & Accessors

Solidity provides the following function visibility specifiers:

- **public**: Functions and state variables with *public* specifier are visible externally and internally. For state variables, accessor functions are created. Functions default to public.
- **private**: Functions and state variables with *private* specifier are only visible in the current contract.
- **external**: Functions with *external* specifier are only visible externally. External functions are part of the contract interface, and can be only called from other contracts and via transactions. For external functions, *f()* does not work, but *this.f()*.
- **internal**: Functions and state variables with *internal* specifier are only visible internally. State variables default to internal.

Internal & External Function Calls

A function in a contract can directly call other functions in the same contract. Only functions of the same contract can be called internally. When functions external to a contract need to be called, the amount of Wei to be sent with the call and the gas can be specified. Box A.3 shows examples of internal and external calls. For an external call, the function to be called must have the modifier *payable* to that we can send a value (in Wei) to the function in the call.

- **A.3: Function calls**

```
contract AddNumbers {
    function add(uint a, uint b) payable returns (uint) {
        return a+b;
    }
}


contract Test {
    AddNumbers adder;
    uint result;

    function setAdder(address addr) {
        adder = AddNumbers(addr);
    }

    function add(uint a, uint b) returns (uint) {
        return a+b;
    }

    function processInternal() {
        //Internal call
        result = add(2,3);
    }

    function processExternal() {
        //External call
        result = adder.add(2,3).value(1).gas(1000)();
    }
}
```

Fallback Function

Fallback function is an unnamed function having no arguments which is called when: (1) None of the other functions matches the given function identifier or (2) A transaction is sent to the contract without any data (contract receives plain Ether). Box A.4 shows an example of a contract with a fallback function.

- **A.4: A contract with fallback function**

```
contract BalanceChecker {
    address owner;

    function BalanceChecker() public
    {
        owner = msg.sender;    // msg is a global variable
    }

    function getContractBalance() constant returns (uint)
    {
        return this.balance;
```

```
    }

    function getOwnerBalance() constant returns (uint)
    {
        return owner.balance;
    }

    //Fallback function
    function () {
        // This function gets executed if a
        // transaction with invalid data is sent to
        // the contract or just ether without data.
        // We revert the send so that no-one
        // accidentally loses money when using the
        // contract.
        throw;
    }
}
```

Constants

Solidity supports constant state variables and constant functions. When a contract with constant state variables is compiled, all the occurrences of the constants are replaced by their values. Constant functions are those which do not modify the state of a contract. Box A.5 shows an example of a contract with constant state variables.

■ **A.5: A contract with constant state variables**

```
contract Test {

    //Constant state variables
    string constant contractName = "Test";
    uint constant deadline = 1481888258;

    //Constant function
    function isExpired() constant returns (bool)
    {
        if(block.timestamp<deadline){
            return false;
        }else{
            return true;
        }
    }
}
```

Events

Events are used to track the execution of the transactions sent to the contract. Whenever an event is called in a contract, the arguments to the event are stored in the transaction log. The event arguments can be indexed by adding the *indexed* attribute before the argument name while declaring an event in the contract. The arguments which are indexed can be searched from the clients, where the watchers can filter the results based on specific values of the indexed arguments. Box A.6 shows an example of a contract with events.

■ **A.6: A contract with events**

```
contract Test {
    mapping (address => uint) amountPaid;

    event Deposit(address _from, uint _amount);
    event Refund(address _to, uint _amount);

    function deposit() {
        amountPaid[msg.sender] = msg.value;
        Deposit(msg.sender, msg.value);
    }

    function refund(address user) {
        if (amountPaid[user] > 0) {
            if(!user.send(amountPaid[user])){
                throw;
            }

            Refund(user, amountPaid[user]);
            amountPaid[user]=0;
        }
    }
}
```

Clients can create watchers (JavaScript callbacks) for the events. A watcher for an event is trigger when the event is called. Box A.7 shows an example of event watchers.

■ **A.7: Watching events using JavaScript**

```
// Watch for a specific event
var event = myContractInstance.Deposit({}, '', function(error, result){
    if (!error){
        console.log(JSON.stringify(result));
    }
});

// Watch for all events
var events = myContractInstance.allEvents('', function(error, result){
    if (!error){
        console.log(JSON.stringify(result));
    }
});
```

Control Structures

The control structures in Solidity are similar to JavaScript except for *switch* and *goto* which are not available in Solidity. The control structures available include *if, else, while, do, for, break, continue, ? :,* and *return*.

Inheritance

Solidity supports multiple inheritance including polymorphism. When a contract inherits from multiple other contracts, the contract code from the base contracts is copied and only the final contract is deployed on the blockchain. Functions can be overridden by another function with the same name in derived class. The overriding function in derived class should have the same number and types of inputs arguments as the function in the base class. Box A.8 shows an example of multiple inheritance where the contract *mortal* inherits from the contract *owned* and the contract *Test* inherits from the contract *mortal*.

■ A.8: Inheritance example

```
contract owned {
  address public _owner;

  function owned() {
    _owner = msg.sender;
  }

  modifier onlyowner() {
    if (msg.sender == _owner) _
  }
}

contract mortal is owned {
  function kill() onlyowner {
    if (msg.sender == _owner) suicide(_owner);
  }
}

contract Test is mortal {
    mapping (address => uint) amountPaid;

    function deposit() {
        amountPaid[msg.sender] = msg.value;
    }

    function refund(address user) onlyowner{
        if (amountPaid[user] > 0) {
            if(!user.send(amountPaid[user])){
                throw; // reverts the transfer
            }

            amountPaid[user]=0;
        }
    }
}
```

Special Variables and Functions

Solidity provides some special variables and functions which always exist in the global namespace. Figure A.1 shows the special variables in Solidity. These variables are used to provide information about the blocks and transactions. Figure A.2 shows the special functions in Solidity. These functions are used to provide commonly used cryptography related utilities (such as hashing).

Variable	Description
block.blockhash(uint blockNumber) returns (bytes32)	Hash of the given block - only works for 256 most recent blocks
block.coinbase (address)	Current block miner's address
block.difficulty (uint)	Current block difficulty
block.gaslimit (uint)	Current block gaslimit
block.number (uint)	Current block number
block.timestamp (uint)	Current block timestamp
msg.data (bytes)	Complete calldata
msg.gas (uint)	Remaining gas
msg.sender (address)	Sender of the message (current call)
msg.value (uint)	Number of wei sent with the message
now (uint)	Current block timestamp (alias for block.timestamp)
tx.gasprice (uint)	Gas price of the transaction
tx.origin (address)	sender of the transaction (full call chain)
this (current contract's type)	The current contract explicitly convertible to address
super	The contract one level higher in the inheritance hierarchy

Figure A.1: Special variables in Solidity

Exceptions

In Solidity the *throw* instruction can be used to manually throw exceptions. When an exception is thrown in a function call, any transfer of Ether in the currently executing call is also reverted. Box A.9 shows an example of using *throw* in a contract to generate an exception. Solidity also generates exceptions automatically. Some of these cases are listed as follows:

1. If an array is accessed beyond its length or a negative index is used (i.e. x[i] where i >= x.length or i<0).
2. If a function called via a message call does not finish properly (i.e. it runs out of gas or throws an exception itself).
3. If a non-existent function on a library is called or Ether is sent to a library.
4. If a contract receives Ether via a public function without the payable modifier.
5. If you divide or modulo by zero (e.g. x / 0 or x % 0).

Function	Description
keccak256(...) returns (bytes32)	Compute the Ethereum-SHA-3 (Keccak-256) hash of the (tightly packed) arguments
sha3(...) returns (bytes32)	An alias to keccak256()
sha256(...) returns (bytes32)	Compute the SHA-256 hash of the (tightly packed) arguments
ripemd160(...) returns (bytes20)	Compute the RIPEMD-160 hash of the (tightly packed) arguments
ecrecover(bytes32 hash, uint8 v, bytes32 r, bytes32 s) returns (address)	Recover address associated with the public key from elliptic curve signature, return zero on error
addmod(uint x, uint y, uint k) returns (uint)	Compute (x + y) % k where the addition is performed with arbitrary precision and does not wrap around at 2**256
mulmod(uint x, uint y, uint k) returns (uint)	Compute (x * y) % k where the multiplication is performed with arbitrary precision and does not wrap around at 2**256
selfdestruct(address recipient)	Destroy the current contract, sending its funds to the given address
<address>.balance (uint256)	Balance of the address in Wei
<address>.send(uint256 amount) returns (bool)	Send given amount of Wei to address, returns false on failure

Figure A.2: Special Functions in Solidity

■ A.9: Exceptions

```
contract Test {
    mapping (address => uint) amountPaid;

    function deposit() {
        amountPaid[msg.sender] = msg.value;
    }

    function refund(address user) {
        if (amountPaid[user] > 0) {
            if(!user.send(amountPaid[user])){
                throw; // reverts the transfer
            }
            amountPaid[user]=0;
        }
    }
}
```

Bibliography

[1] S. Nakamoto, Bitcoin: A peer-to-peer electronic cash system, https://bitcoin.org/bitcoin.pdf, 2008.

[2] *A Next-Generation Smart Contract and Decentralized Application Platform*, https://github.com/ethereum/wiki/wiki/White-Paper

[3] Gavin Wood, *Ethereum: A Secure Decentralised Generalised Transaction Ledger*, http://gavwood.com/paper.pdf

[4] Ethereum Homestead Documentation, http://www.ethdocs.org

[5] David Siegel, *Understanding The DAO Hack for Journalists*, https://medium.com/@pullnews/, June 2016.

[6] Yonatan Sompolinsky, Aviv Zohar, *Accelerating Bitcoin's Transaction Processing Fast Money Grows on Trees, Not Chains*, http://www.cs.huji.ac.il/ avivz/pubs/13/btc_scalability_full.pdf, 2013.

[7] Christian Decker, Roger Wattenhofer, *Information Propagation in the Bitcoin Network*, 13th IEEE International Conference on Peer-to-Peer Computing, 2013.

[8] Vitalik Buterin, *Toward a 12-second Block Time*, https://blog.ethereum.org/2014/07/11/toward-a-12-second-block-time/

[9] Ethereum blockchain platform, https://www.ethereum.org/

[10] MultiChain blockchain platform, http://www.multichain.com/

[11] Eris blockchain platform, https://monax.io/

[12] Solidity Documentation, https://solidity.readthedocs.io

[13] Ethereum JSON RPC, https://github.com/ethereum/wiki/wiki/JSON-RPC

[14] Gavin Wood, Ethereum Experience, http://www.slideshare.net/ethereum/the-ethereum-experience

[15] L. Lamport, R. Shostak, M. Pease, *The Byzantine Generals Problem* ACM Transactions on Programming Languages and Systems, 4 (3), pp. 382-401, 1982.

[16] Vlad Zamfir, *Introducing Casper "the Friendly Ghost"*, https://blog.ethereum.org/2015/08/01/introducing-casper-friendly-ghost/

[17] R3 Corda, http://www.r3cev.com/

[18] Hyperledger, https://www.hyperledger.org/

[19] A. Bahga, V. Madisetti, *Internet of Things: A Hands-On Approach*, ISBN: 978-0996025515, 2014.

[20] Slock.it, https://slock.it

[21] TransactiveGrid, http://transactivegrid.net/

[22] A. Bahga, V. Madisetti, *Blockchain Platform for Industrial Internet of Things*, Journal of Software Engineering and Applications, vol. 9, no. 10, pp. 533-546, 2016.

[23] D. Wu, D.W. Rosen, L. Wang, D. Schaefer, *Cloud-Based Design and Manufacturing: A New Paradigm in Digital Manufacturing and Design Innovation Computer-Aided Design*, Computer-Aided Design, vol. 59, 2015.

[24] X. Xu, *From cloud computing to cloud manufacturing*, Robotics and Computer-Integrated Manufacturing, vol. 28, iss. 1, pp. 75-86, 2012.

[25] Colombo, Armando W and Bangemann, Thomas and Karnouskos, Stamatis and Delsing, Jerker and Stluka, Petr and Harrison, Robert and Jammes, Francois and Lastra, Jose L *Industrial cloud-based cyber-physical systems*, The IMC-AESOP Approach, Springer, 2014.

[26] D. Wu , JL Thames, DW Rosen, D Schaefer, *Enhancing the product realization process with cloud-based design and manufacturing systems*, Trans ASME J Comput Inform Sci Eng, 13(4), 2013.

[27] TestRPC, https://github.com/ethereumjs/testrpc

[28] Ethereum Go Client, https://github.com/ethereum/go-ethereum

[29] Ethereum Python Client, https://github.com/ethereum/pyethapp

[30] Mist Ethereum Wallet, https://github.com/ethereum/mist/releases.

[31] MetaMask, https://metamask.io/

[32] Web3 JavaScript Ðapp API, https://github.com/ethereum/web3.js/

[33] Truffle, http://truffle.readthedocs.io/

[34] Embark, https://github.com/iurimatias/embark-framework

[35] Ether Pudding, https://github.com/ConsenSys/ether-pudding

[36] Crypto-js, https://code.google.com/archive/p/crypto-js/

[37] Apache Cordova, https://cordova.apache.org.

[38] Nils Gura, Arun Patel, Arvinderpal Wander, Hans Eberle, and Sheueling Chang Shantz, *Comparing elliptic curve cryptography and RSA on 8-bit CPUs*, Cryptographic Hardware and Embedded Systems-CHES, pp. 119-132, Springer, 2004.

[39] Vitalik Buterin, *Dagger: A Memory-Hard to Compute, Memory-Easy to Verify Scrypt Alternative*, http://vitalik.ca/ethereum/dagger.html, 2013.

[40] Thaddeus Dryja, *Hashimoto: I/O bound proof of work*, https://mirrorx.com/files/hashimoto. pdf, 2014

[41] Sergio Demian Lerner, *Strict Memory Hard Hashing Functions*, http://www.hashcash.org/papers/memohash.pdf, 2014.

[42] Understanding Ethereum Trie, https://github.com/ebuchman/understanding_ethereum_trie

[43] Donald R. Morrison, *PATRICIA - Practical Algorithm to Retrieve Information Coded in Alphanumeric*, Journal of the ACM, 15(4):514-534, October 1968.

[44] Petar Maymounkov and David Mazieres, *Kademlia: A Peer-to-peer Information System Based on the XOR Metric*, International Workshop on Peer-to-peer Systems (IPTPS'02), 2002.

Index

Printed in the USA
CPSIA information can be obtained
at www.ICGtesting.com
LVHW070344201123
764376LV00006B/34